MICROSOFT TECHNOLOGY SERIES

CURT AUBLEY

Tuning and Sizing NT Servers

Prentice Hall
Upper Saddle River, NJ 07458
www.phptr.com

Library of Congress Cataloging-in-Publication Data

Aubley, Curt.
Tuning and sizing of NT Server / by Curt Aubley.
p. cm.
Includes index.
ISBN: 0-13-095388-1
1. Microsoft Windows NT Server. 2. Client/server computing. I. Title.
QA76.9.C55A93 1998 98-4226
005.4'4769--dc21 CIP

Editorial/Production Supervision: *Eileen Clark*
Acquisitions Editor: *Mary Franz*
Marketing Manager: *Miles Williams*
Manufacturing Manager: *Alexis Heydt*
Cover Design: *Scott Weiss*
Cover Design Direction: *Jerry Votta*
Series Design: *Gail Cocker-Bogusz*

Prentice-Hall, Inc.
A Simon & Schuster Company
Upper Saddle River, NJ 07458

Prentice Hall books are widely used by corporations and government agencies for training, marketing, and resale.

The publisher offers discounts on this book when ordered in bulk quantities. For more information, contact Corporate Sales Department, Phone: 800-382-3419; fax: 201-236-714; email: corpsales@prenhall.com or write Corporate Sales Department, Prentice Hall PTR, One Lake Street, Upper Saddle River, NJ 07458.

Printed in the United States of America

10 9 8 7 6 5 4 3 2

ISBN 0-13-095388-1

Prentice-Hall International (UK) Limited, *London*
Prentice-Hall of Australia Pty. Limited, *Sydney*
Prentice-Hall Canada Inc., *Toronto*
Prentice-Hall Hispanoamericana, S.A., *Mexico*
Prentice-Hall of India Private Limited, *New Delhi*
Prentice-Hall of Japan, Inc., *Tokyo*
Simon & Schuster Asia Pte. Ltd., *Singapore*
Editora Prentice-Hall do Brasil, Ltda., *Rio de Janeiro*

Dedication

This book is dedicated to the memory of my father, Warren

CONTENTS

FIVE NT Server and Memory Performance *165*

EIGHT Putting Theory into Practice: Sizing and Tuning Case Studies *303*

PREFACE

After spending many years working in various UNIX environments, I began working concurrently with a new operating system called Windows NT Advanced Server version 3.1b. Windows NT generated some initial excitement, but it started relatively slow. That has changed. With the release of NT 4.0, this operating system has really built up steam. While researching, testing, benchmarking, and developing new solutions on NT from the workgroup to enterprise level, I am continually collecting troves of information on tuning and sizing NT Server. Developing NT Server-based solutions either as a Senior System Architect for NCR or as Chief of Technology for OAO, the same questions about NT Server arise again and again. Can NT actually be tuned? What size server is required? Will it scale as needed? How do we size it correctly? Why does system performance appear sluggish? How do you determine if NT has run out of resources? How can we help our solution to scale? Anyone developing NT solutions has commonly run into these questions. This book addresses these questions and more.

The goal of this book is to provide a practical approach to tuning and sizing NT Server so that you can immediately begin to maximize your server's overall performance. This book's approach is to discuss server technologies and then explain how NT Server takes advantage of these server technologies. Once this knowledge base is in place it will eliminate the guess work that revolves around tuning and sizing. This enables you to make more intelligent decisions regarding your NT Server's performance and optimization. Instead of providing lists of registry or other NT Server variables that can possibly be changed (or found in the NT Server documentation), specific "rules of thumb" are provided to help you get a jump start in the tuning and sizing of your NT solution.

To help with the integration of all the information provided in this book, the final chapter incorporates in-depth sizing and tuning case studies for Microsoft Exchange, NT File Server, and Microsoft Internet Information Server. These case studies utilize the strategies, methodologies, rules of thumb, bottleneck detection, tuning, and sizing techniques presented throughout this book to highlight the improvements that are possible in an NT Server environment. Again, specific recommendations and results are provided. It is important to note that although numerous specific recommendations are provided, the concepts and principles discussed throughout this book are applicable even as new NT Server versions are released and server technology continues to mature. Of course the tools used to implement these concepts and principals will change. To aid you in keeping up with the new tools that can help your performance improvement efforts, periodically visit *http://www.TuningAndSizingNT.com.*

This web site will also provide a location to share information surrounding the performance of NT Server.

Audience

Tuning and Sizing NT Servers primarily targets System Architects, System and Network Administrators, System Engineers, developers and other IS professionals who develop solutions using NT Server. *Tuning and Sizing NT Servers'* focus is performance. Everyone wants a high-performing server that is big enough to get the job done well, will efficiently use the resources that are available, and is not so overly configured such that they will never use what they have purchased. With these thoughts in mind, performance should always be a consideration when developing a computer-based solution. This book helps those developing and managing NT Server solutions to acquire a better understanding of performance concepts with a focus on actually implementing specific solutions.

This book assumes a general knowledge of NT Server planning, design, and administration. Because of this assumption, this book is targeted for medium to advanced NT experience levels. For some, much of this information will be new. Others may not feel comfortable with some of the advanced "Thinking Outside the Box" sections, while advanced NT gurus may gravitate towards these sections. Working through the book in a sequential manner from Chapter 1 through 8 is recommended since each chapter adds to your overall performance knowledge base. Regardless of your experience level, if you do not work through this book in this manner, review Chapters 1, 2, 3, and 8 and then select the other material as it relates to your particular environment.

Organization

Tuning and Sizing NT Servers jumps right in, with Chapter 1 providing a series of quick tips and ideas that can be implemented immediately. (I became tired of picking up those thick NT Server books and having to read half the book before getting some good, practical hands-on suggestions.) These quick tips are ready to use as is, but are not thoroughly explained in Chapter 1. Chapter 1 does provide those familiar with NT a great place to start in the tuning process, while the beginner should consider this chapter as a prelude of what is to come and then move directly to Chapter 2. Continue reading the subsequent chapters to learn when to really use the quick tips, what they do, how and when to implement them, and more advanced techniques. A structured performance methodology is reviewed in Chapter 2,

"Tuning Strategies and Measurement Gathering." In Chapter 3, Capacity Planning of NT Servers is explored and provides a structured sizing methodology that discusses leveraging NT Server tools and industry standard benchmarks. From there, the chapters follow a general information flow of investigating the server resources (CPU, Memory, Disk, and Networks), how NT Server utilizes these resources, how to size the specific subsystems, detect bottlenecks, and then explores specific tuning recommendations. Leading by example is something I consider important, thus Chapter 8, "Putting Theory into Practice—Sizing and Tuning Case Studies" utilizes the methodologies and recommendations developed throughout this book to develop NT Server solutions based on Microsoft Exchange, File Server, and Internet Information Server.

ACKNOWLEDGMENTS

A tremendous amount of thanks goes to my wife, Diane. Besides being a positive influence during the many hours required to publish this book and helping to keep me rooted in the real world, Diane provided invaluable insight and editing throughout the entire book-writing process.

Special thanks go to my colleague Jim Davis, a Senior Consulting Engineer with NCR. Jim and I spent innumerable hours together working in the lab completing the associated tests and benchmarks for this book. Jim provided expert advice while he endured being my primary sounding board. Special thanks also go out to the outstanding and experienced technical reviewers: Jim Davis—NCR, Lowell Bogard—Lucent, Pam Buffington—Georgia Institute of Technology, Jorj Bauer—University of Pennsylvania, Michael Brown—Motorola, Oren Eshel—E*Trade Group, Glen Seagraves—NCR, Mark Regester—Symbios, Dan Rosenburg—NCR, Buzz Payne—Cisco, Joseph Boyer—Fuji Capital Markets, Haridas Nair—Bluecurve, Kitrick Sheets—MCSB Technology, and Eric Dickman—EEC Systems.

I would like to thank NCR Government Systems Corporation for providing access to the large number of beefed-up NT Servers, Neal Nelson and Associates for the use of their benchmarking software and insight into server technologies, Bluecurve Technologies for providing the enterprise version of their Dynameasure active measurement software, and Network General for providing their classic network Sniffer equipment.

Numerous people at Prentice Hall helped to keep this project ahead of schedule, to all of them I say thanks. Specifically, I am thankful to Eileen Clark for her assistance. She was instrumental in assuring that I kept to the aggressive book-editing schedule.

And finally, I would like to extend a very special thanks to Mary Franz, my primary editor at Prentice Hall. Through conversations and her continuously supportive e-mails, she encouraged me to keep the high level of motivation that was required to make *Tuning and Sizing NT Servers* a reality.

ONE

Instant Rules of Thumb for Tuning and Sizing NT Server

When reading technical material, I hate having to weed through countless pages of information before getting to the really good stuff. That is why I have decided to put some of the practical key points in the beginning of this book. This chapter provides little backup for the recommendations, just key points and "rules of thumb" you can immediately put to use. These key points and rules, along with more advanced techniques for tuning and sizing NT Server, are explored in depth in the chapters that follow. Preview this section before looking at the other chapters. As you read subsequent chapters, these rules of thumb and other tuning and sizing concepts will become more concrete in their usage. Later, this chapter can be used to refresh your memory.

Beware: Knowing what each tuning technique does is more important than just knowing which switch to flip! To fully comprehend the advantages and uses of these rules of thumb, read through the book's chapters. Being informed not just what the tips are but on how and why they influence the behavior of NT Server will help you make more intelligent decisions and spark some alternate tuning ideas. Keep in mind that although these tips can improve your tuning and sizing efforts, they may potentially have adverse effects if implemented incorrectly. The rules of thumb selected were chosen because they are relatively safe to implement and can immediately improve the performance of your NT Server. To say that you'll have an immediate improvement of the performance of your NT Server is a strong statement, but a realistic one when you have an understanding of the workloads occurring in your NT Server solution environment.

Be sure to make two good backups of the registry and understand how to restore the registry before tuning it. (Refer to Appendix A for a refresher on backing up and restoring the registry.) This concept holds true for any tuning, actually; always understand and have a plan to reverse your efforts if needed. Then stress test or benchmark your new configuration to affirm that you have actually improved your server's performance and that it is stable. Remember that the final true test of performance of an interactive application is always the end user's performance perception.

Performance Statistics Gathering: Start the Logs

Without some sort of baseline, either from internal or external metrics, you may never know how much you have improved the performance of your NT Server or how to detect current or potential bottlenecks. The information you collect using NT Server's Performance Monitor (Perfmon) is particularly important in tuning and capacity sizing. Performance Monitor should become one of your favorite tools. Chapter 2, "Tuning Strategies and Measurement Gathering" closely investigates how, when, and why to use the Perfmon-related actions described in this section.

Key Points to Remember When Using Performance Monitor

Starting Performance Monitor (Perfmon)

Action: Start | Administrative Tools | Performance Monitor

Chart Mode

Good for looking at current activity or reviewing logs
Action: File | Chart Mode

Adding Counters to Any Mode

Performance monitor contains a set number of objects. Each object contains subsequent specific counter metrics that can be collected.
Action: Edit | Add to (chart, log, etc.)

Starting Log Mode

Action: To log performance data, start Perfmon

Then, select View|Log, Edit|Add to log. Select all objects using the mouse and shift key, then click Add|Done. To begin the logging session: Select Options|Log, enter the name of your log file (e.g., *test1-perfmon-log*), specify a sampling interval, and then click start. Perfmon uses about the same amount of resources to collect measurements from one object or many objects from NT Server's performance library DLLs, so collect them all except for network segment. DLL—Dynamic Link Library is an NT Server feature that enables executable routines to be stored separately with the .dll extension and to be loaded only by the program that needs them.

Viewing Active Perfmon Logs While Logging Is Occurring

If the copy of Perfmon that is actively being used for logging Perfmon data is used to view the current Perfmon data in any way, Perfmon will stop logging your data. To avoid this inconvenience, launch a second copy of Performance Monitor to view the currently active logging session or real time server data.

Three Action Items to Complete So That All Relative Performance Counters Can Be Collected

1. Add the Simple Network Management Protocol (SNMP) service
   The SNMP service adds network interface object to performance monitor so that Perfmon collects statistics surrounding the network interface card. To add the SNMP service, select Start|Settings|Control Panel|Networks|Services|Add, then add the SNMP service. Once NT Server is rebooted, the SNMP service is activated.
2. Add the Network Tools and Agent
   The Network Tools and Agent adds the network segment object to Perfmon and a network analysis tool to NT Server found under Start|Programs|Administrative Tools Network Monitor. This tool set allows NT Server to collect network-related information for the entire network segment, not just the network interface card of NT Server itself. To add the Network Tools and Agent, select Start|Settings|Control Panel|Networks|Services|Add, then add Network Tools and Agent. Once NT Server is rebooted, these tools are activated.
   Note: Collecting data using either the Perfmon object network segment or the Network Monitor places the selected network interface card into promiscuous mode, which adds additional overhead to your server above and beyond the standard performance monitor application.
3. Run Diskperf
   To monitor disk performance statistics, you must run "diskperf -ye" from a command prompt and reboot the server before disk statistic gathering

is enabled. Options for diskperf can be obtained by typing "diskperf /?" from the NT Server command line.

Determining Which Applications (Processes) Are Running Under NT Server

When performance monitor is started in log mode, it will only collect metrics from processes that are currently running. If a job is started after the logging began, the job generating the load will not be able to be identified. An excellent technique to circumvent this Perfmon limitation is to generate an alert when resource usage levels increase above an acceptable threshold. This alert would then start a second copy of Perfmon so that the guilty process can be identified and dealt with accordingly. Chapter 2 reveals the step-by-step procedure to implement this technique.

NT Server Bottleneck Detection Strategy

Wouldn't it be nice if you could observe just one or two metrics to determine what is going on in your NT Server? Unfortunately, since the server's subsystems are all interrelated, subsequently so are the metrics to observe, even under NT Server. In Chapter 2, "Tuning Strategies and Measurement Gathering," the importance of considering the entire server performance picture when trying to locate an NT Server bottleneck is investigated. There can be more than one server resource area that is contributing to the throttling of NT Server's overall performance. Once all of the major server resource areas are evaluated, focus in on improving the performance of the resource that is farthest to the left in the performance resource chart (Figure 1–1). This strategy will provide the greatest immediate gain to your NT Server's overall performance. Once one server resource is removed as the bottleneck, others may take its place, which will subsequently influence where you focus additional tuning efforts.

General NT Server Observations

1. NT Server typically will run short of memory before any other system resources. Watch this resource closely.
2. Even when you are concerned about another potential resource bottleneck, ensure there is not a memory shortage.
3. Once memory shortages are ruled out, the disk and network subsystems are typically the next sources of contention.

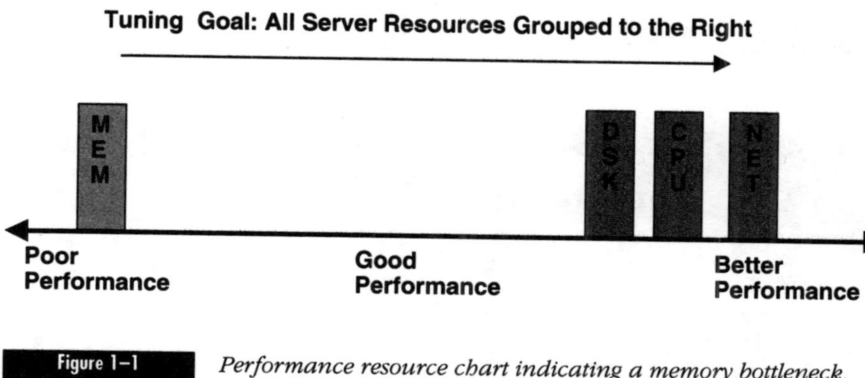

Figure 1–1 *Performance resource chart indicating a memory bottleneck.*

4. You can achieve some of the greatest gains in NT Server performance tuning by properly tuning and sizing the memory subsystem, disk subsystem, and network subsystem; in that order.

Key Performance Metrics to Observe when Detecting Server Bottlenecks

There are a dizzying number of Perfmon objects and counters to consider when sleuthing out NT Server bottlenecks that are throttling overall performance. Listed in the following section is a condensed version of the key metrics to observe when determining if a bottleneck is forming that will throttle back your server's overall performance. All of the metrics outlined here are available when using the default NT Server Perfmon tool. A common concern I hear is that some of these counters always display zero, which is misleading. Ensure that all of the Perfmon counters are turned on as outlined in the section "Three Action Items to Complete So That All Relative Performance Counters Can Be Collected."

These rules of thumb are generic and commonly hold true. As you begin to collect measurements and develop a baseline on your particular NT Server(s), pay particularly close attention to these objects and counters. Any drastic variation from the baseline you develop and/or trends observed over a given period of time, consecutive weeks for instance, can be cause for action. For example, if the Logical Disk: % utilization on a particular disk drive has held steady at 20 percent for four weeks, then suddenly the Logical Disk: % utilization begins to increase at 5 percent each week, investigate and understand what is running on the server. Subsequently, develop an action plan to alleviate this ominous looking condition that is developing before it becomes that bottleneck that slows down your entire system.

Table 1.1 Primary Counters for NT Server memory bottleneck detection.

Object/Counter	Definition	Rule of Thumb for Bottleneck Detection
Memory: Available bytes	Available bytes displays the size of virtual memory currently on the zeroed, free, and standby lists. Zeroed and free memory is ready for use with zeroed memory cleared to zeros. Standby memory is removed from a processor working set but is still available.	NT Server will try to keep at least 4 MB available as seen via this counter. If this value is near 4 MB and pages/sec is high, and the disk drive where the Pagefile is located is busy, there is a memory shortfall. For NT Servers with their memory optimization set to maximizing throughput for file sharing reduce this value to 1 MB.
Memory: Pages/sec	Pages/sec is the number of pages read from the disk or written to the disk to resolve memory references that were not in memory at the time of reference.	This counter can be deceiving, particularly on Enterprise class NT Servers. A high paging activity is fine (>100), unless it is accompanied by a low available bytes indicator and a high % disk time on the paging file disks.
Logical Disk: % Disk Time (for dedicated pagefile.sys disk drive)	Disk time is the percentage of elapsed time that the selected disk drive is busy servicing read or write requests.	If the % disk time is over 10 percent, the available bytes are hovering around 4 MB, and pages/sec is high, the Virtual Memory Manager is using the paging file significantly and the server is experiencing a memory bottleneck. Note the % disk time counter must point to disk drive(s) that contains paging system file(s), pagefile.sys.
Server: Pool Nonpaged Failures	The number of times allocations from nonpaged pool have failed.	If this value is >1 on a regular basis, there is not enough physical memory in the server.
Server: Pool Paged Failures	The number of times allocations from paged pool has failed.	If this value is >1 on a regular basis, there is not enough physical memory in the server or the paging file is too small.

Table 1.2 Primary counters for NT Server disk bottleneck detection.

Object: Counter	Definition	Rule of Thumb for Bottleneck Detection
Logical Disk: % Disk Time	% Disk time is the percentage of elapsed time that the selected disk drive is busy servicing read or write requests.	If this value increases above 60–80 percent, then the response time from the disk drive may become unacceptable. This is the red flag to begin investigating the other disk counters listed below.
Logical Disk: Average Disk Queue Length	Average disk queue length is the average number of both read and writes requests that was queued for the selected logical disk during the sample interval.	If this value is greater than two for a single disk drive and the % disk time is high, the selected disk drive is becoming a bottleneck. This value is an average calculated during the Perfmon sample period. Use this counter to determine if there is a disk bottleneck and the current disk queue length counter to understand the actual workload distribution.
Logical Disk: Current Disk Queue Length	Current disk queue length is the number of requests outstanding on the disk at the time the performance data is collected.	If this value is greater than two for a single disk drive over a sustained period of time and the % disk time is high, the selected disk drive is becoming a bottleneck. This value is instantaneous. Collect granular statistics over time to ensure that there is a sustained problem, not an instantaneous workload increase.
Logical Disk: Disk Transfers/sec	Disk transfers/sec is the rate of read and write operations on the disk.	If this value rises consistently above 80 for a single physical disk drive, observe if the average disk sec/transfer counter is reporting values higher than your baseline or what you consider acceptable. If it is, then disk drive is slowing down the overall server's performance.
Logical Disk: Average Disk sec/Transfer	Average disk sec/transfer is the time in seconds of the average disk transfer.	When the Transfers/sec counter is consistently above 80 for a single disk drive, the average disk sec/transfer should be observed to determine if it is rising above your baseline. A value greater than 0.3 seconds indicates that the selected disk drive's response times is uncommonly slow.

Table 1.2 Primary counters for NT Server disk bottleneck detection. (Continued)

Object: Counter	Definition	Rule of Thumb for Bottleneck Detection
Logical Disk: Disk Bytes/sec	Disk bytes/sec is the rate bytes are transferred to or from the disk during write or read operations.	Sum this counter's value for each disk drive attached to the same SCSI channel and compare it to 80 percent of the theoretical throughput for the SCSI technology in use. If this summed disk/bytes per second value is close to 80 percent, it is the SCSI bus itself that is becoming the disk subsystems bottleneck. Use this data and some math to review the complete disk subsystem data path.

Table 1.3 Primary counters for NT Server Network bottleneck detection.

Object/Counter	Definition	Rule of Thumb for Bottleneck Detection
Network Interface: Output Queue Length	Output queue length is the length of the output packet queue (in packets).	If this value is longer then three for sustained periods of time (longer than 15 minutes), the selected network interface instance is becoming a network bottleneck. Note that this value is not valid in SMP environments as of NT 4 SP3. Look for future service packs to fix this abnormality.
Network Interface: Bytes Total/sec	Bytes total/sec is the rate that bytes are sent and received on the selected network interface, including framing characters.	This value is directly related to the network architecture in use. If the value of bytes total/sec for the network instance is close to the maximum transfer rates of your network, and the output queue length is >3, you have a network bottleneck.
Network Interface: Current Bandwidth	Current bandwidth is an estimate of the interface's current bandwidth in bits per second.	For interfaces that do not vary in bandwidth or for those where no accurate estimation can be made, this value is the nominal bandwidth reported by NT Server. Use this information in conjunction with the bytes total/sec counter to determine the network utilization levels.

Table 1.3 Primary counters for NT Server Network bottleneck detection. (Continued)

Object/Counter	Definition	Rule of Thumb for Bottleneck Detection
Network Segment: % Network Utilization	Percentage of network bandwidth in use on this network segment.	The network architecture in use determines the acceptable level of % utilization. For Ethernet to based network segments, if this value is consistently above the 50–70 percent range, the network segment is becoming a bottleneck and is increasing the response times to everyone using the network.
Network Interface: Packets Outbound and Received Errors	Packets outbound errors received is the number of outbound packets that could not be transmitted/ processed because of network errors.	If this value is >1, the selected network interface is experiencing network problems that are causing the network to slow and potentially become a bottleneck. This problem could be emanating from any NIC or network device connected to the network segment.
Redirector: Current Commands	Current commands counts the number of requests to the redirector that are currently queued for service.	If this number is much larger than the number of network adapter cards installed in the computer, then the network(s) and/or the server(s) being accessed are seriously bottlenecked.
Server: Work Item Shortage	The number of times STATUS_DATA_NOT_ ACCEPTED was returned at receive indication time.	This indicates that NT Server has not allocated sufficient initworkitems or maxworkitems which are causing network limitations.

Table 1.4 Primary counters for NT Server CPU(s) bottleneck detection.

Object/Counter	Definition	Rule of Thumb for Bottleneck Detection
System: % Total Processor Time	% Total processor time is expressed as a percentage of the elapsed time that a processor is busy executing a nonidle thread.	A high value for this counter is not a reason to be alarmed, unless it is accompanied with a server work queue length greater than four or growing with an associated level of processor time greater then 90 percent, then the CPU is becoming a bottleneck. This rule holds true for single CPU NT Servers.

Table 1.4 Primary counters for NT Server CPU(s) bottleneck detection. (Continued)

Object/Counter	Definition	Rule of Thumb for Bottleneck Detection
System: % Total Processor Time	% Total processor time is expressed as a percentage of the elapsed time that a processor is busy executing a nonidle thread.	A high value for this counter is not a reason to be alarmed, unless it is accompanied with an aggregate sustained server work queue length sum greater than two times the number of processors in the server and the processor time is greater then 90 percent. If this is occurring, then the CPUs are becoming a bottleneck.This rule holds true for multi CPU NT Servers.
Server Work Queues: Queue Length	Queue length is the current length of the server work queue for this CPU instance.	If the queue length is >4 or continuously growing with an associated level of total processor time >90 percent, the CPU is becoming a bottleneck. This rule holds true for single CPU NT Servers.
Processor: % Interrupt Time	% Interrupt time is expressed as a percentage of the elapsed time that the processor spent handling hardware interrupts.	This value in itself is not a true indicator of a processor bottleneck. The value of this counter is helpful in determining where to focus your tuning efforts. If this counter is greater than 20 percent and rising compared to your baseline, consider completing diagnostics on the peripheral components to ensure they are operating within acceptable parameters.
Processor: % Privileged Time	% Privileged time is expressed as a percentage of the elapsed time that the processor spent in privileged mode in nonidle threads.	If this value is greater than counter % user time, focus on tuning server resources and investigate how well the application is consuming the privileged time.
Processor: % User Time	% User time is expressed as a percentage of the elapsed time that the processor spent in user mode in nonidle threads.	If this value is greater than counter % privileged time, focus on tuning user/application processes and resources to yield a better return.

Table 1.4 Primary counters for NT Server CPU(s) bottleneck detection. (Continued)

Object/Counter	Definition	Rule of Thumb for Bottleneck Detection
Process: % Processor Time	Process processor time is the percentage of elapsed time that all threads of the selected process used the processor to execute instructions.	Select all processes that are currently running and display them.This technique can quickly show which processes are consuming the highest level of CPU time and thus who might be the culprit for the CPU bottleneck.

Immediate Tuning Tips to Implement

Tables 1.1 through 1.4 are a great quick reference to use when wading through the almost endless counters contained in Perfmon to identify NT Server bottlenecks. The following is a structured methodology to assist the tuning process:

1. Always have a backup of the server, files, and registry before making any changes.
2. Monitor your server and develop a baseline.
3. Proactively monitor your server.
4. Determine what resource is acting like or becoming a bottleneck.
5. Try a single change at a time, when possible, and carefully document all change(s).
6. Benchmark and test your system to determine if the change(s) is helpful and stable.
7. Return to step 3.

This is a helpful methodology to follow when tuning your NT Server solution. Now that the key metrics to observe are presented to help in locating those potential bottlenecks and we have a methodology to follow to assist in the tuning process, let us review general tuning tactics.

Tuning Memory Resources

Selecting NT Server Memory Strategy

NT Server incorporates the facilities to tune its primary memory management strategies. (Chapter 5, "NT Server and Memory Performance," investigates the server's memory architecture and shows how NT Server utilizes memory with much more detail.)

The most common technique to control how NT Server controls its limited memory resources is found under Start|Settings|Control Panel|Network|Services. Select Server, then click Properties. This dialog box offers five options. For most multiuser environments, two options for tuning NT Server's memory strategy are of particular interest: Maximize Throughput for File Sharing and Maximize Throughput for Network Applications. The selection made here can have profound effects on how the server performs, so choose wisely.

OPTION 1: MAXIMIZE THROUGHPUT FOR FILE SHARING.
Select this option only if your NT Server acts as a dedicated file server or its applications exhibit very similar behaviors of a file server. For those environments, this memory strategy provides the greatest level of performance. Do not select this option if this server provides any other services besides that of a file server. If you are running any other applications on the NT Server, such as Microsoft SQL Server, or another memory-intensive application, the server might begin to page (swap information between RAM and the disk) excessively. If this occurs, it will lower the server's overall performance.

OPTION 2: MAXIMIZE THROUGHPUT FOR NETWORK APPLICATIONS.
Select this option for just about every type of server other than that of a file server. NT Server allows less RAM for the dynamic file system cache so that running applications can have access to more RAM. With this option, it is application tuning that generally becomes more important. When you configure applications such as Oracle, Sybase, SQL Server or Microsoft Exchange, you can tune them to use specified amounts of RAM for areas such as buffers for disk I/O or general database caching. Knowing what is running on your system is particularly important here: If you allocate too much memory for each application in a multiapplication environment, moderate paging can turn into thrashing (excessive paging), and you will have one slow system.

Optimizing Virtual Memory

This is a good technique to implement that can make your life a whole lot easier for a variety of tuning and sizing tasks. The paging file system can be split up among sixteen separate pagefile.sys file systems. Typically, splitting the paging file between two–four separate physical disk drives and, if possible, different SCSI channels, is the optimum layout. To accomplish this task, first select two disk drives that are to be dedicated to containing the page file and nothing else. Select Start|Settings|Control Panel|System|Performance. Select Virtual Memory and create two new paging files, one on each disk. After the new paging file systems are in place, remove the default pagefile.sys on the root disk. This will improve your virtual memory performance when NT Server must utilize virtual memory.

When you create the pagefile(s), you are asked to set the initial and maximum size of the paging file. Under Perfmon, observe the paging file: %usage peak parameter. To optimally set the pagefile, set the initial size parameter of the pagefile at % usage peak value. As a corollary to this rule of thumb, at a minimum, set the paging file initial size to twice the size of physical memory and the maximum size for the pagefile to two times physical RAM (to a maximum of 4 GB). This will to minimize spending any resource time extending the size of the paging file and waiting for the paging file extension to complete. Continue to observe your baseline. Constant use of the paging file is one of the major indications of a memory bottleneck.

Remove Unnecessary Processes from the Server

Every bit of RAM counts. Any processes that are not required to service your clients or manage your server should not be running on the system. Typically, areas to tune here are under Start|Settings|Control Panel|Services. Why run the Remote Access Service (RAS) or Spooler (SLOOLSS.EXE) if the server does not perform as a RAS server or has printers connected to it? Any background processes started, even if not active, use RAM and potentially pagefile space.

Schedule Memory Intensive Jobs During Off Peak Hours

This technique always seemed to be a bit of an easy-out strategy to alleviate memory problems, but it is effective and uses resources that may have otherwise been idle. To schedule a job during an off peak hour, use the "at.exe" command from the command prompt. Note, prior to using this command, the scheduler service must be started under Start|Settings|Control Panel|Services. If you do not care for the command line interface of the "at.exe" command that is native to NT Server, the Microsoft Windows NT Resource Kit contains a graphical-based "at.exe" command named "winat.exe."

Control NT Kernel Paging Activities

NT will page some portions of its own kernel to disk, such as the NT executive system drivers to disk when they have not recently been in use, as NT makes room in memory for other processes. This can be helpful for a system with a limited RAM supply. If your server has ample RAM (for example, at least 64 MB more RAM than is normally used by all of the process working sets on the server plus the RAM normally used by the file system cache), then change the following registry entry: HKEY_LOCAL_MACHINE\SYSTEM\CurrentControlSet\Control\Session Manager\Memory Management\DisablePagingExecutive from the default value of 0 to 1. This change will force NT to keep the NT executive (kernel) from paging any of its executive system drivers to disk and insure that they are immediately available.

Purchase More RAM—The Last Resort

More tactics to tune around memory bottlenecks are outlined in Chapter 5, "NT Server and Memory Performance," but when all strategies to tune the memory are exhausted and you have determined that the server is paging excessively, obtain additional RAM for the server. How much RAM to add is a function of current and future system load requirements and anticipated application requirements. To avoid paging, determine how much paging your system does, then add at least that amount. For example, if paging file: % usage max is 20 percent and your paging file size is 1000 MB, consider adding at least 200 MB. Also, when adding the memory to the system, select the RAM size such that it provides the highest density while still providing the highest degree of memory interleaving for growth and performance, respectively.

Tuning Disk Resources

NT Server lets you tune how it uses its disk subsystem and its configuration. In Chapter 6, "NT Server and Disk Subsystem Performance," the server's disk subsystem architecture and how NT Server utilizes the disk subsystem is investigated with much more detail. For now, once the disk subsystem is determined to be an NT Server bottleneck, consider the following tuning options.

Evenly Distribute File System Activity

Review the Perfmon logs regularly to ensure that the disk workload is evenly distributed across the disk subsystem. If % disk time or disk transfers/sec reaches even half of the thresholds mentioned above in the detecting disk bottleneck section, consider spreading the workload on the affected logical drives to other physical drives that are in less demand. One of the most common sources of disk contention is having all applications loaded and running on the root (%SystemRoot%) NT Server disk. The root disk is commonly "c:\", which can quickly become a bottleneck. It is easy to fall victim to this phenomenon, since many applications by default wish to place their information on the root NT Server disk. A tool that is helpful in determining what processes or programs are accessing which files on your server is ntfilmon.exe. This tool is freeware and is available at *http://www.ntinternals.com*.

Allocate Only One Logical Drive per Physical Disk Drive

A technique that helps isolate disk performance problems and improves performance by lowering the head movement rate over the disks is to format only one logical drive per physical drive. For example, if you have three disk drives, create only three logical drives: C, D, and E.

Select the Appropriate Allocation Unit Size (ALU)

Consider matching the file system ALU to the block size of the application you are using. If SQL Server is using a 4 KB block size, when you format a file system on a new disk drive, launch Disk Administrator, create the partition, commit the partition changes, select Format, and then set the ALU to 4096 bytes. Matching the file system block sizes can improve the efficiency of the disk transfers when you use the application. For more ALU size options, use the format command from the command prompt versus the Disk Administrator tool.

Low-Level Format SCSI Disk Drives Before You Start

When using a SCSI disk drive on a new SCSI host bus adapter, always use the host bus adapters tools to low-level format the disk drive before attempting to format the drive under NT Server. The geometric translation in use varies from host bus adapter to host bus adapter. When SCSI disk drives are placed onto a new host bus adapter, check that the correct translation information is being used. Low-level formatting the disk drive with the tools that are provided by the host bus adapter vendor ensures that the translation in use is correct. This will ensure that proper functionality, reported capacity and performance levels are achieved.

Group Similar Disk Workload Characteristics

Either through reading those famous manuals (RTFM) that come with software products or by using Perfmon and ntfilmon.exe (*http://www.Ntinternals.com*), try to determine the characteristics of the disk I/O activities occurring on your server. Determine which applications exhibit sequential activities, random activities, are read intensive, or write intensive. Once you have determined the characteristics of your disk activities, group similar workloads activities on the same disk drives or disk arrays. This is a corollary rule to the Evenly Distribute File System Activity. For example, place large log files on a separate disk drive rather than the general user database area.

Once the workload characteristics are understood and evenly distributed, group disk activities across the disk subsystems utilizing the various Redundant Array of Inexpensive Disks (RAID) levels based on the performance guidelines provided in the next section. For example, to improve the performance of sequential write intensive log files, place them onto a RAID 0, 1, or 0+1 array and avoid RAID 5. For a predominantly random environment that is read intensive, RAID 0 and 5 are good selections. The more you understand your server's environment, the better tuned your NT Server solution will be.

Appropriate Use of RAID

Adding RAID technology to your NT Server's disk subsystem is becoming a more common choice for enterprise servers to increase performance, disk management, and availability. RAID is a particularly excellent choice if multiple disk drives are available and it is not possible to break up the data files across separate disk drives to balance the use of the disk subsystem. NT Server allows for the use of both software- and hardware-based RAID solutions. Use NT Server to implement RAID levels 0 or 1 without any concern of a significant performance overhead penalty for implementing. Do not use NT Server to implement a software-based RAID 5 solution unless there is a significant amount of CPU capacity available that can be allotted for calculating the parity information required for RAID 5. A good rule of thumb is to implement all RAID arrays, especially RAID 5, using a hardware-based solution. Hardware-based RAID solutions offload the RAID calculations to a CPU on the RAID adapter.

The following outlines the performance and fault tolerance tradeoffs of various RAID levels:

RAID 0: Disk Striping

RAID level 0 stripes the disk activity across two or more disk drives. This logical layout provides the advantages of better performance for read, write, random, and sequential environments. The tradeoff for using RAID 0 is that there is no fault redundancy; if you lose one drive in your array you will lose the data for the entire array. In a RAID 0 environment, increasing the number of drives in the array improves the random I/O performance.

RAID 1: Disk Mirroring

RAID level 1 mirrors the disk activity across two or more disk drives. This logical layout provides for better read performance, especially in a multiuser environment, but lower performance in a write intensive environment. This RAID level provides complete data redundancy, even if you are using only two disks. The tradeoff for this redundancy is that the capacity of a RAID 1 mirror is lowered by 50 percent. For example, if you have two 9 GB disk drives in a RAID 1 mirror, there is only 9 GB of usable storage space.

RAID 2, 3, 4 and others

These RAID levels are not commonly used in general computing environments so they are not explored in this book. If you are interested in the other RAID level possibilities, search the Internet for RAID and a myriad of choices are presented.

RAID 5: Disk Striping with Parity

RAID level 5 stripes the disk data with parity information across three or more disk drives. This logical layout provides for better read performance, especially in a multiuser environment, but significantly lowers performance in a write intensive environment. This RAID level provides fault tolerance through the use of parity information, allowing for the loss of one of the RAID 5 arrays member disk drives without the loss of any data.

The tradeoff for this redundancy is that the capacity of a RAID 5 striping with parity is lowered by a factor of 1/(size of a disk drive member). For example, if you have three 9 GB disk drives in a RAID 5 array, there is only 18 GB of usable storage space.

RAID 0+1: Disk Mirroring of Disk Striped Sets

RAID 0+1 stripes data across two or more drives then mirrors those with another stripe set for fault tolerance. This logical layout provides better overall performance than a direct implementation of RAID 1. The tradeoff for this performance improvement and high fault tolerance level is that the capacity of a RAID 0+1 mirror is lowered by 50 percent. For example, if you have two 9 GB disk drives striped and mirrored with another two 9 GB stripes, there is only 18 GB of usable storage space.

Table 1.5 shows the relative performance ratings when comparing the various RAID options using a sector/stripe size of 128 KB. Use this guide when selecting the appropriate performance level that match your server's disk I/O characteristics.

Table 1.5 RAID performance guide.

Raid Level	Random Read	Random Write	Sequential Read	Sequential Write
	Relative Performance Rating			
Stripe (0)	2nd	1st	2nd	1st
Mirror (1)	4th	3rd	4th	3rd
Stripe w/parity (5)	2nd	4th	2nd	4th
Mirrored Stripe Set (1+0)	1st	1st	1st	2nd

Tuning RAID Controller Cache

If there is a built in cache on the RAID host bus adapter and a battery backup unit, the general rule of thumb is to configure it for the write back caching turned on. The default setting for most adapter caches is write through. Having the write back cache enabled is particularly helpful in write intensive environments implemented with RAID Level 5 disk arrays where there are pauses between periods of heavy disk activity. When your environment is characterized by heavy disk write activity, followed by a lull, the write back cache takes advantage of this workload slowdown to write the cached data to disk.

Tuning NT Server Cache Usage

The most common way to control how NT Server uses the available RAM for disk caching purposes is previously outlined in the Tuning Memory Resources section. In particular, the selection of either, option 1, Maximize Throughput for File Sharing, or option 2, Maximize Throughput for Network Applications, drastically affects your server's disk I/O performance. Although it depends on your environment, adding additional RAM will improve the disk I/O performance.

If the server is functioning as a file server and option 1 is chosen, nothing more than a reboot of the server is required to take advantage of the additional RAM. If option 2 is selected, just rebooting the server will improve some disk I/O performance as more RAM is available for NT Server's dynamic file system cache management, but tuning any applications that can be adjusted internally should be revisited. For example, Microsoft Exchange allows the amount of memory it is allowed to use to be easily set via the Exchange Optimizer Program. Examples of tuning an applications disk cache usage is outlined in Chapter 5, "NT Server and Memory Performance," and Chapter 8, "Putting Theory Into Practice: Sizing and Tuning Case Studies."

Disk Adapter Device Drivers and BIOS

This is one of the easiest techniques to implement to improve disk I/O performance. Manufacturers of disk drive adapters are constantly working on removing bugs and improving the performance of their respective disk adapters. Typically, the latest drivers are available via the manufacturers' World Wide Web site. Even before installing NT Server for the first time, check to see that the latest, best performing stable Disk Adapter Device Driver is available. Make it a point to periodically check your manufacturer's web site. It is amazing how much performance you can obtain through the use of improved device drivers. This concept should also be applied to the BIOS or firmware residing on the disk adapter card itself.

SCSI Command Queuing

Some drivers for SCSI adapters have registry settings for SCSI command queuing. By increasing this value, you can improve the performance of the attached disk subsystem. When this value is increased, more SCSI commands can be in the disk device queue. This technique is particularly helpful in disk array environments. Due to the multiple disk drive nature of disk arrays, they are capable of collating multiple SCSI requests in the most efficient manner to achieve higher levels of performance. Use this technique cautiously. Test your performance before and after editing the registry values. For most large disk array (>10 disks) environments, doubling the default value for the driver improves disk performance. Contact the disk adapter vendor for assistance in finding the SCSI command queuing entry in the registry. For example, Symbios SCSI adapters whose default is 32, the SCSI command queue entry is located in the following location: HKey_Local_Machine\System\CurrentControlSet\Services\symc8xx\Parameters\Device\NumberOfRequests (REG_DWORD 32)

File System Selection

Selecting the appropriate file system is important. For this topic, I will stray away from performance for a moment. Under NT Server (NT 4 and above), there are two file system options: NTFS or FAT. If security is a consideration at all, there is only one choice under NT Server, NTFS. If FAT file systems are in use, try to limit their use to disk drives or partitions smaller then 500 GB. For smaller file system sizes that are characterized by many small files, FAT can actually outperform NTFS. FAT file systems are more apt to become fragmented in a shorter period of time and begin to degrade in overall performance for larger file system sizes. Thus, for all file systems larger than 500 GB, use NTFS.

Lower File System Related Overhead

Disabling short name generation on an NTFS partition can increase directory performance significantly if a high number of non-8.3 filenames are in use, which is becoming more common. To disable short name generation, use REGEDIT32.exe to set the registry DWORD value of 1 in the following Registry location: HKEY_LOCAL_MACHINE\SYSTEM\CurentControlSet\Control\Filesystem\NtfsDisable8dot3nameCreation. Let it be known that this will cause problems if legacy 16 bit MS-DOS and MS-Windows-based applications are still in use.

Another registry tunable that can improve file system performance by lowering file system overhead is located in HKEY_LOCAL_MACHINE\SYSTEM\CurrentControlSet\Control\FileSystem\NtfsDisableLastAccessUpdate. Changing the default REG_DWORD value of this key from 0 to 1 will stop NT from updating the last access time/date stamp on directories, as directory trees are traversed.

Like any other file system, NTFS can become fragmented over time on heavily used disks. There are commercial products available to defragment disk drives which significantly improve performance of the file system. Current lists of defragment utilities are available at: *http://www.microsoft.com/infosource*. Included on the CD-ROM is a disk defragmentation tool named diskeeper. The latest version of diskeeper is also available for download from *http://www.sun-belt.com*.

To lessen the impact of fragmentation and take advantage of the physical characteristics of disk drives, try to keep file systems to less than 60 percent capacity. This will allow NTFS to compensate for fragmentation by taking less time to find additional free space as needed and keep a majority of the data in the file system occupying the outer, faster portion of the disk drive platters.

Group Similar Devices on the Same SCSI Channels

To maximize the performance and efficiency of your SCSI channels, group similar devices on the same SCSI bus. By placing an active CD-ROM on the same SCSI bus as a 10 Disk RAID 0 array, the CD-ROM can effectively slow down access to the faster disk array. When SCSI commands are sent to request data from the CD-ROM, which is a slower device than a disk drive, the other devices on the SCSI bus must wait until the CD-ROM (or another slower device) transfer is complete before transferring the data SCSI standard associated with the other devices. A good rule of thumb to follow is to place CD-ROMS on their own SCSI channel, place each tape unit on its own SCSI channel, and group disk drives with similar features (SCSI type, size, rpm, throughput) on their own SCSI channels. Also, avoid configuring SCSI devices using different levels of SCSI standards on the same SCSI channel, as they will be limited to running at the speed of the slowest SCSI standard on the particular SCSI channel. For example, operating Fast and Wide SCSI (20 Mbytes/sec) and Ultra Fast and Wide SCSI (40 Mbytes/sec) on the same SCSI channel limits the SCSI channel to the slower Fast and Wide SCSI speed.

Additional Disk Subsystem Hardware—The Last Resort

As with any resource that has become a bottleneck, additional resources can normally be added during the sizing of the server if you have considered future growth. Always select the fastest components that have a positive life cycle (remember VESA versus PCI years back). For the disk subsystem, this would involve selecting the fastest available disk drives and disk adapter technology available for insertion into the fastest I/O bus available. For example, if there was a need to add three additional disk drives, selecting a PCI-based

SCSI Ultra Fast/Wide Disk Adapter and SCSI Ultra Fast/Wide Disk Drives rotating at 10,000 rpm would be a good choice.

Tuning NT Server's Network Subsystem

The selection of the network architecture in use directly influences the network performance relative to your server. There are many facets of network architecture that can cause a network bottleneck. These facets include client configuration, application design, the physical network, network protocol, and network devices (for example, routers, hubs, etc.). Here, we focus on improving the network performance from NT Server's perspective. More advanced techniques for network subsystems are investigated in Chapter 7, "NT Server and Network Performance."

Balance Server Network Loads

Balance your network load by distributing the more heavily used network segments between two or more Network Interface Cards (NICs). Here, a network segment is defined by the physical connection of other computer systems to the server sharing the same collision domain. Even though network segmentation can involve some new cabling (physical) and subnetting (logical addressing), it is a proven technique to optimize your server's network I/O and is relatively easy to implement. The Network Monitor tool found under Start|Programs|Administrative Tools can aid in determining how to distribute the client systems between the network segments.

Network Protocol and Redirector Binding Selection Order

Another technique that can help you optimize your NT Server's network subsystem performance is to bind only protocols and redirectors (server components other than NT Server "server service") that your network is actually using to your network adapter. Binding is a technique NT Server utilizes to establish a communications channel between the protocol driver (TCP/IP, IPX, etc.) and the NIC itself. Under Start|Settings|Control Panel|Network Protocol, check which protocols (TCP/IP, NetBEUI, etc.) are currently installed. Also, under Control Panel|Network|Services, check which redirectors (RIP for NwLink, RPC support for Banyan, etc.) are installed. Removing unnecessary protocols and redirectors lowers the amount of memory that NT Server requires for network I/O (which can then be used for other tasks) and ensures that your network is not generating any unnecessary traffic, such as unwanted broadcasts.

Network Interface Card Settings

Setting the NIC properly is an area that is commonly taken for granted. Even though various standards defining physical and logical specifications of network communications exist, some compatibility issues always show up when you are not looking. Set your server's NIC and any other network devices your server may communicate with to the best possible network speed setting available. For example, if full duplex 100 BaseTX is available and the other network devices support this setting, choose it. Only as a last resort select auto sensing.

NIC Device Drivers and BIOS Levels

This is one of the easiest techniques to implement to improve network performance and lower server network overhead due to the NIC. Manufacturers of network interface cards are constantly working on removing bugs and improving the performance of their respective network adapters. Typically, the latest drivers are available from the manufacturers' World Wide Web site. Even before installing NT Server for the first time, check to see that the latest, best performing stable Network Device Driver is available. This same concept applies to the BIOS or firmware on the NIC as well. Make it a point to periodically check your manufacturer's web site. You can be rewarded with much better performance with the use of improved device drivers. As with any new software that your NT Server will rely on day in and day out, test the new technology before deploying it into your enterprise.

PERMANENTLY CACHE MAC ADDRESSES

A MAC address is a unique address that a manufacturer burns into NICs, such as a 100BaseT Ethernet card. TCP/IP uses address resolution packets (ARP) broadcasts over the network to associate an IP address with a physical layer MAC address. To lower the number of broadcasts and time required to obtain MAC addresses, you can permanently (until the next reboot, unless a startup script is used) place the associated MAC/IP address pair into memory. Use the following command sequence from the command prompt to implement: "arp -s 137.111.141.101 01-01-01-12-s3-44 (arp -s ip address macaddress)." This feature is particularly helpful when accessing a commonly accessed networked system that uses a static IP address. This is not a suggested technique when the networked system uses dynamic IP addressing (DHCP).

NIC Selections

Select only stable PCI-based NICs for your server. Although it may be tempting to use a NIC based on EISA, ISA, or MCA because the available PCI slots are dwindling, avoid the temptation if the best performance is a consideration. The relative performance difference between an EISA and PCI-based NICs were tested separately using a file transfer intensive environment, in the same NT Server. Table 1.6 illustrates the drastic performance differences between a generic PCI and an EISA-based adapter.

Table 1.6 Comparing PCI and EISA NICs.

Network Technology (Switched Full Duplex Ethernet)	File Transfer Throughput (Mbits/sec)
PCI 100BaseTX	131.0
EISA 100baseTX	9.61

Performance levels achieved always vary based on the workload. But even with a fairly large deviation, which technology would you choose based on these test results?

Controlling Network Users Timeout Period

There are only so many resources allocated for network connections, so if a user strolls away from their desk to enjoy a sunny day, disconnect them. This frees up resources for active users. The command "net config server" lists out the server's current settings. Running the command "net config server /AUTO-DISCONNECT: 10" is how to set the automatic disconnect time to 10 minutes. The registry entry for this value is located at: HKEY_LOCAL_MACHINE\SYSTEM\CurentControlSet\Services\lanmanServer\Parameters\Users

Faster NICs—The Last Resort

When all of the networking components in and around your NT Server solution are running at their optimum level, but more performance is required, consider implementing different network technologies, additional NICs, or changing your network architecture.

Tuning CPU Resources

Tuning the CPU resources may initially conjure up opening your server and trying to determine what you can change, but this is not the goal in this section. NT Server uses a priority based round robin scheduling algorithm to distribute process threads among the CPUs in the server. In Chapter 4, "NT Server and CPU Performance," issues surrounding the server's CPU performance and NT Server's use of scheduling algorithms are investigated, and advanced tuning techniques are explored to tune these resources to your best advantage. Before getting to that level of tuning, there are numerous other techniques presented here that can aid in tuning around CPU bottlenecks.

Ensure That Another Server Resource Is Not Acting as a Bottleneck

The most common occurrence I have encountered when tuning around CPU bottlenecks is the removal of other server resource bottlenecks, not the CPU. If another server resource is acting as a bottleneck, it can appear that the CPU is the actual bottleneck when it is not. Memory bottlenecks, in extreme cases, disguise themselves as CPU problems. When NT Server begins to run out of memory, it can exhibit a condition called thrashing. Thrashing is an excessive contention for physical memory. When this condition occurs, every request for memory results in paging activity to the pagefile on the disk drive(s). This results in an increased amount of CPU activity associated with moving memory pages around, not completing truly productive work. Why waste precious CPU cycles on this activity?

Avoid this condition by configuring a sufficient amount of RAM to avoid thrashing. The highest performing NT Servers I have encountered are sized and tuned with one basic strategy in mind: avoid paging. Paging is considered by many to be acceptable if it occurs infrequently. The more the server pages, the more CPU cycles are wasted on memory operations and the slower the final response times provided to your end users. To improve performance if the server must page, spread NT Server's pagefile across two to four dedicated disk drives sized identically. Refer to Chapter 5, "NT Server and Memory Performance," for the specifics on how to determine if your NT Server is paging and for a step-by-step guide on spreading the pagefile across multiple disk drives.

Offload NT Server CPU Overhead

If the server is running out of CPU processing power, offload NT Server activities that are not required or that can be implemented in hardware. The areas normally associated with CPU overhead that can be removed or offloaded are wasteful hardware components, disk compression, RAID operations, and security auditing.

- **Search for Wasteful Hardware Components**

For enterprise servers, do not be surprised if Processor: % Interrupt Time is around five to twenty percent of the total CPU workload, particularly if the network and disk I/O is very heavy. There are, however, some components that behave better than others. Attempt to obtain NICs that truly support bus mastering and disk host bus adapters that support DMA transfers versus PIO. Some disk and network adapters operate more efficiently than others, thus they require less CPU cycles to operate. Trade magazines provide numerous comparisons of these products. One good source of information is the NT Magazine web site located at: *http://www.ntmag.com*.

- **Do Not Implement Compression**

Compression is nice for notebooks and some workstations, but it has little applicability for an enterprise server. Actively using compression on your server will increase your CPU overhead and slow your disk operations. If you must use compression, relegate its use to drives that are not frequently accessed and are used for archiving only.

- **Offload CPU Intensive Operations**

Whenever possible, offload CPU operations to secondary devices. NT Server allows the native use of software-based RAID 5 implementations. RAID 5 requires constant parity computation every time data is written to a RAID 5 array. Offload this by using a RAID controller with its own CPU for RAID calculations. This frees up CPU cycles for the application instead of wasting them on every disk write activity. Chapter 6, "NT Server and Disk Subsystem Performance," reviews RAID technologies and examines performance issues in depth.

- **Security Auditing Equals CPU Overhead**

Security is important. When increased security levels are required, NT Server auditing is activated (utilizing auditing for tuning is covered in Chapter 2) and a certain level of overhead is introduced onto the server. The amount of overhead introduced is a function of the required level of auditing. The CPU is the server resource that shoulders most of the overhead associated with increased auditing. If auditing is required, do not turn it off. However, be aware that more CPU horsepower may be required to compensate for the increased security to provide the same level of performance experienced without auditing activated.

Remove Faulty Hardware Components

When a hardware device, such as a NIC, interrupts the processor, NT Server's Interrupt Handler will execute to handle the condition, usually by signaling I/O completion and possibly issuing another pending I/O request. Observe the Perfmon counter Processor: Interrupts/sec. If this number begins to grow compared to your baseline when under normal workload, there is a good possibility that a network device has become faulty. When a device becomes faulty, it may begin generating high numbers of interrupts, which inundates the CPU. This wastes precious CPU cycles. Replacing the faulty device will alleviate this situation.

Schedule CPU Intensive Jobs During Off Peak Hours

This technique always seemed to be a bit of an easy-out strategy to alleviate CPU problems, but it is effective and uses resources that may have otherwise been idle. To schedule a job during an off peak hour, use the "at" command from the command prompt. Note, prior to using this command, the scheduler service must be started under Control Panel|Services. To get directions on how to use the at command, type "at /? | more" at the command prompt. Besides the default "at" command included with NT Server there are now friendlier applications to utilize NT Server's scheduler service. The Microsoft Windows NT Server Resource Kit includes a scheduler tool named "winat.exe," which is a friendly GUI front end to the "at" command. Some companies are beginning to introduce more flexible scheduling tools that allow actions to occur based on multiple events besides time. One such tool is Master Minder. Information on Master Minder is available from *http://www.ncr.com*

NT Server Service Packs

Enterprise operating systems are becoming more feature rich and complicated by the minute; subsequently, they are prone to bugs. Microsoft publishes bug fixes or patches such as service packs and hotfixes. Stay abreast of these service packs as they commonly fix various functional problems and occasionally offer performance improvements. Again, as with any new software, test it before it finds its way into a production environment. Don't get discouraged—I have never used an operating system that did not require periodic patches.

Upgrading the CPU(s)—The Last Resort

The obvious way to alleviate processor bottlenecks is to move to a faster CPU. A faster CPU is particularly helpful if you have predominantly single-threaded applications. If you have a multiuser system using multithreaded applications, you can preserve your investment (i.e., not throw out the older CPU when the new one arrives) by adding additional processors. When the Server Work Queues: Queue Length is greater than two times the number of CPUs, your server is a particularly good candidate for additional CPUs. Windows NT Server currently supports up to 32 processors, although 1, 2, 4, and 8 CPU implementations are the most common NT Server implementations.

Sizing and Tuning Specific Server Implementations

The key to any sizing or tuning effort is to understand the types of workloads involved. Once you begin to understand the workloads involved and develop a server baseline, half the battle is already won. Use the previous tuning rules when applicable, but never underestimate the power of an expert for a particular functional area. For example, to improve database server performance, contact or hire an expert for the database in use. Large performance gains are possible by tuning the database design, actual queries, and applications running on the database. Short of hiring a functional area expert, some of the general uses for an NT server are outlined here with additional rules of thumb pertaining to each specific environment. These recommendations for the following server environments are presented here to help jumpstart the performance tuning effort, not as an all-encompassing review of each environment.

NT File Server

Most file server environments are characterized by the following resource usage activity: Memory: Light to Medium, Processor: Light, Disk: Active, and Network: Active. The two key areas to focus on here are disk I/O and network I/O. To size and tune the disk I/O subsystem, estimate the amount of space required, type of usage, and workload. When sizing NT Servers, it is common to consider the use of only one RAID level throughout the entire server configuration. On the contrary, consider using more than one. For example, if 80 percent of the file server workload is for a read environment, implementing a greater than three disk RAID 5: Disk Striping with Parity array will result in better read performance than a single disk and improve the fault tolerance level of the data. If the other 20 percent of the file system's usage are a write intensive environment such as backing up critical files, consider a RAID 1 Mirror. This multiRAID level concept is implemented in Chapter 8's case study, "Microsoft Exchange—Electronic Mail Case Study Solution."

For the networking I/O, select a network adapter that provides the best performance for the network architecture in use. If the environment is Ethernet, obtain a network adapter that supports bus mastering and contains more than one channel on the card to conserve server adapter expansion slots. From a tuning perspective, create the file systems with the appropriate ALU sizes. If some of the file systems provide larger files, such as multimedia files, use a larger ALU size such as 64 Kb. If the file system supports smaller files in a read/write environment, a smaller ALU size, such as 2 Kb, will typically provide the best performance. Use the format command via the command prompt to access these additional ALU options. For example, to format a logical partition "f:" as an NTFS file system with an ALU of 8 Kb, use the command "format f: /fs:ntfs /a:8192".

For NT Server's primary memory strategy, select option 1, Maximize Throughput for File Sharing. This will allow NT Servers cache manager to favor physical memory operations for the caching of I/O operations.

Primary Domain Controller (PDC) and Backup Domain Controllers (BDC)

Most PDC environments are characterized by the following resource usage activity: Memory: Active, Processor: Light, Disk: Moderate, and Network: Moderate. The two key areas to focus on here are memory strategies and network I/O. For NT Server's primary memory strategy, select Maximize Throughput for File Sharing. This will allow NT Servers cache manager to favor physical memory operations for the caching of I/O operations. This will provide the better performance for the PDC/BDC I/O activities.

The primary tuning strategy for PDC/BDC servers centers on the Netlogon service. One of the key activities performed by the Netlogon service is keeping user account databases in sync with all of the BDC servers and the PDC server. Control the load placed onto the PDC and subsequent maintenance traffic generated on the network via the following three registry keys: PulseConcurrency, Pulse, and Randomize. These parameters are found under HKEY_LOCAL_MACHINE\SYSTEM\CurrentControlSet\Services\Netlogon\Parameters. Lower the PulseConcurrency value to limit the number of simultaneous pulses the PDC will send to the BDCs, which in turn lowers the number of concurrent BDC database update requests. This lowers the server loading on PDC and lowers the peak amount of maintenance traffic over the network. However, there is always some type of tradeoff when tuning any server. In this case, the suggested tuning will increase the time required to replicate user account databases throughout the domain. Which is best if based on your requirements and environment.

Microsoft SQL Server

Most SQL server environments are characterized by the following resource usage activity: Memory: Active, Processor: Active, Disk: Active, and Network: Light. The key areas to focus on here are memory, disk, and network I/O. Wow, is it easy to summarize an application server environment by stating, "just watch the entire system," but this is common and just increases the tuning challenge! Having a sufficient amount of memory and properly distributed database activity across the available disk subsystem are the keys to achieving good database performance from an NT Server perspective. For memory strategies, select option 2, Maximize Throughput for Network Applications. This will provide SQL Server access to more memory and provide less memory for NT Server's cache manager to allocate for file system cache operations. This allows SQL Server more control over how memory is allocated.

Because of the high disk I/O levels associated with SQL Server, providing SQL Server with additional memory allows SQL Server to buffer more of its disk I/O operations. This can help to improve SQL Server's overall performance. SQL Server can be tuned using the SQL Enterprise Manager Tool and the Server Configuration option to ensure any additional memory added to the server can be utilized by SQL Server. When configuring SQL Server's memory options, a conservative rule of thumb is to leave at least 64 Mbytes of physical memory aside for NT Server. This will ensure that NT Server does not get starved for memory. If over time you determine that setting aside 64 Mbytes of RAM for NT Server specific operations is excesive, reallocate part of the reserved 64 MB of RAM to SQL Server activities. If the NT Server that SQL Server is operating on a server that is composed of multiple CPUs, change the "SMP Concurrency" to 0. This forces SQL Server to use all of the servers CPUs. If your server is dedicated to SQL Server activities, set the priority boost to 1, which allows the SQL Server to run at a higher priority. Server priority levels are reviewed in Chapter 4, "NT Server and CPU Performance."

Microsoft Exchange

Microsoft Exchange environments are characterized by the following resource usage activity: Memory: Active, Processor: Medium, Disk: Active, and Network: Medium. A simplified view of Exchange is that it is a complex application sitting on top of its own database. This database is already compartmentalized into the following areas: Private Information Store, Public Information Store, Information Store Logs, Director Service, Directory Service Logs, and Message Transfer Agent.

Characterization of the Disk I/O Subsystem

Be sure you have at least two disk drives set aside for the log files. The log files commonly become disk bottlenecks. By dedicating the logs to their own drives, it becomes easier to tune the disk layout and alleviate bottlenecks that may be formed. If a hardware RAID controller with cache is in use, set the controller cache for "write through mode" for drives containing the log files.

Exchange provides an excellent tool, Microsoft Performance Optimize, that determines (most of the time) the optimal disk layout of these compartmentalized databases and adjusts internal registry settings based on available memory, performance tests the optimizer completes on the disk I/O subsystem, and a series of questions asked when the optimizer is run. It is, however, very important to first have all of the RAM, controllers, disks, and file systems set up correctly before running the optimizer. If, after proactively monitoring your server's performance, you decide to implement hardware changes, such as adding additional memory and disks, the optimizer should be rerun to verify the system is still tuned for peak performance.

A key rule of thumb when setting up the optimizer is a selection that allows you to limit the amount of memory that Exchange can use for operation. Select this item and limit Exchange (if on a dedicated server that is running exchange only) to use all of the system memory except for 64 MB. This will ensure that the NT kernel and I/O cache manager have sufficient system resources available. Another key point is to have sufficient disk I/O resources available so that the optimizer can properly spread the various components of exchange across the disk I/O subsystem. In Chapter 8, "Putting Theory Into Practice: Sizing and Tuning Case Studies," sizing and tuning Microsoft Exchange is reviewed in depth in the Electronic Mail Server case study. Advanced memory tuning techniques for Exchange are outlined in the Memory Optimization example: Improving Microsoft Exchange Memory Usage section of Chapter 5, "NT Server and Memory Performance."

Web Servers

There are two primary considerations in Web server resource usage: the type of content that a Web server will provide and the network bandwidth needed to provide it. From a sizing point of view, the projected user demand and Web server content drives the sizing of the network connection and subsequently the other server resource components. A simplified view of a Web server characterization is that a Web server acts primarily either as a Hyper Text Transfer Protocol (http) file server or an application server.

Either one of these characterizations require optimized network I/O and disk I/O. Reference the rules of thumb for NT Server and SQL Server as they relate to the type of Web server in use. In addition to these rules of thumb, Web Servers are typically connected to the Internet, or intranets, which involve wide area networking. To improve the network performance in these environments, adjust the TCP/IP windowing size, which will allow more packets to be sent before receiving an acknowledgment. This setting can be modified through the following registry setting: HKEY_LOCAL_MACHINE\SYSTEM\CurrentControlSet\Services\Tcpip\Parameters\TcpWindowSize. The setting of this value is highly dependent on the network architecture in use. For most network mediums, the window size should be a multiple of the maximum TCP segment size in use.

Specific to the Web server Internet Information Server (IIS), there are numerous strategies that can influence IIS performance. Regardless of the Web server characteristics, set NT's memory strategy to option 2: Maximize Throughput for Network Applications. This allows for more flexibility in tuning IIS and lowers the probability that any of the IIs working set will be paged to disk. As you observe the IIs web server, if there is available memory, the IIS cache size can be increased. This is set under HKEY_LOCAL_MACHINE\SYSTEM\CurrentControlSet\Services\MemoryCacheSize. Similar to an Exchange or SQL Server environment, when setting the cache value for IIS, ensure that enough memory is set aside for the NT kernel and dynamic cache management. To control how long IIS objects can spend in cache, adjust the following registry key: HKEY_LOCAL_MACHINE\SYSTEM\CurrentControlSet\Services\

ObjectCacheTTL. For a relatively static IIs site, triple the default value. For IIS sites that are more dynamic, 1.5 times the default value is a good starting point.

More advanced tuning techniques for Microsoft Internet Information Server (IIS) are outlined in the Web Server Case Study located in Chapter 8, "Putting Theory Into Practice: Sizing and Tuning Case Studies."

Sizing Rules of Thumb

The following rules of thumb for sizing an NT Server should be used as general guidelines before the final NT solution is configured. It is possible to provide a good sizing estimate by utilizing sound, logical sizing techniques which any good IS professional can apply. Follow this structured sizing methodology when developing a new NT Server solution:

1. Define objective(s).
2. Understand requirements needed to meet your objective.
3. Determine loading characteristics.
4. Determine performance requirements.
5. Understand future business requirements.
6. Understand future server architectures.
7. Configure the server.
8. Stress test and validate the server configuration.
9. Proactively follow the Tuning Methodology during validations testing
10. Deploy the server into production.
11. Proactively follow the Tuning Methodology after the server is deployed.

Each of the above steps influences both the type and amount of server hardware needed to be configured to meet your needs for today and tomorrow. Each of these steps are reviewed in Chapter 3, "Capacity Sizing."

Historical information obtained from NT Servers running similar applications and experiencing similar workloads are an excellent source of sizing information. In lieu of having historical information available, review Chapter 3's Capacity Sizing Industry Standard Benchmark section. This section focuses on how to extrapolate from Industry Standard Benchmarks when initially sizing your NT Server solution.

Some of the NT Server specifics sizing concerns that I commonly encountered are presented below.

Sizing Disk Subsystems

The primary areas to consider when sizing the disk subsystems are capacity, availability, and performance. Consider each of these factors jointly when configuring your I/O subsystem.

Disk Subsystem Capacity

Capacity is the initial concern for the disk subsystem, but too often its relationship to availability and performance are not taken into consideration. Capacity is the easiest resource to calculate when using the sizing methodology. For this example, consider a database that requires 27 GB of actual (usable) disk space for all of its components (logs, dataspace, userspace, index areas, etc.). Three 9-GB disk drives are an economical choice to meet this capacity requirement.

Disk Subsystem Availability

The availability requirement indicates the data is important enough to need some type of data protection, while keeping cost of the server in the realm of reality. When selecting which RAID strategy to meet your availability needs, refer to the RAID definitions earlier in this chapter (Appropriate Use of RAID) to determine which RAID configuration provides the availability needed. RAID arrays that provide fault tolerance protection do so at a cost of disk capacity. A RAID 5 array can provide adequate data protection against the loss of a single disk drive, but at the disk capacity cost of 1/(size of one of the member disks in the RAID 5 array). For example, a four 9-GB RAID 5 disk array yields 27 GB of usable data space.

Sizing Disk Subsystem Performance

General

The required transaction rate is very important when determining your physical and logical disk I/O layout. The transaction rate refers to the number of transfers/sec or input/output operations (I/O's) per second that the server must provide to meet the desired disk subsystem performance requirement. Disk drives from the same vendor's disk family, regardless of the disk capacity, provide similar levels of performance. A 9-GB disk drive provides more disk capacity than a 4-GB disk drive, but it does not necessarily provide more performance.

A 7200 RPM Fast and Wide SCSI-2 based disk drive can typically sustain up to 100 I/Os per second in a mixed workload environment and 2 Mbytes/sec transfer rates. When grouped together into a RAID array, the array typically supports the aggregate of these performance factors. For example, a three disk RAID 0 array can support approximately 300 I/Os per second and 6 Megabytes/sec of throughput. This is where the old saying that more spindles (disk drives) provide better performance comes from. These specifications are rules of thumb used for basic planning. The actual performance will vary significantly based on client loads and application design.

Disk Subsystem Selection

Using these rules of thumb outlined above, an initial estimate can be made to determine if a specific disk configuration will support your environment. Although it is more economical to use the largest capacity disk drives available, this strategy may not provide the performance required. **Not taking this information into account when configuring your disk I/O subsystem is the most common mistake I have encountered!**

For example, if you were developing a new NT Server solution to estimate the I/Os per second it must support, review historical performance metrics from Perfmon for a similar environment. Specifically, check Perfmon's Logical Disk: Transfers/sec counter. This counter provides a good indication of I/Os per second the disk subsystem is experiencing. If the similar server is satisfactorily supporting 100 users across a four 4-GB RAID 5 disk array and the transfers/sec counter indicates a value of 200, a new server's four 9-GB disk array should support similar workload needs. However, if the new server will need to support an additional 100 users with similar work habits, the four 9-GB disk array will probably not support your needs. To support the estimated 400 I/Os per second for your environment, additional disk drives will need to be configured into the four 9-GB disk array or a second disk array will need to be configured. More detailed information on determining transfers/sec for RAID arrays is investigated in Chapter 6, "NT Server and Disk Sysbsystem Performance."

SCSI Bus Implementation

When considering how to configure your SCSI buses, review Table 1.7.

Table 1.7 Various SCSI bus characteristics.

Technology	Theoretical Transfer Speed Mbytes/sec	Realistic Transfer Speed (Estimated Real world performance) Mbytes/sec
Ultra Fast/ Wide SCSI-3	40	32
Fast/Wide SCSI-2	20	16
SCSI-2	10	8

Avoid configuring fast SCSI devices (disk drives) on the same SCSI bus as slow devices (tapes, CD-ROMs), this can potentially slow down access to your faster devices if all devices are active on the bus at the same time.

Determining the Number of Disk Drives per SCSI Bus

The number of disk devices (disk drives or arrays) to configure per SCSI bus is a function of your environment. To determine the throughput of your disk devices, there are two primary options. First, you could use various third party testing tools outlined in Chapter 2. Secondly, you could use Perfmon. To use Perfmon when determining the throughput of each disk device, explore Perfmon's logical disk objects: bytes/sec. Then use the estimated SCSI Real World transfer speed chart when configuring the number of disk drives per SCSI bus. For example, if you notice that each of your disk devices is providing 4 Mbytes/sec, and you have four devices, your SCSI channel must support 16 Mbytes/sec. If these four disk devices are connected to a Fast/Wide SCSI-2 bus, which (from the chart) will support 16 MB/sec, configure any additional disk devices on a second SCSI bus.

If you do not have any historical data for your environment, a good rule of thumb when configuring the number of disk drives per SCSI bus is to estimate that each disk drive will provide 2 Mbytes/sec of data throughput. Remember that the throughput actually achieved is highly dependent on client load, application design, disk adapter model, and disk drive model.

Sizing the CPU(s)

The primary object when sizing the model and number of CPUs is related directly to the type of workload in the projected environment. The typical rule of thumb here is to configure the fastest CPU that is economically feasible and is supported by the application you wish to run. Business requirements and required resources to support NT Server based applications are increasing constantly. Starting with the fastest possible CPU and a server architecture that can support multiple CPUs provides better long-term investment protection.

NT Server is a multiprocess and multithread enabled operating system. Without any real applications running under NT, there are multiple active processes and threads. Thus, additional CPUs are normally helpful to a degree. Consider your NT Server a candidate for a multiple CPU configuration if the following conditions are relevant to your environment:

- More than one major application running at a time
- The application is multithreaded and was designed for a Symmetric Multi Processing (SMP) environment
- Utilizing the Tuning Methodology, you have determined that the server is CPU bound and the Server Work Queues: Queue Length is greater than two times the number of CPUs on the server.

Configure enough CPU resources to drive all of the server's resources. For example, configuring a single CPU server that is connected to three ATM networks and 200 GB of disk drives in a high transaction rate environment is an unbalanced server and configured in an unrealistic manor. Develop the server configuration such that the CPU is kept "fed." This is achieved by ensuring there is enough CPU cache, Main Memory (RAM), and I/O channels for the disk and network devices. NT Server can easily be slowed by its weakest component in the data path that is not providing the data requested by the CPU. More information on factors that influence CPU perrformance is located in Chapter 4, "NT Server and CPU Performance."

Sizing Network I/O Subsystems

NT Server requires good network performance, as the network is the primary means in which clients request services. This topic is reviewed in depth in Chapter 7, "NT Server and Network Performance."

NETWORK SELECTION

A common misconception when configuring the network I/O subsystem is a misunderstanding of actual throughput that the network can provide and the network characteristics needed to meet the requirements (see Table 1.8).

Table 1.8 Common Network Information.

LAN Network Technology	Throughput Megabits/sec	Throughput Megabytes/sec	Topology Media Access (Protocol Characteristics)
Ethernet (10BaseT)	10	1.25	CSMA/CD
Token Ring (16MB Ring)	16	2	Token Passing
Ethernet (100BaseT)	100	12.5	CSMA/CD
FDDI	100	12.5	Token Passing

Note that there are two key pieces of information presented above to consider when configuring the server's network I/O. First, the theoretical throughputs of all of the various networks are typically referred to in bits/sec, not bytes/sec. Mixing up bits/sec and bytes/sec is surprisingly common. When determining the aggregate network requirements of the clients the server is supporting, always keep this in mind.

Second, consider the Topology–Media Access method of each network type. Each network type displays different response time characteristics under higher utilization levels. In an Ethernet environment, as the average network utilization increases above 20 percent, a Network General Expert Sniffer will generate an event that the network usage is becoming a potential bottleneck. At which % utilization Ethernet performance degrades depends on your environment and the published reference you use. When Ethernet utilization rises above the 50-70 percent range, response times increase dramatically due to the associated network congestion.

The Number of Clients per Network

A simplified rule of thumb for the number of clients to connect per network segment is to determine what is the worst case acceptable throughput for each network client, then divide that amount into the selected network throughput. For example, if each client should have no less then 1.5 Mbits/sec of available bandwidth, and the network supports 100 Mbits/sec, the segment could possibly support 66 clients. Unfortunately this simple calculation does not take into account the network media characteristics, but it does provide for a good starting point for the maximum amount of clients per network segment. Utilizing historical and industry standard benchmarks greatly aid in sizing the number of clients per network segment.

Server Network Interface Card Selections

The type and number of network cards is obviously dependent on the network architecture in which the server will be deployed. As before, there are two techniques to obtain the information needed to determine the amount network bandwidth the server requires.

If historical performance information is not available, survey your environment to determine required bandwidth and the subsequent number network interface cards. For example, suppose you are sizing a Web server and have a goal of supporting 50,000 hits per eight-hour workday. The server network interface must be able to sustain 139 Kbits/sec of throughput. For this example, one 10 BaseT Ethernet card would easily support the network bandwidth requirement. If this web server is destined to deliver content over the Internet, call your internet service provider (ISP). I'll let your local ISP help you configure the WAN connection to the Internet for right now. In Chapter 8, a web server connected to an Intranet/Internet over LAN connections is examined.

The second method to determine the bandwidth needed for the server to support is by reviewing the Perfmon Network Interface: Bytes Total/sec for clients in their current environment. Summing the bytes/sec average values up for the total number of clients you have can provide you with a network sizing reference point.

Sizing Memory Requirements

Vendors try their best to provide realistic information on memory requirements for servers that run their software applications. Unfortunately, they are trying to sell a product as well, thus their estimates for server resources tend to be on the skinny side, to say the least. But for a starting point, be sure you take into consideration the following:

- all applications that the server is running
- NT Server's requirement
- NT Server File System Cache use
- the number of concurrent users the server is supporting
- the amount of server resources configured (CPU, Disk, Network etc.)

To determine a good memory size starting point, sum the vendor recommendations for all of the above areas. For example, if you were implementing a database and web server for 60 concurrent users, consider:

- clients performance expectation. For most environments, larger amounts of RAM will yield higher levels of overall performance
- all applications that the server is running.
  Database Application—16 MB
  Web Server—16MB
- NT Server's Requirement
  32 MB
- NT Server File System Cache
  32MB
- The number of concurrent users the server is supporting
  60 * 250 Kbytes of RAM for each connection

Summing the metrics together suggests a starting memory size for the server of 111 Mbytes. 111 Mbytes is not quite a power of two and it would be difficult to configure a Server with this exact amount of RAM, thus use a 128 Mbyte RAM server configuration as the reference point. The best place to find the information on the amount of RAM required by an application is often from the software vendor directly. Remember however, that if a software vendor provided default RAM requirements that were too large they might scare customers away.

If you wish to consider an alternate view of sizing a server's memory, check out the Server Memory Assessment Engine on-line tool from Kingston Technology at *http://www.kingston.com/servermap/*. This on-line tool walks you through a questionnaire with a goal of making a memory sizing recommendation at the end. It is a helpful tool for a second or third opinion, but as before, keep in mind that Kingston is a company that specializes in selling RAM. Do not be surprised by the results. Review Chapter 3, "Capacity Sizing" for techniques to determine if your server configuration will really meet your objectives.

At a minimum, regardless of the application environment, consider the following CPU/Memory ratios when configuring your server's memory:

Table 1.9 CPU/Memory ratios.

Number of CPUs	Minimum Amount of RAM (Mbytes)
1	64
2	128
4	256
6	512
8	1024 (1GB)

This will help to insure that the CPUs are kept properly fed with data. This table is based on Intel Pentium PRO class processor performance levels or above.

Implementing Server Memory

When obtaining memory for your server make every effort to purchase the highest density available which still provides memory interleaving. Obtaining higher density memory provides a better utilization of available memory slots for future memory expansion. Of course, if you think that the amount of RAM required by operating systems and software applications will actual decrease in the future, skip the previous rule of thumb.

Memory interleaving is typically available in two flavors, two-way and four-way interleaving. Use four-way interleaving whenever possible, since it significantly improves the overall performance of your RAM-based memory resource. When finally choosing the type of memory for the server, select the fastest available RAM that employs physical error checking and correcting functionality. Specific RAM chip(s) speed is referenced by the amount of time it takes the CPU to access the RAM. For example, choose 60 ns RAM over 70 ns RAM. When making this selection, ensure that the RAM technology in use is not proprietary. Using proprietary RAM chips can cause acquisition and pricing challenges later in the server's life cycle.

Summary

In this chapter, tuning and sizing NT Server was reviewed from the perspective of immediate actions that can be completed to improve the overall performance of your NT Server solution. Although not all encompassing, this chapter provides a reference to the concepts and methodologies presented throughout the other chapters of this book. Some of these tuning suggestions may already be familiar while others may be new. By reviewing the subsequent chapters in this book, these tuning tips and rules of thumb are explored in more depth. This may lead you to reconsider some of the most common tuning tactics while introducing you to new tactics you may not have considered.

T W O

Tuning Strategies and Measurement Gathering

Goals for Tuning NT Server

In theory, NT Server was designed as a self-tuning easily administered operating environment. That's why there is a selection under Start|Administrative Tools for that "server optimization" application that automatically tunes your system so that it runs at its very best. What? You aren't familiar with that built in NT Server tool?! Of course you're not, because it does not exist. NT Server does a good job of self-tuning itself. Many of NT Server's system parameters are dynamically set either while the server is running or during the boot process, based on the server resources available. In achieving this goal, NT has succeeded in apparently removing many traditional administrative requirements, but it also obscures many tunables in the process. This approach provides more of a one-size-fits-all solution, which is in essence an average solution that fits many customer requirements. Average is a little easier to implement.

As NT Server moves into the enterprise, supporting hundreds to perhaps thousands of users while running multiple applications, fewer and fewer solutions fit into the "average NT Server mold." Average solutions provide average results. NT can still provide a solid average solution and work well, but who wants an average solution? As NT moves into the enterprise, it becomes increasingly important to properly tune and size your server.

There are many reasons why you may want to tune your NT Server. They include but are not limited to:

- Efficient use of resources
- Maximizing your return on investment

- Managing system loads and resources
- Getting more work done
- Troubleshooting performance problems
- Obtaining capacity sizing and planning data for the future expansion of existing servers
- Removing bottlenecks that may limit NT Server's scalability
- Understanding how to develop future NT Server based solution architectures

In short, the goal of tuning any NT Server is to remove any current or potential server bottlenecks that may be throttling its overall performance. By tuning your NT Server, you insure that your server is performing and scaling to the absolute highest levels possible.

The Big Picture: Understand the Entire Architecture

Unless you work in a very secure environment with a single server, and access that server by sitting at the console, there will be many other factors (listed below) that can influence how well a server appears to be performing. This concept of how the performance of a server is perceived by the end user is very important. End users do not care what is contributing to poor performance; they just want the response times to be as fast as possible, and the computer always to work. Thus, the performance of a server is ultimately dictated and judged by the client's perception as they sit down at their workstation and try to complete their business requirements. Obviously, investigating every facet of an Information Systems (IS) architecture is beyond the scope of just one nominally thick book, but I wanted, at a minimum, to point out key areas that can influence a clients perception. These areas are:

- Client application
- Client workstation (specifically video performance)
- Network connection to the workstation
- Type of network protocol in use
- Number of network devices between the client workstation and the server
- Type of network devices between the client workstation and the server
- Placement of NT resources (PDC, BDC, WINS, DNS, etc.)
- Server application
- Method of communication between client application and server application (middleware)
- Database configuration

- Database queries
- Server performance

So, what areas can you tune? There are numerous areas of an NT Server solution that you can tune. What benefits you obtain from your efforts depend greatly on what you decide to tune and when you decide to tune. The following is a list of typical server areas you should consider tuning, and the performance gains you might expect to obtain from your tuning efforts:

- Server configuration (100x)
- Disk I/O layout (50x)
- Database configuration (50x)
- Database query tuning (50x)
- Server application (30x)
- NT Server settings (30x)
- Network subsystem (25x)
- NT kernel (registry) tuning (5x)

These performance improvements represent both the relative performance improvements compared to the other tunable areas, and in some cases may actually improve overall performance by the factor indicated. Of the tunable areas listed, I will focus on server configuration, disk subsystem layout, network subsystem, NT Server settings, network I/O, and NT kernel (registry settings) tuning. Additionally, some server applications and hardware technology will be analyzed in conjunction with the above mentioned areas.

Tuning Strategy

There are two "laws" of tuning that always seem to pop up: (1) The Law of Tradeoffs, and (2) The Law of Diminishing Returns. For example, change the system settings for the NT cache to favor the file system cache, then application performance may suffer, and vice versa; there is always some type of tradeoff. (NT Server's file system cache is investigated in depth in Chapter 5, "NT Server and Memory Performance.") Consequently, there is only so much tuning that can be done, until you reach a point when the time required to obtain the performance gain is too consuming and is not worth additional effort. Typically, the greatest gains are achieved at the start of the tuning process.

Tuning techniques can be viewed as *performance engineering*, which sounds very scientific. But tuning and sizing can be a real challenge because it is not completely scientific; computer performance is part art and part science. Why? There are two primary aspects of computer performance that are in a constant state of flux: people and technology. People, or the clients your servers are supporting, can and do change the way they do business, especially when the demands placed on their business change. Technology is constantly changing as well. What you implement today may quickly become outdated tomorrow. Thus, at some point, you have to make a decision to understand the future business needs and technology that are on the horizon, then implement your architecture taking these factors into consideration. Once you understand the concepts for tuning and sizing presented in this book, they can be used continuously, even as business needs and technology changes.

Even though the environment around the server may be constantly changing, a scientific approach can be taken. When developing a tuning strategy or methodology, think about why you might tune a server. Remember the goal that you are trying to achieve is to ensure that your server is performing at the absolute highest performance level possible.

Practical Guidelines

Here the focus is on practical real world techniques. In a university environment, people develop elaborate methodologies that can take a fairly long time to implement, thus spending vast quantities of time squeezing every last gram of performance out of each system resource. While this may be beneficial in a university environment, solutions need to be implemented smartly and quickly in the business world. This does not imply that long-term analysis is not helpful, you just need to be realistic. Long-term performance logging is helpful for tuning and even more helpful in sizing.

Hardware is relatively inexpensive when compared to staffing costs; therefore, keeping a server reasonably well tuned will provide an excellent return on your investment. Since technology changes rapidly and client requirements and dreams often increase, the information gained from working with your current server is indispensable. This tuning and sizing information can aid in sizing additional server resources, configuring your next server, or may even influence the next information systems architecture that is put into place.

Tuning Methodology

Spending your time making one resource of your server fly is worthless if other resources of your server are causing the actual bottleneck. A bottleneck is any server resource that limits the other server resources from running at their peak. Server resources include processors (CPUs), disk subsystems (dsk), memory (mem), network subsystems (net), operating systems, and applications.

Having realistic expectations when tuning a server helps to keep you sane. Many resources can be sized and tuned, such as the disk I/O layout or file system cache strategies under NT Server. Other aspects may be out of your immediate control, such as the algorithm used for scheduling by the NT Server operating system itself, applications for which you do not have access to the source code, or applications that do not allow internal resource adjustments.

Focus your efforts in areas where you can make the greatest gain with the least amount of effort. Review the Performance Resource Chart (PRC) shown in Figure 2–1.

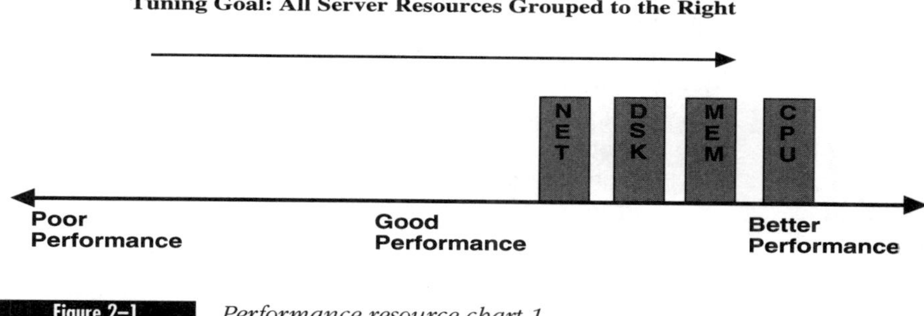

Figure 2–1 *Performance resource chart 1.*

The ultimate goal when tuning a server to run at its absolute best is to have every server resource running at its optimal level such that it is not a significant limiting factor for any other resource. This would mean trying to get all of the server resources to the far right hand side of the PRC as shown in Figure 2–1, and having well designed applications. A perfect server would have each resource side by side, grouped at the right hand of the chart, indicating that each resource is running at its optimal level.

Figure 2–1 shows a balanced, well-sized and tuned server. Figure 2–2 (PRC 2) shows an unbalanced system, where the network subsystem is the limiting factor for the server. Adding more resources to other areas of the server in this example would not improve the server's performance.

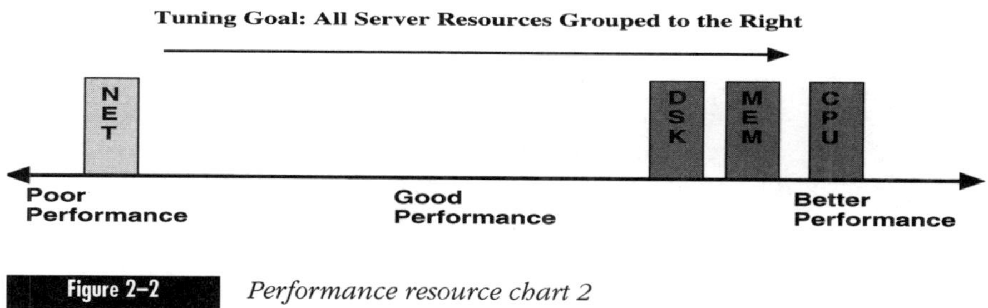

Figure 2–2 *Performance resource chart 2*

Look at the performance chart with a simplistic view. If I was walking on this performance line, the farther I can push all of the server resources to the right, the better the performance for the entire server. Although these figures show the four primary server resources, the same PRC concept applies when tuning other server resources such as applications. To achieve this goal, keep the tuning methodology in mind when trying to tune your system:

1. Always have a backup of the server, files, and registry before making any changes
2. Monitor your server and develop a baseline
3. Proactively monitor your server
4. Determine what resource is acting like or becoming a bottleneck
5. Try a single change at a time, when possible, and carefully document all change(s)
6. Benchmark and test your system to determine if the change(s) is helpful and stable
7. Return to step 3

Always ensure that you have the appropriate files backed up and understand how to restore your system back to its original state in the unlikely event that the tuning change you have made doesn't quite work out like you had planned. It is alarming to learn of the number of people who state that their server is completely backed up, but when I inquire if they have ever tried to actually test restoring their system, either data files or registry hives, I get a blank stare. (Backing up and restoration of the registry is provided as a refresher in Appendix A).

Being proactive about monitoring your server is monumental if you ever want to tune a server well. As you monitor your server over time, you will begin to have a better understanding of what is normally running on your server and the performance characteristics of your server. These last two points are helpful for performance tuning and eventual sizing either expansions to your current server or deployment of a new server or architecture.

Conceptual Walk-Through of the Tuning Methodology

Deciding which resource is the bottleneck determines where to spend your cycles. For example, look at Figure 2–2. Notice that the network resource is at the undesirable far left position of the chart. This should be the obvious area to focus your efforts. Perhaps you change from a shared Ethernet 10 BaseT (10 Megabit/second) environment to a 100 Mbit/sec switched Ethernet environment. This change may shift the entire PRC outlook by moving the network resource to the middle of the chart, half way between the disk subsystem and memory resources as shown in the Performance Resource Chart 3 in Figure 2–3.

If, after continued monitoring of the server, the server resources are still distributed roughly the same as showed in Figure 2–3, change the focus of your tuning efforts. Focusing any more effort on the network subsystem resource is not going to yield any more gains! Do not waste your valuable time. Although it might be fun to play with that new ATM card and associated

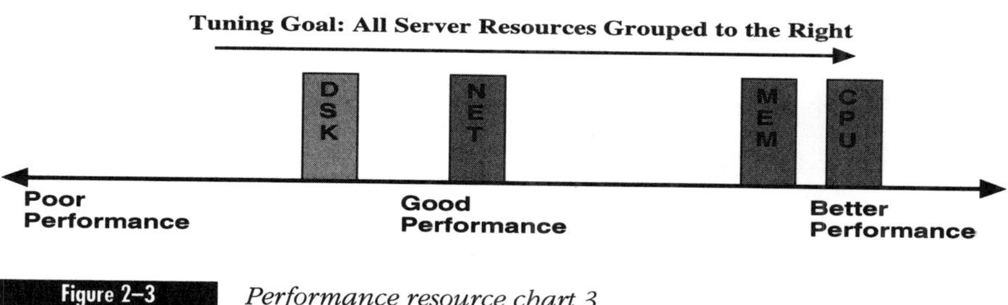

Figure 2–3 *Performance resource chart 3*

switches, it will not improve the performance that the server is providing to your clients because the network is not the server resource throttling back your server's overall performance. As you improve one resource of your server, eventually another resource becomes the new bottleneck. Remember that all server resources are closely interrelated.

If, after more proactive monitoring of your server, it is observed the disk subsystem is now the cause of the new bottleneck, the focus should be turned to removing it. Unfortunately, some people miss this. Do not fall into this trap of concentrating on improving the performance of the wrong server resource (even if it is fun). This warning is crucial to the tuning methodology, sizing servers, and getting servers to scale. Each of the major server resources is reviewed in depth in later chapters to help in identifying NT Server bottlenecks.

I have worked at locations where we determined that adding memory and tuning some applications would greatly improve the performance of the server, which it did. I returned a week later to find that even more RAM was added to speed things up, since it worked before. This did not help. The customer was concerned that the system was not scaling. Was this true? No, because the memory resource was no longer the bottleneck! After following a structured and sound tuning methodology, other bottlenecks were discovered, and attention was focused on removing those bottlenecks. Other resources, which were not inhibiting overall server performance, were kept in check through proactive monitoring.

Developing a Baseline

How do you determine how well a system is running? End users are typically not shy, to say the least, about expressing their opinions when applications appear to be running slowly. Being flogged by an end user is something that any IS staff member would like to and can avoid. Following the tuning methodology previously outlined can help in avoiding having the end user as the primary mechanism for determining when performance problems are at hand.

Developing a performance baseline for your server is the first real step in assuring your server is running at its very best. Once a solid performance baseline is developed, it becomes easier to determine if the end users are actually experiencing a system or server slowdown or, if they are just having a bad day and have decided to share this fact with others. It also helps you to determine if your tuning techniques are effective. There are two primary techniques in developing a performance baseline. The first is to run specific tests or benchmarks on your server before and after placing the server into production, in essence, taking the servers pulse to ensure it is still operating within acceptable parameters.

The second primary technique in developing a baseline is to collect server resource statistics on the server(s) that are in use. The primary tool included in NT Server for developing a performance baseline of server resource usage is the performance monitor. Using these two techniques in concert (benchmarks and baseline tests) helps to determine when there is a problem, or potential problem, and have the server information (performance monitor logs) available to determine what is causing the bottleneck. For larger environments, there are other third-party tools that can be helpful in developing baselines and monitoring server performance but are not normally available to everyone working with NT Server due to economics. Three such third-party technologies that come to mind are Hewlett-Packard's OpenView (*http://www.hp.com*), Platinum Technology's Server Vision (*http://www.platinum.com*), and Computer Associates' UniCenter TNG (*http://www.ca.com*).

Specific Tests to Run When Developing a Baseline

How can you tell if that disk array you added is actually installed correctly and now improving your disk I/O performance? What about that new network interface card? It is easy to state that something is running much faster or slower, but it is more difficult to actually prove it. In an ideal world or in some larger environments that I have worked, the common rule of thumb is to build an exact prototype which encompasses the applications, network architecture, clients, and servers and test your solution before you place it into production. This technique ensures that the solution works and that it meets desired performance requirements. Common tools to accomplish this level of testing are Remote Terminal Emulators and Remote Workstation Emulators.

These tools can be set up to stress your prototype with increasing user loads which emulate the actual type of work that is indicative of your environment when your solution is placed into production. These tools help you to determine such information as response time for the end user and throughput of the server in use. I highly recommend that these types of tools be used for large rollouts. Once you test your configuration in a prototype or lab environment, you can determine how well your server and network architecture will perform before production. Thus if in the production environment something seems slow, you can reuse these tools to determine if your solution is actually running slowly.

Not everyone has the time or budget to run the elaborate tests mentioned above to help when developing a baseline. There are, however, other more economical tests that are also available to check the pulse of your server to ensure it is performing like it should. Even in a small environment, the following baseline tests can be run. This example and subsequent examples throughout this book use tools from both the NT Workstation and Server Resource Kits. These kits include invaluable information on the architecture of NT Server, troubleshooting hints, and helpful software tools. I strongly recommend that anyone who actually performs any type of hands on work with NT Server, obtain these resource kits.

Before your server is placed into production, try the following simple tests to determine how your disk and network I/O are performing. The electronic copies of these scripts can be found via *http://www.TuningAndSizingNT.com,* or on the CD-ROM included with this book.

TESTING LOCAL DISK I/O PERFORMANCE: LocalDiskTest.bat

```
@echo off
REM # Turn off stdout echo
REM ##################################################
REM #
REM # Script: LocalDiskTest.bat
REM #          Simple file transfer and time
REM #
REM # Goal:   Take a server's pulse by copying a file
REM #         between local disk drives
REM #
REM ##################################################

REM # Easy way to create a 10 MB file
REM # creatfil.exe command from NT Resource Kit
REM # Clear screen to start
REM #
cls
echo Creating 10MB test file to test disk transfer
  time
echo on
creatfil c:\temp\testfil2start.ded 10000
@echo off

REM # Check size of File created
REM #
@Echo on
```

```
dir c:\temp\testfil2start.ded
@echo off

REM # copy file to locally connected disk
REM # timethis command located on NT Resource Kit CD-ROM
REM #
@echo on
timethis "copy c:\temp\testfil2start.ded
  d:\temp\testfil2end.ded"
@echo off

REM # Cleanup
REM #
del c:\temp\testfil2start.ded
del d:\temp\testfil2end.ded
REM #############
REM # End Script
REM #############
```

When run on a Pentium Pro 128 MB, Fast and Wide SCSI-2 disk-based system, this test produced an elapsed time of 3.696 seconds, which translates to a throughput measurement of 2.77 MB/sec. You can easily customize the basic parameters of size and number of iterations in the above script to make it more reflective of your environment. Note that small files will most likely be cached and will not measure true physical disk performance.

TESTING LOCAL DISK AND NETWORK I/O PERFORMANCE: DiskAndNetworkTest.bat

```
@echo off
REM # Turn off stdout echo
REM ##################################################
REM #
REM # Script: DiskAndNetworkTest.bat
REM # Simple file transfer and time
REM #
REM # Goal: Take a network server's pulse by copying a
REM #       file to a remote server
REM #
REM ##################################################

REM # Easy way to create a 10 MB file
REM # creatfil.exe command from NT Resource Kit
REM # Clear screen to start
REM #
cls
echo Creating 10 MB test file to test disk transfer time
```

```
echo on
creatfil c:\temp\testfil2start.ded 10000
@echo off

REM # Check size of File created
REM #
@Echo on
dir c:\temp\testfil2start.ded
@echo off

REM # Create Network Connection
REM #
net use k: \\megatron\c$

REM # copy file to network connected disk/share
REM # timethis command located on NT Resource Kit CD-ROM
REM #
@echo on
timethis "copy c:\temp\testfil2start.ded
  k:\temp\testfil2end.ded"
@echo off

REM # Cleanup
REM #
del c:\temp\testfil2start.ded
del k:\temp\testfil2end.ded
net use k: /delete
```

When this script was run between a Pentium Pro 128 MB SCSI disk-based server and a Pentium 100 128 MB, SCSI-based server on a dedicated 10 BaseT network, this test resulted in an elapsed time of 12.017 seconds, translating to a throughput measurement of 0.852 MB/sec. This test was completed on a dedicated network, a baseline network, in an ideal environment.

We now know the best performance we can achieve under ideal conditions for this baseline environment. This becomes our ideal baseline. Although this baseline test was completed in an ideal environment, it makes common sense to use the systems that depict your environment. Once the servers are placed into production, run the script again and compare the production results against the ideal environment results at various times throughout the day. This can be accomplished by having this script run periodically throughout the day using NT's scheduler service and redirecting the script output to a log file. Accomplish redirecting the script output by using the following command series from the command prompt: "LocalDiskTest.bat 1>> LocalDiskTest.log 2>> LocalDiskTest.error". The >> operator appends the output of the NT batch script to a file so previous data is not lost. For this example, the standard out (1) information is sent to its own log file and standard error (2) is sent to its own error file.

NT Server does not start the scheduler service by default. To start the scheduler service, open Start|Settings|Control Panel|Services and double click on the scheduler service. Set the service to startup automatically. Once you reboot your server, the scheduler service will be active and then you will be able to use the "at" command from the command prompt to schedule your periodic network server Disk and Network I/O Performance baseline tests. Here is an example of using the "at" command to run the DiskAndNetwork-Test.bat periodically every day at 1:30 PM, 3:30 PM, and 2:00 AM:

```
c:\at  13:30 /interactive /every:M,T,W,Th,F,S,Su
  "cmd /c c:\users\curt\bin\DiskAndNetworkTest.bat 1>>
  c:\logs\performance\DiskAndNetworktest.log
  2>>c:\logs\errors\DiskAndNetworktest.error"

c:\at  15:30 /interactive /every:M,T,W,Th,F,S,Su
  "cmd /c c:\users\curt\bin\DiskAndNetworkTest.bat 1>>
  c:\logs\performance\DiskAndNetworktest.log
  2>>c:\logs\errors\DiskAndNetworktest.error"

c:\at  2:00 /interactive /every:M,T,W,Th,F,S,Su
  "cmd /c c:\users\curt\bin\DiskAndNetworkTest.bat 1>>
  c:\logs\performance\DiskAndNetworktest.log
  2>>c:\logs\errors\DiskAndNetworktest.error"
```

The NT Server Resource Kit also includes "winat.exe," which provides a friendly GUI-based front end to the "at" command. When using "winat.exe," do not put the command in quotes. By analyzing the results of the baseline server's pulse you have created, you can decide what is acceptable and what is not. If the production baseline becomes unacceptable, you can take the appropriate actions, then rerun the server pulse test to determine if your efforts to remove the bottleneck are successful. A look at locating disk subsystem bottlenecks is revealed in Chapter 6.

EXPANDING THE BASIC SERVER PULSE TEST

This simple example was chosen since this is something that everyone can easily implement and is something that almost all servers need to do: transfer files to another computer. These simple scripts can be expanded using one of the more robust scripting languages available for NT Server, such as Perl for NT. As NT moves into the enterprise, however, nice GUI interfaces are in helping new administrators get up to speed on administrating a single or small group of servers are, anyone managing or testing a large NT Server rollout appreciates the power of a good scripting language. Most GUI-based tools shipped with NT Server are designed to be used sitting at the console, and manually repeating task after task. Manually intensive tasks are prone to developing problems. For example, checking a registry entry on 300 servers via a GUI without making a mistake is a challenge, and is time consuming without the aid of a good scripting language. Perl provides Win32 modules to accomplish helpful administrative tasks. I hack Perl scripts in UNIX environments as needed, and have found it helpful in NT Server environments as well. Perl for NT is available from the NT Server Resource Kit, but an even better source is to download a copy of Perl from *http://www.activestate.com*. By downloading Perl, you are sure to get the latest release.

Using Perl and the resource kit, you can easily customize the NT batch script DiskAndNetworkTest.bat to calculate the throughput of your test, log the data into a friendlier log file format, and send an alert to NT Server's Event Viewer (Start|Programs|Administrative Tools|Event Viewer). Later in the Alert and Monitor Service section, I add an optional module to this script, which enables it to start a copy of Performance Monitor in logging mode on the local and remote servers. This helps in isolating why the file transfer is below an acceptable baseline. Here is an example Perl and NT Batch script customization of DiskAndNetworkTest.bat. These two scripts, PulseTest.bat and BaseLineCheck.pl,work in concert, with explanatory comments included in the scripts.

TESTING LOCAL DISK AND NETWORK I/O PERFORMANCE: PulseTest.bat and BaseLineCheck.pl

PulseTest.bat

```
@echo off
REM # Turn off stdout echo
REM ######################################################
REM #
REM #
REM # Goal: Take a network server's pulse by copying a
REM #       file to the remote server
REM #
REM # Script: Simple file transfer and time
REM #         Batch Scripts called by Perl script
REM #         Baseline.pl for data manipulation
REM #
REM # Note: Coordinate any changes between batch
REM #   and BaselineCheck.pl Perl script
REM #
REM #   -baseline value of acceptable transfer times
REM #    is influenced by size of file transferred
REM #   -Values Set in BaseLineCheck.pl (self explained)
REM #   baseline, outputfile, baselinelogfile, remote
```

```
REM #   host
REM #   -Values Set in TestPulse.bat
REM #   testfile2.ded - this is file to be transferred
REM #   to the network share remote host
REM #
REM ##################################################


REM # Easy way to create a 10MB file
REM # creatfil.exe command from NT Resource Kit
REM #
creatfil c:\temp\testfil2.ded 10000

REM # Check size of File created and pass exact file to
REM # Perl script
REM #
dir c:\temp\testfil2.ded

REM # Set network share
REM # If this is changed, change remotehost name in
REM # BaseLineCheck.pl
REM #
net use k: \\megatron\c$

REM # copy file to network connected disk/share
REM # timethis command located on NT Resource Kit CD-ROM
REM #
timethis "copy c:\temp\testfil2.ded
  k:\temp\testfil2.ded"

REM # Cleanup
REM #
del k:\temp\testfil2.ded
net use k: /delete


REM #############
REM # End Script PulseTest.bat
REM #############
```

```
BaseLineCheck.pl

#########################################################
#
#
#   Perl Script: Rapid Prototype/Example for taking
#     baseline measurements from outside your server
#     Error checking for empty results, etc. left for
#     reader
#
#   What Script Does:
#      BaseLineCheck.pl is typically run from the NT
#      scheduler via the at command:
#      c:\>at 21:02 /interactive /every:M,T,W,Th,F,S,Su
#      cmd /c
#      c:\users\curt\bin\baselinecheck.pl
#      1>>c:\temp\output.txt
#      2>>c:\temp\output.txt
#
#      This Perl script calls the NT batch script
#      PulseTest.bat which creates and times the
#      transfer of a 10 MB file to a remote server
#      This script then compares the corresponding timing
#      results to the designated baseline and logs the
#      results in a log file and sends an alert to the
#      NT event logs if the results are lower
#      than the baseline specified.
#
#   Key Notes:
#      -Ensure this file (BaseLineCheck.pl) and NT
#       batch script
#       PulseTest.bat are in the same directory
#      -Only one file is not cleaned up, but it is over
#      written
#      c:\temp\output.txt. Use for debugging if needed
#
#########################################################

# Initialization
#
$pulsetestlocation="c:/users/curt/bin/PulseTest.bat";
  #Path to .bat
$remotehost="megatron"; # For log, indicate name of
                        # remote Server
$baseline=700000;       # Minimum acceptable performance
                        #  (Bytes/sec)
                        #  e.g. baseline value
```

```
$outputfile="c:/temp/output.txt"; # Where
                                 # PulseTest.bat sends
                                 # temporary
                                 # data temporary test
                                 # results
$performanceunacceptable=0;      # Set performance test flag
                                 # 0 - indicates acceptable
                                 #      Performance
                                 # 1 - indicates unacceptable
                                 #      Performance
$baselinelogfile="c:/users/curt/logs/baseline.log";
                                 # Where to place results


# Call NT Batch script to tun PulseTest.bat
#
system("$pulsetestlocation > $outputfile");


# Open temporary results file $outputfile from
  PulseTest.bat
#
open(IN, "$outputfile") ||
  die "cannot open $outputfile: $!";

# Get data from PulseTest.bat
while (<IN>)
    {
    if (/Elapsed/)
        {
        chomp($_);       #Get time results
        $time=$_;
        }
    if (/Start/)         #Get date of tests
        {
        $temp_date=$_;  }
     if (/File/)#   Get size of file sent
      {
      chomp($_);
      $size=$_;
  }
    }

# Close file
close(IN);

# Determine Transfer Time Values
# Removing colons and normalize data
```

```
#
$hour=substr($time, 28, 2);
$min=substr($time, 31, 2);
$sec=substr($time, 34, 10);
$date=substr($temp_date, 28, 20);
$total_time= ($hour*3600) + ($min*60) + ($sec);

# Remove Commas and such to determine transfer file
#  Size for throughput calculation
#
$_=substr($size, 28, 20);
tr/0123456789//cd;
$filesize=$_;

# Finally, determine throughput
#
$throughput=$filesize/$total_time;


# Check to see how measured throughput compares to
#  minimum acceptable throughput
#
# If Transfer speed unacceptable,log the event
#  to NT Server event log and baseline performance log

# Normalize data for comparison
#
$throughput1=sprintf("%.2f",$throughput);
$baseline1=sprintf("%.2f",$baseline);

if ($throughput1 lt $baseline1)
  {
    $performanceunacceptable=1; # Set flag so that
                                # baseline log updated
                                # w/error

  use Win32::Eventlog;          # Send error to NT
  Event log
  {
       my $number, $EventLog;
         # open the event log.

       Win32::EventLog::Open($EventLog , "Performance
Baseline Perl App", '') || die $!;
              # define the event to log.
        $Event =
      {
         'EventType' => EVENTLOG_INFORMATION_TYPE,
```

```
            'Category' => 0,
          'EventID' => 0x1003,
            'Data' => '',
            'Strings' => "Unacceptable performance! Base-
  line: $baseline1 but measured Throughput
  $throughput1 bytes/sec",
        };
          # report the event and check the error
            $EventLog->Report($Event) || die $!;
        }
#--
#-- Enter Code here to Start Perfmon Monitor Service
#-- Module if so desired
#--
  }

# Get This System's Information
#
use Win32;
$computername=Win32::NodeName;

# Print results to performance baseline log file (or
  database)
#
open(LOGFILE, ">> $baselinelogfile") ||
  die "cannot open $baselinelogfile: $!";

if ($performanceunacceptable eq 1)
    {
    printf LOGFILE "Error: Below Baseline($baseline1
    bytes/sec)-";
    }

printf LOGFILE "$date, $computername Net Throughput to
  $remotehost: $throughput1 bytes/sec \n";

close(LOGFILE);

#####################################################
#
# BaselineCheck.pl Ends Here
#
#####################################################
```

This tool is introduced here to help in developing comparisons for your environment and sends exceptions to the Event View to save the time of constantly checking the server pulse output baseline file. Once you begin to understand the characteristics of your environment, you can choose the thresholds that are not acceptable, and have these unacceptable thresholds sent to NT Server's Event Application Log for easier notification. In the next section, Performance Monitor, I will outline how to automatically start Performance Monitor to aid in determining why the servers under test have fallen below the baseline.

The most important concept that you should remember from Specific Tests to Run When Developing a Baseline, is to take the time to develop a suite of tests that measure the quantitative performance of your server or server subsystems. Thus, you will more accurately be able to determine the health of your server, and if your tuning efforts are effective.

Free and Commercially Available Tools for Baseline Development

The tests mentioned above are by no means thorough benchmarks, and some people are not interested in modeling their environments using Perl and NT batch scripts. There are always other options. The NT Server Resource Kit provides comprehensive tools such as the "Response Probe" tool, which provides for more elaborate exercising of your disk subsystem to take a server's pulse. Another friendlier tool I have found helpful, is the free disk test software package Galileo from Intel. Galileo is available via ftp at *ftp.intel.com* or *http://developer.intel.com/design/servers/devtools/iometer.*

Two commercial software packages that are excellent for large-scale prototyping are the "Neal Nelson Business Benchmark for NT," available from Neal Nelson and Associates, (phone 312-755-1000) and "Dynameasure Enterprise" Bluecurve *http://www.bluecurve.com*. Both of these tools are used throughout this book for hands on examples. Bluecurve has provided a limited copy of their software on the CD-ROM that accompanies this book so that you take it for a test drive and test your environment. These commercial testing tools can help you model your environment even closer. Commercial benchmarks are explored in depth in Chapter 3, "Capacity Sizing."

Performance Statistics Gathering: Start the Logs

It is now time to review the second primary technique to developing a performance baseline. The first was running specific tests or benchmarks on your server before and after placing it into production; in essence, taking a server's pulse to ensure it is operating within acceptable parameters. The second primary technique in developing a baseline is to collect resource statistics on the server(s) that are in use. The primary tool included in NT Server for developing a performance baseline of server resource usage is the Performance Monitor.

But before we begin to review Performance Monitor, there are several other helpful tools that are included in both NT Server 4.0 and the NT Resource Kit.

Event Viewer

If all of your server's hardware and software components are not working properly, they will never be able to perform well. Analogous to a car with an eight cylinder engine, if only five of the eight cylinders are running correctly, the biggest concern is not the top speed you will be able to obtain in the race, but if you can race at all.

NT Server's Event Viewer, found under Start|Programs|Administrative Tools|Event Viewer, allows for a quick check to see if all applications, services, drivers, and hardware components, etc. have started and are operating correctly. The Event Viewer provides a centralized logging point for most of NT Server's functions. The Event Viewer is broken down into three primary areas: system, security, and application. Make it a point to review these on a regular basis. Before a server is ready to enter production, I always reboot a few times and Ensure that the Event Viewer logs are clear of any errors. Start with a system that is operating correctly.

Windows NT Diagnostic Tool

Another helpful tool is Windows Diagnostics (see Figure 2–4). This tool, winmsd.exe, is accessed from the console via Start|Programs|Administrative Tools|Windows NT Diagnostics. This is one of the easiest methods to determine operating system version, service packs installed, resource usage, and memory use. For example, the Memory tab shows how much total (or actual) physical memory you have, what is available, and what the file system cache is currently using. There is other information displayed under the memory tab, but being able to quickly observe the amount of memory available provides a quick indication if further investigation is needed or not. If the available amount of memory is hovering around four to five MBytes and the pagefile.sys in use value is greater than 25 percent of available RAM, I would skip to Chapter 5, "NT Server and Memory Performance," for an in-depth investigation.

As NT Server is deployed onto larger enterprise class servers using the Intel CPU architecture, hardware resource usage becomes more important. Here, hardware usage is defined as interrupts, I/O ports, DMA, and memory resources. Under Windows NT Diagnostics, you can quickly see how these resources are used. Even with plug and play PCI enabled BIOSs, most servers today have server tools that must be executed before NT Server is booted. These tools are usually executed from a DOS diskette or partition to ensure the hardware resources are set up correctly. These tools take a hardware perspective of the server. Using the Windows NT Diagnostics tool, you get NT Server's software perspective of what is in the server and how NT is using the

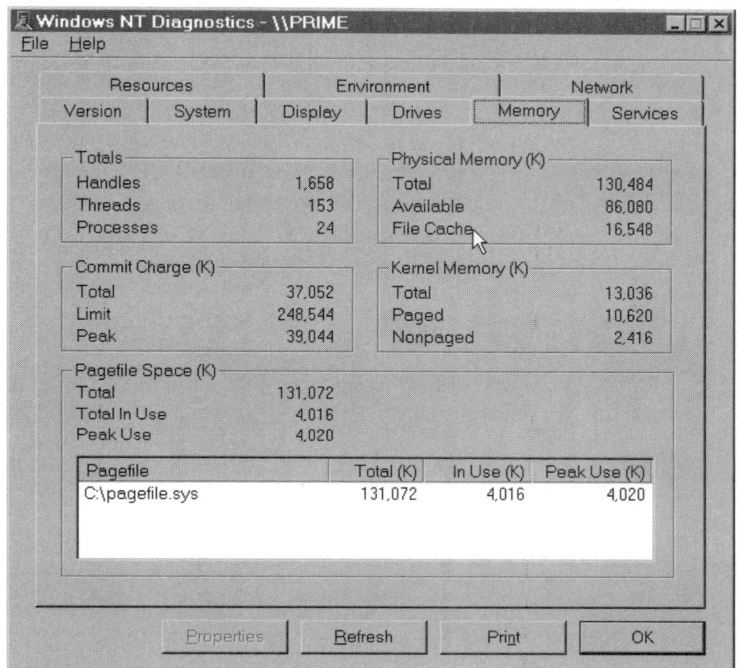

Figure 2–4 *Windows NT Diagnostics tool (winmds.exe)*

resources. Sometimes, the server hardware and operating system tools do not quite match; thus, it is important to check both when putting your NT solution into place for performance and troubleshooting. Windows NT Diagnostics has both a graphical mode (winmsd.exe) and a command line mode (winmsdp.exe) so that it is easy to redirect all of the tool's data to a log file for future reference. In the following chapters, we explore the relationship between hardware resources and their interaction with NT Server.

Task Manager

Task Manager is the best software performance tool addition to NT from NT Server 3.51 to 4.0. Although the information provided by Task Manager was available by using a combination of Resource Kit tools, they were neither as friendly nor installed by default. To launch Task Manager, right click the NT Server tool bar and select Task Manager. Task Manager is a tool that provides a current look at what is running on your server from three different views: applications, processes, and performance. Task Manager provides an instantaneous (almost) view of what is running on your server. Since Task Manager does not have a file-logging mode, this tool is not helpful for long term or baseline logging, but it is very helpful in solving active performance problems.

For example, perhaps the server has suddenly become CPU bound at about the same time an end user mentions some of their applications have gone astray. Using Task Manager's process view, you can quickly determine which processes are running amok, and watch their system usage. Using Task Manager process view, you can quickly determine if the processes in question are continually using more RAM, how much CPU time they are accumulating, and then kill them off if needed by right clicking on the process and selecting End Process. Task Manager is very similar to the UNIX tool "top" in depicting what processes are running and which resources they are consuming.

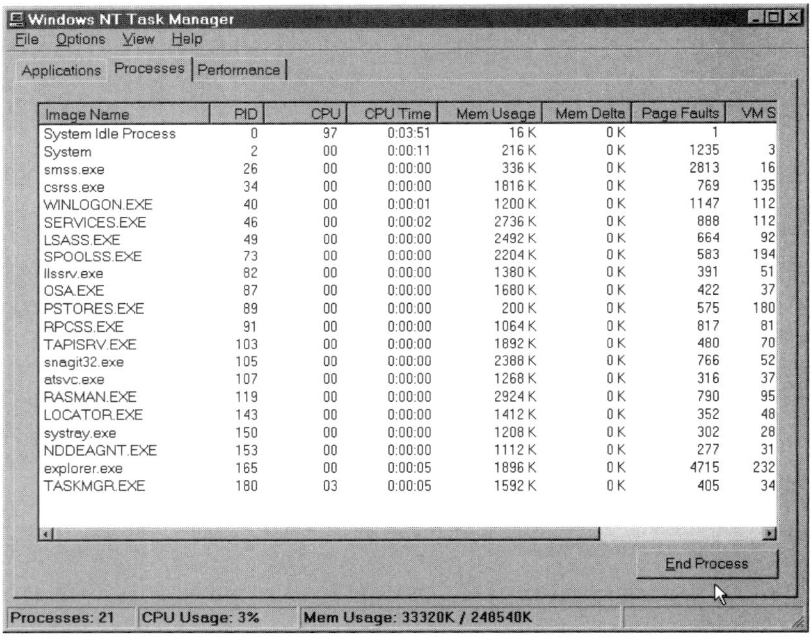

Windows NT Task Manager
File Options View Help
Applications Processes Performance

Image Name	PID	CPU	CPU Time	Mem Usage	Mem Delta	Page Faults	VM S
System Idle Process	0	97	0:03:51	16 K	0 K	1	
System	2	00	0:00:11	216 K	0 K	1235	3
smss.exe	26	00	0:00:00	336 K	0 K	2813	16
csrss.exe	34	00	0:00:00	1816 K	0 K	769	135
WINLOGON.EXE	40	00	0:00:01	1200 K	0 K	1147	112
SERVICES.EXE	46	00	0:00:02	2736 K	0 K	888	112
LSASS.EXE	49	00	0:00:00	2492 K	0 K	664	92
SPOOLSS.EXE	73	00	0:00:00	2204 K	0 K	583	194
llssrv.exe	82	00	0:00:00	1380 K	0 K	391	51
OSA.EXE	87	00	0:00:00	1680 K	0 K	422	37
PSTORES.EXE	89	00	0:00:00	200 K	0 K	575	180
RPCSS.EXE	91	00	0:00:00	1064 K	0 K	817	81
TAPISRV.EXE	103	00	0:00:00	1892 K	0 K	480	70
snagit32.exe	105	00	0:00:00	2388 K	0 K	766	52
atsvc.exe	107	00	0:00:00	1268 K	0 K	316	37
RASMAN.EXE	119	00	0:00:00	2924 K	0 K	790	95
LOCATOR.EXE	143	00	0:00:00	1412 K	0 K	352	48
systray.exe	150	00	0:00:00	1208 K	0 K	302	28
NDDEAGNT.EXE	153	00	0:00:00	1112 K	0 K	277	31
explorer.exe	165	00	0:00:05	1896 K	0 K	4715	232
TASKMGR.EXE	180	03	0:00:05	1592 K	0 K	405	34

End Process

Processes: 21 CPU Usage: 3% Mem Usage: 33320K / 248540K

Figure 2–5 *Task Manager's process view*

Understanding what processes are normally executing on your server is helpful when troubleshooting performance problems. Task Manager is a great tool to instantly observe what processes are running on your server. Figure 2–5 provides an illustration of the extensive information that Task Manager can quickly provide. In this snapshot, the following fields are shown:

- **Image Name**—depicts the processes that are in memory and can be run on the CPU
- **CPU**—current CPU usage
- **CPU Time**—accumulated CPU time since the process was started

- **Memory Usage**—the amount of physical RAM the process is currently occupying
- **Memory Delta**—the difference in the current amount of RAM since the last sample
- **Page Fault**—how often the process requested data or code that was not in the process's working set

The Performance Monitor can provide similar information, although it is not as easy to use as Task Manager, but its data can be logged. When looking at these outputs, some of the processes that are presented may seem obvious to some and alien to others. The following is a listing and definition of the common processes that run in the background after an NT Server installation, before additional applications and services are running or installed.

Common Background Processes Running Under NT Server

Microsoft Windows NT Workstation Resource Kit, Microsoft Press, pps. 279–280)

SERVICES • This process is shared by the Windows NT Services Control Manager, which starts all services, and a group of Windows NT 32 bit services, including Alerter, Clipbook Server, Computer Browser, Event Viewer, Messenger, Server and Workstation, and Plug and Play.

CSRSS • Client Server Runtime Subsystem provides text window support, shutdown, and hard error handling to NT environment subsystems.

EXPLORER • A segment of the user interface which lets users open documents and applications from a hierarchical display.

IDLE • Process that runs to occupy the processors when they are not executing threads. Idle has one process per CPU.

LLSSRV • License Logging Service, the service that logs the licensing data for license manager in NT server.

LSASS • Local Security Administration Subsystem runs the local security authority component of NT security subsystem. This process handles aspects of security administration on the local computer, including access and permissions. The Net Logon Service shares this process.

NDDEAGNT • Network DDE Agent, handles requests for network DDE services.

NTVDM • NT Virtual DOS Machine which simulates a 16 bit environment for MS-DOS and 16 bit Windows applications.

PERFMON • Performance Monitor executable

RPCSS • Remote Procedure Call (RPC) Subsystem which includes RPC service and locator—services process is shared by NT services control manager, which starts all services.

SMS • Session Manager Subsystem.

SPOOLSS • Spooler Subsystem that controls despooling of printer data from disk to printer.

SYSTEM • Contains system threads that handle lazy writing by file system, virtual memory modified page writing, working set trimming, and similar system functions.

TASKMGR • Task Manager executable.

WINLOGON • Logon process executable manages log on/off and remote Performance Monitor data requests.

Performance Monitor

Since Performance Monitor is the primary tool to utilize when tuning and sizing NT Server, it is wise to become intimately familiar with it. Locating a server bottleneck or sizing a server for increased workloads is not cut and dried. Monitoring only one server resource at a time can help you narrow in on a bottleneck or a trend, but to understand what is really happening, it is important to comprehend the relationships between the server resources. Individual server resources are explored in-depth in later chapters, but to gather the actual data needed to see these relationships, you should be familiar with what the Performance Monitor can and cannot do for you.

Performance Monitor, a software tool that measures the usage of server resources in either real time or over a period of time and can log resource usage information into a file. Defined with the standard NT Server operating system are a series of objects that have subsequent counters associated with them. For example, one such object is the Processor Object, which has numerous counters associated with it such as % Processor time, % User Time, etc. Performance Monitor is extensible, which allows vendors to add additional functionality to the Performance Monitor tool through the addition of more objects and subsequent counters. When some applications for NT Server are installed, such as Internet Information Server (IIS), an entirely new set of objects are installed in addition to the default Performance Monitor objects to help analyze and tune that particular application.

In this section I will not list every possible counter, since this information can easily be obtained from the Performance Monitor itself, or from the Microsoft Windows NT Workstation and Server Resource Kits. What I will cover is the primary modes of operation when using Performance Monitor, key pieces of information about using Performance Monitor that are not always apparent, and primary counters you should become familiar with at a minimum. The individual counters under Performance Monitor are reviewed in more detail in the later chapters that delve into the individual server resources.

Understanding the Effects of Performance Monitoring Measurement

Regardless of what is being measured, do not add so much overhead to the server such that what you are measuring is being heavily affected by the tool you are measuring with. This was more of an issue back in the days of the Intel 80386 and 80486 based server days than the more recent Pentium II, Pentium Pro, and DEC Alpha based NT servers of today. The NT Kernel is always collecting statistics on the objects that can be collected by Performance Monitor, regardless of whether Performance Monitor is running or not (except for a few cases that will be addressed). Thus, it does not matter if you are logging one or all of the objects available, the load placed on the server is not substantial, unless the sampling period is set to less then five seconds between samples. However, when Performance Monitor is run in Chart Mode, it does use more CPU cycles than the other modes of operation due to updating the real time graphical display.

Activating Essential Performance Monitor Counters

My disk counters always display zero. Wow! Those disks are never bottlenecks! Not quite. There are some important objects and counters that are not started, or installed, by default. To ensure that all relative performance counters can be collected, complete the following actions:

1. Add the SNMP Agent service under Start|Settings|Control Panel|Network|Services|Add select SNMP Service. Adding this service installs the network interface segment object to Performance Monitor
2. Add the Network Tools and Agent under Start|Settings|Control Panel|Network|Services|Add select Network Tools and Agent. This will install the network segment object to Performance Monitor and the real time Network Monitor based application.
   Network Segment is the only Performance Monitor object that may negatively affect your server's networking performance. Collecting data using this object places the selected network interface card into promiscuous mode. Promiscuous mode forces the selected network interface card to read every packet that it observes on the network segment it is attached to regardless if the network packet is destined for the server or not. This will add additional overhead to your server above and beyond the standard Performance Monitor application. The network segment counter is a useful tool, although care should be taken when it is activated. Use this counter on an as needed basis to investigate network bottlenecks. Do not run it all of the time.
3. To monitor disk performance statistics, you must run "diskperf -ye" from a command prompt and reboot the server before disk statistic gathering is enabled. Diskperf has several options, typing "diskperf /? | more" at

the command line provides explanations for all of the diskperf options. The "-y" option suggested sets the server to start disk performance counters when it is restarted. The "-e" option enables the disk performance counters used for measuring performance of the physical drives in striped disk sets.

To launch Performance Monitor, or Perfmon as I will refer to it, select Start|Administrative Tools|Performance Monitor. There are four primary modes of operation when using Perfmon: Chart Mode, Log Mode, Alert Mode, and Report Mode. You can select any of these modes from the View menu selection and add additional counters for observation in the selected mode by Edit|Add.

Perfmon Chart Mode

Chart Mode is a good mode to use when you want to determine what is currently happening on your server or to analyze a Perfmon log file. Using Chart Mode's graphical output is helpful when viewing the different server resource relationships. Although each server resource is investigated closer in later chapters, a question I get quite often is, "What counters should be observed when trying to understand what is going on with my server?" Under the Task Manager section, Processes view, any process that is currently running under NT Server is listed. This same process information is also logged under Perfmon. But what about monitoring the other primary resources? If you add too many counters to the graphical workspace view, it is difficult to make heads or tails of what the heck is going on, even if it might look impressive to the common passerby or for executive presentations.

Key Perfmon Counters To Observe

Perfmon allows you to save your workspace under File|Save workspace. Once you save your workspace as a .pmw file, it is easy to set-up a desktop shortcut (icon) to this view. Thus, when the .pmw icon is double clicked, a copy of Performance Monitor with the saved workspace settings is launched. To set up a shortcut to a specific .pmw file, right click an open area of the server console, select new|shortcut, browse the file system to locate the .pmw file that was saved, and then name your shortcut. Using this technique, I created .pmw files for each of the primary server resources so that it is easy to observe key server relationships with a few clicks of the mouse. Copies of these .pmw files ar3e on this book's accompaning CD-ROM. Future updat4es are available at http://www.TuningAndSizingNT.com. These .pmw files are: cpu-resources.pmw, disk-resources.pmw, memory-resources.pmw, and network-resources.pmw (see Figures 2–6 through 2–9).

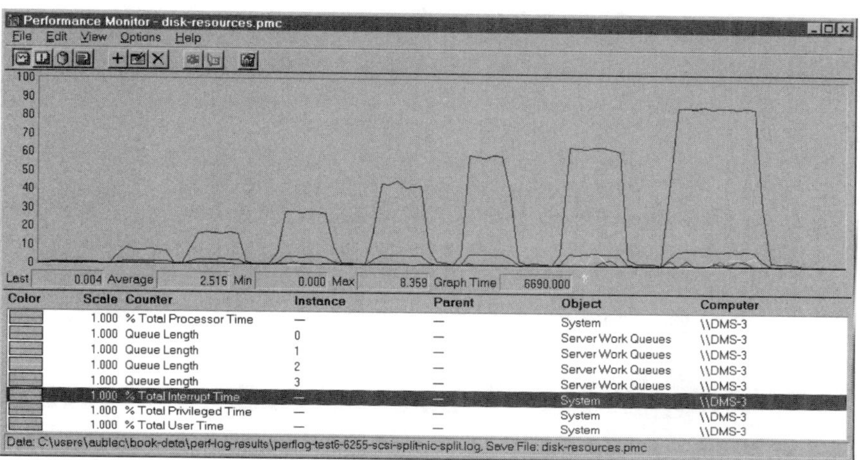

Figure 2–6 *Key Perfmon CPU counters to observer: CPU-resource-usage.pmw.*

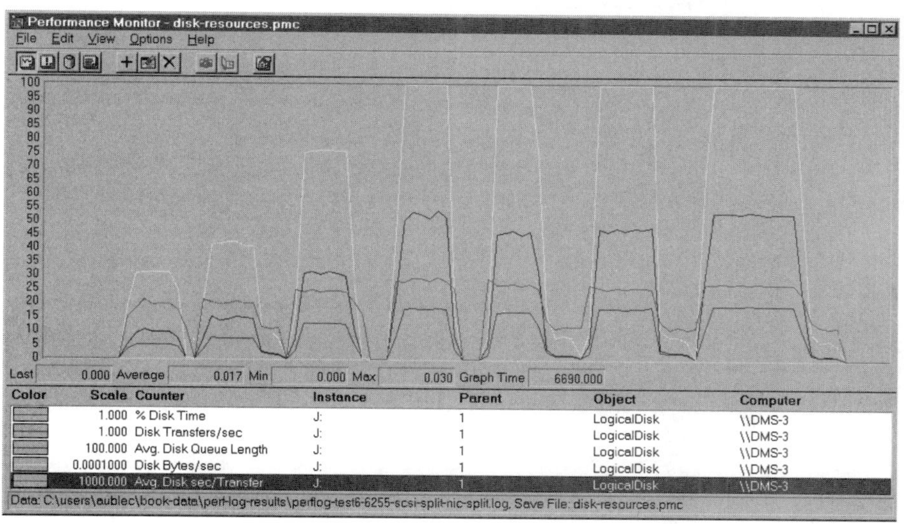

Figure 2–7 *Key Perfmon disk counters to observer: Disk-resource-usage.pmw.*

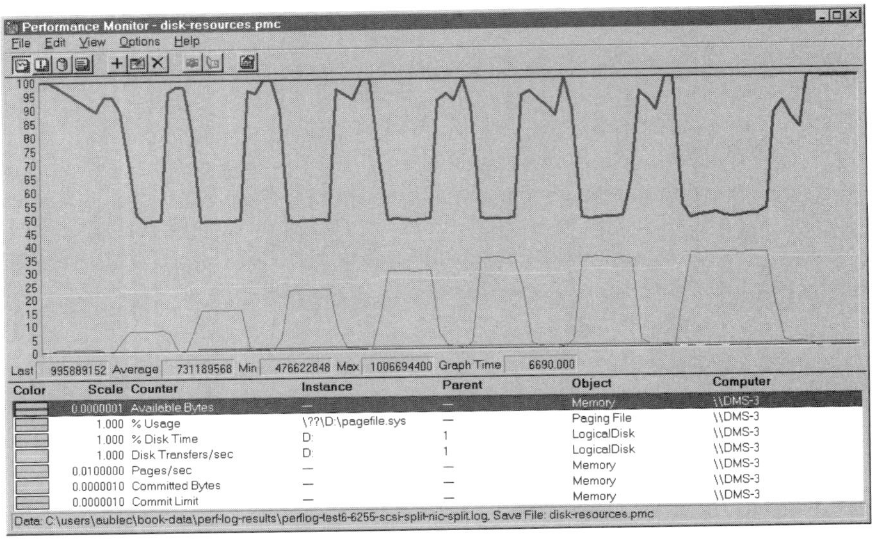

Performance Monitor - disk-resources.pmc
File Edit View Options Help
100
95
90
85
80
75
70
65
60
55
50
45
40
35
30
25
20
15
10
5
0
Last 995889152 Average 731189568 Min 476622848 Max 1006694400 Graph Time 6690.000
Color Scale Counter Instance Parent Object Computer
0.0000001 Available Bytes — — Memory \\DMS-3
1.000 % Usage \??\D:\pagefile.sys — Paging File \\DMS-3
1.000 % Disk Time D: 1 LogicalDisk \\DMS-3
1.000 Disk Transfers/sec D: 1 LogicalDisk \\DMS-3
0.0100000 Pages/sec — — Memory \\DMS-3
0.0000010 Committed Bytes — — Memory \\DMS-3
0.0000010 Commit Limit — — Memory \\DMS-3
Data: C:\users\aublec\book-data\perf-log-results\perflog-test6-6255-scsi-split-nic-split.log, Save File: disk-resources.pmc

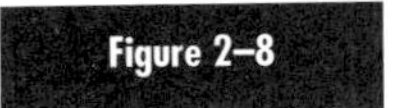

Figure 2–8 *Key Perfmon memory counters to observer: Memory-resource-usage.pmw.*

Performance Monitor - disk-resources.pmc
File Edit View Options Help
125000000
112500000
100000000
87500000
75000000
62500000
50000000
37500000
25000000
12500000
0
Last 5.244 Average 1523434 Min 0.000 Max 3973318 Graph Time 6690.000
Color Scale Counter Instance Parent Object Computer
10.000 Bytes Total/sec 3 — Network Interface \\DMS-3
0.0000001 Output Queue Length 3 — Network Interface \\DMS-3
1.000 Current Bandwidth 3 — Network Interface \\DMS-3
1.000 Packets Outbound Discarded 3 — Network Interface \\DMS-3
1.000 Packets Outbound Errors 3 — Network Interface \\DMS-3
1.000 Packets Received Discarded 3 — Network Interface \\DMS-3
1.000 Packets Received Errors 3 — Network Interface \\DMS-3
Data: C:\users\aublec\book-data\perf-log-results\perflog-test6-6255-scsi-split-nic-split.log, Save File: disk-resources.pmc

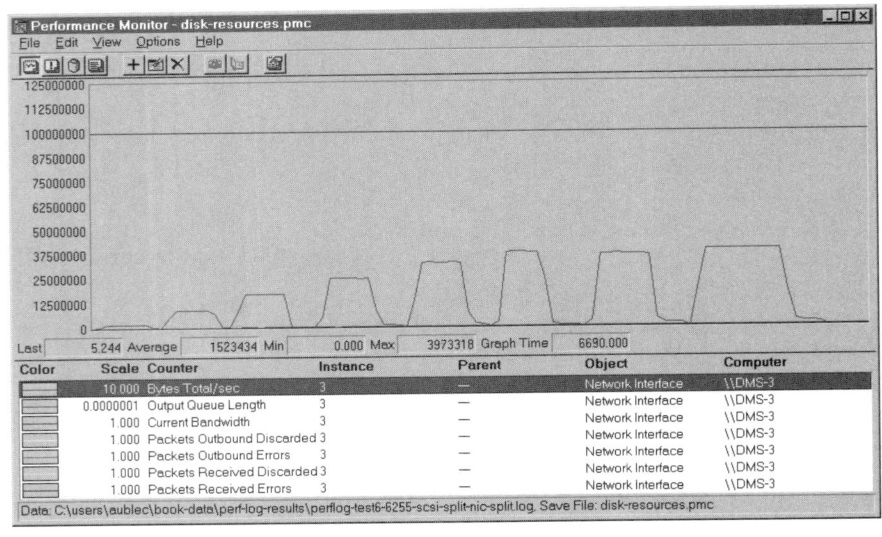

Figure 2–9 *Key Perfmon network counters to observer: Network-resource-usage.pmw.*

Note that you may need to customize these Perfmon workspace files for your specific environment. If your server environment differs from the examples illustrated—in areas such as network or disk subsystems—you may need to change the number of instances (the actual physical device) in Perfmon. Even though these are good counters to observe when gaining an immediate understanding of server resource usage, you should experiment with others. There are numerous other objects and counters available under Perfmon which can provide additional detailed insight into the performance of your server; just remember to understand what you are measuring.

Perfmon Log Mode

Perfmon's Log Mode allows for the long-term collection of NT Server performance data. Collection of long-term data facilitates the detection of bottlenecks, system trends, and baseline comparison analysis.

To begin logging data with Perfmon, start Perfmon, then select View|Log, Edit|Add to log. Select all objects using the mouse and shift key, then click Add|Done. To begin the logging session select Options|Log, enter the name of your log file (e.g., *server19-perfmon-log*), specify a sampling interval, and then click Start. Perfmon uses about the same amount of resources to collect measurements from one object or many objects from NT Server's performance library DLLs, so collect them all, except for the network segment. Select the network segment counter only if you suspect a network problem. The server will need extra CPU cycles and memory available to process all of the incoming packets. Extra resources are required because the network interface card is placed into a promiscuous mode of operation by the network segment counter. Enough performance data is available from the network interface object (installed when the SNMP Service was added earlier) to help in detecting general network bottlenecks even without the network segment counter.

If the copy of Performance Monitor that is currently being used for logging is used to view the current data in any way, it will stop logging your data. To avoid this inconvenience, launch a second copy of Performance Monitor to view the currently active logging session or real time server data. Another quirk of Perfmon is that when it is started in logging mode, it only logs those processes that were currently active when logging was started. Thus, if a new application was spawned after logging began, Perfmon would detect and report the increase in server resources, but you would not have a clue as to which process was causing this increase. To work around this quirk, review the Alert and Monitor Service section later in this chapter.

When to Collect Perfmon Data

When should performance data be collected? The ideal answer is all of the time, since you may need the data for future sizing requirements or to troubleshoot a problem. The two major stumbling blocks when running Perfmon all of the time are disk space and dynamic activity on the server. When you log data, you need to place it somewhere. Table 2.1 outlines the amount of data that is logged when all objects are selected for measurement. Use this chart for general planning purposes only. The number of processes that are currently running and the addition of Performance Monitor objects (that may have been added via additional application installations) influence the amount of data logged.

Table 2.1 Logged data selected for measurement.

Performance Monitor Log Growth Rate

Time	Sampling Period	Log File Size (Mbytes)
60 Minutes	5 sec	25.71
1 Day	5 sec	616.90
60 Minutes	1 minute	2.15
1 Day	1 minute	51.41
60 Minutes	15 minutes	.142
1 Day	15 minutes	3.42

The frequency of the sampling period depends on your environment and what you want to accomplish. Obviously, the shorter the sampling period, the better the chance that any temporary workload surges on the server will be discovered. Conversely, the amount of disk space used can become prohibitive. If you were developing a prototype, a more frequent sampling rate would provide the increased granularity required to understand your workload characteristics. For general server health, four out of five engineers surveyed recommend a sampling period between 15 to 30 minutes. After reviewing the 15–30 minute sampling period data, there may be times that you start a copy of Perfmon with a higher sampling period to isolate problem areas. It is also possible to use a less granular, say 60 minute sampling rate, and then tie that sampling system to a finer sampling rate using Perfmon's Alert Mode.

Alert Mode and Monitor Service

Under Perfmon's Alert Mode you can easily set thresholds for various server resource parameters that in turn trigger other events. This is helpful to reduce the amount of time required to review the performance logs. This tool can become even more powerful when coupled with the Performance Monitor service that is included with the Microsoft Windows NT Server Resource Kit. Using these two tools in concert, you can start a second copy of Perfmon to log current data at a higher sampling rate for a given amount of time. This can help lower the amount of data normally collected (i.e., only collect granular data when needed). These tools also aid in working around that quirk in Perfmon that causes only processes that are currently active during the startup of Perfmon in logging mode to be collected. It is in this environment when the second copy of Perfmon earns its keep. The second copy of Perfmon only starts when the first copy detects an increase in server usage; thus, when the second copy starts, there is a high degree of probability it will log the currently active process guilty of causing the increased (for good or bad) load.

Setting Up the Monitor Service

Sounds great, but how do you make this happen? First, set up the scheduler service as stated earlier so we can use the "at" command, then set up the Monitor Service. Copy the monitor.exe and datalog.exe files from the Microsoft Windows NT Server Resource Kit CD-ROM into the %SystemRoot%\system32 directory (commonly C:\winnt\system32), then install the service by typing "monitor setup" at the command prompt. Next, start a copy of Perfmon in Log Mode, select all of the counters you desire (I like to select all of them since [except network segment] the one needed is usually the one not selected). Then, under Perfmon Options|Log, choose a location for the output log to be written. At this point, select File|Save Log Settings as monitor-log-settings.pml into the %systemroot%\system32 directory. Back at the command line, type in "monitor \\`yourComputer` monitor-log-settings.pml". The monitor service is now installed to use the Perfmon Log settings that you have defined. This is all that is needed to begin using the monitor service from the Performance Monitor Alert view.

Alert Mode and Monitor Service Example

Let's now walk through an example together. In reviewing your performance logs, you notice sporadic surges in CPU usage that do not follow any noticeable trends. To get a better understanding of this phenomenon, select a counter to key on to determine when the CPU is overloaded, which can then be used by the Perfmon's Alert View to trigger an additional action. Once Perfmon is started, select View|Alert, then select Edit|Add and highlight Server Work Queue object. In the Alert selection, enter Alter, if over 2, then add the program to run the first time the alert is detected with "c:\users\curt\bin\monitor-start.bat". The batch file, c:\users\curt\bin\monitor-start.bat, will start the Monitor Service, which subsequently runs a second copy of Perfmon in logging mode. This setup procedure is illustrated in Figure 2–10.

```
Echo off
REM #####################################################
REM #
REM # Batch Script starts Monitor Service which
REM # launches Perfmon in log mode
REM #
REM #####################################################

C:\winnt\system32\monitor start 1>> c:\temp\moni-
  tor.log 2>>c:\temp\monitor.error2
```

Batch File: monitor-start.bat

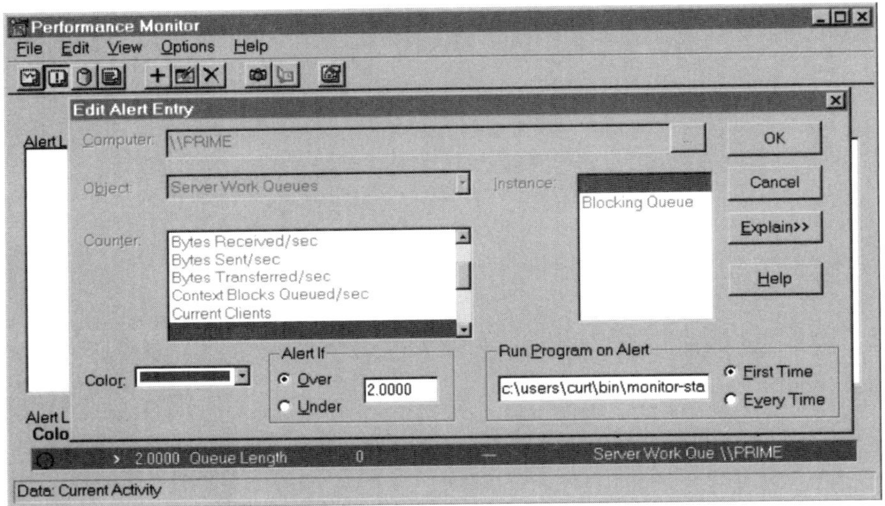

Figure 2–10 *Alert Mode and Monitor Service example.*

Additional Perfmon and Monitor Service Techniques

Staying with the same concept on launching Perfmon as needed, there are two other helpful techniques for using the monitor service to activate Perfmon in logging mode. The first technique is to start Perfmon only during those times of day when you want some extra performance monitoring. To accomplish this, install the monitor service as instructed above, then use the "at" command to start and stop the service.

```
C:> at \\prime 9:30 /every: M,W,F "monitor start"
C:> at \\prime 10:30 /every: M,W,F "monitor stop"
```

The second technique is to add the following Perl command to the BaseLineCheck.pl script explained earier. This will start the monitor service on both of the servers that are being checked to aid in determining why the response time between the servers fell below the baseline.

```
#########################################################
#
# Start Perfmon Monitor Service Module
#
# Note: Remember to have the monitor service properly
# installed on both servers
#
#########################################################

# Call NT Batch script to start the Monitor Service
#
system("c:\winnt\system32\monitor \\$remotehost
  start  >> c:\temp\monitor.log");
system("c:\winnt\system32\monitor \\$localhost start
  >> c:\temp\monitor.log");

####################
# End Module Addition
####################
```

Report Mode

To ease the analysis of large log files, combine Perfmon's Report Mode and time window functions. Perfmon's Report Mode provides the mechanism to review specific data values from log files while the time window function assists in targeting certain portions of your log file by time/date stamp. To analyze a Perfmon log file using this technique, you must first select a log file to analyze under Options|Data From and then choose the log file for analysis. To enter Report View, select View|Report then add the objects and counters you would like to review from Edit|Add.

To now determine where in the log file you wish to obtain the specific data values, switch back to Chart Mode by selecting View|Chart Mode. Use Edit|Add to select the objects and counters to view. Unfortunately, adding counters to the Report Mode does not implicitly add them to the Chart Mode also; thus, the values must be added to both. Chart Mode is good for spotting the areas in a timeline where there may be a problem, but it is difficult to determine the exact values for the time period in question. As illustrated in Figure 2–11 select the Edit|Time Window to zero in on the area of concern.

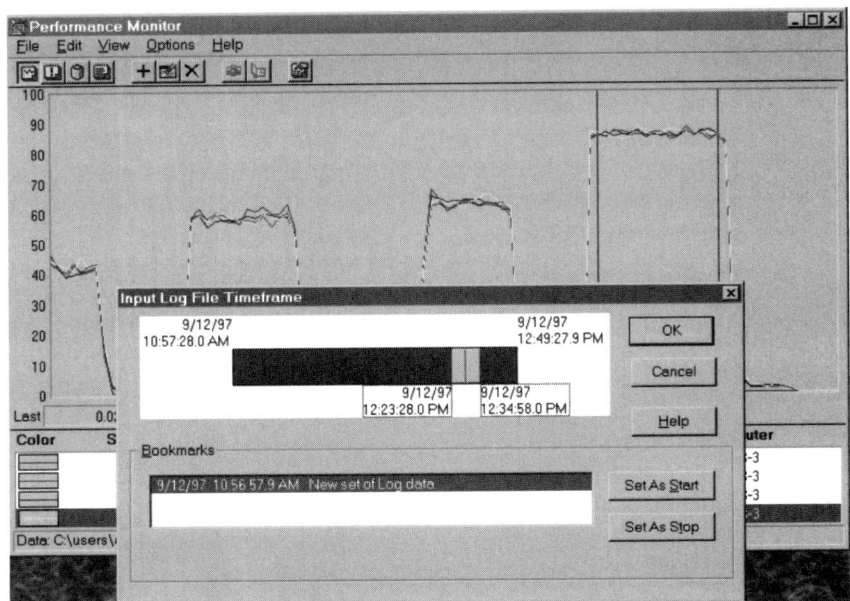

Figure 2–11 *Controlling Perfmon's time window.*

Now, switch back to Report Mode, and you will notice the objects and counters have changed, reflecting the new time window selection under Chart Mode (see Figure 2–12).

By having all of the key metrics to monitor available in one easy view, analysis of the data is much more manageable. Having great data available is useless if you are not aware and familiar with the tools required to leverage the data to your advantage.

Using Accounting to Zero in on Resource Usage

What word comes to mind when server accounting is mentioned? Overhead! is the most typical response. Accounting does add a certain amount of overhead to the server. The amount of overhead incurred is a function of the level of accounting that is turned on and the amount of load placed on the server. This is a direct proportional relationship. The more accounting options selected and the more the server is used, the higher accounting overhead percentage there is. Accounting is typically associated with security, but here we use accounting to our advantage to zero in on who is behind processes that are placing a load onto the server. By selectively choosing which server accounting metrics to collect, server accounting can be helpful while not introducing a significant overhead onto the server.

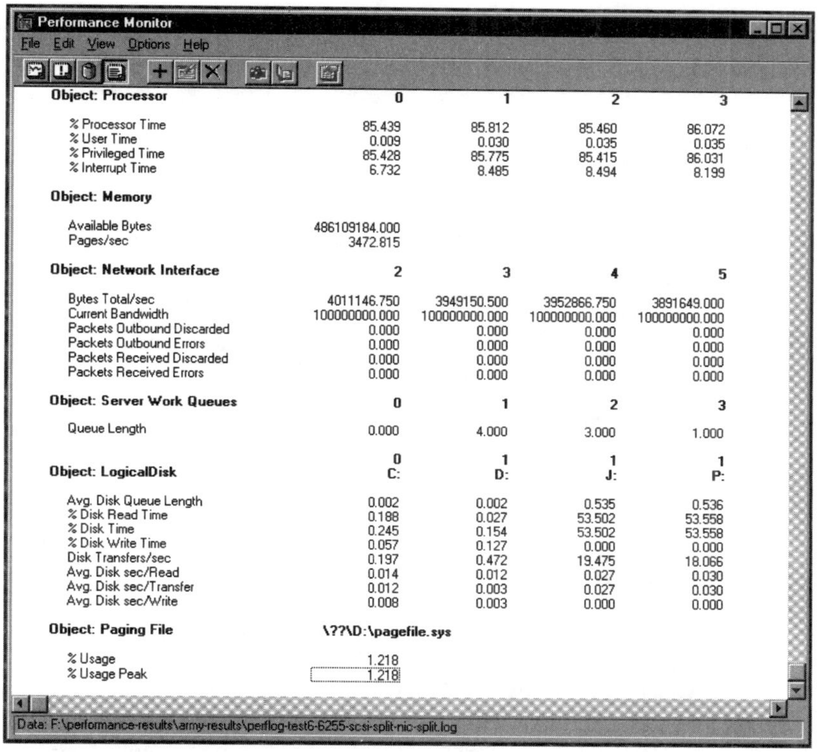

Performance Monitor

File Edit View Options Help

Object: Processor	0	1	2	3
% Processor Time	85.439	85.812	85.460	86.072
% User Time	0.009	0.030	0.035	0.035
% Privileged Time	85.428	85.775	85.415	86.031
% Interrupt Time	6.732	8.485	8.494	8.199
Object: Memory				
Available Bytes	486109184.000			
Pages/sec	3472.815			
Object: Network Interface	2	3	4	5
Bytes Total/sec	4011146.750	3949150.500	3952866.750	3891649.000
Current Bandwidth	100000000.000	100000000.000	100000000.000	100000000.000
Packets Outbound Discarded	0.000	0.000	0.000	0.000
Packets Outbound Errors	0.000	0.000	0.000	0.000
Packets Received Discarded	0.000	0.000	0.000	0.000
Packets Received Errors	0.000	0.000	0.000	0.000
Object: Server Work Queues	0	1	2	3
Queue Length	0.000	4.000	3.000	1.000
Object: LogicalDisk	0 C:	1 D:	1 J:	1 P:
Avg. Disk Queue Length	0.002	0.002	0.535	0.536
% Disk Read Time	0.188	0.027	53.502	53.558
% Disk Time	0.245	0.154	53.502	53.558
% Disk Write Time	0.057	0.127	0.000	0.000
Disk Transfers/sec	0.197	0.472	19.475	18.066
Avg. Disk sec/Read	0.014	0.012	0.027	0.030
Avg. Disk sec/Transfer	0.012	0.003	0.027	0.030
Avg. Disk sec/Write	0.008	0.003	0.000	0.000
Object: Paging File	\??\D:\pagefile.sys			
% Usage	1.218			
% Usage Peak	1.218			

Data: F:\performance-results\army-results\perflog-test6-6255-scsi-split-nic-split.log

Figure 2–12 *Perfmon's report view.*

What are the typical areas that are audited? Process tracking and file use. Use process tracking to help in determining who is running which background process. Perfmon or Task Manager can alert you to the fact that an application is running, but it does not provide information on who is running the application. This information is important when trying to load balance your server either by controlling which server the application is run on or by determining when is the best time to run a particular application.

Process Tracking

To activate process accounting, select Start|Administrative Tools|User Manager| for Domains|Policies|Audit and then select the metrics you wish to audit. This is where you can select process tracking and file and object access. For process tracking, after selecting process tracking and clicking OK, all process success/failures are logged into the Event Viewers security display. Figure 2–13 illustrates the output for process tracking from the Event Viewer.

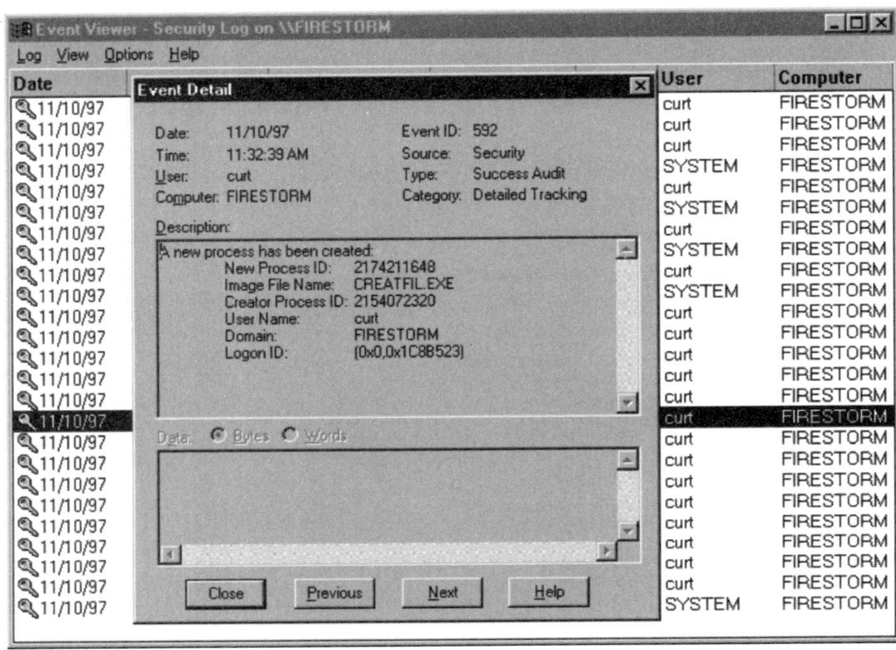

Figure 2–13 *Using auditing to track process usage.*

What you search for varies from environment to environment. In Figure 2–13 we tracked who was creating large temporary files.

Tracking File Access

To determine what files on a volume are being used, enable file auditing. To track a file's access characteristics, set up accounting as mentioned above under User Manager for Domains and select File and Object Access. Then select the file or files whose access characteristics you wish to track with the NT Server explorer application by right clicking the chosen file(s), and select properties. Under properties, select security and auditing to determine what type of file accesses you want to track. Once this file auditing is set, check the Event Log security view periodically to determine if any file accesses were accessed. In Figure 2–14 we determine who was accessing a particular file and when it was accessed.

Ntfilmon.exe

Sometimes you may not know what files to track, or even what files are being accessed on a particular volume. Understanding which files are accessed on a particular volume becomes important when trying to load

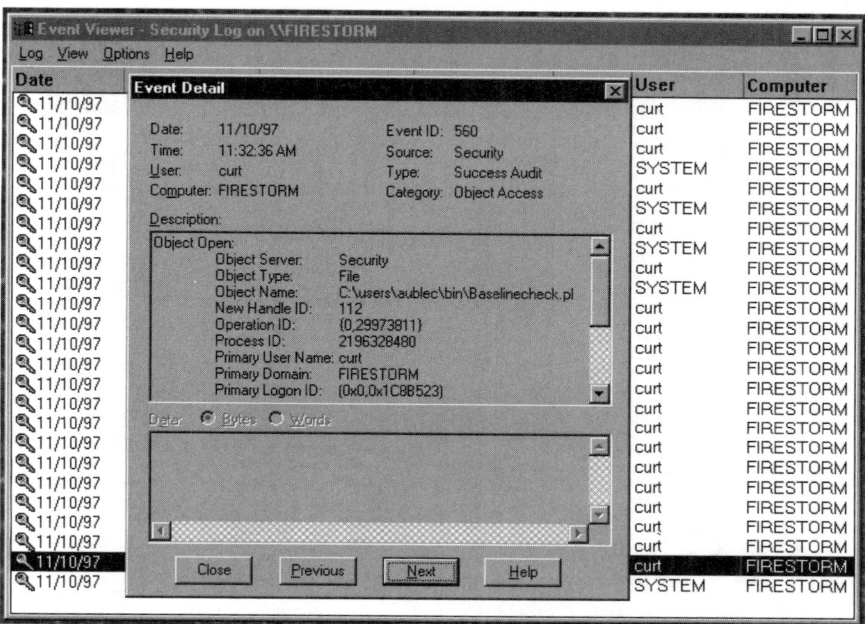

Figure 2–14 *Using accounting to track file access.*

balance your disk I/O subsystem. For this task, try the freeware tool Ntfilmon.exe from the *http://www.ntinternals.com* website. This is an excellent tool used to investigate which files are being accessed and which processes are responsible for this access. Figure 2–15 displays an example output from the Ntfilmon.exe tool.

Putting It All Together: The Environment

Now that we have the strategies, methodologies, and even some code to help in the development of your baselines and the monitoring of your server's performance, let us walk through an example. Let's say that Diane has developed an NT solution that encompasses 25 NT servers connected through a local area network servicing 1000 clients. Due to time constraints, she decides to develop an ideal baseline using the two primary mail servers before they are placed into production. She runs the BaseLineCheck.pl and PulseTest.bat tests (both shown previously) and finds her throughput measures 920,000 bytes/sec, which she feels is acceptable.

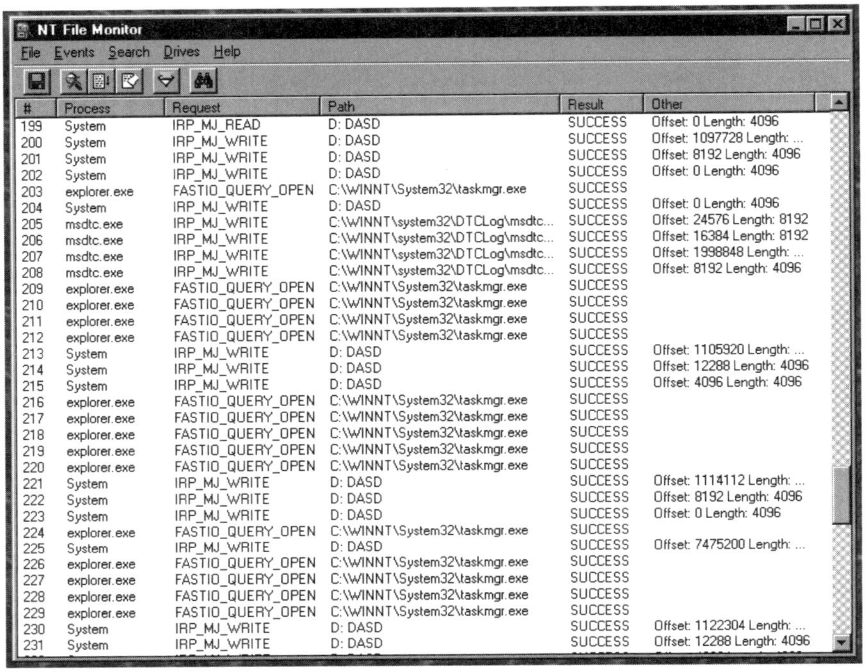

NT File Monitor

File Events Search Drives Help

#	Process	Request	Path	Result	Other
199	System	IRP_MJ_READ	D: DASD	SUCCESS	Offset: 0 Length: 4096
200	System	IRP_MJ_WRITE	D: DASD	SUCCESS	Offset: 1097728 Length: ...
201	System	IRP_MJ_WRITE	D: DASD	SUCCESS	Offset: 8192 Length: 4096
202	System	IRP_MJ_WRITE	D: DASD	SUCCESS	Offset: 0 Length: 4096
203	explorer.exe	FASTIO_QUERY_OPEN	C:\WINNT\System32\taskmgr.exe	SUCCESS	
204	System	IRP_MJ_WRITE	D: DASD	SUCCESS	Offset: 0 Length: 4096
205	msdtc.exe	IRP_MJ_WRITE	C:\WINNT\system32\DTCLog\msdtc...	SUCCESS	Offset: 24576 Length: 8192
206	msdtc.exe	IRP_MJ_WRITE	C:\WINNT\system32\DTCLog\msdtc...	SUCCESS	Offset: 16384 Length: 8192
207	msdtc.exe	IRP_MJ_WRITE	C:\WINNT\system32\DTCLog\msdtc...	SUCCESS	Offset: 1998848 Length: ...
208	msdtc.exe	IRP_MJ_WRITE	C:\WINNT\system32\DTCLog\msdtc...	SUCCESS	Offset: 8192 Length: 4096
209	explorer.exe	FASTIO_QUERY_OPEN	C:\WINNT\System32\taskmgr.exe	SUCCESS	
210	explorer.exe	FASTIO_QUERY_OPEN	C:\WINNT\System32\taskmgr.exe	SUCCESS	
211	explorer.exe	FASTIO_QUERY_OPEN	C:\WINNT\System32\taskmgr.exe	SUCCESS	
212	explorer.exe	FASTIO_QUERY_OPEN	C:\WINNT\System32\taskmgr.exe	SUCCESS	
213	System	IRP_MJ_WRITE	D: DASD	SUCCESS	Offset: 1105920 Length: ...
214	System	IRP_MJ_WRITE	D: DASD	SUCCESS	Offset: 12288 Length: 4096
215	System	IRP_MJ_WRITE	D: DASD	SUCCESS	Offset: 4096 Length: 4096
216	explorer.exe	FASTIO_QUERY_OPEN	C:\WINNT\System32\taskmgr.exe	SUCCESS	
217	explorer.exe	FASTIO_QUERY_OPEN	C:\WINNT\System32\taskmgr.exe	SUCCESS	
218	explorer.exe	FASTIO_QUERY_OPEN	C:\WINNT\System32\taskmgr.exe	SUCCESS	
219	explorer.exe	FASTIO_QUERY_OPEN	C:\WINNT\System32\taskmgr.exe	SUCCESS	
220	explorer.exe	FASTIO_QUERY_OPEN	C:\WINNT\System32\taskmgr.exe	SUCCESS	
221	System	IRP_MJ_WRITE	D: DASD	SUCCESS	Offset: 1114112 Length: ...
222	System	IRP_MJ_WRITE	D: DASD	SUCCESS	Offset: 8192 Length: 4096
223	System	IRP_MJ_WRITE	D: DASD	SUCCESS	Offset: 0 Length: 4096
224	explorer.exe	FASTIO_QUERY_OPEN	C:\WINNT\System32\taskmgr.exe	SUCCESS	
225	System	IRP_MJ_WRITE	D: DASD	SUCCESS	Offset: 7475200 Length: ...
226	explorer.exe	FASTIO_QUERY_OPEN	C:\WINNT\System32\taskmgr.exe	SUCCESS	
227	explorer.exe	FASTIO_QUERY_OPEN	C:\WINNT\System32\taskmgr.exe	SUCCESS	
228	explorer.exe	FASTIO_QUERY_OPEN	C:\WINNT\System32\taskmgr.exe	SUCCESS	
229	explorer.exe	FASTIO_QUERY_OPEN	C:\WINNT\System32\taskmgr.exe	SUCCESS	
230	System	IRP_MJ_WRITE	D: DASD	SUCCESS	Offset: 1122304 Length: ...
231	System	IRP_MJ_WRITE	D: DASD	SUCCESS	Offset: 12288 Length: 4096

Figure 2–15 *Using NTFilmon.exe to track all file accesses*

Example Strategy and Tactics

The NT solution is placed into production, and Diane runs BaselineCheck.pl and PulseTest.bat at various times throughout the work week using the NT Server scheduler. Since Diane does not know what is normal for her environment, she sets the minimum acceptable baseline value equal ($baseline) to a low value of 100 bytes/sec in the BaseLineCheck.pl script so that no alerts are generated. After seven days of collecting data, this is what her baseline.log file looks like:

```
Mon Nov 03 14:00:00, PRIME Net Throughput to megatron:
  834012.05 bytes/sec
Tue Nov 04 14:00:00, PRIME Net Throughput to megatron:
  851417.64 bytes/sec
Wed Nov 05 14:00:00, PRIME Net Throughput to megatron:
  834759.93 bytes/sec
Thu Nov 06 14:00:00, PRIME Net Throughput to megatron:
  851346.86 bytes/sec
Fri Nov 07 14:00:00, PRIME Net Throughput to megatron:
  852764.82 bytes/sec
```

```
Mon Nov 10 14:00:00, PRIME Net Throughput to megatron:
  809550.16 bytes/sec
Tue Nov 11 14:00:00, PRIME Net Throughput to megatron:
  771665.41 bytes/sec
```

After reviewing the performance monitor logs for the selected servers and not noticing anything out of the ordinary, she takes the average of the baseline.log results. Since Diane is overloaded with other projects to complete and does not want to be alerted every time there is a slight change in the PulseTest.bat, she factors in an 18 percent surge rate to determine an approximate value of 700,000 bytes/sec as an acceptable performance baseline. Diane then starts the scripts, allowing them to run without intervention and without constant monitoring. Several weeks pass by and while checking NT Server's Application Event Log (a valuable tool to check your servers health), she finds the following (see Figure 2–16):

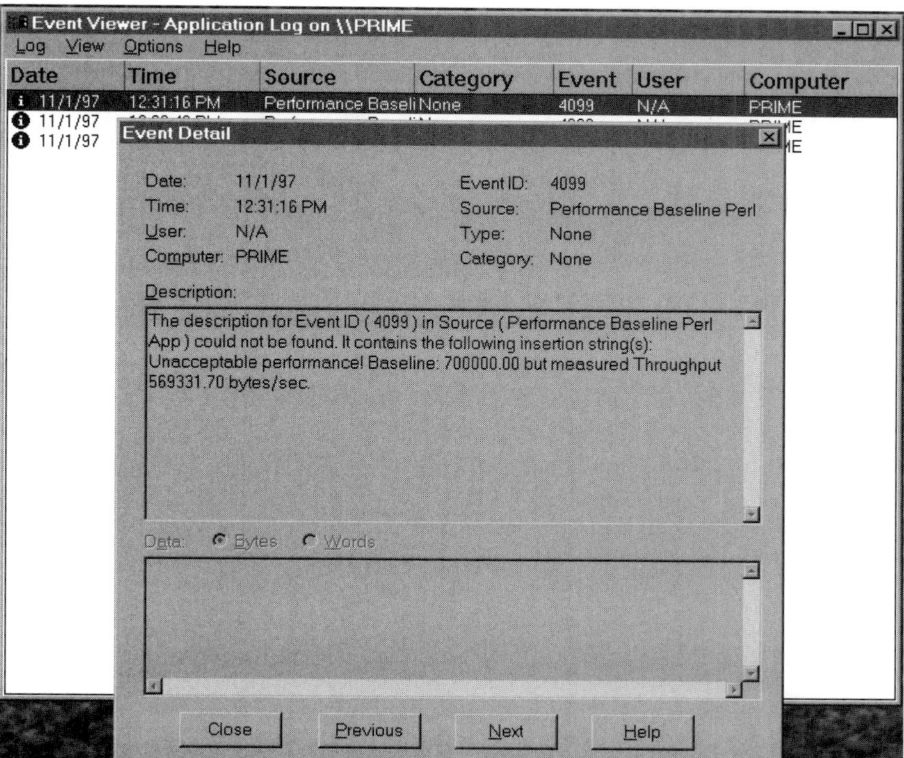

Figure 2–16 *NT Server's Application Event Log.*

Diane then reviews the baseline.log file for any time/date patterns associated with the unacceptable performance levels shown in the Application Event Log.

```
Error: Below Baseline(700000.00 bytes/sec)-Wed Nov 12
  14:00:00, PRIME Net Throughput to megatron:
  587998.85 bytes/sec
Error: Below Baseline(700000.00 bytes/sec)-Thu Nov 13
  14:00:00, PRIME Net Throughput to megatron:
  582977.51 bytes/sec
Error: Below Baseline(700000.00 bytes/sec)-Fri Nov 14
  14:00:00, PRIME Net Throughput to megatron:
  569331.70 bytes/sec
Mon Nov 17 14:00:00, PRIME Net Throughput to megatron:
  735632.18 bytes/sec
Tue Nov 18 14:00:00, PRIME Net Throughput to megatron:
  709092.17 bytes/sec
Error: Below Baseline(700000.00 bytes/sec)-Wed Nov 19
  14:00:00, PRIME Net Throughput to megatron:
  587998.85 bytes/sec
Error: Below Baseline(700000.00 bytes/sec)-Thu Nov 20
  14:00:00, PRIME Net Throughput to megatron:
  582977.51 bytes/sec
Error: Below Baseline(700000.00 bytes/sec)-Fri Nov 21
  14:00:00, PRIME Net Throughput to megatron:
  569331.70 bytes/sec
```

Zeroing In On the Performance Problem

Diane plans to spend the weekend at work hoping to fix this impending performance problem before end users begin to complain. To help in locating the problems, she adds the Performance Monitor Activation module in the BaseLineCheck.pl script. This starts a copy of the performance monitor whenever the PulseTest.bat test returns performance levels below the designated baseline, which will help in determining why the server slowdowns are occurring.

After reviewing the Perfmon logs generated by the monitor service and Perl scripts, she finds that the CPU on the systems were pegged at 100 percent and the server work queues were backing up during the same time periods as the baseline test. Reviewing the Process object under Performance Monitor, she notices that a stored procedure database program was being started by the scheduler that was very CPU intensive. The program being run was for data not required until the following day. Cleverly, Diane changed the scheduled run time for this program to off peak business hours. This small change now allowed the system to be more responsive, exhibiting characteristics that were now back to the normal baseline Diane had observed earlier. Case closed, Diane saves the day and has a nice weekend away from the office.

Summary

In this chapter, the strategies and methodologies for tuning NT Server were reviewed. Once this foundation was in place, key tools to help in implementing these performance strategies were then reviewed. Examples using the information provided were investigated that not only exhibited the use of the strategies and technology presented, but proved that an understanding of what is occurring in your NT Server and surrounding environment is crucial as well. It is important to understand that as either hardware or software technology changes, the strategies outlined in this chapter can be applied.

THREE

Capacity Sizing

Goals of Sizing

If you wanted to determine the configuration of a new NT Server solution to meet your needs for today and tomorrow, where would you start? If a vendor's sales literature states that only 16 MB of RAM is required to run the application, will that really be enough? These are only a few of the questions that will be addressed in this chapter. Sizing encompasses several areas, which include:

1. Developing a specific server configuration to meet the NT Server solution requirements.
2. Adding additional capacity to an existing NT Server configuration.
3. Staying one step ahead of the demand for your NT Server.

If money were not an object, everyone would purchase the largest and latest server technology without a blink of an eye. Unfortunately, when developing a solution that might encompass 300 servers, spending an extra five thousand per server results in an extra 1.5 million dollars. Even if the environment is smaller, few people want to spend their budgets on solutions that do not meet their requirements or on hardware that sits around unproductively.

Reality of Sizing

Similar to tuning, capacity sizing and planning is part art and part science. Sizing an NT Server to provide a solution is a challenge if a sound approach is not followed. When working to size a server for a new environment, the first volleys in discussions tend to start something like this:

System Engineer: So, what business problem are you trying to solve?

Customer: We want a new database server for our business. How many users can an NT server support?

System Engineer: I would like to learn more about your environment. What type of users will use the server and what is the concurrency rate?

Customer: We do not know yet. So how many users can the server support?

System Engineer: We will need to complete some investigations into your environment before determining the number of users that the server might support.

Customer: Ok, so how many users will it support?

Interesting paradox isn't it. The system engineer could just choose an arbitrary number based on his or her own experience or extrapolate from a commercial benchmark, but how do you know if this selection will pertain to the customer's environment at all? You don't. Until the environment that the server will support is understood, it is unrealistic to provide a realistic answer, never mind an initial NT Server configuration or solution architecture.

Sizing Methodology

As we prepare to size an NT server solution, we will gather a significant amount of information and make various assumptions. We will avoid the paradox above by learning as much about the requirements as possible. But why make any assumptions? How many and the type of assumptions made depends upon your environment, timeline, and economics. If you study a problem and model it long enough with the most sophisticated mathematical algorithm, you still will not size a server perfectly. Why? Similar to tuning, there is a primary aspect of sizing that is in a constant state of flux: people. People, or the clients your servers are supporting, can, and do, change the way they do business, especially when the demands placed on their business change.

Perhaps you planned on having 100 order entry personnel working concurrently 70 percent of the time. When suddenly their "talking mouse" products takes off. Overnight, the company adds another 100 order entry contractors working concurrently 90 percent of the time. This would drastically influence the workload on the server and your sizing estimates. Business requirements and end users' habits perennially change as they adapt and change to their environment. This will subsequently influence your server load, which will change your sizing characteristics. Brian Wong (*Configurations and Capacity Planning for Solaris Servers*, Sun Microsystems, A Prentice Hall Title, 1997) stated, "...an SE can tell you what the system cannot do, not guarantee what it will do." The human factor is what makes sizing and tuning based on both art and science.

Fortunately, it is possible to provide a good sizing estimate by utilizing sound, logical sizing techniques, which any good IS professional can apply.

Follow this structured sizing methodology when developing a new NT Server solution.

1. Define objective(s).
2. Understand requirements needed to meet your objective.
3. Determine loading characteristics.
4. Determine performance requirements.
5. Understand future business requirements.
6. Understand future server architectures.
7. Configure the server.
8. Stress test and validate the server configuration.
9. Proactively follow tuning methodology during validations testing
10. Deploy the server into production.
11. Proactively follow tuning methodology after the server is deployed.

Each of the above steps influences both the type and amount of server hardware needed to be configured to meet your needs. Figure 3–1 presents a graphical representation of the sizing methodology:

From here we will explore each step of the sizing methodology in more detail. Even as we look at the methodology in more detail, *keep in mind that every environment is different*. So, if in the explanation of one of these steps, you do not see an area being addressed that you are concerned with, feel free to expand it! There is no substitute for experience. Use this methodology as a framework in helping to develop your solution, not as gospel. In Chapter 8, "Putting Theory Into Practice: Sizing and Tuning Case Studies," we will apply this methodology to several sizing case studies.

Exploring the Sizing Methodology in Detail

1—Define Objective(s)

Defining the server's objective is straightforward. Why do you require this server? What part of the solution will the server perform? This list can get long quickly, but some of the possibilities include: Primary Domain Controller (PDC), Backup Domain Controller (BDC), Domain Name Server (DNS), File

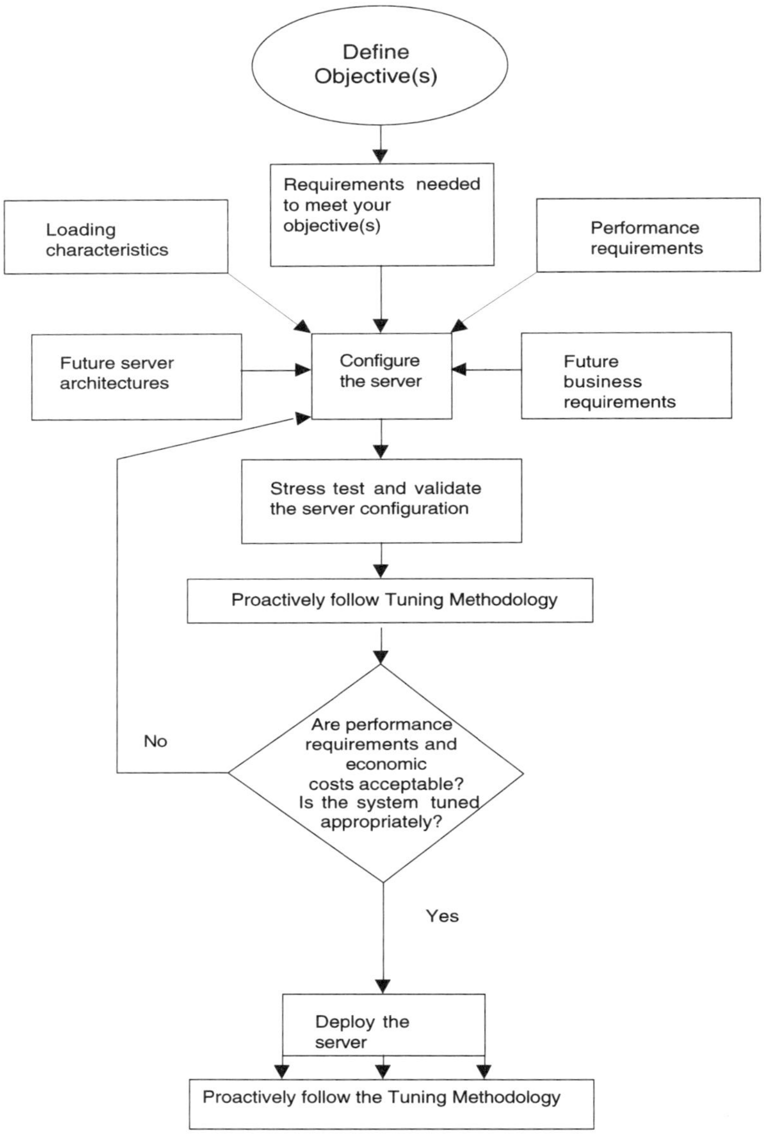

Define Objective(s)

Requirements needed to meet your objective(s)

Loading characteristics

Performance requirements

Future server architectures

Configure the server

Future business requirements

Stress test and validate the server configuration

Proactively follow Tuning Methodology

Are performance requirements and economic costs acceptable? Is the system tuned appropriately?

No

Yes

Deploy the server

Proactively follow the Tuning Methodology

Figure 3–1 *Sizing methodology.*

Server, Print Server, Web Server, Mail Server, Database Server, etc. Defining your objective helps to determine where in your overall system architecture that it makes sense to locate it. For example, placing a departmental file server close to the actual users can help in lowering network latency when accessing the server and help to control network traffic patterns. (Latency is defined as the time spent waiting for a result. Typically, it is the end user waiting for a result.) The tradeoff for this example is an increased server management complexity that can be associated with managing distributed server architectures.

Once the objective is defined, it becomes easier to characterize the type of workloads the server will experience. The workload characterization directly affects tuning NT Server. Understanding the load characterization also is the key to the initial server configuration which is illustrated through step-by-step examples in Chapter 8. Although NT Server lends itself to distributed application architectures, it is becoming more common to see numerous server functions being combined into fewer, but larger, NT Super Servers. This makes the need for understanding the various types of load characterizations even more important.

2—Understand Requirements Needed to Meet Your Objective

The primary questions to answer in this step are:

- which application(s) will meet your objective(s)?
- what are the availability requirements?
- what are the disk subsystem storage requirements?

If you were developing a database application, you would need to decide which database to use, such as Teradata, Oracle, SQL Server or one of the many others. There is a plethora of questions surrounding making a decision on which application to use. Some of the most common questions are scalability of the product, references of other customers using the product in similar environments, development environments, future plans for the product, and so on. The application that you choose to meet your objective will affect which types of server resources are needed to support running the application.

Just as NT Server has a minimum recommended server configuration, set somewhere around an Intel 80486 CPU with at least 16 MB of RAM (which I'm sure everyone thinks is realistic), so will other applications that your are considering. Remember that when a vendor mentions the minimum configuration needed to run the application, they typically really mean the MINIMUM just to make it run. In the case of Microsoft, this minimum hardware recommendation is sometimes referred to as the "Microsoft Dream Sheet." Add 100 concurrent users and the suggested minimum server resource requirements are tossed out the window.

How important the objective is you are fulfilling and the budget that you have typically drive availability requirements for the server. If the server were a local file and print server, the server configuration would most likely require a lower factor of availability. At the other end of the spectrum, if the solution is a Web server that processes transactions for your retail outlet on the Internet, a clustered solution may be advisable to ensure the solution has a very high availability rating. A server is typically defined as a critical server in your architecture which, if the server were to fail, the business would lose revenue or seriously affect productivity.

Storage requirements are self-defining. As we will see in Chapter 6, "NT Server and Disk Subsystem Performance" and Chapter 8's case studies, availability, capacity, and performance requirements will greatly influence the final server configuration.

3—Determine Loading Characteristics

Determining loading characteristics of the server can take time and occasionally be laborious, but it is extremely important. The loading characteristics typically drive the bulk of the server resources needed to provide a solution that runs in a manner that is acceptable to both the end users and the business. Key information you want to obtain when trying to determine the loading characteristics includes:

- number of total users
- number of concurrent users (users that are actually requesting something from the server at the same time)
- transaction rates
- read or write environment disk subsystem characteristics
- size of records
- type of work the user will complete (order entry, mailing out electronic advertisements, home accounts usage, research, etc.)

There are two primary techniques when collecting workload information: historical collection on existing servers and estimation without existing servers. As you might guess, it is preferable to collect historical information from servers currently running similar applications to your own planned environments. This is when the concepts from Chapter 2 come into play.

If you have already been collecting server statistics, you can determine how the current server is performing and extrapolate possible future loading requirements. If you haven't been following the methodologies outlined in Chapter 2, it is not too late to start. Occasionally, it is possible to meet with other businesses that have implemented a similar solution to your own and subsequently obtain their performance metrics to determine loading characteristics.

If you do not have historical data to rely on, you can survey the current and/or potential end users to estimate what future workloads will be encountered. You can accomplish this through a variety of methods such as e-mailing out questionnaires to determine work habits or enlisting the support of several good interns to question the end users and complete the surveys you have developed. In either case, a reasonable estimate is possible which will help provide you with an initial starting point.

4—Determine Performance Requirements

The two most common measurements of performance are response time and throughput. Response time is what the end user experiences. How long does it take for the server to respond to my request? Always remember that between the server and the end user, there are several layers of a system architecture (other than the server) that may influence the end users perceived response time. Throughput is the amount of work that the server can complete in a defined amount of time. These two concepts are somewhat opposing in nature. If a server is very busy completing a high amount of work, the throughput is good. Unfortunately, if the server is busy completing a high amount of work, an end user's request will not be serviced as fast. Conversely, if the server is not busy completing a high level work, for example, its throughput level is lower at the moment, the server will be able to service that end user request in a timely fashion, thus providing good response time.

For any interactive application that is ultimately used daily by an end user, there is only one true measure of performance: response time. It does not matter what type of scientific, engineering mumbo jumbo jargon is used to explain what is happening on the server or the network, if the end user requires a five second or less response time, then that is the standard they will expect. Working with your clients to determine acceptable response times can both drive the server configuration and establish a metric of your job performance.

Working with the customer to set realistic performance expectations is important. If you and the customer decide subsecond response is the ultimate performance metric, then be sure you quantify when this is realistic. If you are setting up a database to support an order entry environment, quantify your performance metric for both response time and user concurrency rate. Concurrency rate is the amount of time concurrent users are actively working with the server. You may support 200 users with your server, but only 50 of them are ever accessing the server at the same time. This is a 25 percent concurrency rate. For example, agree that subsecond response time will be provided for local users (LAN connected) when less than 100 users are accessing the server concurrently. Many NT Server environments are deployed in a client server fashion, which allows a single NT server to support more users than if they were logged directly into the server, as is the case in some UNIX and NT Server Citrix/Hydra multiuser environments.

Throughput metrics for server environments is a more applicable measure of performance when the supporting application is not interactive or most of the work is completed offline in a batch mode. Some example throughput metrics for a server are quantified by the number of mail messages the server can process per hour, or the number of accounting queries that can be completed per eight hour evening time window so that they are available the next business day.

5—Understand Future Business Requirements

Whenever someone mentions futures, I think of psychics or palm readers. Although some people believe in this, I prefer to look at more scientific futures. When thinking about business requirement futures, revisit steps 1 through 4 and ask yourself, "Will my business objectives be the same?" "How much growth do I anticipate?" For business futures, the two areas of concern are deciding if the server will need to support additional applications and if the workload will increase. Both of these areas will affect your server architecture. If your future looks stable, perhaps a 1–2 CPU NT Server will suffice. If the business is rapidly growing, perhaps a 2–8 CPU NT Server should be considered. By spending time understanding future business requirements before sizing the server, future server growth can easily be planned for instead of reacted to.

6—Understand Future Server Architectures

As technology rapidly advances, vendors look to deploy newer technology in an effort to garner market share. In completing this mission, new technologies are developed and individual vendors or vendor consortiums attempt to leverage these technologies so that they evolve into standards either by lobbying the various standards groups (IEEE, The Open Group, etc.) or by sheer market share. Why be concerned about this when configuring your server? If the technology which is chosen quickly becomes discontinued or never develops a growing market presence, you can find yourself either (a) locked into a single vendor which causes drastically higher prices for parts and upgrades, or (b) not having anywhere to purchase parts. You may recall some years ago when two new I/O bus standards were emerging: PCI and VESA. At that time, you could have purchased a PCI-based SCSI host adapter or a VESA-based SCSI host adapter. If you had chosen the VESA-based SCSI adapter, today you would have a difficult time locating additional good, competitively priced VESA-based SCSI controllers.

The moral of this story: Consider all of the technologies your server will need to support today and tomorrow to meet your requirements. Deciding which technology will win or lose in the long run is a formidable task. If you adhere to technologies that follow both industry group standards and a promising market share forecast, you will most likely be safe. Key factors to consider when choosing a server technology to configure are shown in Table 3.1.

Table 3.1 Key factors to consider when choosing a server technology.

Key Server Factor	Definition
Service and Support	Warranty options, technical support for software, technical support for hardware, etc.
CPU Scalability	Number, speed, and future caches that are planned to be supported
Memory Scalability	Maximum amount and types of memory supported
I/O Scalability	Number of peer I/O (PCI today) busses the server can scale to and available I/O slots
Internal Disk Capacity	Number of internal disk drives the server will support
External Disk Array Support	Number of external disk drives the server will support
Redundant Array of Inexpensive Disks (RAID) Support	Both internal and external RAID devices
Communication Adapter Support	LAN and WAN connectivity
Fault Tolerance Features	Hot pluggable power supplies, redundant fans, etc.
Server Management Features	Adherence to server management standards such as DMI, SNMP, etc.

7—Configure the Server

Finally, to the good stuff. At this point, you can configure the server. Choose the server resources required in meeting your objective, with consideration for steps 1 through 6, and obtain the server. As you configure the server, look at each individual resource to meet the overall server configuration. Software and hardware vendors are good sources of information for suggested configurations from which to begin your configuration efforts. Reviewing relevant industry benchmarks also can help in providing insight into the initial configuration. Industry benchmarks are explored in-depth later in this chapter. The following steps are presented to help in guiding you through the actual server configuration process. Case studies in Chapter 8 provide examples that help to solidify the configuration process.

- **Server Configuration Process**
  Having some sort of idea on how each server resource works and relates to the overall server performance is helpful when configuring your server. Chapters 4 through 7 review each server resource in greater detail. Then, in Chapter 8's case studies, this methodology is thrust into action as facets of several server scenarios are sized, configured, tuned, and stress tested.

a. **Application Characteristics Review**
Complete some research on how the application typically behaves. For example, Microsoft Exchange environments are characterized by the following resource usage activity: Disk: Active, Memory: Active, Processor: Medium, and Network: Medium. Even closer review of the application in use may dictate network or disk subsystem design.

b. **Review Each Server Resource**
Disk I/O Requirements

When sizing disk I/O environments consider availability, capacity (available disk storage), and performance requirements. Understanding the disk I/O subsystem characteristics (usage and workload of the disk I/O sub-system) is helpful for initial layout and future tuning of the disk I/O subsystem.

CPU Requirements

When sizing the level of CPU power required, keep in mind the application requirements and processing power that is required to drive supporting disk and network subsystems.

Memory Requirements

When sizing the amount of memory to place into the server, consider all application and operating system requirements. Sizing the memory subsystem is an additive process. Some memory resources are shared between processes running under NT Server, but to be on the safer, conservative side of sizing, consider sizing the memory subsystem as an additive process. Take into consideration operating system requirements, NT Server file system cache needs (dynamic disk buffer cache), and application needs. Application memory requirements are more than just the memory space needed to run the application.

Application memory also encompasses memory needed to support its data sets and users. For example, a database engine may have a per user memory requirement such as 0.250 Mbytes per user. For example, if the database will support 500 users, an additional 125 Mbytes of memory would be needed on top of any other memory requirements.

Network I/O Requirements

The amount of data that the server provides and the characteristics of the applications in use dictates the type and number of network interface cards. Access patterns of the server influences the type of protocol to use. Token passing protocols such as FDDI exhibit better degradation characteristics than shared bus protocols such as Ethernet. Also, select a network adapter that provides the best performance for the network architecture in use. If the environment is Ethernet, obtain a network adapter that supports bus mastering and contains more then one channel on the card to conserve server peripheral expansion slots.

c. **Initial Hardware Configuration and Tuning**
In this step the initial configuration of the server hardware configuration begins to take shape based on steps a and b.

d. **Initial Software Configuration and Tuning**
In this step, the initial software configuration of the server configuration begins to take shape based on steps a and b.

e. **Initial Tuning**
Reviewing the load characteristics and completing research on the application in use is helpful when tuning the hardware and software. Review Chapter 1 as a reference and guide to tune the server before stress testing or deploying the NT Server.

f. **Server Architecture Relationship Check**
This is a final common sense check of a server. Review Chapter 1 as a reference before stress testing or deploying the final NT Server configuration. Look for configurations options that are just strange, such as a server with 4 GB of RAM, one disk drive, and one CPU. Try to avoid starting with a server bottleneck. Completing some basic arithmetic of the I/O subsystem for a worst case scenario can help to disqualify poor disk I/O designs.

g. **Future Business and Server Architectures Check Review**
Will the server have room to grow if needed? Steps 5 and 6 of the sizing methodology point out that it is important to obtain this information. This step is the actual contingency planning. If the server will need to support an increased role in the future, how will you actually

accomplish meeting those goals? For example, if the server needs 1 GB of RAM today, but will need to support 2 GB in the future, pay close attention to the density of the RAM initially purchased. Selecting a density of RAM that fills all available memory slots today will not support increasing the memory size in the future without throwing away or redeploying the current investment. A better strategy is to obtain higher density SIMMs/DIMMs today. Then, as memory is needed in the future, it can be added to the current configuration versus removing the old RAM.

8—Stress Test and Validate the Server Configuration

This is a crucial step before actually deploying the server. How can you be sure that the server will meet your performance requirements and run correctly with various applications running simultaneously under load without crashing? In the tuning methodology outlined in Chapter 2, we reviewed taking a baseline of your server before deploying it into production to determine what performance level was possible in a nonproduction environment. This information was then used when taking the server's pulse in the production environment for comparison and to aid in determining if tuning is necessary.

This is the same concept used for sizing, but when initial sizing is your goal, do not just take the server's pulse. To determine if the server will withstand the types of stress and workloads that you expect it to support in production, stress the server in the most realistic manor possible. This preproduction load testing becomes your validation baseline. If the validation baseline proves to be unacceptable, do not deploy the server. Revisit the requirements and configuration, then use the tuning methodology (sizing methodology, step 9) to tune your server before it enters production. Continue this iterative process until you can meet the desired performance levels.

Now that you have developed your validation baseline, which includes measurements such as response time, throughput, and server resource usage, you can feel comfortable that your solution will meet your current requirements. You also have a baseline reference for future tuning efforts. But why stop there? Is meeting the performance requirements under the current workload really good enough? What if there is a landslide of increased server load? Will the server seize up faster than a truck transmission without transmission fluid? Or will the server support the additional load gracefully until it begins an honorable death?

To determine if the server will support additional workloads, it is important to take into consideration future business requirements, and then stress your server accordingly. By stressing the server past its breaking point, you gain enormous amounts of insight to future capacity planning and tuning. Figure 3–2 illustrates a server's breaking point.

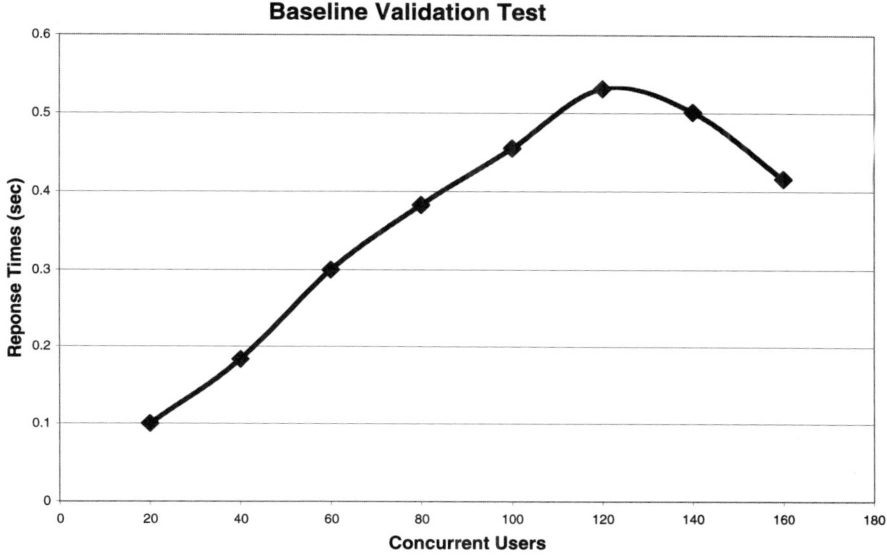

Figure 3–2 *Stressing your server.*

The "knee" in the curve represented in Figure 3–2 is a classic illustration depicting the beginning of the end for an NT Server. This graph shows that a resource on the server became a bottleneck as the load increased past 120 users.

Obviously, a curve depicting a slowly decreasing degradation slope is desirable. What defines acceptable and unacceptable performance are the business requirements. The rate of degradation is helpful for planning since it indicates how well the server can weather a load storm.

If your business requirements define supporting 100 concurrent users today, and 200 in three months, it would be nice to have a validated baseline that shows not only if the server will support 100 users today, but the 200 users of tomorrow. Through iterative testing and using the tuning methodology in conjunction with a server-loading tool, you can identify server bottlenecks, tune around them, and obtain the highest level of performance from the current configuration. In Chapter 8's case studies, we explore these concepts with real examples. Once this iterative testing and tuning no longer yields significant gains, review the data to determine which server resources will require additional hardware or software changes to meet the projected workloads. If the server's architecture has met its realistic scalability limit, consider distributing the increasing workload to additional servers as appropriate. In this manner, even if your server solution only meets today's needs, you can budget and plan for the upgrade to support the projected workload increases of tomorrow.

9—Proactively Follow the Tuning Methodology During Stress and Validation Testing

Tuning and sizing techniques work best when they are utilized in concert. Use the tuning methodology when load testing your server solution prior to deployment. It is much easier to tune around server bottlenecks before a server is running a mission-critical application. Another benefit of this technique is the development of the server's pulse baselines. These server pulse baselines are used for future comparisons of server resource usage. Even if it is not possible to load test your server prior to deployment, review Chapter 1 tuning recommendations before deploying the server into production.

10—Deploy the Server into Production

Why state the obvious? This step defines itself. I wanted to show a clear distinction between baseline validation and tuning of the preproduction server and the deployed server. It is much easier to tune and validate a server before it enters production.

11—Proactively Follow the Tuning Methodology After the Server Is Deployed

Environments do change. The information gathered following the tuning methodology is helpful for staying one step in front of user demand by identifying current load demands and potential server bottlenecks. Also, use this information when developing and sizing future server solutions and when adding additional capacity to your current server(s).

Benchmarks Are Your Friends

Historical data and user surveys are great techniques to obtain information that will influence the sizing and configuration of your server. But, where can you obtain information about sizing and performance of new technologies? Industry Standard benchmarks! Industry benchmarks help to cause marketing chaos for the decision maker, but they also can come to the rescue of that same decision maker. If you understand what the industry benchmark results represent and how to use them to your advantage, they can be a useful weapon to your sizing arsenal. Always remember that while no one benchmark can fully characterize overall system performance perfectly, the results of a variety of realistic benchmarks can give valuable insight into expected real performance for sizing and tuning efforts.

What Are Industry Standard Benchmarks?

In basic terms, a benchmark is any measurable reproducible test. Sounds simple, because the concept is simple. What is not simple is developing benchmarks that measure what you want them to measure and agreeing upon how that measurement is to be taken. Various vendors from time to time do agree on, or at least support, various benchmarks. If there is enough support for a particular benchmark, they can become industry standard benchmarks. Now, in theory, if one vendor runs standard benchmark A and another vendor runs standard benchmark A, you should be able to compare the results in an apples-to-apples comparison. Since these industry benchmarks carry, in a manner of speaking, bragging rights along with them, they transform into marketing engineering. Vendors will always want to "one up" their respective competition, which results in continuous benchmarking efforts of the latest server hardware and software technologies. Thus, the leapfrog effect. This is an advantage to you! In a way, you have a team of the best engineers from every vendor trying to make their server solutions run faster and faster.

There are several standard industry benchmarks that are publicly released and are beneficial to any tuning and sizing efforts. Several of the most common industry benchmarks for the NT Server environment are reviewed, explaining what they are and how they might be helpful. Some industry standard benchmarks are produced by industry consortiums, such as the Transaction Processing Council (TPC) and the Standard Performance Evaluation Corporation (SPEC). Some companies develop and sell their own benchmarks. This class of benchmarks become industry standards through their marketing efforts and market share. Two commercial benchmark vendors include AIM and Neal Nelson & Associates. Other benchmarks are available free of charge from groups like Ziff Davis and various universities. Personally, I have found that you get what you pay for when considering the quality of the benchmark used.

The baseline validation tests that are described in the sizing methodology is also a benchmark, a very specific benchmark that depicts a particular environment—yours. Benchmarking a server in your specific environment is the best way to determine if the server will meet your requirements. The number of benchmarks available today is ever increasing as new technologies are introduced.

Where Do Benchmarks Fit in the Sizing Methodology?

You can gain valuable insight into the server sizing configurations and software tuning techniques from the many industry standard benchmarks available. Industry standard benchmark results are updated frequently. Once the pertinent information is obtained, apply that information to the various steps outlined in the sizing methodology. Industry standard benchmark information is most applicable to step 7, configuring the server. If the loading characteristics (step 3) and performance requirements (step 4) are similar to that of the benchmark environment, the benchmark provides an immediate basis to extrapolate from for the initial server configuration created in step 7 configuring the server. Even if the industry standard benchmark that is similar to your environment does match exactly, server sizing information and software tuning information can still be extrapolated from them and be applied to the sizing environment in steps 7 and 9. Always insure you select the appropriate industry benchmark that emulates your environment the closest.

Transaction Processing Council (TPC)

TPC produces various server benchmarks that are run by the major server vendors. There are four primary TPC benchmarks: TPC-A, TPC-B, TPC-C, and TPC-D. As benchmarks improve, so does the server technology that is under test. Thus, if the server technology has improved but improvements are not made to the current benchmark technology, the validity of the benchmark results become suspect. Currently, the TPC-A and TPC-B benchmarks fall into this category of benchmarks and are no longer actively supported by the vendor community. For this discussion, both of these benchmarks are omitted since results on current server platforms are no longer published. Information on the definitions and results of the TPC benchmarks is available on the Internet at *http://www.tpc.org*. TPC-C and

TPC-D can be applicable to the NT Server database environment, if you understand what the benchmark is intended for and for what it measures. Although audited, I can not recommend making any type of purchase decisions solely on the results of any industry standard benchmarks such as the TPC based benchmarks.

TPC-C Explanation

The TPC-C benchmark focuses on transaction-based database server environments. The TPC-C benchmark defines that five different transactions are active on the system. The benchmark defines throughput as how many new-order transactions per minute a server can support while keeping the response times for these transactions less then five seconds. Thus, the primary measurement of the TPC-C benchmark is a measure of maximum sustained system performance. Therefore, for a 1000 transaction C actions per minute (tpmC), a server is generating 1000 new-order transactions per minute while fulfilling the rest of the TPC-C transaction mix workload.

Most NT Server based TPC-C benchmark solutions are designed for a client/server environment. In this environment, the clients support the major portion of the front-end application processing requirements and the server supports the database from which the application requests information. If you extrapolate information from the TPC-C benchmark test results, remember how the solution architecture is defined and the type of transaction the server is supporting. Consider yourself lucky if your environment matches directly up to the TPC-C environment, because it then becomes a little easier to use the TPC-C to your advantage when sizing your server. If you have a client/server database environment (which many NT database solutions are), but your transaction model does not line up exactly with the TPC-C model, TPC-C benchmark results can still be helpful.

EXAMPLE TPC-C RESULTS

Figure 3–3 depicts a TPC-C Executive summary downloaded from the TPC Web site:

NCR	NCR WorldMark™ 4300S C/S w/5 S26 Clients		TPC-C Rev. 3.3 Report Date: June 2, 1997
Total System Cost	TPC-C Throughput	Price / Performance	Availability Date
$ 778,970	9116 tpmC	$ 85.45 per tpmC	August 1997

Processors	Database Manager	Operating System	Other Software	Level of Concurrency
(4) Pentium Pro 200	Microsoft SQL Server v.6.5 Enterprise Edition	Microsoft Windows NT 4.0 Enterprise Edition	NCR TopEnd 2.04.01, Microsoft Internet Connector License, Microsoft Visual C++, Microsoft SQLServer Programmers Toolkit	7800 users

Clients

Server

(1) NCR 4300 R
(1) 6250 RAID modules of (20) 9G disks
and (3) 6250 RAID modules of (20) 4G disks

(1) NCR 4300 R
w/ 4 processors, CDROM,
(3) 4GB Drives, and (2) 6250
RAID modules of (20) 4G disks

(5) NCR S26's

System Components	Server Quantity	Server Description	Clients Quantity	Clients Description
Processors	4	Intel PentiumPro/200	5	Intel Pentium Pro/200
Memory		w/ 512K 2LC each		w/256K 2LC
Disk Controllers	4	1024 Megabytes	5	512 Megabytes
Disk Drives	4	NCR PCI QuadSCSI	5	Integrated SCSI
	103	4GB Drives	5	2GB SCSI
CDROM Drive	20	9GB Drives		
PC Connectivity	1	SCSI		
	429	Linksys 10B 20 port HUBS	5	SCSI
Network Adapters	3	Linksys 100B 4 port HUBS	20	PCI 10/100Ethernet
	1	PCI 10/100 Ethernet		

Figure 3–3 *Executive Summary.*

NCR WorldMark 4300S c/s Microsoft SQL Server 6.5	TPC-C Rev. 3.3 Report Date: June 2, 1997

Description	Product ID	Third Party Brand	Pricing	Unit List	Quantity	Extended List	Extended 5 Year Maint
Server Hardware							
4300S/2 P6 200, 0MB DIMM	3447-4922-8090			18,750	1	18,750	8,980
2 200MHz/512	F027			8,300	1	8,300	840
Memory Upgrade, 1GB DIMMs	F120			34,000	4	136,000	0
Quad SCSI Adapter (4DF)	F129			2,550	4	10,200	0
HD Disk- 4GB 7200 F/W Hot Plug	F343			1,600	3	4,800	960
Ethernet Adapter PCI 10BaseT	F143/F144			225	1	225	40
Monochrome Monitor, 14" VGA	3298-2131-8090			215	1	215	108
Disk Solution							
RACKMOUNT CABINET(STAGED' 4300R	6250-6100-6690			2,050	1	2,050	6,375
SCSI 68P HD TO 68P HD - 15 FT	1415-C078-0030			250	12	3,000	0
Series 4 controller - 64 MB cache	6250-F058			12,180	12	146,160	67,200
Series 4 disk array module	6250-F200			13,740	6	82,440	0
4.2GB 7200RPM SCA DISK DRIVE	6250-F204			1,600	100	160,000	0
9.1 GB 7200RPM SCA DISK DRIVE	6250-F309			2,450	20	49,000	0
					Subtotal	621,140	84,503
Server Software							
Microsoft NT Server v. 4.0 Enterprise Editio		Microsoft	1	3,999	1	3,999	0
Micrososct SQL Server 6.5 Enterprise Edition		Microsoft	1	7,999	1	7,999	0
Microsoft Internet Connector License		Microsoft	1	2,999	1	2,999	0
Microsoft Software Maintenance		Microsoft	1	10,475	1		10,475
					Subtotal	14,997	10,475
Client Hardware							
S26 XLP	3426-7600			4,500	5	22,500	7,015
200MHz uni-proc	3426-F044			1,500	5	7,500	1,430
128MB SIMM Kit (2x64MB)	3426-F109			3,500	20	70,000	0
F/W 2GB Hot Plug Drive	3426-F344			1,200	5	6,000	900
Ethernet Adapter, PCI	3426-F143/F144			225	20	4,500	0
Monochrome Monitor, 14" VGA	3298-2131-8090			215	5	1,075	540
US/North American Power Cord	3404-F050			0	5	0	0
					Subtotal	111,575	9,885
Client Software							
Microsoft Windows NT Server v. 4.0		Microsoft	1	809	5	4,045	0
Microsoft SQL Workstation w/ Programmers Toolkit		Microsoft	1	499	1	499	0
Visual C++ 32-bit edition(subscription)		Microsoft	1	499	1	499	0
TopEnd 2.04	D906-A210-0000			5,000	5	25,000	1,025
					Subtotal	30,043	1,025
User Connectivity							
Linksys 20-port 10BaseT Hubs	65360304	Linksys	2	180	390	70,200	0
SPARE 20 port Hubs	65360304	Linksys	2	180	39	7,020	0
Linksys 8-port 100BaseTX Hubs	65360303	Linksys	2	555	1	555	0
Spare Linksys 8-port 100BaseTX Hubs	65360303	Linksys	2	555	2	1,110	0
					Subtotal	78,885	0
					Discounts	(164,476)	(19,083)
					Total	$692,165	$86,805

1: Microsoft - Client/server software maint. shown bundled under Server Softwa
2: Dataflex - Hubs have a 5 year warranty.
Audited by Information Paradigm, Inc.
Hardware is currently available, Software available March 1997.

Five-Year Cost Of Ownership:	778,970
tpmC Rating:	9,116.00
$/tpmC:	$85.45

Prices used in TPC benchmarks reflect the actual prices a customer would pay for a one-time purchase of the stated components. Individually negotiated discounts are not permitted. Special prices based on assumptions about past or future purchases are not permitted. All discounts reflect standard pricing policies for the listed components. For complete details, see the pricing sections of the TPC benchmark specifications. If you find that the stated prices are not available according to these items, please inform the TPC at pricing@tpc.org.

Figure 3–3 *Executive Summary (continued)*

EXTRAPOLATING TPC-C RESULTS

TPC-C executive summaries are available for a myriad of server platforms. Occasionally check this website for the latest information. Vendors add and withdraw benchmark results over time. Using this executive summary, let's review some of the notable pieces of information and point out facts that you might find applicable for any environment.

- Server configuration CPU, RAM, DISK, Network
  four CPUs needed for calculations and to drive large external disk arrays
- 4 GB of RAM
  Large amounts of RAM required for operating system and database application. This large amount of RAM improves overall performance by allowing the database to cache in RAM actions that may have needed disk access
- 120 external disk drives
  Increased number of disk drives used to support high transaction rate
- Sixteen available external SCSI channels
  Doing the math, this works out to ten disk drives per Ultra Fast/Wide SCSI-2 channel
- 1 100BaseT Network Interface Card
  Even supporting a high number of concurrent users, this client/server based benchmark does not require a high network bandwidth environment
- Maximum number of concurrent users supported: 7800
- Version of operating System: NT 4.0 Enterprise edition
  NT Server Enterprise edition allows the application access of 3 GB of RAM with 1 GB of RAM reserved for the operating system
- TPC-C throughput 9116 tpmC
- Price/Performance $85.45
- Database: Microsoft SQL Server v6.5 Enterprise edition
- Other software: Top end middleware and transaction monitor
  This middleware technology lowers the number of concurrent connections required to service the emulated end users

From this information it is possible to extrapolate key pieces of information such as the disk I/O configuration. Here, 120 external drives are needed, not due as much to capacity requirements, but to transaction rate requirements. Regardless of the size of the disk drives, individual disk drives can only support so many input/output transactions per second. Thus, the need for an increased number of disk drives. Keep this in mind when configuring a database or any transaction-based environment. More specific disk I/O rules of thumb examples are pointed out in Chapters 1 and 6.

TPC-C SIZING PITFALLS

There are some drawbacks to using TPC-C information to help size your configuration. TPC-C benchmarks are expensive for vendors to run, thus limiting the number of available TPC-C configurations you can reference to aid in sizing your server. This particular solution architecture uses five high powered PCs to emulate 7800 users, which is not quite realistic and can greatly influence the network architecture in use. For an Ethernet environment, which is a CSMA/CD-based protocol, increasing the number of actual concurrent client systems will increase the number of network interface cards needed in the server to support the higher network transaction loads. For additional information on NT Server network subsystem performance and technologies review Chapter 7, "NT Server and Network Performance."

The low numbers of real clients has another, somewhat negative effect when using TPC-C results to help size your server: active connections. Most TPC-C benchmarks utilize some type of transaction processing (TP) monitor, in this case it is Top End. Using a transaction monitor can greatly aid in managing your system. One way a transaction monitor accomplished this is by multiplexing the connections into the database, in essence lowering the number of active connections into the database. If you are not using a transaction monitor, the subsequent increase in active connections into the database server increases the load on the server and lowers the number of concurrent users that can be supported. How much the load is increased on the server is application dependent, but I will typically lower the number of concurrent users supports by at least 25 percent just to be safe.

FURTHER INFORMATION ON TPC-C

TPC-C is best used to approximate server solutions of similar environments. Even if your environment is not a perfect fit to the TPC-C environment, look between the lines to gain configuration and sizing insights. For more in-depth information on TPC-C benchmark results, full disclosure reports are available but are quite thick, thus I omitted including one here. Full disclosure reports provide specific information on any tuning completed above and beyond the default installation of the software used for the benchmark. It is a good exercise to review these reports as they provide insight into which areas to investigate when tuning NT Server and the various database engines.

TPC-D

TPC-D is mentioned here more for its future NT Server applicability than for its current applicability. The TPC-D benchmark focuses on the data warehousing environments. The data warehouse environment is generically summarized as complex, query decision support requests of very large databases. This benchmark is run against specific database sizes ranging from 1 GB to

1 TB. There are some NT Server benchmarks in the 100 GB arena, which provide reasonable price and performance. Here, NT Server shows its strength in the price area more so than the performance area. To date, no NT Server-based benchmarks have been published providing leading performance values in any of the larger more realistic data warehouse databases sizes of 300 GB and 1 TB.

TPC-D benchmarks exercise CPU, memory, and disk I/O subsystems significantly. Because of this fact, if your database environment is very stressful across the primary server resources, review the TPC-D executive summary reports and review the server configuration. These server configurations show powerful but well-balanced solutions. Well balanced refers to the fact that there is enough CPU and disk subsystems configured to move data or, in essence to feed intense CPU operations and also provide enough CPU power to support significant disk I/O throughput.

For large data warehouse environments, NT currently is not demonstrating much proof that it can support such an environment. NT Server may become more of a consideration in this space as the NT Server operating system matures, database technology running under NT Server matures, and the hardware that NT supports becomes even more scalable.

The Standard Performance Evaluation Corporation (SPEC)

SPEC is a nonprofit corporation that publishes a variety of benchmarks intended to help evaluate different areas of computer performance. The SPECweb96 benchmark suite is particularly relevant for the NT Server environment. Information and results for SPEC benchmarks is available from *http://www.spec.org*.

SPECWEB96

SPECweb96 is a standardized benchmark test designed to measure a server's ability to act as a World Wide Web server. The workload for this benchmark simulates the accesses to a web service provider, where the server supports the home page for a number of different organizations. This benchmark reports the throughput that a World Wide Web server can support. Here the throughput is defined as the sustained number of hypertext transfer protocol (HTTP) operations per second.

To understand what this throughput result is really providing, let's review the benchmark a little closer. This test is set up such that multiple client machines are configured to access a web server under test. The load on the web server is increased until the server software is saturated with hits and the response time degrades significantly. This point of saturation is then reported as the maximum number of HTTP operations per second that the web-server software can sustain and is the metric reported.

SPECWEB96 CONSTRUCTION

SPECweb96 is constructed as a collection of four classes of home page files ranging in the following workload sizes: less than 1 KB, 1 to 10 KB, 10 to 100 KB, and 100 KB to 1 MB. There are several files in each class, with sizes distributed evenly through the range for that class. SPECweb96 directs 35 percent of its activity to the smallest class, 50 percent to the 1-to-10-KB class, 14 percent to the 10-to-100-KB class, and one percent to the largest files. Within each class there are nonlinear distributions of accesses, reflecting the fact that certain files are more popular than others.

As with the TPC-C benchmark, vendors disclose executive summary reports of their SPECweb96 results. Here is a sample report:

Table 3.2 NCR 4300 SPECweb96 Results

NCR: WorldMarkTM 4300 Server—1191 SPECweb96
Microsoft: Internet Information Server 3

Throughput ops/sec	Response msec	Throughput ops/sec	Response msec
121	11.1	726	11.4
242	10.3	844	11.9
363	10.2	967	12.9
485	10.4	1084	14.7
605	10.9	1191	20.1

General Availability Dates

Hardware	Aug-96
Operating System	Aug-96
HTTP Software	Dec-96

System Hardware

Vendor	NCR
Model	WorldMarkTM 4300 Server
Processor	200 MHz Pentium Pro
# of Processors	2
Primary Cache	8 KB I + 8 KB D
Secondary Cache	512 KB (I+D)
Other Cache	None
Memory	2GB
Disk Controllers	NCR PCI Quad SCSI Controller
Disk Subsystem	NCR 6255 external RAID
Other Hardware	None

Table 3.2 NCR 4300 SPECweb96 Results (Continued)

NCR:WorldMarkTM 4300 Server—1191 SPECweb96 Microsoft: Internet Information Server 3	
System Software	
Operating System	Windows NT Server 4.0
Other Software	None
File System Type	NTFS
HTTP Software	
Vendor	Microsoft
HTTP Software	Internet Information Server 3
# of "threads"	1
Server Cache	default
Log Mode	standard
Network	
# of Controllers	4
Network Controller	DEC DEFPA-UA FDDI controller/PCI Adapter
# of Nets	4
Type of Nets	FDDI over UTP
Network Speed	100 Mb/ps
MSL (sec)	30
Time-Wait (sec)	60
Load Generators	
# of Generators	7
# of Processes Each	5
Model	HD Victoria
Processor	200 MHz Pentium Pro
# of Processors	1
Memory	64 MB EDO per HD Victoria
Network Controller	DEC FDDIcontroller/PCI Adapter (3 DEFPA-MA, 4 DEFPA-UA)
Operating System	Windows NT Server 4.0 w/SP3 and post-SP3 hotfix tcpip
Compiler	Microsoft Visual C++ 4.2
Benchmark Configuration	
Max Requested Load	1210
Max Fileset Size	761

Table 3.2 NCR 4300 SPECweb96 Results (Continued)

NCR: WorldMarkTM 4300 Server—1191 SPECweb96 Microsoft: Internet Information Server 3	
Test Sponsor	
Tested By	Mindcraft, Inc.
License Number	10
Test Date	Jun-97
Operating System Notes	
<> Service Pack 3 from May '97 installed	
<> tcpip.sys patch from NT hot fix after Service Pack 3	
Network Notes	
<> three nets at half duplex, each net with two clients chained via the DEFPA-MA FDDI controllers	
<> one client connected directly to the server on the fourth NIC	
Other Notes	
<> BIOS Setting: PCI Line Prefetch=disable (default=enable)	
<> BIOS Setting: Address Bit Permuting=enable (no default)	
<> Added registry entry: Tcpip/Parameters/TcpTimedWaitDelay=60 (default=240)	
<> Added registry entry: Tcpip/Parameters/MaxFreeTcbs=85000 (default=2000)	
<> Added registry entry: Tcpip/Parameters/MaxHashTableSize=65536 (default=512)	
<> Added registry entry: Inetinfo/Parameters/ObjectCacheTTL=4294967295 (default=30)	
<> Added registry entry: Inetinfo/Parameters/ListenBackLog=1024 (default=15)	
<> Added registry entry: Inetinfo/Parameters/LogFileFlushInterval=60 (default=30)	
<> Added registry entry: NDIS/Parameters/ProcessorAffinityMask=0 (default=#FFFFFFFF)	
<> NT System Properties: Application Performance set to "No Boost" (default=midway)	
<> Five 4.3 GB Fast/Wide SCSI disks in an external RAID array	
<> Two internal 4.3 GB Fast/Wide 7200 RPM disks on a separate controller	
<> RAID Disk Array configured as RAID 0, 1 logical drive for benchmark data, 50%/50% read/write acceleration	
<> One SCSI disk with D: partition for OS, one SCSI disk with E: partition for web server logging.	

APPLYING SPECWEB96 RESULTS

So, how can this information be helpful in sizing and configuring your NT Servers acting as web servers? This benchmark (and benchmarks similar in nature) can help significantly if you keep in mind what is actually tested. The obvious information provided is that if you are looking to support 1191 static HTTP requests per second or 102,902,400 hits/day, you know the exact NT Server configuration needed. While 102,902,400 hits/day may sound impressive, remember this assumes your traffic load is spread across the entire 24-hour day. Configuration information to take note of here is the significant memory and network I/O sizing required to support these levels of hit rates.

SPECWEB96 CONCERNS

The primary concern when using the SPECweb96 results is the content type of the benchmark; static pages. If your web server environment is more dynamic in nature, perhaps through the use of CGI scripts, ActiveX, JavaScript, or other dynamic page generation techniques, using the SPECweb96 results when sizing an NT server can be more of a challenge. If you keep in mind the big picture or end result, it really is not that difficult to be able to leverage SPECweb96 results to your sizing advantage.

When dynamic pages are generated, the web server may still serve up the same amount of information that was served in the static environment. It is the generation of this dynamic content that requires additional server resources. SPECweb96 provides information on the base platform configuration required to serve static pages at a specific performance level. You must then tune your server resources and add additional server resources to support the increased load caused by the dynamic page generation. Take note that the SPECweb96 environment is normally run intranet style or from local high speed LANs. This is an important consideration when developing the network architecture required to support higher hit rates. This SPECweb96 Executive report shows the use of FDDI rings. FDDI used here provides 100 Megabits/sec of bandwidth per network interface card (NIC). This bandwidth is important, but what is even more important is the token passing protocol that FDDI uses which enables the FDDI NIC to provide a much more graceful degradation curve under heavy loads versus a network protocol such as Ethernet.

SPECWEB96 FUTURE WEB SIZING EXAMPLE

SPECweb96 information is also helpful for future sizing. Perhaps you are planning for an increase in static hit rates at your website beyond your current configuration. Will additional resources allow your software/hardware solution to support additional hits? Review the *http://www.spec.org/osg/web96/results* pages and look for a configuration that might be similar to what you are interested in. Again, running benchmarks are expensive, so the available list of varied configurations to choose from may be limited. On the positive side, there is a list. The previous SPECweb96 server configuration results used above were based on a NCR 4300 2 CPU Intel Pentium Pro, NT Server, using

Internet Information Server 3.0 (IIS 3.0) web server based solution. Scanning the SPEC website I found an HP benchmark result run after the NCR benchmark. The HP LX Pro configuration was run using IIS in a 4 CPU Intel Pentium Pro configuration.

Both the NCR 2 CPU server and the HP 4 CPU server are based on similar, if not the same, Intel motherboard for these particular SPECweb96 results. With this knowledge (perhaps somewhat of insider based knowledge that is available if you dig down into websites far enough) the HP results can be used to help size the current NCR configuration. This is a surprisingly common occurrence between many of the Intel CPU Server Vendors.

Here are the HP results from the SPEC website.

Table 3.3 HP Netserver 6/200 SPECweb96 Result

HP: HP Netserver 6/200 LX Pro—1733 SPECweb96

Microsoft: Internet Information Server 3.0

Throughput ops/sec	Response msec	Throughput ops/sec	Response msec
180	6.9	1081	9.5
360	7.0	1260	10.6
541	7.4	1442	12.0
720	8.0	1621	14.8
901	8.7	1733	17.3

General Availability Dates

Hardware	Aug-97
Operating System	Nov-97
HTTP Software	Mar-97

System Hardware

Vendor	HP
Model	HP Netserver 6/200 LX Pro
Processor	200Mhz PPro
# of Processors	4
Primary Cache	8KBI+8KBD on chip
Secondary Cache	1MB(I+D) off chip
Other Cache	
Memory	2048MB
Disk Controllers	1 F/W/U SCSI
Disk Subsystem	1 HP D3582A, 6 HP ST34501WC
Other Hardware	

Table 3.3 HP Netserver 6/200 SPECweb96 Result (Continued)

HP: HP Netserver 6/200 LX Pro—1733 SPECweb96 Microsoft: Internet Information Server 3.0	
System Software	
Operating System	NT Server 4.0 w/SP3
Other Software	tcpip.sys patch from NT hot fix after SP 3
File System Type	
HTTP Software	
Vendor	Microsoft
HTTP Software	Internet Information Server 3.0
# of "threads"	Default
Server Cache	Default
Log Mode	Combined Network
# of Controllers	4
Network Controller	DEC DEFPA-MB FDDI PCI UTP Adapter
# of Nets	4
Type of Nets	FDDI
Network Speed	100Mbit/s
MSL (sec)	30
Time-Wait (sec)	60
Load Generators	
# of Generators	11
# of Processes Each	3
Model	HP Vectra XA
Processor	200MHz PPro/256KB
# of Processors	1
Memory	96MB
Network Controller	DEC DEFPA FDDI over UTP
Operating System	NT 4.0 Workstation SP3
Compiler	Visual C++ 5.0
Benchmark Configuration	
Max Requested Load	1800
Max Fileset Size	927
Test Sponsor	
Tested By	Hewlett-Packard
License Number	3
Test Date	Aug-97

Table 3.3 HP Netserver 6/200 SPECweb96 Result (Continued)

HP: HP Netserver 6/200 LX Pro—1733 SPECweb96 Microsoft: Internet Information Server 3.0
Operating System Notes
<> Windows NT 4.0 Service Pack 3, tcpip.sys patch from NT hot fix after Service Pack 3
Network Notes
<> The DEC DEFPA-MB cards are dual attach station (DAS) FDDI over category five twisted pair. <> No hubs were employed, each of the four networks is connected as a ring using both attachments. <> Each network included one card in the SUT and two of the clients. <> Clients 1(prime) 2 on 1st segment, clients 3, 4 and 5 on 2nd, 6, 7 and 8 on 3rd, 9, 10 and 11 on 4th.
Other Notes
<> Performance Boost for Foreground Application=NONE –Do not raise the priority of the foreground application, default is halfway. <> Disable IIS Windows NT Challenge/Response –Disables IIS user information encryption, default is enabled. <> Added Registry Entry InetInfo/Parameters/LogFileFlushInterval=0x3c –Makes the log file flush interval 60 seconds, default is 30. <> Added Registry Entry InetInfo/Parameters/LogFileBatchSize=0x2000000 –Forces the log file flush size to be MIN(60 sec,32 MB), default is 64 KB. <> Added Registry Entry InetInfo/Parameters/ObjectCacheTTL=0xea60 –Keeps IIS open descriptors active at least 16.6 hours, default is 30 sec. <> Added Registry Entry InetInfo/Parameters/MemoryCacheSize=0x2000000 –Ups the cache open descriptor table to 32 MB, default is 3 MB. <> Added Registry Entry InetInfo/Parameters/ListenBacklog=0x19 –Specifies maximum active connections to hold in server queue, default is 15. <> Added Registry Entry InetInfo/Parameters/MaxPoolThreads=1 –Specifies maximum network request threads per processor, default is 10. <> Added Registry Entry InetInfo/Parameters/PoolThreadLimit=4 –Specifies maximum pool threads in system, default is 2 * #MB. <> Added Registry Entry Tcpip/Parameters/MaxFreeTcbs=0x186a0 –Increases the TCB timewait table to 120000 entries, default is 2000. <> Added Registry Entry Tcpip/Parameters/MaxHashTableSize=0x10000 –Sets TCB hash table size to 65,536 entries, default is 512. <> Added Registry Entry Tcpip/Parameters/TcpTimedWaitDelay=0x3c –Sets TIME_WAIT parameter to 60 seconds (non-RFC 1122), default is 240. <> Set NDIS/Parameters/ProcessorAffinityMask to 0 –Forces processor that handled interrupt to also handle that DPC, default is any processor. <> One 4 GB 7200 RPM disk for OS, 3 4 GB 10 KRPM disk for web pages, 1 4 GB 10 KRPM Drive for IIS logs, 1 4 GB 10 KRPM Drive for Pagefile

Reviewing this data closely indicates that an increased hit rate is possible. This HP LX Pro configuration yielded a SPECweb96 result of 1733 compared to the earlier NCR result of 1191. This is an improvement of over 45 percent. Is this perfect scalability? No. Does it allow a single server to support an increased static http workload? Yes. Looking closely at the NCR and HP configurations and reviewing the server resources yields the following differences (Table 3.4).

Table 3.4 HP and NCR SPECweb96 results.

	NCR	HP	Primary Difference
CPU	2 200MHx Pentium Pro w/512k L2 Cache	4 200MHx Pentium Pro w/1MB L2 Cache	2 CPUs and increase of L2 cache from 512K to 1MB
DISK	Similar	Similar	N/A
Network	Similar	Similar	N/A
Software Configuration	Similar	Similar	N/A

This information indicates what it will take to expand the current 2 CPU server to support an increased level of web-based workloads. The initial server SPECweb96 results reviewed were for the NCR 4300. To consider scalability possibilities, it would be ideal to find another NCR 4300 with an expanded configuration. While NCR had not yet published additional larger SPECweb96 results based on NCR 4300 configuration, during the time I researched this matter, HP had. Both servers are Intel-based, using very similar configurations, which allows for the leverage of the new HP data information to be used when considering an increase in the sizing of the current NCR 4300 in use. If the content on the NCR 4300 in use included dynamic page generation, consider increasing the number of CPUs, amount of memory, disks, etc., to compensate or change the overall web deployment architecture.

For this example, NCR and HP servers are used. Your environment may utilize different vendor's servers. Which vendor makes the server is irrelevant. What is relevant here are the sizing concepts presented and the applicability of these concepts to your specific environment.

NetBench

The Ziff-Davis Benchmark Operation produces a series of benchmarks that encompass a variety of areas, which can be downloaded from their website: *http://www1.zdnet.com/zdbop/zdbop.html*. Of these benchmarks, NetBench is a helpful benchmark when testing NT Servers as file servers. NetBench exercises network file I/O requests in a file server environment producing a bytes/sec server I/O throughput score. The NetBench benchmark program measures how well a file server handles typical office productivity application file I/O requests workloads by stressing the file server with various client types. The clients exercise the NT Server with requests for network file operations. Each client tallies how many bytes of data it moves to and from the server and how long the process takes. The client then uses this information to calculate its throughput for that test mix.

The primary benefit of this benchmark is that several trade magazines run this test suite against numerous vendors' servers, thus a fair amount of data is available. I doubt there is any coincidence that most of the magazines using the Ziff-Davis benchmarks fall under the Ziff-Davis ownership umbrella. These published results are beneficial for determining sizing configurations of NT file servers and determining the number of office environment clients the NT file server can support. The following is an excerpt from the October 21, 1997 issue of PC magazine (*http://zdnet.com/pcmag/features/cheap/cheaps3c.htm*).

ANALYZING NETBENCH RESULTS

Figure 3–4 depicts various departmental servers under a NetBench load. There are two key characteristics of the servers evaluated above: throughput and cli-

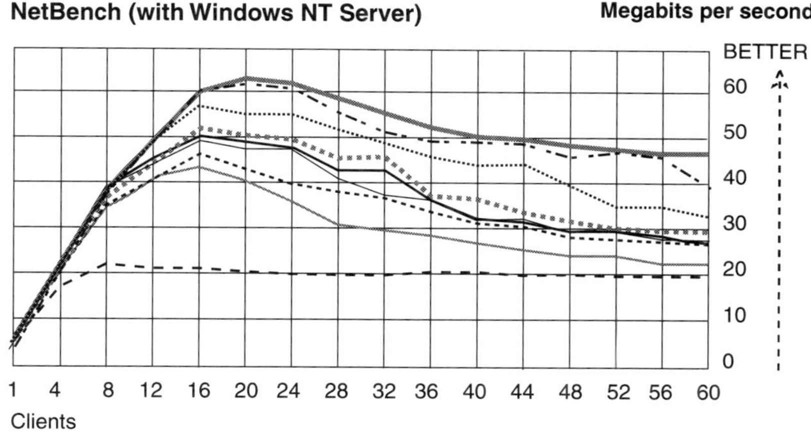

Reprinted from PC Magazine October 21, 1997. © 1997 Ziff Davis

Figure 3–4 *NT Server NetBench results.*

ents supported. Although each server provided varied amount of network throughput, the top performing servers provide a maximum network I/O throughput of just over 60 Megabits/sec. Supported throughput began to fall when more then 20 concurrent clients were requesting service. These departmental servers were configured roughly the same with a single Pentium Pro or Pentium II CPU, 128 MB of RAM, two 10/100 network interface cards, and two 4 GB hard disks in a RAID Level 1 mirrored configuration. The total network load for each benchmark test was a 60-node network divided into two identical 30-client segments.

NetBench places particular stress onto the network and disk I/O subsystems which is indicative of what you find in a file server environment. File server testing is highly susceptible to the choice of the network and disk components along with the server configurations. So what sizing information can be gleaned from the chart above? It depends on your environment. If your requirements indicate the need to support 60 concurrent clients while sustaining 20 Megabits/sec of network throughput, then the basic server configuration provided here will meet those requirements. If, however, your requirements dictate supporting 60 concurrent clients while sustaining a throughput requirement of 50 Megabits/sec, none of the server configurations evaluated by PC Week will meet your requirements. Note that to meet the 50 Megabit/sec requirement, even the best server solution evaluated above would be regulated to supporting 40 concurrent clients, split between two network segments. If requirements dictate the need for a high client count and high throughput rate, the information provided is a good starting point when determining what will and will not work.

NETBENCH LIMITATIONS

The limiting factor for this benchmark is twofold: the workload mix and client loads. As with other benchmarks, if your environment is not indicative of general office productivity applications, the results provided by this benchmark are less helpful. Generating a significant amount of load is prohibitive in a NetBench environment due to the large number of client PC's required to generate workload levels high enough to properly stress higher end servers. Higher end NT Servers can be equated with work horses, not race horses. If high enough workload levels are not attained on larger NT Server configurations, the server's real capabilities will not be properly tested.

Where Do Historical Baselines Fit in the Sizing Methodology?

Historical baselines are particularly useful when applied to steps 3 and 7 of the sizing methodology. In step 3, Determining loading characteristics, having historical information on which to base the loading analysis is quite helpful and is explained below. Once you understand the characteristics of the loads that the server will need to support, configuring a server to meet your requirements becomes more realistic, since you can leap directly into placing an optimum configuration together.

Using Historical Baselines

In several locations throughout this chapter, the use of current performance logs from Perfmon was alluded to. In Chapter 2, the use of Perfmon generated performance logs was described. How can you use these Perfmon logs to your advantage for longer-term capacity sizing and planning? Perfmon allows performance data to be exported into a variety of formats from File|Export Chart. Available export formats include tabular delimited fields (.tsv) and comma separated fields (.csv). These export formats can be imported into a database of your choice for more advanced and long term analyses to determine future trends. A slightly less complex but helpful method is to export this information into a spreadsheet. Once the data is inside of the spreadsheet, you can then exploit some of the spreadsheets trend analysis capabilities.

To generate a disk I/O analysis graph similar to Figure 3–5, follow these steps:

1. Launch Perfmon by selecting Start|Administrative Tools|Performance Monitor.
2. Select Options|Data|From and then choose the log file.
   Note: You must already have created a log file for this step.
   Refer back to Chapter 2 for the steps associated to create a log file using Perfmon.
3. Under Logical Disk Object, select % Disk Time.
4. Under File|Export Chart, save your data in the .tsv file format.
5. Launch your spreadsheet; this example is based on Microsoft Excel.
6. Open the .tsv file you exported and follow the Excel's data import wizard.
7. Highlight the performance data % Disk Time and Time/Date Stamp.
8. Select Chart Wizard and follow the wizards steps to create the graph.
9. Once the graph is created, right click on the % Disk Time data series.
10. While the data series is selected, right click the data series and choose add trend line.
11. For this example, I used a linear trend line.
12. Right clicking the newly created trend line allows access to trend line Format|Options.
13. Under options, enter in the number of units for future forecast.
14. Congratulations, you now have a capacity sizing projection chart!

Following the steps on generating a disk I/O analysis graph, a disk I/O trend analysis for use in capacity planning was created.

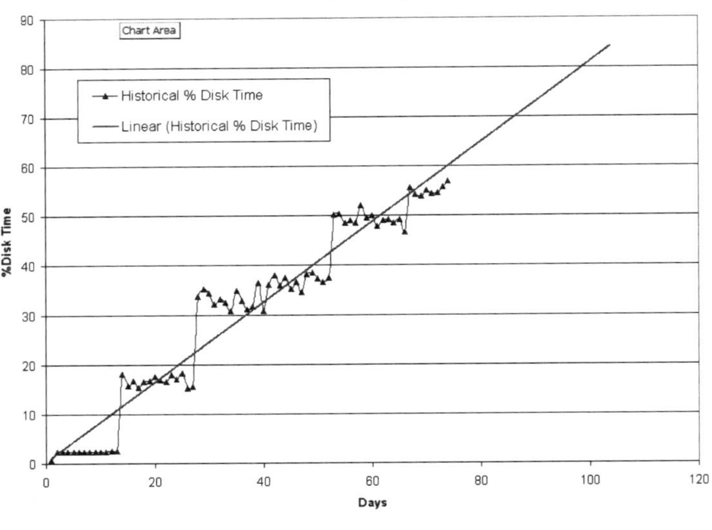

Figure 3–5 *A disk I/O trend analysis.*

This graph depicts one disk drive's percent disk time historical usage and 30 day projected % Disk Time usage. The disk usage for this drive is steadily increasing, with a current % Disk Time hovering in the 50 percent range. A 50 percent utilization is acceptable, but as the % Disk Utilization increases past the 60–80 percent utilization range, disk response time begins to exponentially increase [Patterson and Hennesey, *Computer Architecture: A Quantitative Approach,* p. 545]. If disk response increases, so will the associated activity that requires that disk request. Thus, the final response time the user experiences will also increase, which is what we want to avoid happening on a regular basis.

So what do you do with this data? Head back to Chapter 2, "Tuning Strategies and Measurement Gathering" and use the tuning methodology in conjunction with Chapter 6, "NT Server and Disk Subsystem Performance" to determine possible solutions to this pending disk bottleneck. Some of the solutions can encompass techniques ranging from changing this configuration from a single disk device to a RAID device, tuning the allocation unit size (ALU), or redistributing some of the disk workload to other disk devices in the server. If the solution involves the purchase of additional hardware resources, use this trend analysis to help justify the decision.

There is, however, an assumption made here that this disk usage pattern will continue into the future. This is where the art of sizing comes into play, since you will have to take into consideration factors such as future business requirements and continued use of this application by end users as the company grows.

This same capacity planning technique can be used to project the future capacity usage and potential bottlenecks for all of the major server resources. What should you analyze and graph? Chapter 1 has several tables that outline detection of server bottlenecks. Use these tables as a guide when deciding which Perfmon objects to use for sizing trend analysis. The same Perfmon objects that are helpful for detecting server bottlenecks are also helpful for sizing servers as well. For convenience, some of the key Perfmon objects and counters to consider for capacity planning and trend analysis are charted in Table 3.5.

Table 3.5 Key Perfmon objects and counters.

Object/Counter	Definition	Rule of Thumb for Bottleneck Detection
Memory Counters		
Memory: Available bytes	Available bytes displays the size of virtual memory currently on the zeroed, free, and standby lists. Zeroed and free memory is ready for use with zeroed memory cleared to zeros. Standby memory is removed from a processor's work set but is still available.	NT Server will try to keep at least 4 MB available as seen via this counter. If this value is near 4 MB and pages/sec is high, it is likely there is a memory shortfall.
Memory: Pages/sec	Pages/sec is the number of pages read from the disk or written to the disk to resolve memory references that were not in memory at the time of reference.	This counter can be deceiving particularly on Enterprise class systems. A high paging activity is fine (>100), unless it is accompanied by a low available bytes indicator and a high % Disk Time on the paging file disks.
Disk Counters		
Logical Disk: % Disk Time	% Disk time is the percentage of elapsed time that the selected disk drive is busy servicing read or write requests.	If this value increases above 60–80 percent, then the response time from the disk drive may become unacceptable, thus the selected disk instance is becoming a bottleneck.
Logical Disk: Average Disk Queue Length	Average disk queue length is the average number of both read and write requests that were queued for the selected disk during the sample interval.	If this value is >2 for a single disk drive and the % Disk Time is high, the selected disk drive is becoming a bottleneck.

Table 3.5 Key Perfmon objects and counters. (Continued)

Object/Counter	Definition	Rule of Thumb for Bottleneck Detection
Logical Disk: Disk Bytes/sec	Disk bytes/sec is the rate bytes are transferred to or from the disk during read or write operations	If the sum of these two counters is greater then 80 percent of the SCSI channel speed in use, the SCSI channel in use may be causing an I/O system bottleneck.
Network Counters		
Network Interface: Bytes Total/sec	Bytes total/sec is the rate that bytes are sent and received on the selected network interface, including framing characters.	This value is directly related to the network architecture in use. If the value of bytes total/sec for the network instance is close to the maximum transfer rates of your network, and the output queue length is >10, you have a network bottleneck. Output queue length is currently (as of SP3) only valid for non-SMP based servers.
CPU Counters		
System: % Total Processor Time	Total processor time is expressed as a percentage of the elapsed time that all processors are busy executing nonidle threads.	A value for this counter is not a reason to be alarmed. Unless it is accompanied with a server work queue length >2 times the number of CPUs in the server or growing with an associated level of processor time >90 percent, then the CPU is becoming a bottleneck.
Server Work Queues: Queue Length	Queue length is the current length of the server work queue for this CPU instance.	If the queue length is >2 times the number of CPUs in the server or continuously growing with an associated level of processor time >90 percent, the CPU is becoming a bottleneck.

Of course, this capacity sizing technique is only helpful if you proactively monitor and keep accurate records on the servers that are managed. So why not track performance logs of at least your most crucial servers? Keeping good records is the key to staying one step ahead in the capacity planning game!

How Server Architecture Relationships Affect Server Configurations

Throughout this chapter, the focus has been on determining the requirements of each server component. From a configuration standpoint, each server resource (CPU, memory, disk, and network) is covered in more detail in later chapters with specific recommendations. For now, let's take a step back and look at the entire server architecture as it relates to the final configuration.

When configuring your server, it is important to understand the relationships of the various server components and how data is moved in a server. Once you begin to understand these relationships, it is possible to size balanced NT Server configurations that do not introduce bottlenecks before you even begin. Standard high volume (SHV) server boards produced by Intel are what many of today's hardware manufactures OEM for the basis of for their 4 CPU NT Super Server implementations. Figure 3–6 illustrates a logical SHV-based server.

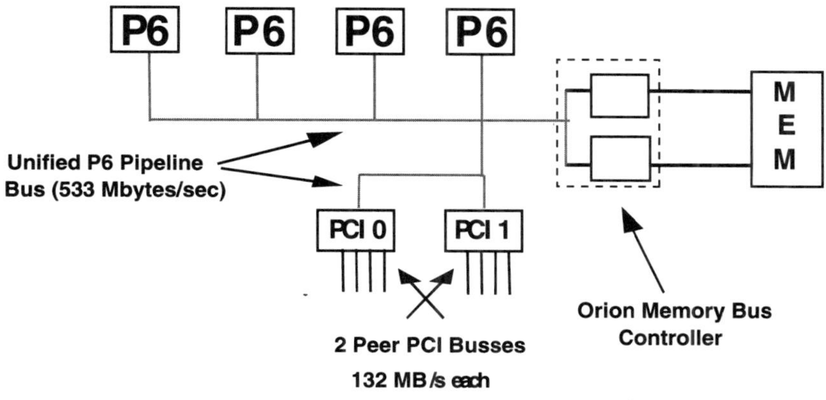

Figure 3–6 *SHV-based server.*

The server's primary system bus (P6) operates at 66 MHz or 533 Mbytes/sec. Attached to the P6 bus are up to 4 Pentium Pro CPUs operating up tp 200 Mhz, up to 4 GB of RAM (currently rated at 60ns), and two peer PCI I/O buses operating at 133 Mbytes/sec. Understanding the speeds and feeds of the server is less important at the moment than understanding the relationships between them. Let's look at these speeds and feeds from two perspectives: (1) the time it takes to get data to the CPU, and (2) how data gets from the I/O subsystem to the CPU. The time it takes to get data to the CPU drastically affects the server's overall performance (see Table 3.6).

Table 3.6 Time needed to obtain data from server resources

Resource	Time (nanoseconds)
CPU to L1 cache	2
CPU to directly connected L2 Cache	2
CPU to indirectly connected L2 Cache	4
CPU to Main Memory/RAM	50–70
CPU to Disk Drives	9,000,000–35,000,000
CPU to Network Connected Disk Resource	10,000,000–250,000,000

Nanoseconds are a small quantity of time that are difficult to put into perspective. Figure 3–7 takes a graphical look at access times compared to the various server resources outlined in Table 3.6.

To help put this into perspective, let's scale these nanoseconds into seconds. Now, if you needed a piece of information to complete your job and go home, and the information was in Level 2 cache, it would take all of two seconds to gather the data and then shortly thereafter you would go home. If the information you required was on the disk drive, you would have to wait 9,000,000 seconds or 2,500 hours. Which would you prefer? The primary

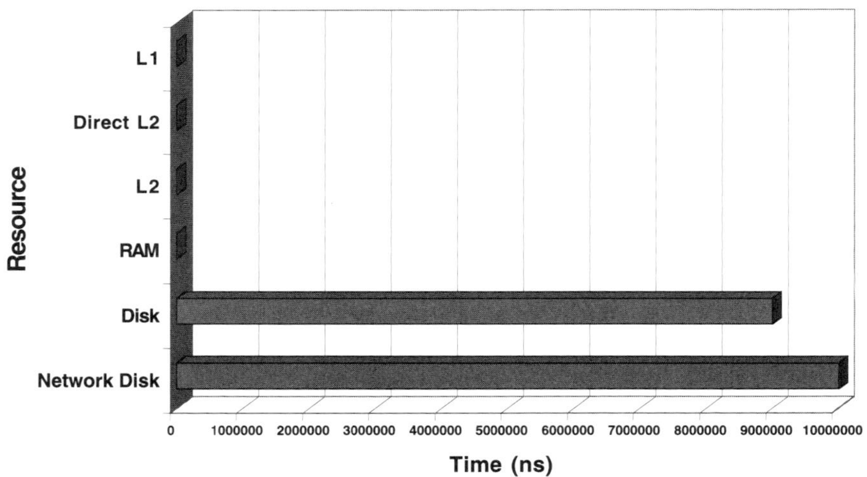

Figure 3–7 *Access times.*

objective of this simplified graph is to drive home the importance of the time required to get data from sources other than cache or main memory.

Amazing, isn't it? While the CPU waits for data from disk, it could be sitting around idle. Keeping a CPU properly presented or "fed" with data allows the CPU to be more efficient. The reference to efficient here is in the context that the CPU is running a productive action versus sitting and waiting for the data it needs.

Properly Sizing Memory

This fact becomes even more important as enterprise NT Servers begin to appear. Determining the appropriate amount of RAM to configure will greatly affect your server's performance. To keep a Pentium Pro CPU class NT Server based properly fed, 64 MB of RAM per CPU at a minimum is required. With 64 MB of RAM, NT's entire working set (24 MB) can fit into memory, there is some application space available, and there is still some RAM available for NT Server's file system caching. Now, of course, permanently saved data on disk drives will need to be accessed at some point, but it would be prudent to avoid accessing the disk drives unless absolutely necessary. Every time the server must access the disk, the CPU could wait the equivalent of driving several times from NY to LA before the CPU can continue. Having enough RAM available to avoid constantly traveling to the disk for data drastically improves the server's performance.

Server I/O Relationships

Now let's look at how data gets from the I/O subsystem to the CPU. Different server architectures are capable of providing certain levels of theoretical I/O performance. The SHV architecture can support a very large amount of external disk arrays. In theory, one SHV based server can support in excess of 7 TB external disk drives. Now, if all of this data is actually active and usable is another story. The NCR 4300 TPC-C executive summary report previously reviewed illustrates one particularly large configuration, which supported 120 disk drives for 632 GB of disk space. The NCR 4300 4 way Super Server is based on the Intel SHV server board.

The SHV I/O subsystem is limited to 2 peer PCI buses, which in essence, feed a single faster P6 system bus. These access speeds you cannot influence, but you should be aware that you could easily influence how the I/O system is used. When considering the I/O layout, think of plumbing (we'll skip the various I/O overheads for now). Consider Figures 3–8 and 3–9.:

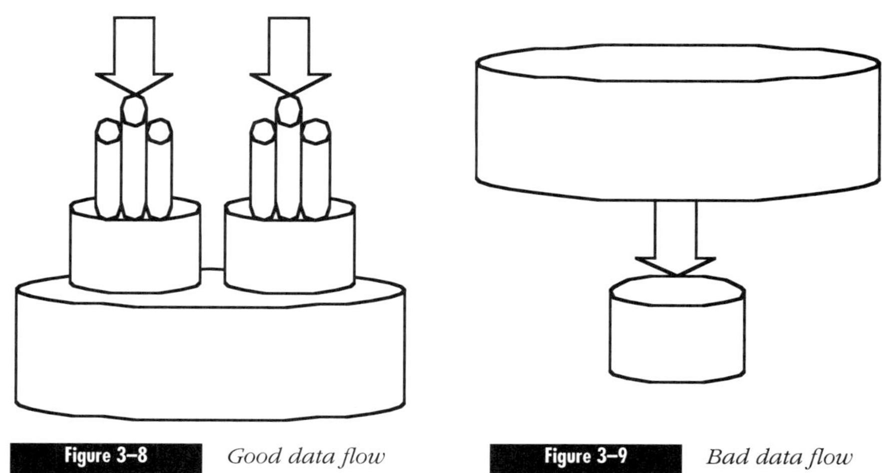

Figure 3–8 *Good data flow*

Figure 3–9 *Bad data flow*

Obviously you would want to avoid Figure 3–9. This is the same concept when configuring the I/O subsystem. Following the sizing methodology and Chapter 7, along with some experience, you can determine how many I/O devices will be active at one time. For a worst case scenario, you can consider all I/O devices active at the same time (however unlikely). If your server will support 6 PCI I/O cards and the configuration calls for 3 ATM network cards (~60 Mbytes/sec), and 3 Quad Ultra Fast and Wide SCSI cards (~480 Mbytes sec), there is a problem. The aggregate I/O throughput of these devices ~540 Mbytes/sec will greatly overflow the 266 Mbytes/sec available from the two peer PCI buses available in an SHV based server. The moral of the story: *Even if the server specifications state that the server can be configured in a certain manner, it is not always wise to do so.*

Server CPUs Drive More Than Applications Alone

Now that we have considered the sizing relationship of the main memory and I/O subsystem, never forget the CPU processing power required to drive the entire server. Driving high levels of I/O requires a significant amount of processing power. The amount of CPU power required to accomplish this should lower once I20 technology comes of age. More detailed information on these two topics are provided in Chapters 5 and 7. Until then, keep in mind that you must share the direct processing power needed for application calculations with the processing power required to drive the I/O subsystem.

This concept of ensuring that there is enough CPU processing power becomes relevant when, after following the sizing methodology, you determine the need for an NT Server to provide very high levels of I/O throughput. Perhaps the requirements call for a communications application driving multiple ATM lines in conjunction with another application requiring high processing requirements. At that point, sizing requirements may have outgrown the SHV architecture and a more scalable server design that supports higher numbers of CPUs, PCI buses, and memory should be considered. With the introduction of commodity priced 8 CPU based servers, choosing a more scalable server platform is much more realistic than years past. Another option, commonly used before the advent of higher scaling commodity Intel CPU based servers for the NT environment, is distributing the application(s) among multiple super servers as needed to meet the requirements.

Sizing Summary

In this chapter we explored a sizing methodology that can be used when sizing any NT Server for your solution regardless of the current technology level in use. NT Server sizing aids such as using Industry Standard Benchmarks and historical data trend usage, were covered to help in gaining a more realistic start in your sizing efforts. In addition to these areas, server architecture relationships were investigated which provide insight into the relationships of server resources while using the extensive capabilities and limitations of modern SHV servers as a reference example. Understanding server architectures leads to properly sized and configured NT Servers that provide realistic, well-balanced, and scalable solutions.

F O U R

NT Server and CPU Performance

If you want to tune or size an NT Server, having an understanding of how the server hardware, operating system and applications actual work is important. When you understand how these various components are trying to complete their respective tasks, it becomes much more evident how to help them complete their tasks by tuning and sizing the server resources for maximum performance. This is exactly what is presented in the following chapters. Descriptions, explanations, and examples are provided to help you understand how the server components interact. Armed with this information, some of the "black magic" of tuning and sizing is removed and more effective tuning and sizing tactics are employed. It is tempting to just jump in and start adding this or tuning that. Knowing which "knob to turn" to tune NT Server is good; understanding when to "turn a tuning knob" and why it will help is better.

CPU

The Central Processing Unit (CPU) is the glamour queen of any server. It is the single most important resource in the server, as it processes various requests from server applications and subsequent end users. In this chapter, CPU performance is investigated from several perspectives. First, general CPU architectures are reviewed to determine the relative performance of several available CPU models and what, from server architecture perspective, influences the CPU performance. Then we'll look at how NT Server takes advantage of the CPU. Once our foundation of CPU knowledge is established, we determine when CPU bottlenecks are occurring while running NT Server and then explore sizing the CPU subsystem. Once the CPU subsystem is sized and we understand how to clearly identify bottlenecks, we continue to build upon our foundation by examining how to tune around them.

It is common for businesses to assume that if they add another CPU, the overall performance of their server will increase. As shown in the upcoming chapters, adding another CPU does not always improve performance unless it is the bottleneck that is throttling NT Server's performance. This fact is exemplified in each of the case studies provided in Chapter 8. The case studies demonstrated that additional or faster CPUs were not required to improve the performance of the servers. This concept is mentioned throughout this book a million times because it is very important (okay, a million may be a slight exaggeration). Too often I have read published documents that mention, "we added a CPU, but it did not improve the performance. This software/hardware/application does not scale..." Although this is occasionally true, it is my experience that more often than not, the CPU is not the limiting factor. I hope you remember to take this into consideration before making the decision to increase the speed or number of CPUs in your server.

CPU Architecture Review

This section covers some of the key server architecture factors that influence CPU effectiveness, relative performance of CPUs available today, and guidelines on the selection of a CPU. This section is not a low-level complex review of CPU and server architectures in which you need a doctorate in computer engineering to understand. If you are curious about lower level details of computer architectures, read John Hennessy and David Patterson's excellent book on this topic titled ***Computer Architecture A Quantitative Approach***.

Microsoft and Intel focus on high volume to generate their revenue. This results in servers with generally lower price points, which provide excellent price/performance results. Intel developed a Standard High Volume (SHV) server motherboard, which is the basis of many of the 1-4 Pentium Pro CPU based servers on the market today. Intel's SHV design is referenced here to explain various factors influencing CPU performance. This is not an endorsement of Intel-only server solutions; however it is a popular architecture that provides a good reference to illustrate server architecture principles. Figure 4–1 presents a logical illustration of an SHV motherboard.

Current Intel CPU offerings operate at internal clock speeds up to 400 Mhz. The system bus on the SHV motherboard operates at 66 Mhz. The system bus provides the data path between the CPU, memory, and the I/O subsystem. Obviously, there is a bit of a discrepancy between the speed at

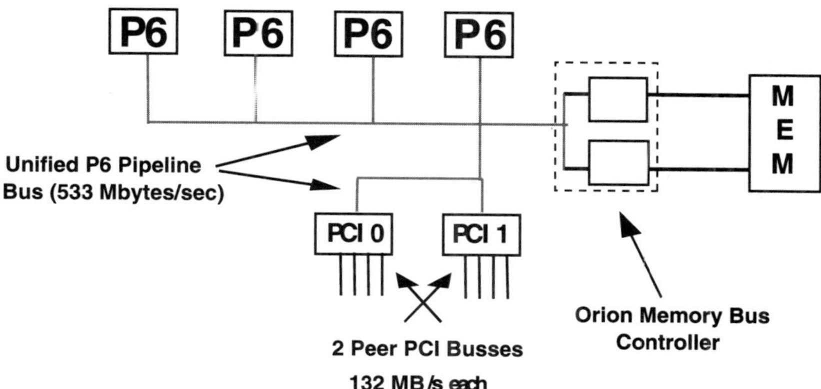

Figure 4–1 *Logical view of an Intel SHV architecture.*

which the system bus operates and the speed at which the CPU(s) operate. For a CPU to be effective, both data and instructions must be moved into the CPU in a fashion such that it can be kept productive performing the requested tasks. When data that the CPU requires is not available, it waits. This is commonly referred to as a CPU wait state. Under NT Server, while a CPU waits for data or is not busy operating on another task, NT Server's system idle process occupies the CPU. You can see the system idle process under task manager, process view.

COMPARING CPU ARCHITECTURES

The CPU can be in a waiting mode for a variety of reasons, such as waiting for a disk operation, network operation, or memory operation. In an effort to keep the CPU processing efficiently, data and instructions must constantly flow into the CPU as requested; in essence, keeping the CPU fed. To accomplish this task, a memory hierarchy is created. The memory hierarchy is constructed of Level 1 cache, Level 2 cache, and main memory (RAM). The type, size, levels, and speed of each level of the memory hierarchy is dictated by a combination of the CPU and server architecture in use. Economics are reflected in the memory hierarchy, as each faster level of cache (where L1 is faster then RAM) is more expensive than the next to implement. Table 4.1 lists the relative speeds and sizes of various levels of memory access.

COMPARING THE PENTIUM PRO AND PENTIUM II CPUS

Both the Pentium Pro and Pentium II CPUs employ Dual Independent Bus (DIB) architectures which allows the CPU to access its second level cache without traversing the system bus. This allows the CPU to access to the L2 cached data at higher speeds and lowers the amount of data traveling the system bus. The Pentium Pro's L2 cache is actually built on the same chip as the

Table 4.1 Relative speed and sizes of various levels of memory access

	Pentium Pro	Pentium II	Pentium Pro	Pentium II
Cache Level	Cache Sizes	Cache Sizes	Speed at which cache is accessed	
L1	8KB data, 8KB instructions	16KB data, 16KB instructions	Chip Speed	Chip Speed
L2	256KB, 512KB, 1MB	512KB	Chip Speed	1/2 of Chip Speed
Main Memory (RAM)	1-8GB	1-2GB	60ns	60ns

Note: The data specifications for all Intel processors are obtained from the Intel Corporation website *http://www.intel.com*

CPU itself. This allows the Pentium Pro to access the L2 cache at core speed, which is the speed at which the CPU is operating. Intel's Pentium® II processor combines the power of the Pentium Pro processor with the media enhancement of Intel's MMX™. The Pentium II, however, does not access its L2 cache at core speed, but at one-half of the core CPU speed. This doubles the amount of time required to access its L2 cache compared to the Pentium Pro. Figure 4–2 illustrates of the Pentium II CPU and Dual Independent Bus.

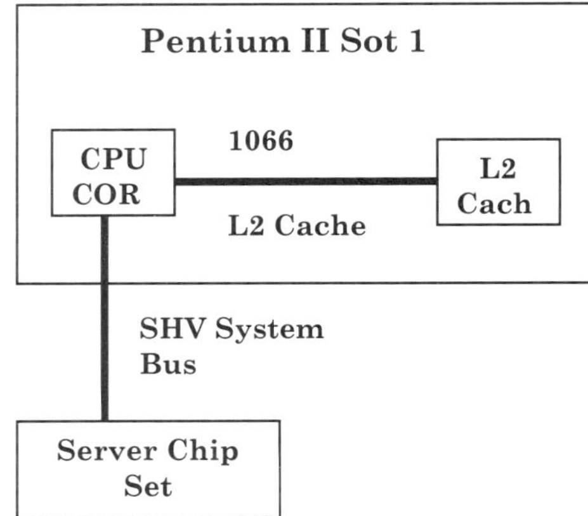

Figure 4–2 *Pentium II dual independent architecture.*

Note: The data for this picture was obtained *http://developer.intel.com/design/PentiumII/prodbref/dibtech.htm* then modified.

HELPING YOUR SERVER SCALE

Increased cache sizes keep the CPU fed at a higher rate; thus, the CPU can complete more work in an efficient manner. Cache size is an important consideration when selecting a CPU. What is also important is the fact that larger CPU caches result in less data traversing the server's system bus, in essence lowering the system buses' congestion levels. With CPU speeds doubling in performance every 18 months (Moore's Law), CPUs are capable of completing more and more work at a faster pace. A problem occurs if the ratio between the system bus speed and CPU speed becomes so disparate that the system bus becomes the limiting factor for server performance, not the CPU. When this occurs, server manufacturers tend to do one of two things: increase the size of the cache on the CPU, and/or replace the system bus.

Planning Around CPU and System Bus Bottlenecks

Based on the above concepts, the choices made when purchasing a server influence your return on investment or length of time the server can meet your needs before throwing parts away. If, when using the sizing methodology from Chapter 3, you discover that only one or two CPUs are required, a smaller cache should be sufficient. In single or double CPU environments, a larger cache is not normally that beneficial from a price/performance point of view. The server's system bus is typically not saturated in smaller servers because of the fact there are not enough I/O buses available to saturate it. It is common for the latest generation of CPU technology to be introduced in workstations and smaller servers first. Then, as the motherboard designs catch up, they become capable of supporting the latest CPUs.

This is currently the case between the Pentium Pro and Pentium II CPUs. From a pure CPU to CPU comparison, the Pentium II provides slightly better performance. Applications that rely on L2 cache may perform better with larger and faster L2 caches provided by the Pentium Pro CPU. Many of the database engines available today, particularly Oracle, displays this type of improved performance with larger and faster caches. The Pentium II CPU is only available in servers supporting one or two CPUs. If your processing requirements are greater than two Pentium II CPUs can provide, then the Pentium Pro is a better choice. Pentium Pro based servers running NT Server can currently support up to eight Pentium Pro CPUs. The increase in performance provided by the Pentium Pro is exemplified in TPC-C results. Four, six, and eight CPU Pentium Pro based servers currently provide the highest published TPC-C results in the NT Server space.

Choose L2 Cache Sizes Wisely

If, when using the sizing methodology, you determine that you wish to start with two CPUs or four CPUs and definitely plan to increase the number of CPUs in the future, opt for the fastest CPU with largest cache size possible. Don't be misled here, you want the fastest CPU that the server can support in a greater than two CPU arrangement. But, after selecting your CPU, if you have a choice between 512 K cache and a 1 MB cache, and it is economically feasible, select the larger cache version of the fastest CPU. Using this strategy, better long-term performance will be available as more and more CPUs are placed onto the server's system bus. For example, when the initial Pentium Pro CPUs were available, many four CPU capable servers were initially configured with two CPUs and the smaller 256 KB caches. This worked well in the one or two CPU environments. In fact, it provided much better price/performance than their 512 KB cache counterparts.

Unfortunately, when the server was completely configured with four CPUs all using 256 KB sized caches, performance scalability was severely limited compared to similarly configured four CPU servers with the 512 K cache. The CPUs were not the limiting factor, the small cache and stressed system bus were the bottleneck culprits! In the short term, budgets were provided with a modest saving by obtaining CPUs with the smaller cache sizes. In the long term, businesses who configured their servers with the Pentium Pro CPU and 256 KB caches that wanted to reap the full performance of a four CPU NT server, lost their initial investment by having to replace their 256 KB cache CPUs with 512 KB cache CPUs. This was not a mandatory requirement, it was only a requirement if they wanted significantly better scaling.

As CPU technology advances and SMP based system bus technology does not, do not be surprised as newer CPUs introduced for the current server technology are introduced with larger and larger caches. Vendors are just trying to stretch the life cycles of their products. I use Intel CPUs for the examples in this chapter, but this is a general computer industry observation of numerous vendors; thus, this is not an Intel specific observation. When caches get particularly large, the vendor is compensating for lower system bus speeds that are getting closer to saturation. As long as you obtain the performance level you require, the CPU system bus relationship is only a trivial fact. But it can also be a prelude that a new overall server architecture is right around the corner.

CPU Technology Is Always Changing

I have encountered various vendors' propaganda which states that the next generation Intel CPU will provide significantly higher levels of CPU performance than the current Pentium II/Pentium Pro CPU family. Taking advantage of this higher level of CPU performance requires a faster server system bus. The next generation of Intel SHV board that will support the Intel's Deshutes CPU is based on a 100 MHz-system bus and higher bandwidth I/O buses. Until this next generation of SHV based servers arrive, if you require higher levels of processing power, consider servers based on increased numbers of CPUs. There are several vendors now shipping creatively designed one to eight CPU Pentium Pro based servers that are based on hybrid designs of Intel's current SHV.

Comparing CPU Performance

Factors such as the internal CPU instruction set, internal design, cache design, number of instructions the CPU completes per clock cycle, and so on, all influence the performance of a CPU. The speed (MHz) of a specific CPU does not directly translate into guaranteed higher levels of CPU performance unless you compare CPUs in the same family generation. Notice that the slower Pentium Pro 200MHz CPU actually outperforms the Pentium MMX 233Mhz CPU (see Table 4.2).

Table 4.2 Relative CPU performance levels

CPU	iCOMP index 2.0
Pentium II - 400 MHz	440
Pentium II - 300 MHz	332
Pentium II - 266 MHz	303
Pentium II - 233 MHz	267
Pentium Pro – 200 MHz (256KB cache)	220
Pentium - 233MHz (MMX)	203
Pentium Pro – 180 MHz	197
Pentium - 200MHz (MMX)	182
Pentium - 166MHz (MMX)	160
Pentium - 150MHz (MMX)	144
Pentium - 200MHz	142
Pentium - 166MHz	127

Note: Data obtained from *http://www.ideasinternational.com/benchmark/intel/icomp.html*

This chart illustrates the relative performance of different Intel CPUs from the perspective of the Intel iCOMP Index 2.0 suite. The iCOMP® index provides a relative measure of microprocessor performance. It is not a benchmark, but a collection of benchmarks used to calculate an index of relative processor performance and is published by the Intel Corporation on the website *http://www.intel.com*. iCOMP Index combines five benchmarks: CPUmark32*, NortonSI-32*, SPECint95*, SPECfp95*, and the Intel Media Benchmark.

These types of synthetic benchmarks, such as those encompassed in iCOMP, are helpful to use when comparing CPUs because they exercise both CPU and associated memory subsystems extensively. What they do not measure is overall server performance. Because of this, it is not possible to make a direct extrapolation between the synthetic benchmark result and the amount of performance that you can expect in your server. If your environment is very computationally intensive, you can make a partial extrapolation from a CPU focused synthetic benchmark. Generally, the performance associated with fielding these CPUs could actually be more or less, depending on your environment. The CPU(s) are, however, one major factor which affects the servers overall performance.

Look at the Big Picture for CPU Selection

Let's step back and look at the big picture. To get the longest life possible out of your server, the basic rule of thumb is to obtain the fastest, highest density components and use them to populate a server that will support the increased workloads and performance levels you define at a price you can afford. There is always a tradeoff somewhere. For CPUs, the economic tradeoff is the timeliness of the technology. As new CPUs are introduced to the market, they are initially priced much higher than current technology. Also in conjunction with the introduction of a new CPU, the older CPU technology price will erode and become more attractive. Now a decision is required: Choose the newer technology at a premium price or wait until the next generation?

If you are deploying a brand new server and the highest levels of performance are required, newer technology will normally provide a good long-term return on investment while immediately meeting your performance needs. If you are considering upgrading the type and/or number of CPUs in your current server, first ensure that the CPU(s) are the bottleneck (stay tuned, we look at this later in this chapter). Then consider waiting a release or two until upgrading CPUs. When the new CPU release provides a 10 percent or better relative performance gain, the upgrade is realistically justified. (Of course, there is also the traditional bragging right associated with having the latest and greatest technology that must always be considered.)

Should I Upgrade?

The overall performance a new CPU(s) provides for your environment is the real determining factor when selecting the CPU to meet your requirements. Just because one CPU is faster than another CPU in a benchmark that only tests the CPU and memory performance, it is not a good indication that your server will benefit from such an upgrade. Running the stress and validation tests developed for your environment (outlined in the sizing methodology) with the new CPU technology installed is the best way to benchmark your server. In this way, you can determine exactly how much improvement can be expected in your environment when you upgrade CPUs. Once you have this information, you can make a decision on whether the cost of the new CPU(s) justifies the associated performance upgrade it delivers.

When you do not have your own stress test or benchmark to use, consider extrapolating from Industry Standard Benchmarks (outlined in Chapter 3.) For example, if your environment is representative of a large client server transaction based database and you determined that the CPU subsystem is the bottleneck throttling your server's overall performance, review a relevant benchmark to your environment, such as the TPC-C database benchmark. Table 4.3 tracks various TPC-C results:

Table 4.3 Comparing overall server performance with the TPC-C benchmark.

Base Configuration (Type of CPUs)	Number of Client Systems	Performance Level (tpmC)	Amount of Memory	Number of Disks	NT Server Release Level	Databases Release
Configuration 1 4 - Pentium Pro 166 MHz/512 K cache	3	6,043	2 GB	112	NT 4	SQL Server 6.5
Configuration 2 4 - Pentium Pro 200 MHz/512 K cache	4	7,368	2 GB	114	NT 4	SQL Server 6.5
Configuration 3 4 - Pentium Pro 200 MHz/512 K cache	5	9,116	4 GB	123	NT 4 Enterprise Edition	SQL Server 6.5 Enterprise Edition

From these TPC-C results you can deduce that upgrading from Configuration 1, using 4-166 MHz Pentium Pro CPUs, to Configuration 2, using 4-200 MHz Pentium Pro CPUs, yielded over a 21 percent improvement in the number of transactions supported. What is particularly nice about comparing results of Configuration 1 and 2 is that the configurations between both tests are very, very similar. With the CPUs being the primary difference between the configurations, it is a good estimation that the new CPUs are what provided the additional level of performance.

Be careful when reviewing benchmark results published by vendors. Many times it is not only one facet of the server that has changed, but also a version of database software, or a major hardware change such as an additional 1 GB of memory, or combination thereof. When comparing servers using Industry Standard Benchmarks, select the benchmark that is as close to your own environment as possible. Then take into consideration differences in the configuration so that you are not comparing apples to oranges. For example, comparing Configuration 3 and Configuration 1 provides little, if any, indication that upgrading the CPU was the primary reason that for the 50 percent performance improvement. The addition of 2 GB of memory, 11 more disk drives, and a different version of the database, are just a few things that may have influenced the final results.

NT Server and the CPU

Now that we have established a general understanding of relative CPU performance and a few factors that influence CPU performance, let's investigate how NT Server takes advantage of the processing power of the server hardware. With an understanding of both the hardware and the operating system, it becomes much easier to detect, then tune around, CPU bottlenecks. NT Server is a time sharing, multiprocessing operating system that employs preemptive multitasking and soft affinity [Optimizing Windows NT, NT Server Resource Kit]. Before we look at the details on how NT Server accomplishes this bold statement, let's take a quick review of processes, threads, and context switching.

Processes, Threads, and Context Switching

In NT Server, a process is an object that represents an instance of an executing program (application). Each process must have at least one or more threads of execution. Each thread object executes a program code for the process. The schedulable entity by the NT Server kernel is the thread object, not the processor object.[1] A context switch is the action that takes place when the processor switches from one executable thread to another executable thread. These explanations are dry, but solidify our foundation of knowledge.

NT Server and a Single CPU Environment

So how does a single CPU NT Server multitask? Actually, it doesn't, if you consider multitasking as the completion of several threads concurrently. The CPU actually switches between threads so fast, it just appears that the threads

---

1. p. 1,129 paraphrase from Windows NT File System Internals, O'Reilly, Rajeev Nagar

are running concurrently. Some processes are monolithic, which means that the process does not spawn multiple threads of execution, just one—itself. Multithreaded processes or applications are composed of many threads of execution, some of which can run concurrently. When a context switch occurs under NT Server, it is expensive from the CPU's point of view because of the associated housekeeping required to change from running one thread to another. Switching between threads in the same process is less CPU expensive than switching a completely new single threaded process. Thus, NT Server can still multitask on a single CPU server when there are monolithic and multithreaded applications running concurrently.

NT Server and Multiple CPU Environment

When a server contains greater than one CPU in a Symmetric Multiprocessor (SMP) environment, NT Server takes advantage of these additional CPUs by executing threads across the multiple CPUs at the same time. An SMP designed server is one in which all server resources are shared and each CPU is equal in its control of the server; for example, there is not a master CPU that the other CPUs must report to. In multiple CPU server environments, true multitasking is accomplished. That is, two or more threads can be running at the same time. NT Server is capable of supporting 32 processors in an SMP configuration. 32 CPUs? Yes! NT Server is designed to support 32 CPUs. What most people purchase is an NT Server package that can support one to four CPUs. One to eight CPU servers are becoming more common. To take advantage of these additional CPUs currently, you must obtain NT Server Enterprise Edition. NT Server is actually licensed on a per-user *and* per-CPU basis.

In years past, vendors would obtain special licensees for the server hardware when supporting greater than four CPUs. Vendors such as NCR and Sequent have produced high-end servers that ran NT in the 1–16 CPU range for several years. It is only recently that the volume and marketplace for enterprise servers has reached a point to catch Microsoft's interest; thus, the mass market commercial release of NT Server Enterprise Edition. By the way, the Hardware Abstraction Layer (HAL) for each server that supports greater than four CPUs, is proprietary. For that matter, every HAL is proprietary. There are some standards that hardware must abide by for NT Server to run on it, but for the most part, the HALs are proprietary. This is a nice feature of NT Server to provide this HAL technique so that it can run on various vendors' server platforms. Before an NT Server CD-ROM is cut, Microsoft obtains HALs, drivers, and so on. from various vendors and places this information on the NT Server CD-ROM. Thus, if you ever load NT Server and need an HAL provided directly from the manufacturer, it is most likely caused by the server being leading edge technology and the HAL not being available at the time the NT Server CD-ROMs went to manufacturing. If this is the case, most venders will provide the HAL for you. This concept is also relevant for thge device drivers associated with newly released peripherals.

Processes and Threads Running Under NT Server

There are multiple processes, containing one or more threads, running under NT Server at all times. Take a look for yourself by starting Task Manager. Start Task Manager by depressing ctrl-alt-delete at the same time and then choose Task Manager. Select processes|tab|view, select columns, then select threads. You can now view the processes running under NT Server and the associated number of threads each process is running. Figure 4–3 depicts a Task Manager view of a relatively idle NT Server.

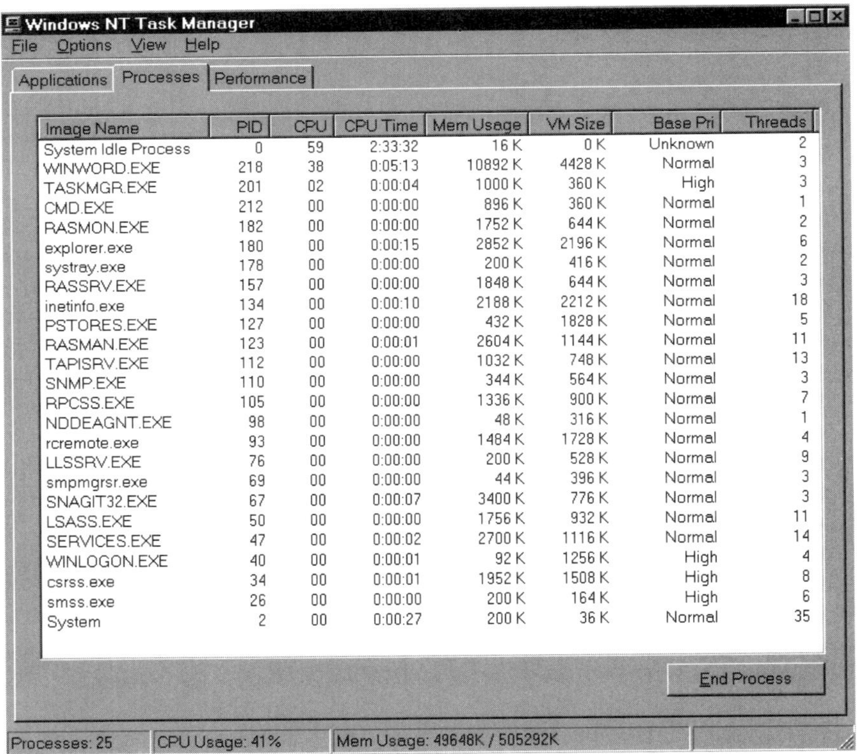

Image Name	PID	CPU	CPU Time	Mem Usage	VM Size	Base Pri	Threads
System Idle Process	0	59	2:33:32	16 K	0 K	Unknown	2
WINWORD.EXE	218	38	0:05:13	10892 K	4428 K	Normal	3
TASKMGR.EXE	201	02	0:00:04	1000 K	360 K	High	3
CMD.EXE	212	00	0:00:00	896 K	360 K	Normal	1
RASMON.EXE	182	00	0:00:00	1752 K	644 K	Normal	2
explorer.exe	180	00	0:00:15	2852 K	2196 K	Normal	6
systray.exe	178	00	0:00:00	200 K	416 K	Normal	2
RASSRV.EXE	157	00	0:00:00	1848 K	644 K	Normal	3
inetinfo.exe	134	00	0:00:10	2188 K	2212 K	Normal	18
PSTORES.EXE	127	00	0:00:00	432 K	1828 K	Normal	5
RASMAN.EXE	123	00	0:00:01	2604 K	1144 K	Normal	11
TAPISRV.EXE	112	00	0:00:00	1032 K	748 K	Normal	13
SNMP.EXE	110	00	0:00:00	344 K	564 K	Normal	3
RPCSS.EXE	105	00	0:00:00	1336 K	900 K	Normal	7
NDDEAGNT.EXE	98	00	0:00:00	48 K	316 K	Normal	1
rcremote.exe	93	00	0:00:00	1484 K	1728 K	Normal	4
LLSSRV.EXE	76	00	0:00:00	200 K	528 K	Normal	9
smpmgrsr.exe	69	00	0:00:00	44 K	396 K	Normal	3
SNAGIT32.EXE	67	00	0:00:07	3400 K	776 K	Normal	3
LSASS.EXE	50	00	0:00:00	1756 K	932 K	Normal	11
SERVICES.EXE	47	00	0:00:02	2700 K	1116 K	Normal	14
WINLOGON.EXE	40	00	0:00:01	92 K	1256 K	High	4
csrss.exe	34	00	0:00:01	1952 K	1508 K	High	8
smss.exe	26	00	0:00:00	200 K	164 K	High	6
System	2	00	0:00:27	200 K	36 K	Normal	35

Figure 4–3 *Viewing processes running under NT Server with the Task Manager*

Notice how even the Microsoft Word process (winword.exe) contains two threads.

Determining Which Process is Associated with Which Application

When you start Task Manager or Perfmon in the process view, you can view which processes are running under NT Server. In Chapter 2, a list of the common processes running under NT Server is provided. Some processes are easy to associate with their application. For example, when Task Manager is started, the process TASKMGR.EXE shows up in the Task Manager process view. Sometimes it is difficult to determine or distinguish which process is associated with a particular application. If the process is not well known, ensure all new applications are stopped. Start Task Manager and take note of the currently running processes. Now, start your application. Again, review Task Manager; the new process will be added to Task Manager's process list. Understanding what processes are running on your server and what application they are associated with becomes important later in this chapter when trying to isolate CPU usage patterns.

NT Scheduler and Priority Levels

Now that we have all of these process threads running around, how does NT Server coordinate which thread or threads get to use the CPU? The NT Server's Microkernel includes the scheduler. The Microkernel schedules ready threads for processor time based upon their dynamic priority, a number from 0 to 31 that represents the relative importance of the task. NT Server uses a priority based round robin scheduling algorithm to distribute threads among the CPUs on the server. The higher the priority number, the higher the thread's priority level. The base priority of a thread varies only within plus or minus two from the base priority of its process. The highest priority thread always runs on the processor, even if this requires that a lower priority thread be preempted. This allows NT Server processes to complete background tasks that are needed to keep the server running. Threads will run on the CPU until they reach the end of their quantum (slice of time the thread is allowed to run on the CPU), become I/O bound, or are preempted by a higher priority thread. Most applications started by users run at the normal priority level. Table 4.4 shows NT Server's priority levels.

NT Server's scheduler tries to be fair about who gets access to CPU resources in an effort to ensure that all threads do get access to the resource. On a CPU bound server, it is possible that some threads become starved for CPU attention. Refer back to the Task Manager Figure 4–3. You can see the relative priority levels for the various processes. Notice how some processes are running at real time priority levels (16-31) such as the SERVICE.EXE process. Chapter 2 has a listing of common processes and what they are responsible for. If you are interested in an even more detailed process view that

Table 4.4 NT Server priority levels

Base	Priority class	Thread priority
31	Real-time	Time critical
26	Real-time	Highest
25	Real-time	Above normal
24	Real-time	Normal
23	Real-time	Below normal
22	Real-time	Lowest
16	Real-time	Idle
15	Idle, Normal, or High	Time critical
15	High	Highest
14	High	Above normal
13	High	Normal
12	High	Below normal
11	High	Lowest
10	Normal	Highest
9	Normal	Above normal
8	Normal	Normal
7	Normal	Below normal
6	Normal	Lowest
6	Idle	Highest
5	Idle	Above Normal
4	Idle	Normal
3	Idle	Below normal
2	Idle	Lowest
1	Idle, Normal, or High	Idle
0	Reserved for Operating System	

Data obtained from Thread Priorities in Windows NT [Windows NT Workstation Resource Kit, Microsoft, page 106]

shows the priority levels for each thread, run pviewer.exe from the NT Workstation Resource Kit.

Consider the scheduler as a traffic cop standing in the front of a single file line to see a teller. The customers in the line are ready-to-run threads, and the teller is the CPU. When you get into the line is important, but the traffic cop can move anyone to the front of the line based on how important the cop feels the customer is (priority). This is annoying, but necessary. If a person gets to the teller and makes a request that is completed by another division of the bank, such as loans, that person is sent back to the line and other customers are serviced first. If a service requested by Customer Q can be completed by another person in line, that person is rushed to the front of the line. If the teller is fast enough, perhaps working at 100 percent of his capacity, he will be able to service everyone without a long line forming. The bank owners are elated; they are getting a great return on their teller investment. Conversely, when the teller cannot keep up with the service requests, the line grows. The bank owners (not to mention the customers in line) are, to say the least, frustrated.

Under NT Server, if the ready queue is consistently greater than four or two times the number of CPUs in the server, then the CPU is becoming a bottleneck since it is not able to keep up with demand. Conversely, a CPU running near 100 percent of its capacity is not a bottleneck, if the queue is not greater than two-to-four threads and growing. In this environment, you are getting the most out of your CPU investment. You have purchased the CPU resources; You should have them completing productive work as often as possible!

Affinity

In the CPU Performance section above, we mentioned that the CPU provides the best possible performance if the data it requires can be found in the L1 or L2 cache. When the data is not available in the cache, the system bus is traversed to obtain the data from either the memory or I/O subsystems. This slows down the CPU from completing the thread's request. If this is an SMP based server with more than one CPU, the extra data on the system bus can slow down the other CPUs since only one request can traverse the system bus at a time.

To increase the chances of a cache hit, NT Server employs soft affinity when assigning threads to processors. If all other factors are equal, NT Server tries to run the thread on the CPU it last executed on. If the CPU last executed on is not available, the NT Server Microkernel dispatches the thread to the next available CPU. This concept is soft affinity, which is implemented inside of NT Server. Conversely, hard affinity binds a particular thread or process to a specific CPU permanently. The more successful NT Server's Microkernel is in applying the soft affinity strategy, the more efficient and better performing the entire server becomes. Providing good server performance is not entirely on NT Server's shoulders. How well the application is designed, including effective use of cache, also influences the server's performance just as much, if not more than NT Server itself.

Detecting CPU Bottlenecks

Recall from Chapter 2 that it is important to consider the entire server performance picture when trying to locate an NT Server bottleneck. There can be more than one server resource area that is contributing to the throttling of the server's overall performance. Once all of the major server resource areas are evaluated, focus in on the resource that is farthest to the left in the Performance Resource Chart introduced in Chapter 2 and repeated here in Figure 4–4 for reference. This strategy will provide the greatest immediate gain to the server's overall performance. For this discussion, all other server resources have already been investigated and determined not to be a bottleneck throttling back the server's performance. Remember to revisit the Performance Resource Chart after tuning around a CPU bottleneck. Once one server resource is removed as the bottleneck, others may take its place, which will subsequently influence where you focus additional tuning efforts.

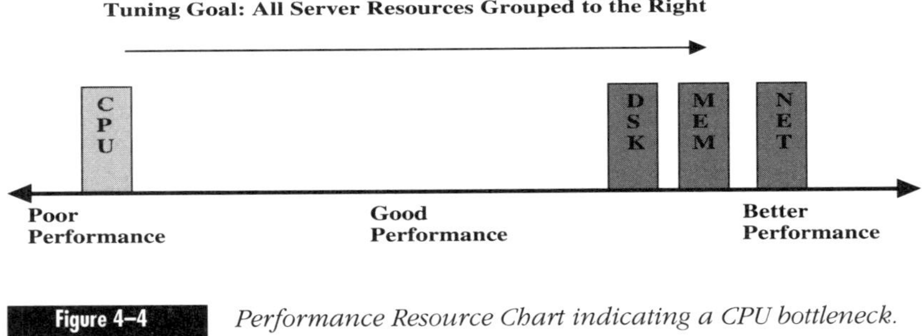

Figure 4–4 *Performance Resource Chart indicating a CPU bottleneck.*

Detecting Single CPU Server Bottlenecks

Now that you are properly armed with information regarding server CPU performance and how NT Server takes advantage of server iron, let's focus on detecting CPU bottlenecks while running NT Server. The two tools described in Chapter 2: Task Manager and Perfmon, are your best friends when trying to locate a CPU bottleneck.

From the information provided here on how NT Server utilizes the CPU, it should be apparent that a server whose CPUs are running at near 100 percent is not bottlenecked by the CPU. So when is the CPU the bottleneck in a server? When the CPU is not keeping up with the workload being requested of it, the CPU has become the bottleneck that is throttling back the overall server's performance. To determine if this is happening on a **single** CPU server, review the relationship of the following counters under Perfmon: Processor: % Processor Time and Server Work Queues: Queue Length. Perfmon defines % Processor Time as "a percentage of the elapsed time that a processor is busy executing a non-Idle thread." It can be viewed as the fraction of the time spent doing useful work. Each processor is assigned an Idle thread in the Idle process which consumes those unproductive processor cycles not used by any other threads. Perfmon defines Server Work Queues: Queue Length as "the current length of the server work queue for this CPU. A sustained queue length greater than four may indicate processor congestion. This is an instantaneous count, not an average over time."

Basically, if the CPU is busy completing productive work, is running at a high capacity level greater than 90 percent, and the Server Work Queues are consistently greater than four or growing, then the CPU is the unquestionable bottleneck throttling back the server's performance. If this condition only occurs during occasional load storms it can be tolerated. However, if this condition continues for long periods of time, such as for several hours during normal business hours, end users response times will increase; that is, it will take longer for requested tasks to complete. When the CPU becomes a bottleneck, even a simple task, such as responding to a network request from an end user, takes longer to complete since the network requests must wait in line to get service from the CPU.

Detecting Multiple CPU Server Bottlenecks

This same concept applies when looking for CPU bottlenecks in a multiple CPU server configuration, with the addition of some third grade math. When using Perfmon: Processor: % Processor Time in a multiple CPU server, there is a counter instance for each CPU in the server. Looking at each instance is helpful for tuning, but for bottleneck detection it is easier to use System: % Total Processor Time. Perfmon's definition for % Total Processor Time is: "the average percentage of time that all the processors on the system are busy executing non-Idle threads. On a multiprocessor system, if all processors are always busy this is 100 percent, if all processors are 50 percent busy this is 50 percent and if one-quarter of the processors are 100 percent busy this is 25 percent. It can be viewed as the fraction of the time spent doing useful work. Each processor is assigned an Idle thread in the Idle process which consumes those unproductive processor cycles not used by any other threads." Unfortunately, there is not an all encompassing Perfmon counter for Server Work Queues: Queue Length. For CPU work queue length, you must review each instance under Server Work Queues: Queue Length. You have a CPU bottleneck if the % Total Processor Time is greater then 90 percent and the aggregate queue length is greater than two times the number of CPUs in the server.

Yes, the book definition would extrapolate out to four times the number of CPUs in the server, but it is my experience that for multiple CPU environments, a 2x recommendation is a more realistic indication of a CPU bottleneck. For example, in a four CPU server, if the % Total Processor Time is greater then 90 percent and the processor queue length is greater than eight, then the CPUs are the bottleneck throttling back the server's overall performance.

Using the Server Work Queues: Queue Length Counter Effectively

Tradeoffs are everywhere. I don't know if you noticed a small fact in the Perfmon Queue Length definition that states, "This is an instantaneous count, not an average over time." To use this counter effectively, you must run Perfmon in both a granular fashion and for extended periods of time. Being an instantaneous counter, this counter only reports what is happening at one point in time. Thus, if your sampling period is broad, you may be missing the times when the run queue is longer than you might want and you are only catching it when it is short. This concept is referred to as the Nyquist effect.

To avoid this, Perfmon must be run at a higher sampling rate. How high of a sampling rate you run Perfmon depends upon your environment, but when isolating server work queue problems, I run Perfmon at five-second intervals. Any lower than five-second intervals and Perfmon begins to influence server performance beyond acceptable levels. This is something that is observable and is actually an example of the Heisenberg principle which states that you cannot measure something without affecting it (the server) some manner.

Here, we try to keep the amount that we affect the server to a minimum. Running Perfmon at a sampling rate of five seconds all of the time is unrealistic since it would create some enormous Perfmon log files. Typically, you want to sample at a five-second rate when the CPU usage is greater than 80 to 90 percent. (Refer to Chapter 2, Alert Mode and Monitor Service section for an example of using Perfmon's alert mode.) Running a second copy of Perfmon for a dedicated amount of time at a five second sampling interval helps to zero in on CPU bottlenecks. This also helps to detect which process(s) may be guilty of using all of those precious CPU cycles.

Artful CPU Bottleneck Detection and Tuning: % User and % Privileged Time

Okay, you think it can't be that easy to detect a CPU bottleneck, but it really is. Of course computer performance is part art. (I have to say that at least once a chapter.) There are times when knowing your server environment is more important than just following the rule of thumb above in the Detecting

Single CPU Server Bottlenecks for CPU Bottlenecks section. Reviewing other factors associated with CPU performance and the types of applications running on your server, allows you to determine when a faster CPU upgrade may be prudent.

NT Server has two basic modes of operation: user mode and kernel (privileged) mode. The primary difference between these modes is that if a process needs access to something controlled by NT Server, such as access to a disk drive, the process that is running in user mode must make a system call to the NT kernel. Kernel mode is a privileged mode of operations where the code has direct access to all memory, user mode processes, and hardware.[2] When the NT Server kernel is processing the user mode process's request, it is doing so in privileged mode. For Intel based CPU architectures, this means that privileged mode is running in ring mode 0, which allows it access to lower level functions. (This factoid was even on the Microsoft NT Server exam.)

By watching Processor: % Privileged Time and Processor: % User Time, you can determine how often the CPU is running in privileged or user mode. Perfmon defines Processor: % Privileged Time as "the percentage of processor time spent in Privileged Mode in non-Idle threads. The Windows NT service layer, the Executive routines, and the Windows NT Kernel all execute in Privileged Mode. Device drivers for most devices other than graphics adapters and printers also execute in Privileged Mode. Unlike some early operating systems (DOS), NT Server uses process boundaries for subsystem protection in addition to the traditional protection of User and Privileged modes. These subsystem processes provide additional protection. Therefore, some work done by NT Server on behalf of your application may appear in other subsystem processes in addition to the Privileged Time in your process."

Perfmon defines Processor: % User Time as "the percentage of processor time spent in User Mode in non-Idle threads. All application code and subsystem code executes in User Mode. The graphics engine, graphics device drivers, printer device drivers, and the window manager also execute in User Mode. Code executing in User Mode cannot damage the integrity of the Windows NT Executive, Kernel, and device drivers. Unlike some early operating systems (DOS), Windows NT uses process boundaries for subsystem protection in addition to the traditional protection of User and Privileged modes. These subsystem processes provide additional protection. Therefore, some work done by Windows NT on behalf of your application may appear in other subsystem processes in addition to the Privileged Time in your process."

---

2. *Windows NT File Systems Internals: A Developers Guide*, O'Reilly, Nagar

Applying Artful CPU Tuning

So how does one use this knowledge? Look at the following two Perfmon charts.

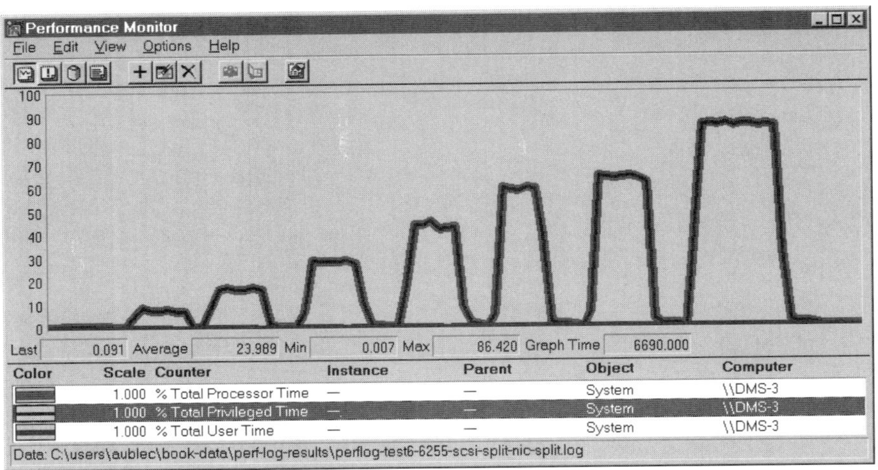

Figure 4–5 *Perfmon Chart illustrating privileged mode hogging the CPU.*

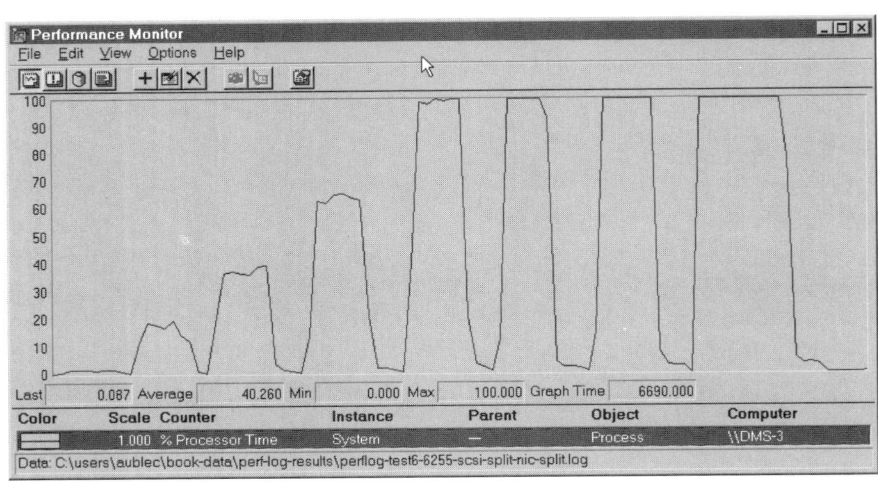

Figure 4–6 *Perfmon Chart: The guilty process hogging privileged mode CPU operations.*

Each peak in this Perfmon graph (Figure 4–5) represents an increased user load on the server. The user load levels are 1, 20, 40, 60, 80, 100, 120, and 200. Notice that the system process in Figure 4–6 using close to all of the CPU. The system process contains system threads that handle lazy writing by file system, virtual memory modified page writing, working set trimming, and similar system functions. This particular server was working as a video file server. As such, most of its processing is dedicated to providing file services, which are a privileged mode of operation. This now makes sense as to why the system process was so busy; it was busy providing services surrounding serving video files for 200 users.

The CPU usage depicted above is quite heavy. To determine if faster CPUs would improve the server's performance to the end users, we ran this exact test a second time with faster CPUs. Even with the faster CPUs, the server did not provide any tangible overall performance improvements to the end users. The tests which we ran provided two key pieces of information.

- A faster CPU can provide support for more disk drives and networks, but it does not make disk drives or networks run any faster.
- If a majority of the processing time is spent in privileged mode, follow the criteria stated above to determine if the CPUs are the bottleneck.

If, however, the % User Time is high (>60 percent) and the % Privileged time is low (<40 percent), determine what type of application is running on the server. If you have a server application that completes a high number of calculation requests of the CPU and the Perfmon statistics gathered do not quite meet the rule of thumb criteria for a CPU bottleneck, a faster CPU will help your performance.

Let's try to explain this concept with a little more detail. Normally, when a CPU is running at greater than 80 percent of its capacity and no threads are waiting in the server queue, you are getting a good return on your investment. When none of the other server resources are bottlenecks and the CPU is running as fast as it can, the CPU is the bottleneck. This may sound strange. The CPU is not a bottleneck in the traditional sense that is defined here; the CPU is keeping up with the requested workload. What has happened is that the CPU cannot help the server complete its workload any faster. When this occurs, one way to help your application complete its computations faster is to provide it with a faster CPU. Of course when you do this, you must closely watch the other server resources to ensure that the bottleneck has not shifted. You can always make your application code more efficient, too, if you have access to the source code.

Ideal Environment for Artful CPU Detection and Tuning

In this example, there are multiple applications running and the CPU is running at a high rate, close to 90 percent. The server work queue is zero, and all process activity is occurring in user mode.

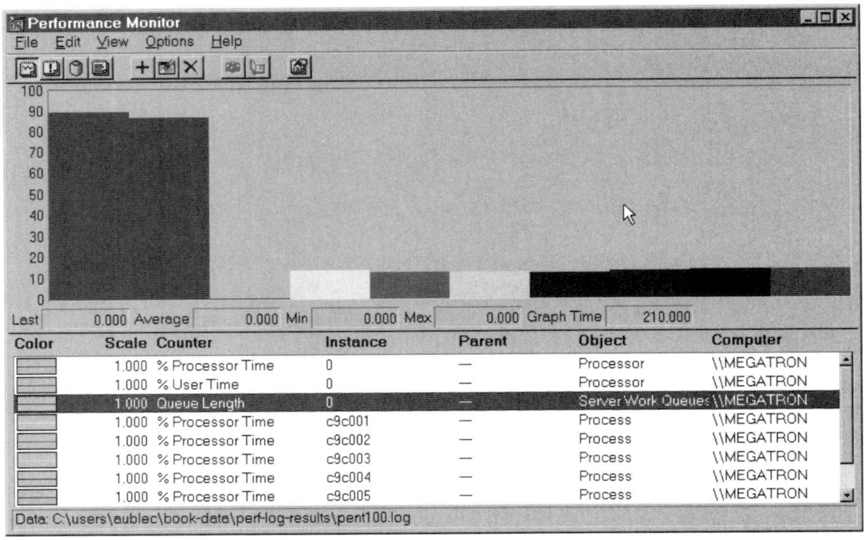

Figure 4–7 *Perfmon screenshot of a server that is a candidate for artful tuning.*

This is a perfect example of when artful tuning can be applied. The CPU is not the bottleneck in this example. All of the server resources were checked to ensure that they were not the cause of any bottlenecks. This server is just flat out running as fast as it can. To improve the performance of this server workload, a faster CPU upgrade was implemented. This provided faster response times for this NT Server environment.

Another option to improve performance would have been to work with the developer of this application to produce a more efficient application. This is a good option if you can arrange access to the source code. If you cannot arrange for access to the source code, and a higher level of performance is required, follow the artful tuning technique to determine when a server is a candidate for a faster CPU to help overall performance.

Artful Tuning II: Adding Additional CPUs

Later in this chapter server scaling is discussed. For now, though, when might a server be a candidate for multiple CPUs? When an application is designed to support multiple threads at the same time or there are multiple applications running on the server concurrently. If either of these cases pertain to a server environment and the current CPU is a bottleneck (greater than 90 percent CPU utilization and a server work queue length greater than four), the server is an excellent candidate for a second CPU. If, after the addition of the second CPU, performance improves but there is a still a CPU bottleneck occurring, consider the addition of even more CPUs. Be careful when adding additional

CPUs that the other NT Server resources are up to the task of supporting the increased processing power. In particular, watch the memory and disk subsystem closely for possible bottlenecks, as they must be capable of feeding the CPUs at a high rate to keep them productive.

This Artful Tuning II technique was applied in the server environment depicted in Figure 4–7. Over 20 separate applications were running in this environment. The addition of a second, third, and fourth CPU improved the length of time that the server was able to support an increased workload without an increase in the end users response time. Additional memory and disk subsystem resources were added to take advantage of the third and fourth CPUs.

Remember that when you tune your server without understanding what your server is doing, you are guessing. Avoid guessing whenever possible, since it lengthens the time it takes to get your server running at its peak. Without knowing your environment, it is close to impossible to know if implementing this nontraditional CPU bottleneck removal techniques will be effective or not.

Interrupt Driven CPU Bottlenecks

When a device on the server such as a network interface card needs servicing, it generates an interrupt to the CPU. Using Perfmon, you can observe both the number of interrupts that are being generated by using the counter Processor: Interrupts/sec and determine the percentage of the CPU that is being used to service the interrupts by observing Processor: % Interrupt Time. Perfmon defines % Interrupt Time as "the percentage of elapsed time that the Processor spent handling hardware Interrupts. When a hardware device interrupts the Processor, the Interrupt Handler will execute to handle the condition, usually by signaling I/O completion and possibly issuing another pending I/O request. Some of this work may be done in a Deferred Procedure Call (see Processor: % DPC Time.) However, time spent in DPCs is not counted as time in Interrupts. Interrupts are executed in Privileged Mode, so this is a component of Processor: % Privileged Time. This counter can help determine the source of excessive time being spent in Privileged Mode." Perfmon defines Interrupts/sec as "the number of device interrupts the processor is experiencing. A device interrupts the processor when it has completed a task or when it otherwise requires attention. Normal thread execution is suspended during interrupts. An interrupt may cause the processor to switch to another, higher priority thread. Clock interrupts are frequent, periodic, and create a background of interrupt activity."

On an Intel CPU-based server operating without any workloads, it is normal to observe at least 100 interrupts per second. This is caused by the Intel CPU processor clock interrupts. On a heavily loaded server supporting 200 users the interrupts/sec can easily reach much higher levels. High interrupt levels are shown in Figure 4–8.

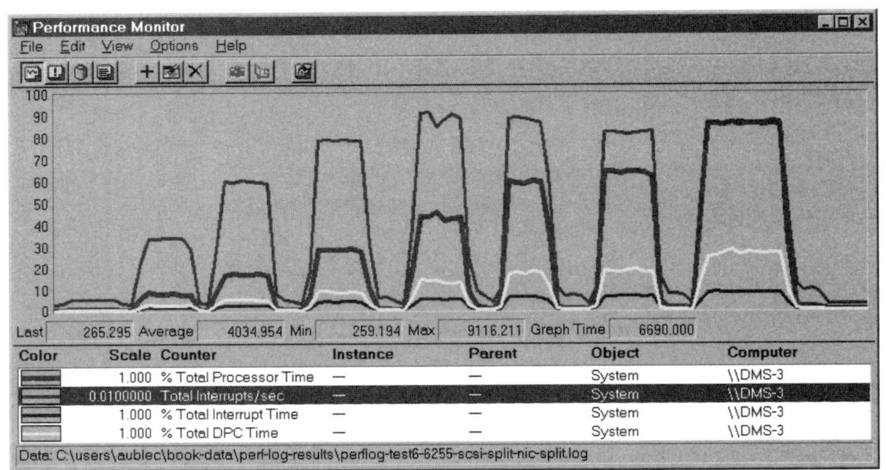

Figure 4–8 *Acceptable high interrupt/sec rates when supporting 200 concurrent users.*

This Perfmon graph is from an NCR 4300 server configured with four 100 BaseT NICs, 1 GB of RAM, four Pentium Pro 200 MHz/512 K cache CPUs, and 40 4-GB disk drives under a maximum load of 200 concurrent users. The interrupts/sec are actually off of the Perfmon scale, noted by the 0.01 scale factor. Under the heaviest load, the total Interrupts/sec were over 9000. This test was run repeatedly to verify the results. On every test run under the full 200-user load, the interrupts/sec levels were roughly the same. Thus, for this workload, 9000 interrupts per second consumed 10 percent of all the CPUs for immediate action (shown by the % Total Interrupt Time) and 30 percent of the CPU for deferred requests (shown by % Total DPC Time). This is the baseline for this server.

Baselines Are Important for Bottleneck Detection

If the interrupts/sec in this example ever increased significantly over the baseline 9000 interrupts/sec for the same workload, it would be a flag that there is a problem with a hardware device. When a hardware device begins to generate high rates of unjustified interrupts, it consumes precious CPU cycles. To the extreme, the hardware device can actually be the cause of an interrupt-driven CPU bottleneck. To tune around this problem, you must troubleshoot your server hardware and remove the component that is malfunctioning. This in itself can be difficult. The server's Power On Self Test (POST) or network driver loop back test (normally found under Start|Settings|Control Panel|Networks|Adapter) are helpful in tracking down hardware problems. If NT Server detects the problem, check NT Server's event log for errors that might lead you to the troublesome critter.

There is no steadfast rule of thumb stating if the number of interrupts per second is over XX amount, you have a hardware problem. Just as in this example, whether you have a problem or not is based on your environment and the baseline you develop. Whenever the interrupts/sec start to increase and the workload is the same as usual, it is time to investigate and troubleshoot your server's hardware devices.

Sizing CPU Subsystems

Sizing the type and number of CPUs required is directly related to the type of workload in the projected environment. The typical rule of thumb here is to configure the fastest CPU that is economically feasible and is supported by the application you wish to run.

Sizing the CPU subsystem is an additive process. Take into account each major activity that is occurring on the server. To help in determining the amount of processing power you need, follow the sizing methodology outlined in Chapter 3. Use of historical data, stress testing your solution, extrapolating from Industry benchmarks, or CPU configuration based on what the server you have will support, are all good techniques to utilize when sizing the CPU subsystem. These techniques are used in the case studies in Chapter 8.

Avoid running applications in emulation mode. Emulation is really synonymous to slow. Emulation mode is a technique where an application executable runs on a CPU that it does not natively support. To compensate for this, CPU level instructions are converted from the current CPU architecture to another CPU architecture. This is typically completed by special software on the server and adds overhead to an application since the application must traverse another layer of waiting before actually getting responses from the server's CPU. Business requirements and required resources to support NT-based applications are increasing constantly; thus, starting with the fastest possible CPU and a server architecture that can support multiple CPUs provides better long term investment protection.

Even without any real applications running under NT, there are multiple active processes and threads; thus, additional CPUs are normally helpful to a degree. Consider your NT Server a candidate for a multiple CPU configuration if the following conditions are relevant to your environment.

- More than one major application running at a time
- The application is multithreaded and was designed for a Symmetric Multiprocessing (SMP) environment
- Utilizing the tuning methodology, you have determined that the server is CPU bound and the Server Work Queues: Queue Length is greater than two times the number of CPUs in the server

Configure enough CPU resources to drive all of the server's resources. One area that is overlooked when sizing the amount of CPU power required for a solution is the amount of CPU power required to drive the disk and network I/O subsystems. Stress tests and historical data are the two best sources of information to determine how much CPU power is required.

CPU Sizing Example

For example, if you wanted to develop a server solution that supported 200 total concurrent end users with file services and some application services, you could extrapolate part of the CPU sizing information from Chapter 8, "Sizing and Tuning Case Studies."

In the file server case study, we find that when supporting 50 concurrent users, 48 percent of the capacity of a 200 MHz Pentium Pro CPU was used. The final File Server configuration included a 10-disk external disk array, 128 Mb of RAM, and a single 100 BaseTX NIC. Extrapolating from this, to support 200 users (four times as many) would require: two Pentium Pro CPUs running at 96 percent of capacity, 512 MB of RAM, 40 disk drives, and four 100 BaseT NICs.

How well do sizing extrapolations work? This extrapolation is very close to what was actually needed when I worked with a video file server supporting 200 concurrent users. The only item that was slightly higher than expected was that 3.2 CPUs are actually required instead of two. This was due to the fact that other applications were running concurrently on the server. Fortunately, we learned about these increased processing requirements by stress testing the server before deployment. Being somewhat conservative, we actually configured four CPUs to support possible workload storms.

Configure Enough RAM When Sizing the CPUs

New operating systems and applications always want more and more memory. But this is the CPU chapter. Why is it important to configure enough memory should be apparent from the discussion of CPU performance at the beginning of this chapter. In short, if enough memory is not configured, you do not keep the CPU fed. If the CPU must wait for data, it is not productive. Configuring a 200 Mhz Pentium Pro based server with 16 MB of RAM will never keep the CPU fed. If you were to do this, you might as well not waste money on the Pentium Pro and purchase a less expensive 100 Mhz Pentium CPU. Why? By not having enough memory available to keep the Pentium Pro fed, you slow it down significantly. Does the performance level really lower to that of a 100 MHz Pentium? Well not exactly, but the performance level does drop drastically. I hope this point is clear. For a single CPU Pentium Pro class CPU or above, configure at least 64 Mbytes per CPU as a minimum.

Tuning Strategies for Removing CPU Bottlenecks

At first glance, it would appear that tuning an NT Server to remove a CPU bottleneck is impossible and the only possibility is upgrading to faster or additional CPUs. This is a typical response. Purchasing more hardware is a valid technique and we will discuss when it is appropriate to upgrade or add CPUs. But I do not care for typical responses. The case studies presented in Chapter 8 moves step-by-step through the strategies and tactics involved with tuning various areas of NT Server and clearly show what levels of performance improvements are associated with each tuning step implemented.

In this section we will review the strategies surrounding CPU tuning and then get into the specifics. I cannot stress the importance of how critical it is to not just know which "operating system knob to tweak," but to understand why something can or may need to be changed. Following are the primary strategies to consider when tuning around a CPU bottleneck.

- Ensure another server resource is not acting as a bottleneck
- Remove unnecessary workloads
- Offload server CPU overhead
- Upgrade to faster CPUs
- Add additional CPUs
- Help NT Server to control process priorities
- Help NT Server control process affinity

Hands on Tactics for Tuning Around CPU Bottlenecks

Ensure Another Server Resource Is Not Acting as a Bottleneck

The most common occurrence I have encountered when tuning around CPU bottlenecks is the removal of other server bottlenecks, not the CPU. If another server resource is acting as a bottleneck, it can appear that the CPU is the actual bottleneck when it is not. Memory bottlenecks in extreme cases disguise themselves as CPU problems. When NT Server begins to run out of memory, it can exhibit a condition called thrashing. Thrashing is an excessive contention for physical memory. When this condition occurs, every request for memory results in paging activity to the Pagefile on the disk drive(s). This results in an increased amount of CPU activity associated with moving memory pages around, not completing truly productive work. Why waste precious CPU cycles on this activity?

Avoid this condition by configuring a sufficient amount of RAM to avoid thrashing. The highest performing NT Servers I have encountered are sized and tuned with one basic strategy in mind: avoid paging. Paging is considered by many as acceptable if it occurs infrequently. The more the server pages, the more CPU cycles are wasted on memory operations and the slower the final response times provided to your end users. To improve the performance if the server must page, spread NT Server's Pagefile across two to four dedicated disk drives sized identically. Refer to Chapter 5, "NT Server and Memory Performance" for the specifics on how to determine if your NT Server is paging and a step-by-step guide on spreading the Pagefile across multiple disk drives.

REMOVE UNNECESSARY PROCESSES

Use Perfmon, Process: % Processor Time, and search for applications that are consuming CPU time and ensure that these applications are really required for server operation. Or, start Task Manager and click on the CPU column. Task Manager will list the processes that are using the highest level of CPU performance at the top of the chart. A good rule of thumb here is to remove exotic screen savers. Do not run screen savers such as 3D pipes (or any 3GL screen savers) on any servers. They consume precious server resources and look awful when the server begins to slow down. Consider locking the console, logging out, and turning off the monitor.

Also, look for runaway applications. If an application is not responding and appears to continuously hog resources, kill the process using Task Manager.

This tactic is implemented in Chapter 8's file server case study. Several nonessential background processes and services were removed. Using this tactic not only removes stress on the CPU, but also frees up the memory these processes and services were using. Keeping a baseline of what processes are running on your server helps to identify unwanted and unknown processes.

More applications are taking advantage of NT Server's services as a mechanism to start background processes. NT Server can actually run with only workstation and server services started. All other services are not actually required for NT Server operation. Keeping the EventLog service active is a good idea for monitoring the health of your server and applications. Any services not required for the operation of your server should be disabled.

OFFLOAD SERVER CPU OVERHEAD

If the server is running out of CPU processing power, offload NT Server activities that are not required or can be implemented in hardware. The areas normally associated with CPU overhead that can be removed or offloaded are wasteful hardware components, disk compression, RAID operations, and Security Auditing.

- **Search for Wasteful Hardware Components**

For enterprise servers, do not be surprised if Processor: % Interrupt Time is around five to twenty percent of the total CPU workload, particularly if the network and disk I/O is very heavy. There are, however, some components that behave better then others. Attempt to obtain network interface cards that truly support bus mastering and disk adapters that support DMA transfers versus PIO. Some disk and network adapters operate more efficiently than others; thus, they require less CPU cycles to operate. Trade magazines provide numerous comparisons of these products. One good source of information is the NT Magazine website located at: *http://www.ntmag.com*.

- **Do Not Implement Compression**

Compression is nice for notebooks and some workstations, but it has little applicability for an Enterprise Server. Actively using compression on your server will increase your CPU overhead and slow your disk operations. If you must use compression, relegate its use to drives that are not frequently accessed and are used for archiving only.

- **Offload CPU Intensive Operations**

Whenever possible, offload CPU operations to secondary devices. NT Server allows the native use of software based RAID 5 implementations. RAID 5 requires constant parity computation every time data is written to a RAID 5 array. Offload this by using a RAID controller with its own CPU for RAID calculations. This frees up CPU cycles for the application, instead of wasting them on every disk write activity. Chapter 6, "NT Server and Disk Subsystem Performance" reviews RAID technologies and examines performance issues in depth.

- **Security Auditing Equals CPU Overhead**

Security is important. When increased security levels are required, NT Server auditing is activated (utilizing auditing for tuning was covered in Chapter 2) and a certain level of overhead is introduced onto the server. The amount of overhead introduced is a function of the required level of auditing. The CPU is the server resource that shoulders most of the overhead associated with increased auditing. If auditing is required, do not turn it off. However, be aware that more CPU horsepower may be required to compensate for the increased security to provide the same level of performance experienced without auditing activated.

UPGRADE TO FASTER CPUS

If the CPU is running at or near 100 percent and all of the other server's resources are not bottlenecks, then the server is running at its very best. If an even higher level of overall performance is required, it may be time to upgrade the CPU, the server components, or even the server itself.

The obvious way to alleviate processor bottlenecks is to move to a faster CPU. If your application is known to be compute intensive and your Processor: % User Time dominates your server's processing environment, you are a prime candidate to reap the benefits of a faster CPU. Once the CPU is upgraded, do not forget to check the server resources to ensure that the bottleneck has not shifted with the addition of a faster CPU. Have you ever seen someone upgrade to a faster CPU yet nothing improves or it get worse because there is now a memory or other resource bottleneck? Talk about disappointment!

If you have a multiuser system using multithreaded applications or multiple single threaded applications, you can preserve your investment (for example, don't throw out the older CPU when the new one arrives) by adding additional processors. A discussion on this topic is next.

ADD ADDITIONAL CPUs

Additional CPUs for NT Server, or any server operating system for that matter, can spark serious debates. In a perfect world, if the server is CPU bound, adding an additional CPU would improve performance 100 percent. This is considered linear scaling. Figure 4–9 illustrates perfect and not so perfect scaling.

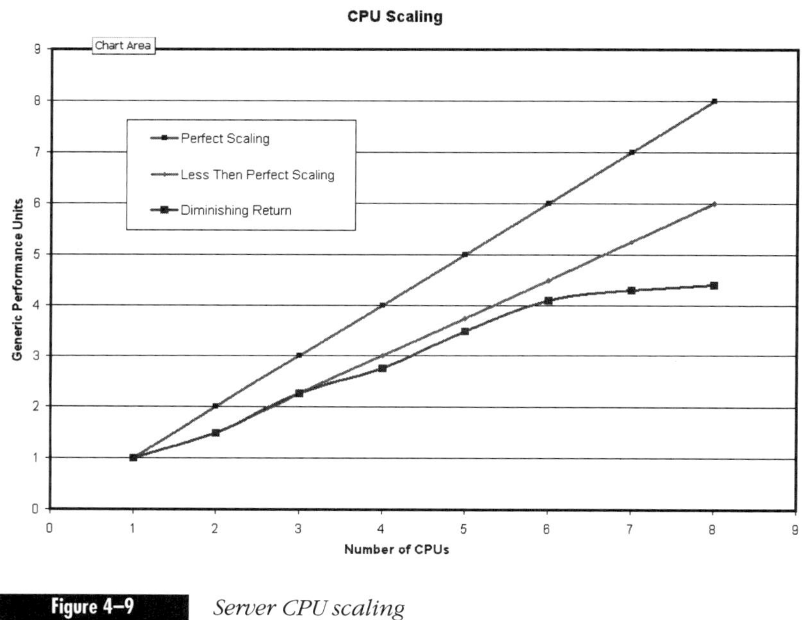

Figure 4–9 *Server CPU scaling*

My view of scaling is that if your performance increases enough to justify the cost of the additional CPUs, the server scales. Perhaps a simple view, but I have worked with many people who prefer to add a little more power to their current server versus purchasing a completely new server due to the hardware and management costs associated with a new server. How well your server scales is closely tied to your environment. Factors such as the server application, server hardware, communications, client application, and NT Server itself directly influence how well your server will scale. From a generic point of view, if the Server Work Queue in your environment is greater than two times the number of CPUs in your server, then your environment is a candidate for additional CPUs. You may also be a candidate for more CPUs if you have multiple single threaded applications running on your server.

Adding more CPUs does not directly dictate that your server will run faster. Why add more CPUs if the server is not running faster? Because the server can complete more work before the performance service level degrades. I once heard a general statement that summed this concept up well, "Servers are more like workhorses then racehorses." Although the response time may or may not improve to the end user when multiple CPUs are used, the server will provide the same level of good response times to more users than before the addition of multiple CPUs. If your goal is faster response times to an increased number of end users, consider both faster and additional CPUs.

DETERMINE IF MULTIPLE CPUS ARE HELPING

To test how well an application under NT Server scales, disable all CPUs except for one and start Perfmon in logging mode with all counters activated. Run the application and measure the performance of the application. Tools to complete this type of test are outlined in Chapter 2 and implemented in Chapter 8. Collect all of the Perfmon data and measure performance results of the application. Ensure that there are no server bottlenecks besides possibly the CPU. Add another CPU and rerun the same test. Review your data. In this manner, you can determine how well additional CPUs are affecting the application's performance. After continued iterative testing, you will come to a point where additional CPUs are added but performance is not improved. This is the point to which the single application scales. This same technique can be applied when operating multiple applications on one server.

Nothing Is Better Than Proof

If you have followed the rules above when deciding to add more CPUs, you have a better than average chance that your overall performance will improve. But, there is nothing like a good stress test that emulates your environment to determine what level of performance is achieved when adding additional CPUs. If your own stress test is not in your future, typical applications that take advantage of four or more CPUs are the many database engines available for NT Server.

The folks at the NCR(http://www.ncr.com) benchmarking center in Columbia, South Carolina published some excellent performance results regarding scaling databases on an NCR 4300 running NT Server and an Oracle database. Bluecurve Corporation's (http://www.bluecurve.com) Dynameasure stress testing tool was used to stress test both a 4 CPU and an 8 CPU NCR 4300 with their Oracle database workload. Table 4.4 shows the configuration of the servers and results.

There is more to these results than just propaganda. First, it shows that in an appropriate environment, very good scalability is obtainable. In fact, these results are near perfect. Secondly, these results demonstrate that it is important not only to increase the number of CPUs, but the other server

Table 4.5 Scaling database results.

Configuration	NCR 4300 #1	NCR 4300 #2
Number of 200 MHz/1MB cache CPUs	4	8
Amount of Memory (RAM)	512 MB	1 GB
Disk Drives	6 (1 for NT, 5 for Database)	12 (1 for NT, 11 for Database)
Operating System	NT Server Enterprise Edition	NT Server Enterprise Edition
Average Response Time	0.350 seconds	0.140 seconds
Bluecurve Transactions per second	227	447

resources as well. There is no doubt that if the four additional CPUs were added, but the other server resources were not properly increased, that contention for resources would have occurred creating bottlenecks in the server that would have inhibited overall performance and scaling of NT Server.

Helping NT Server to Control Process Priorities

NT Server does a good job of controlling process priorities. But every environment is different, and a good systems engineer and/or administrator knows their own environment best. You can tune CPU performance by using Task Manager to identify the process that is consuming most of the CPU time or not obtaining enough CPU time, then adjust priority levels accordingly. We reviewed NT Server's 31 distinct priority levels. A process starts with a base priority level and its threads can vary two levels higher or lower than its base. If you have a particularly busy CPU, you can control a process's priority level under Task Manager|Processes. Right click the process then select Real-time and High, Normal, or Low priority. Be careful when you set the processor's priority to real time—the process can become selfish and never release the CPU. If the process won't release the CPU, your server might become unstable; a selfish process is particularly dangerous on a single CPU server.

To implement priority changes on a more permanent basis (priority level changes using Task Manager results are only in place until the next time a server reboots), use the start command. The start command can be placed in shell/batch scripts that are run at server startup or directly from a command prompt. To review the start command's options, enter "start /? | more" from NT's command prompt.

Controlling NT Servers CPU Quantum Allotment

Under NT Server 4.0, there is a point-and-click application applet for influencing the quantum of foreground and background applications. On the Performance tab of Control Panel|System, you can select the performance boost for the foreground application from none to maximum on a sliding scale. This sliding scale adjusts the default quantum level of applications when you start them. For dedicated servers with larger applications running in the background, change this "foreground application boost" setting to none.

If this selection does not appear to provide the additional quanta required, you can fine tune NT Server's quantum level using ntfrob. This tool can be downloaded from *http://www.ntinternals.com*. Ntfrob allows for more control over NT Server's quantum levels than what NT Server provides natively. For busy, heavily loaded servers, try a background quantum of 360 and a foreground quantum of 120. This will allow each thread a slightly longer amount of time on the CPU to complete its processing. The "quantum" control feature is available in NT Server 5 Alpha release. I am curious if it will stay.

Use this tool with care. If you change the quantum greatly, the server's console can become unresponsive. This is definitely a tool you will want to try in a test environment before fielding your server.

Schedule CPU Intensive Jobs During Off Peak Hours

This technique always seemed to be a bit of an easy-out strategy to alleviate CPU problems, but it is effective and uses resources that may have otherwise been idle. To schedule a job during an off peak hour, use the "at" command from the command prompt. Note, that prior to using this command, the scheduler service must be started under Control Panel|Services. To get directions on how to use the at command, type "at /? | more" at the command prompt. Besides the default "at" command included with NT Server there are now friendlier applications to utilize NT Server's scheduler service. The Microsoft Windows NT Server Resource Kit includes a scheduler tool name winat.exe, which is a friendly GUI front end to the "at" command. Some companies are beginning to introduce more flexible scheduling tools that allow actions to occur based on multiple events besides time. One such tool is Master Minder. Information on Master Minder is available from *http://www.ncr.com*.

NT Server Service Packs

Enterprise operating systems are becoming more feature rich and complicated by the minute and, as such, they are prone to bugs. Microsoft publishes bug fixes or patches such as Service Packs and hotfixes. Stay abreast of these Service Packs as they commonly fix various functional problems and occasionally offer performance improvements. As with any new software, test it before it finds its way into a production environment. Don't become discouraged; I have never used an operating system that did not require periodic patches.

Thinking Outside of the Box

Advanced Tuning Techniques: Helping NT Server Control Process Affinity

If your are not feeling bold and adventurous, skip to the next chapter. This section is definitely for those who want to really tune their CPUs and improve their server's overall performance. NT Server's Microkernel provides good general management of thread allocations to the various CPUs in an SMP based server environment. On multiprocessor computers, the NT Server Microkernel distributes thread-processing requests over all processors based on thread level priority. Often, even though NT Server utilizes soft affinity, threads still end up running on more than one processor. For some environments that rely heavily on cache performance, NT Server and the applications running on your server can use assistance to take full advantage of your server's resources.

In the beginning of this chapter the importance of cache hits and keeping unneeded data off the system bus was discussed. To help NT Server do a better job accomplishing this, hard affinity can be applied to permanently bind a process or threads to a specific CPU or set of CPUs. When hard affinity is set, the designated process and associated threads are forced to always return to the same processor.

This tuning technique is not for all environments. A good rule of thumb is that applying affinity is always applicable when there are multiple applications running on the server or when multiple instances of a database are in use on the same server. For example, while I was working in one particular customer environment, they used four instances of Oracle running concurrently on the same server. The performance provided by the four CPU server was okay, but nothing to write home about. In an attempt to improve the server's performance, each Oracle instance was bound to its own CPU. All other processes and threads were under normal NT Server control. So what was the result? A significant increase in overall performance was achieved. How could we be sure that applying hard affinity to the Oracle was what actually improved the server performance? The stress test workload remained the same and no other tuning attempts or other changes were made.

Actual Test Results

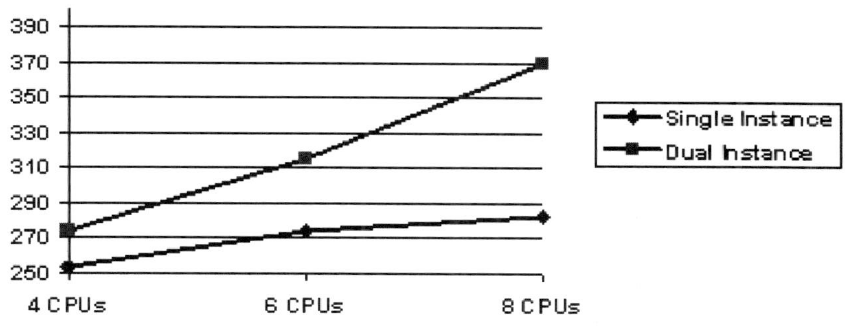

Figure 4–10 *Hard affinity performance gains.*[*]

*. from NCR White Paper: "Windows NT Scalability on NCR Servers

Figure 4–10 illustrates the performance gains associated with applying hard affinity to an eight CPU Pentium 133 MHz based server running single and dual instances of Microsoft's SQL Server database. The y-axis depicts performance workload units, where the bigger the number, the better the performance achieved. The performance gain was greatest when eight CPUs were used, although performance increased a good amount on the four and six CPU tests.

For more information on these types of tests when using hard affinity in multiple application environments, check out the white paper, "Getting the Biggest Bang for Your Windows NT Server: Running Multiple Applications on a single CMP Server" available at *http://www.ncr.com/products/multiapp.doc*. NCR and Microsoft published this interesting paper that explores in detail the hard affinity concepts discussed here. It highlights the benefits of using hard affinity concepts in the appropriate environments and how applying hard affinity can make a night and day difference in overall performance.

There are two tools available to apply hard affinity that I am aware of: NT Server provides one natively under Task Manager, and the other is NCR SMP Utilization Manager. An evaluation copy of the NCR SMP Utilization Manager is included on the CD-ROM accompanying this book.

Use a Sound Affinity Tuning Methodology

Regardless of which tool is used to apply hard affinity, it is important to follow a methodical approach when implementing this CPU tuning tactic. Run your application(s) and develop a performance baseline. Then apply hard affinity to one application at a time or to one portion of an application at a time. Once the hard affinity is applied, test the performance of your application. If the performance improves, move onto the next application or application component. As you continue your testing, log what is working and what is not. Eventually you will have a matrix (see Table 4.6).

Table 4.6 Hard affinity test log.

	Application Distribution			
	Microsoft IIs Web Server	**SQL Server Instance 1**	**SQL Server Instance 2**	**Custom Application 1**
CPU 1	X			
CPU 2	X			
CPU 3		X		
CPU 4		X		
CPU 5			X	
CPU 6				X

Determining the correct mix takes time and is definitely for those people who want the highest level of performance from their server. This is not an administration nightmare. Of the two tools mentioned to apply hard affinity, process and thread affinity changes made with the NCR SMP Utilization Manager are persistent. The NCR SMP Utilization Manager is started as a service when NT Server boots. The combination of these two facts allows SMP Utilization Manager to automatically rebind the application processes and threads whenever the server boots so that additional manual intervention is not required.

NT Server Affinity: Task Manager

To use NT Server's Task Manager to apply hard affinity, start Task Manager by depressing ctrl-alt-delete and selecting Task Manager. To select affinity for a process, left click the process name in the Task Manager Processes tab, then click the highlighted name with the right mouse button. Now you can select one or more processors from the CPU list based on how you wish to best apply hard affinity for your environment. Task Manager is limited to applying hard affinity at the process level as it does not provide a mechanism to apply affinity at the thread level. Figure 4–11 depicts limiting the MAD.EXE process to CPUs 2 and 3.

It is convenient to have this tool built into NT Server, but it requires manual intervention. There is currently no mechanism under Task Manager to

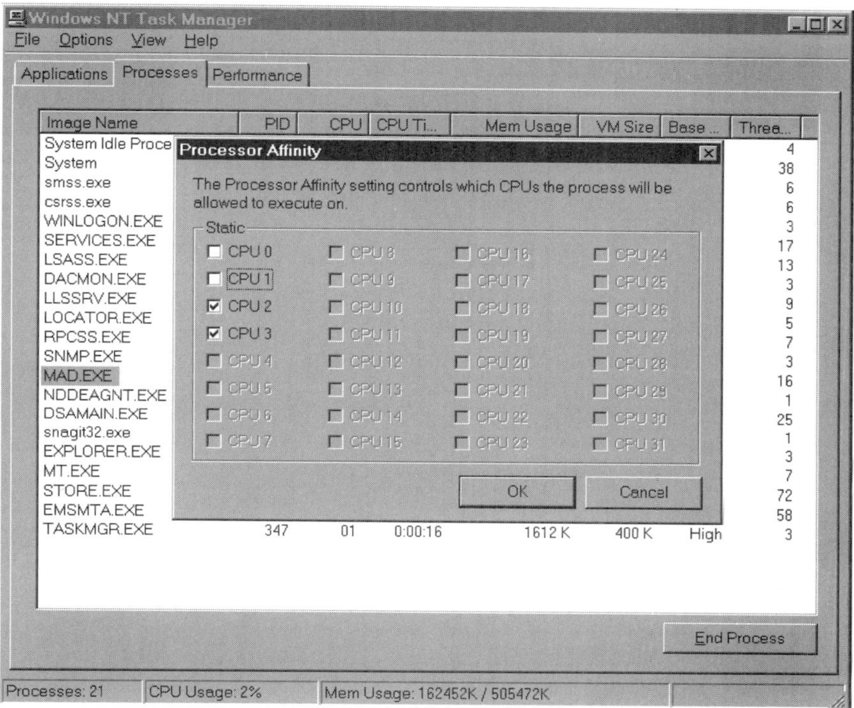

Figure 4–11 *Using NT Server's Task Manager to apply hard affinity.*

automatically reapply the hard affinity settings you configured if the server reboots. Thus, if the server reboots, you must manually reallocate the hard affinity settings to the CPUs as needed. One other caveat I observed when using this tool compared to the NCR SMP Utilization Manager was that the Task Manager affinity settings could not be applied to some of NT Server's background services. This limits some of the usefulness of this tool since it is helpful to apply affinity to some of NT Server's background services on larger SMP configurations.

Some other common sense points about using either NT Server's Task Manager or NCR SMP Utilization Manager:

- Do not use both tools at the same time to apply hard affinity. Use one or the other, but not both. Using both can cause problems with your server.
- If your server does not have more then one CPU, neither tool will allow for binding processes. This makes sense, since all processes are already bound to a CPU in a single CPU server.
- The process that you wish to apply hard affinity to must already be started.

NCR SMP Utilization Manager

Instead of rewriting how to use NCR's SMP Utilization Manager here, review the on-line help file. The help file provides friendly and intuitive step-by-step instructions on using this tool. What I will cover are some main points about this tool. A trial version of this tool is included on the CD-ROM with this book.

There are two major end-user visible portions of the NCR SMP Utilization Manager: the service and the GUI. The service (smpmgrsr.exe) auto starts at installation time, while the GUI starts when you either double click on the NCR SMP Utilization Manager icon, or you run it from the command line (c:\ncrsmpmgr\smpmgrgui.exe). Having the service available is a nice feature, since once you finally achieve that perfect balance of applying hard affinity to various processes, your work is not wasted. The hard affinity settings are both dynamically set upon hitting the apply button and are reapplied whenever the server is rebooted. If this is a standardized server whose configuration is duplicated throughput your enterprise, the registry settings can be replicated to similar NT Servers in your enterprise. This is when a good scripting language is helpful to automate this task or you can use the SMP Utilization Manager.

Processes are made of one or more threads. When using NCR's SMP Utilization Manager, you can control affinity at the process or thread level. If you wish to have all threads of a process set to a particular CPU, select the process and apply hard affinity. If you wish to control specific threads of a process set to a particular CPU, select the particular thread and apply hard affinity. This provides very fine grain control of your application.

Figure 4–12 depicts using the GUI portion of NCR's SMP Utilization Manager to apply hard affinity to the SYSTEM.EXE process, limiting its use to only two CPUs.

Partitioning NT Server

We have described how to use the technique of hard affinity to improve overall server performance. You can also use this technology to partition or control how much CPU power certain applications are allowed to have access to. For example, if you were running both Microsoft's IIS web server and SQL Server's database on the same four CPU server, you could use the SMP Utilization Manager to bind IIS so that it only uses two CPUs in the server and then set hard affinity so that SQL Server uses the other two CPUs. In this manner, you can divide the computer processing power between two applications. Beware that you must also ensure that the other resources are properly configured as well. Each application should be administered to have their own dedicated disk drives and memory range limited.

So what are the benefits of such a partitioning arrangement? First, by partitioning all of the various server resources, you lower the possible contention for resources and improve the performance of multiple applications run-

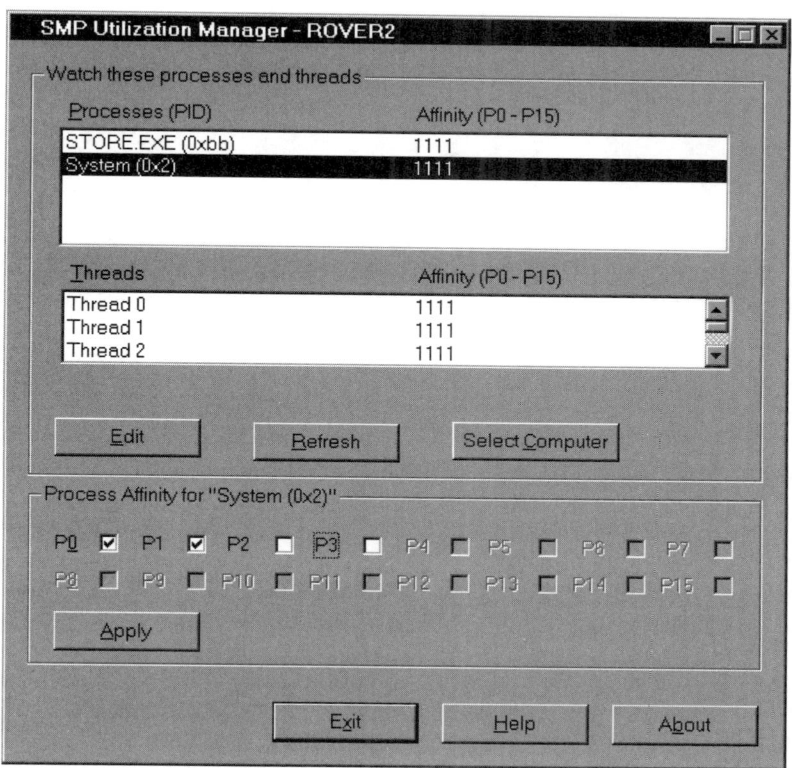

Figure 4–12 *Using Utilization Manager to apply hard affinity.*

ning on the same NT Server. Secondly, ease of management. You now only have one server to purchase and administer versus two. Finally, as NT Server moves into centralized locations, you can assure a customer of how much processing power they have access to.

Summary

In this chapter CPU performance was investigated from both hardware and software perspectives. If you take anything away from this chapter, remember at least two points. First, understanding not only what to change when tuning NT Server, but why it should be changed. This enables you to more effectively tune your NT Server. Secondly, by understanding what is happening in your environment, it is possible to tune NT Server's CPU performance.

F I V E

NT Server and Memory Performance

NT Server's memory subsystem allows for an amazing amount of tuning flexibility. This chapter's goal is to discuss how memory resources are used under NT Server so that we can develop insight into how to best tune around memory bottlenecks. We start by reviewing memory technology to ensure that you get the most out of a server's memory subsystem. Then we look at how NT Server utilizes the memory subsystem. Once this foundation is in place, general sizing guidelines for determining the amount of RAM required for your server are reviewed. To finish up this chapter, we look at how to detect memory bottlenecks and various tactics to implement for tuning around them.

Memory Technology Review

RAM is the gateway to maximum NT performance. In Chapter 4, "NT Server and CPU Performance," the importance of properly sized and utilized cache was stressed. When the data that the CPU requires is not found in cache, it looks to main memory (RAM). Random Access Memory (RAM) is accessed over the server's system bus. Accessing required data from RAM is tremendously faster than needing to touch a physical device such as a disk drive. Data found in memory is accessed at an average speed of 60 ns. Data located on a physical disk drive has an average access time of 11 msec. Think of this as the difference between walking to the TV to change the channel versus running a 26 mile marathon to change the channel. Which would you prefer?

Obviously, at some, point data must be brought in from the disk subsystem. We'll look at disk subsystems in-depth in Chapter 6. For now, once the data is in memory, you want to access the data at the highest speed possible. When implementing workstation technology, there is more RAM options available than in the server space. Why? Single user versus multiple user support. If a workstation hiccups, one person is annoyed. If a server hiccups, many users are affected. It is almost a guarantee that one of the customers serviced by the hiccuping server is someone that controls your raise or bonus at the end of the year. Over time, many of the new technologies introduced in workstations make their way into servers as the technology matures, server motherboard designs improve, and error control techniques are matched up with the newer RAM technology. This lag time of adding technology upgrades and RAM error control slows the introduction of new RAM technologies into servers compared to new RAM technologies introduced into workstations. As CPU power has increased, vendors have recognized the need to develop faster access to the memory subsystem if this increased CPU power is to be unleashed.

SIMM and DIMM Server Memory

How can errors occur in RAM? RAM is actually composed of dynamic random access components that must be kept charged or data is lost. To compensate for the possibility that a RAM component might lose a charge, a variety of error-checking technologies are available for server memory subsystems. The most common is the Error Checking and Correcting (ECC) based RAM. Using an ECC based memory subsystem, if an error is detected, it is corrected before doing any real harm. Today, ECC memory is available in either Single Inline Memory Modules (SIMM), or Dual Inline Memory Modules (DIMM). The primary difference between SIMM and DIMM memory is wider data path density and higher memory capacity. DIMM memory modules essentially double the data path provideds compared to SIMMs. Also, with DIMM technology, more memory can now be squeezed into a smaller space. This affords the server motherboard to support twice the RAM capacity than with SIMM technology. DIMM memory is composed with 132-pin connectors while SIMM memory utilizes 72-pin technology. To support higher DIMM memory modules, the server motherboard must be able to accommodate the different DIMM pin outs. Those servers that usually accommodate either memory technology configure memory through the use of a daughter card attachment directly into the memory bus connector that attaches into the motherboard (not a PCI slot). The Standard High Volume (SHV) motherboard design (used as a reference in Chapter 5 manufactured Intel) is an example of a server motherboard that supports either DIMM or SIMM memory modules through the use of a daughter card. Using DIMM technology, NT Super Servers are now capable of physically supporting up to 8 GB of RAM, even if NT Server 4.0 is only capable of taking advantage of the first 4 GB. NT 5 on 64-bit based servers (DEC Alpha today, Intel Merced in the future) should be able to address all 8GB of RAM.

DIMM Performance Alert

Be careful when using the newer, high density DIMMs in servers that previously were using SIMM memory modules. To effectively use the DIMM technology and provide similar performance levels as their SIMM counterparts, the BIOS level on the server may require updating. Check with the hardware vendor. Typically, although not always, new BIOS versions are downloadable from the vendors website.

DRAM Future

DRAM is implemented using several different technology types. At their core, all of these different memory types are similar. They differ mostly in the way that they are organized and how the memory is accessed. The oldest or conventional DRAM DIMM uses the standard memory addressing method, where the first row's address is sent to memory and then the column address. At least six members of the current and upcoming DRAMs are included in the field of next-generation memory: Fast Page Mode, EDO, SDRAM, SDRAM II (DDR), Direct Rambus, and SLDRAM. The following is a list of various RAM technologies—slowly working their way up into the server technology arena—that you should be aware of:

Fast Page Mode (FPM) RAM

Fast page mode memory is slightly faster than conventional DRAM. While standard DRAM requires that a row and column be sent for each access, FPM RAM works by sending the row address just once for many accesses to memory in locations near each other, improving access time. This is the most common DIMM implementation.

Extended Data Out (EDO)

EDO DRAM technology shortens the read cycle between memory and the CPU. On computer systems designed to support it, EDO memory allows a CPU to access memory 10 to 20 percent faster than comparable fast page mode chips.

Synchronous DRAM (SDRAM)

With asynchronous DRAMs such as EDO or FPM, it is common to add extra wait states to the access timing for the CPU to compensate for memory that was too slow. Synchronous DRAM uses a clock to synchronize signal input and output on a memory chip. The clock is coordinated with the CPU clock so the timing of the memory chips and the timing of the CPU are "in synch." SDRAM is tied to the system clock and is designed to be able to read or write from memory in burst mode at one clock cycle per access (no wait states) at memory bus speeds of up to 100 MHz or even higher. Synchronous DRAM saves time in executing commands and transmitting data, thereby increasing the overall performance of the computer. In pure memory speed tests, SDRAM is about 50 percent faster than EDO memory, with estimated server memory performance gains of around 25 percent.

SDRAM II (DDR)

Double-data rate SDRAM is a faster version of SDRAM that is able to read data on both the rising and the falling edge of the system clock, thus doubling the data rate of the memory chip. Think of the system clock as the pendulum of a cuckoo clock. In SDRAM, when the pendulum swings left, data is transferred. In SDRAM II, data is transferred when the pendulum swings to the left and to the right.

Direct Rambus

RDRAM is a design developed by a company called Rambus, Inc. RDRAM is extremely fast and uses a narrow, high-bandwidth channel to transmit data at speeds about ten times faster than standard DRAM. Two other flavors of RDRAM are also under research: Concurrent and Direct RDRAM. Concurrent is based on the fundamental design of the standard RDRAM, yet is enhanced to increase speed and performance. Direct is also based on RDRAM, yet through additional enhancements it will be even faster than concurrent RDRAM.

SLDRAM (SyncLink)

SLDRAM is a "joint effort" DRAM that may be the closest speed competitor with Rambus. Development is coordinated through a consortium of twelve DRAM manufacturers and system companies. SLDRAM is an enhanced line extension of SDRAM architecture that extends the current four-bank design to 16 banks. SLDRAM is currently in the development stage and is scheduled for production in 1999.

It is important to understand that even though the relative performance between the RAM technologies affects overall server performance, there is never a guarantee that your server's performance will improve by the amount shown between the various technologies. It is safe to state that some performance improvements will be achieved when implementing the newer technologies.

Table 5.1 Various relative performance levels of RAM technologies reviewed.

	FPM	EDO	SDRAM	DDR SDRAM	SLDRAM	Direct RDRAM
Peak Band-width	66 MB/sec (60–80ns access)	66 MB/sec (50–60ns access)	125 MB/sec (7–15ns access)	200 MB/ sec	400 MB/sec	1.6 GB/sec
MHz	66 MHz	66 MHz	125 MHz	200 MHz	400 MHz	800 MHz
Standard Body	JDEC	JEDEC	JEDEC	JEDEC	SLDRAM Consortium	Rambus
Availability	1995	1995	1997	1998	1999	1999

Source for chart and memory definition extrapolations:
(*http://www.kingston.com/tech/memo19.htm* and *http://www.PCGuide.com*)

RAM Performance Considerations

The primary consideration when obtaining RAM is that you want it to be as fast as possible. No surprise here. The most obvious RAM characteristic to take notice of is the speed at which the RAM operates. Pay close attention when selecting RAM for your server; be sure that you are obtaining the fastest ECC supported memory possible that the server's chipset and bus can support. A nanosecond is only a billionth of a second. So, what's a nanosecond between friends? Quite a bit if you consider that the memory subsystem is being accessed millions of times a second; each access adds up. Consider paying close attention to your configuration and ensure that 60 ns RAM was delivered versus 80 ns RAM; you have now improved every potential RAM access by 33 percent. In reality, due to the various timing considerations between the CPU and the memory subsystem, the effect that this selection has on overall server performance is less than this calculated comparison. Regardless of the exact performance, it is worth the effort to obtain the fastest memory possible as it will provide server performance improvements of varying magnitudes depending on your environment. Although a rarity, do not mix and match different RAM modules within the same server. If the server does function, it will be throttled by the speed and access technique of the slowest memory module.

RAM Interleaving

Interleaving is a memory technique that can improve your server's performance. In general, the purpose of interleaving is to take advantage of the potential memory bandwidth of the entire available RAM subsystem.[1] Memory chips can be organized into banks to read or write multiple words of data at a time rather than one word of data at a time. By providing more data per memory access, the effective memory access speed is improved and potentially less memory accesses are required over the system bus. Less data having to traverse the server's system bus is always a good thing.

NT Servers normally support one-, two-, and four-way interleaving. Avoid one-way interleaving. Four-way interleaving provides the highest level of performance. In achieving the various interleaving levels there are some tradeoffs. SIMM Memory must be configured in even memory bank sets. To achieve higher interleaving levels when the amount of RAM is relatively small in the server, lower density SIMMs memory modules must be used. When you use lower density memory modules, the maximum amount of RAM that can be configured in the server is limited due to the available memory slots being filled.

To avoid this, apply the sizing methodology from Chapter 3 and pay close attention to future business requirements. If the future business requirements will require supporting higher amounts of RAM, use the highest density RAM possible that meets your current requirements. Using this strategy yields a memory subsystem that can be interleaved and will allow for the projected growth without trading out lower density memory modules in the future. For this concept to be effective, you may need to slightly over-configure the memory subsystem initially and let your workload catch up. In the short term, this is more expensive. In the long term, it is more cost effective.

How NT Server Utilizes Server Memory

The Virtual Memory Manager (VMM) in conjunction with the Cache Manager (CM) are the primary NT Server components that manage memory usage. When a program is started, which we will refer to as a process, hard page faults are generated to bring the data from the disk subsystem into the memory subsystem. A soft page fault occurs if the process's request for data or instructions can be resolved by the VMM in physical memory, without traveling to the disk subsystem. As each process is brought into memory, the physical memory that the process occupies is referred to as its working set.

---

1. *Computer Architecture: A Quantitative Approach, 2nd edition*; Morgan Kaufman Publishers, Inc., San Francisco, CA, ISBN: 1-55860-329-8, Hennessy & Patterson, 1990, 1996, p. 431.

It is not efficient to bring every bit of a process's actual code into memory, since many pieces of the process's code that reside on the disk drive are not required for the process to complete its task. The VMM brings in pages of memory required by the process on an as-needed basis. The size of a page of memory varies by operating system and CPU architecture in use. For NT Server running on an Intel-based CPU, pages are 4 Kbytes in size. By using this paging strategy, NT Server conserves physical memory and allows multiple processes to simultaneously use the memory subsystem. As a process needs either data or program code from the disk, the VMM generates additional hard page faults (and soft page faults) as additional pages of memory are used. In this manner, the working set of each process can grow.

Virtual Memory

NT Server 4.0 is based on 32-bit code: this provides 2^32 possible memory addresses or 4 GB of usable memory space for each process. This is not exactly true though. NT Server sets aside memory space for operating system specific tasks, which also must reside in this same 4 GB of usable space. To achieve this, NT Server 4.0 Standard Edition's VMM divides the 4 GB range of addresses allocated to each process into two halves. A 2 GB range is dedicated to user-mode virtual addresses, called user space, and another 2 GB range containing kernel-mode virtual addressees, called kernel space, which is shared between all processes.[2] The 2 GB of user mode virtual addresses are not accessible by other processes in the server (unless you are employing interprocess communication) while the kernel-mode addresses are dedicated to operating system activities which are shared among all processes running on the server. These operating system activities include kernel mode actions requested by the processes.

Why is this important? Unless you always have 4 GB of RAM in the server, NT Server must map this 4 GB data space into nonexistent physical RAM space that is referred to as virtual memory. The process thinks it has access to a full 2 GB of physical memory even when that much RAM may not be physically available. When physical memory is no longer available, the VMM utilizes NT Server's Pagefile.

Pagefile

The Pagefile is an area on the disk subsystem where memory pages are placed when enough physical memory (RAM) is not available. You can see the actual Pagefile area on the disk drive by enabling the Windows NT Explorer to view hidden files under view|folder and then select the "show all

2. File System Internals; ISBN 1-56592-249-2, p. 198

files" option. The actual Pagefile shown under Explorer is named pagefile.sys. The pagefile.sys is sometimes referred to as the physical (non-RAM) portion of virtual memory. The VMM begins paging data to the Pagefile when a process requests more physical memory than is currently available on the server; for example, all of the physical memory is already allocated to other processes. To make room in physical memory, the VMM cuts down or trims the working set of another process whose pages have not recently been referenced. When a process's working set is trimmed, VMM pages the trimmed process's memory information onto the Pagefile. Thus, in the future, if the process that was trimmed needs its data back, the VMM can page the copy of the process's data back into physical memory from the Pagefile.

NT Server configures the Pagefile when you initially install the operating system. The default size of the Pagefile is physical memory plus 12 MB. The Pagefile is then placed on the root disk drive (the drive where %SystemRoot% lives). For smaller servers that do not page often and do not have particularly heavy loads placed on them with respect to their capacity, this strategy is adequate. What happens if a process needs more virtual memory then the Pagefile is configured for, or if the Pagefile is heavily used?

PAGEFILE SIZE LIMITS VIRTUAL MEMORY AVAILABLE TO A PROCESS

When a process uses code or data paged into physical memory, the VMM reserves space for that page on the Pagefile residing on a physical disk drive just in case the page of data needs to be paged out of physical memory. This does not mean that the Pagefile is used, an area of it is just reserved for its possible future use. Physical memory under NT Server 4.0 needs to be backed by the Pagefile; thus, the size of the Pagefile limits the amount of data that can be stored in memory.[3] **This is important to remember.**

Even though the dedicated, theoretical virtual memory space available to a process is 2 GB, in reality the virtual memory available to the process is limited by the maximum size of the Pagefile that is configured. This is true for the other sharable 2 GB of Virtual Memory reserved for NT Server operating system operations also. When a process requests memory that is beyond what the VMM can actually map to the Pagefile, a virtual memory conflict occurs. This results in an error code being returned to the application. You can observe the current memory limit on your NT Server by looking at Perfmon's memory object commit limit counter. Perfmon defines the commit limit as "the size (in bytes) of virtual memory that can be committed without having to extend the paging file(s). If the paging file(s) can be extended, this is a soft limit." This information is also available under Task Manager|Performance, in

---

3. paraphrased from *Windows NT 4.0 Workstation Resource Kit*, ISBN 1-57231-343-9, p. 393,

the lower left-hand corner under Commit Charge Limit. This same Task Manager page provides a quick look at how much total physical memory is configured in the server, how much of it is currently available, and how much memory is being used by the file system cache.

CONFIGURING THE PAGEFILE FOR MAXIMUM PERFORMANCE

Under Start|Settings|Control Panel|System|Performance |Virtual Memory|Settings are the configuration settings for the Pagefile where you can set an initial and maximum size for the Pagefile. To lower the possibility of virtual memory conflicts from occurring on enterprise class servers, configure the initial and maximum size of the Pagefile to twice the amount of physical memory found in the server, up to the 4 GB RAM limit.

Why configure a Pagefile so large? Two important reasons: functionality and performance. From a functionality perspective, you do not want an important server application to suddenly feel boxed in and stop running because of a virtual memory limitation. This statement is based on the concepts presented in the **Pagefile Size Limits Virtual Memory Available to a Process** section above. Microsoft Knowledge base article Q171793 (*http://www.microsoftt.com/kb*) alludes to the fact that in larger server memory configurations, having a Pagefile smaller than actual physical memory will "affect the total memory commit size for applications." Personal experience has shown this to be true.

From a performance perspective, defining a large Pagefile is a strategic decision. NT Server can dynamically increase the size of the Pagefile on the fly, up to the Pagefile's maximum size setting, which is great! This is how NT Server helps to avoid virtual memory conflicts. Unfortunately, when NT Server grows past the initial Pagefile setting, it requires resources to complete this task of growing the Pagefile. If the server requires the Pagefile to be resized, it is a good bet that memory resources are already becoming scarce. When NT Server dynamically resizes the Pagefile, this causes the server to use even more resources during a server's time of need. This adds even more performance problems to the already besieged server.

The VMM writes pages of data to the Pagefile in a sequential fashion. The VMM employs a read-ahead caching strategy when working with the Pagefile to move potential memory pages back into physical memory. The VMM hopes that the next page requested from the Pagefile is already back in memory, thus only incurring a less costly soft page fault. For this strategy to be most effective, the Pagefile located on the disk drive must be contiguous. Contiguous data implies that the data is grouped together on the same area of the disk drive such that less physical disk movement is required to obtain the data. When NT Server dynamically adds more space to the Pagefile, there is no guarantee that the additional Pagefile space will be placed onto the disk drive in a contiguous fashion in respect to where the current pagefile.sys is located. When this happens, the Pagefile becomes fragmented on the disk subsystem it resides on. Now, when memory pages are written to or read from the new dynamically grown Pagefile, additional performance will be lost as the heads on the disk drive must wander around the disk drive to access the Pagefile. More techniques for improving virtual memory performance are located in this chapter's **Tuning Around Memory Bottlenecks** section.

NT Server's File System Cache

NT Server utilizes file system caching to improve I/O subsystem performance. So why include this information in the chapter on memory performance? The file system cache uses the same physical memory that applications would like to use.

What is the file system cache? NT Server dynamically allocates an area of physical memory to cache data written and read from the I/O subsystem. The area in the virtual memory hierarchy where the VMM places the file system cache used by the CM is in the upper 2 GB or kernel accessed memory area which is shared among all processes. In this manner, all processes have access to the file system cache. The goal of the file system cache is to lower the number of times that the physical devices attached to the server's I/O subsystem must be accessed. By lowering the number of times that the physical subsystem must be accessed, less time is required to obtain the requested data, and overall server performance is greatly improved.

How The File System Cache Is Implemented

When a process requests data from the disk subsystem, the I/O Manager works in conjunction with the Cache Manager (CM) to obtain the requested data. The file system cache is beneficial for both read and write environments. When the I/O manager requests that data files are to be written to the disk subsystem, the CM steps in. The CM groups the modified data in its cache before actually writing it to the disk subsystem. This is referred to as a lazy write. A lazy write provides improved responsiveness to the application and subsequently the end user, since they do not have to wait for the data to be physically written to disk. Another positive effect grouping disk writes in cache has is that when the CM does write the data to the disk subsystem, it is written in larger chunks. In this manner, the disk I/O is more efficient and there is a better chance that the data will be written to disk in a contiguous fashion. This technique of grouping data into a larger chunk before writing it to disk is sometimes referred to as deferred or lazy commit.

For some environments, applications manage caching of their own data and prefer that the file system cache does not get involved. This occurs in applications such as an Oracle Database, Microsoft's SQL Server, and

Microsoft Exchange, to name a few. One method applications use to avoid file system cache intervention is to specify the FILE_FLAG_NO_BUFFERING parameter.[4] This is not a flag set in the registry, but a flag that the application sets when requesting I/O operations of NT Server's I/O Manager.

File System Cache in a Read Intensive Disk I/O Environment

When the CM's predictive algorithms detects sequential reading characteristics occurring, it employs the same read-ahead cache strategy that the VMM employs when working with the Pagefile. When a process requests data from the disk subsystem, additional data that is originally requested by the process is actually read from the disk subsystem and placed into the file system cache. When this strategy is effective, it provides significant performance advantages to the server since data requests by processes are filled in memory (soft page fault) versus the disk subsystem (hard page fault). If other processes are not making memory requests, the file system cache's working set can grow to use all available memory that NT Server has to offer. When I state all available memory here, I really mean every last bit of available memory.

File System Cache Investigated

Using the Nelson Business Benchmark Suite for Windows NT, the file system cache concept was tested. Neal Nelson and Associates commercially produces this benchmark suite. Unfortunately, the company's website is not available to the general public, but they can be reached at (312) 755-1000. The Business Benchmark provides a suite of 30 tests for exercising either NT or UNIX servers. Each test measures a different area of NT performance ranging from a simulated database environment to specific, disk subsystem stress tests. Each test is run under increased workload levels to a published maximum of 50. To specifically illustrate the merits and pitfalls of NT Server's file system cache, "Test 18: 1024 byte Sequential Reads from NT Files" was selected to exercise the server up to a load level of 20 copies. This 20-copy load level equates to approximately 400 light users. This stress test was run on a NCR S46 configured with NT Server 4.0, SP3, 2 200MHz Pentium Pro CPUs, 3 Ultra-Fast/Wide SCSI-2 Disk Drives (NT, Page file, work disk) and 128 MB of RAM. As each workload level test is run from 1 to 20, as reported by the benchmark, larger and larger working set files are used by the benchmark. The following are the throughput levels achieved (see Figure 5–1).

---

4. *Optimizing Windows NT: Microsoft Windows NT Resource Kit 3.5*, Microsoft Press, ISBN 1-55615-655-3, 1995, p. 182.

Under light loads, throughput levels to a single disk drive ranged between 33 and 40 Mbytes. This is fantastic! A single disk drive that provides this level of performance. Not quite! To help in understanding what is happening during this test, refer to Figure 5–2.

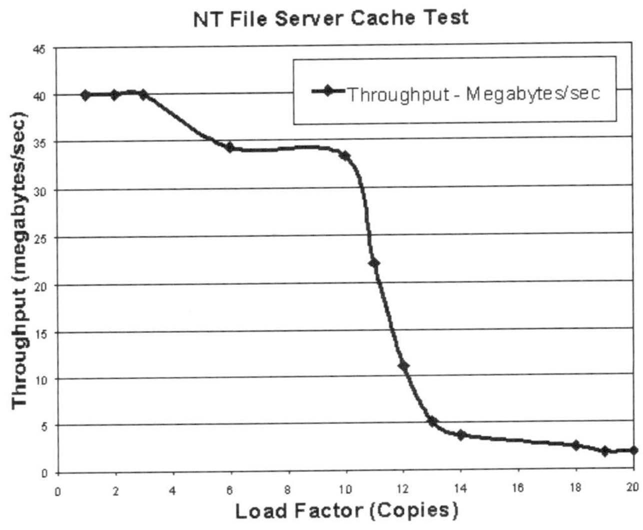

Figure 5–1 *NT Server file system cache test results.*

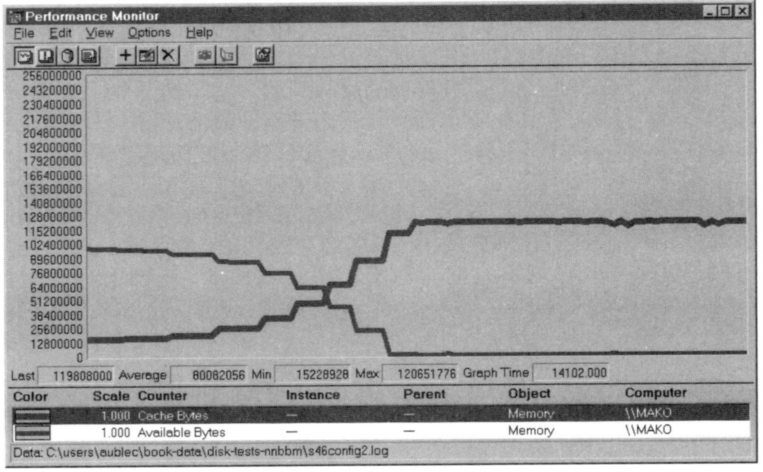

Figure 5–2 *NT Server file server cache Perfmon logs.*

Analyzing the File System Cache Results

So what is happening here? Up until load factor 10, performance is fantastic. At load factor 10, the benchmark began to use a work file with a size greater than the server's available RAM of 128 Mbytes. After load level 10, the work file size continues to increase, thus the file system cache becomes less and less effective in caching the requested data. By the time the benchmark reached load level 15, which uses a work file size of 331 Mbytes, NT Server's file system cache is defeated since the work file is bigger than the file system cache and physical reads from the actual disk drive are occurring. In addition to the larger work file sizes as the benchmark load increases, the number of multiuser requests increases too. Suddenly, performance is down to 1.8 Mbytes/sec of throughput.

Looking at the Perfmon results in Figure 5–2, the following two counters from the Memory object are shown: available bytes and cache bytes. NT Server's Perfmon defines the cache bytes counter as "the number of bytes currently in use by the system cache. The system cache is used to buffer data retrieved from disk or LAN. The system cache uses memory not in use by active processes in the computer." Available bytes is defined by Perfmon as "the size of the virtual memory currently on the Zeroed, Free, and Standby lists. Zeroed and Free memory is ready for use, with Zeroed memory cleared to zeros. Standby memory is memory removed from a process's Working Set but still available. Notice that this is an instantaneous count, not an average over the time interval."

When reviewing this Perfmon graph, it is important to observe that NT Server committed every possible byte of memory to the file system cache. You can observe how the file system cache (Cache Bytes) dynamically grows as the load generated by the benchmark increases. Do not get discouraged, this is what the file system cache is supposed to do. The file system cache grows so that it can cache more and more of the disk I/O activity. Also, although not shown in this Perfmon graph but reflected in the benchmark results, the server's performance degraded as the load increased even further because the server began to increase its paging activities from load levels 15 to 20.

Under the lighter loads, less than load level 10, the file system cache directly contributed to great disk subsystem performance as it dynamically increased its size to meet requested tasks. But, as the workload increased, the file system cache became less and less effective. This illustrates the positive and negative influence that the file system cache can have. Properly sized and tuned, the file system cache is a great ally. Improperly tuned, it can lead to lower overall performance, due to its exhibited behavior of using so much memory for file system cache operations that the server begins to run short of memory needed for NT Server itself. This fact was also illustrated and investigated in Chapter 8's case studies. To understand how to control the file system caches behavior for you advantage, read on to this chapter's **NT Server Memory Strategies** section.

Thrashing: Extreme Paging at Its Worst

What is wrong with paging? Nothing actually, it is part of normal NT Server operations. However, the degree of paging is important, if you have any interest in performance. Paging can occur at increased levels on busy servers. If a process requests a page of data, and there is no physical memory for that page to be placed, the VMM will trim the working set of another process to make room in physical memory for the new page of data. When this occurs, the least recently used data from the processes working set is stolen (removed) from physical memory and sent (paged) to the Pagefile. Later, if the process whose memory was stolen requires the data that is resident on the Pagefile back, the VMM will page this data back into physical memory.

A problem occurs when the VMM must move data back into physical memory for processes, and to accomplish this, it must trim the working set of another process that will soon need that data again. Now when the other process turns around and requires its data back, which is in the Pagefile again, the VMM must now trim the working set of another process to get the requested page back into physical memory. Having the VMM write data to the Pagefile often is not that serious of a condition. What is serious is when the VMM must frequently read and write to and from the Pagefile (a hard page fault) to fulfill the requests of multiple processes, which are all clamor for physical memory.

When contention for physical memory occurs in the vicious cycle described above, the VMM is trimming the working set of one process just to fulfill another process's memory requests at a very high rate. As this occurs, all of the server resources are placed under increased stress just to complete memory operations. More CPU cycles are needed to move the data into and out of memory (both physical and virtual), versus being used for productive work. The disk where the Pagefile resides becomes active at ever higher rates. This undesirable condition of memory contention is referred to as thrashing. This thrashing condition commonly clouds the detection of the real server bottleneck. Under the worst circumstances on a heavily loaded server, thrashing can make it appear that there is a CPU or disk bottleneck when, in reality, there is a memory bottleneck.

NT Server Memory Strategies

NT Server allows you to influence how the memory subsystem is used. By wisely selecting NT Server's memory management strategy, you influence how much memory NT Server uses for various processes working sets in memory. Properly setting NT Server's memory strategy is the first step in avoiding thrashing. For most multiuser enterprise environments, two options for tuning NT Server's memory strategy are of particular interest: Maximize Throughput for File Sharing and Maximize Throughput for Network Applications. These options are chosen by selecting Start|Settings|Control Panel|Network|Services|Server, then selecting the optimization level (memory management strategy). When you make your selection, the server power must be cycled. Which is a fancy way to state, "reboot the computer." What NT Server's GUI server interface actually does is tune the registry.

The following is the registry variable that is altered and what the associated possible values are:

HKEY_LOCAL_MACHINE/System/CurrentControlSet/Control/Session Manager/Memory Management/LargeSystemCache

REG_DWORD

Range: 0, 1, 2, and 3

Default: 2

Values:

0–Minimize memory used.

1–Balance (cache and working sets have equal priority).

2–Maximize throughput for file sharing (the cache has a higher priority).

3–Maximize throughput for network applications (the other working sets have higher priority).

[This information obtained from *NT Workstation Resource Kit* online documentation]

Maximize Throughput for File Sharing

When you select Maximize Throughput for File Sharing, NT Server favors the working set of the file system cache over the other processes working sets running on your server. This gives priority for space in memory to the file system cache. With this setting, if the VMM needs to trim a process work set, it will select other processes before the file system cache process. Yes, the file system cache is similar to other processes in the fact it has a working set that can be trimmed.

When using Maximize Throughput for File Sharing, NT Server uses all available memory for the file system cache (dynamic file system cache allocation). We showed how NT Server actually goes into this mode in the benchmark example above and in Chapter 8's file server case study. This option is good when you use your NT Server only as a file server or other server application that exhibits file-server-like characteristics. Allocating all memory for the file system cache generally enhances disk and network I/O performance. Other instances when it is good to use NT Server's default Maximize Throughput for File Sharing setting are: dedicated file servers, primary domain controllers, backup domain controllers, and print servers.

When Not to Use Maximize Throughput for File Sharing Memory Strategy

Using Maximize Throughput for File Sharing is not suggested when you are running multiple applications under NT Server. When you start a client/server application, such as Microsoft SQL Server or another memory-intensive application, the server might begin to thrash. Remember that when Maximize Throughput for File Sharing memory strategy is in use, the VMM favors the file system cache over the other processes on the server. Thus, if you are running processes which are demanding memory or which you have allocated memory to and the file system cache is demanding memory, somebody loses. This loss will be in your applications performance.

If the server you are fielding is under constant heavy loads and the memory subsystem is paging or thrashing, use one of the techniques outlined in this chapter's **Tuning Around Memory Bottlenecks** section to remove the memory bottleneck. If you are unable to tune around the memory bottleneck, consider changing the memory strategy. When a high load on the server is characterized by heavy I/O subsystem use, the file system cache (growing to use all the server memory) actually becomes a hindrance. When all of the memory in the server is used, the server will begin to potentially page heavily. When this occurs, the paging activity loads outweigh the benefits of the file system cache. To avoid allowing the file system cache from using all of the server's memory in this environment, it is better to use the Maximize Throughput for Network Applications memory strategy.

When to Use Maximize Throughput for Network Applications

The second primary option for tuning NT Server's memory strategy is Maximize Throughput for Network Applications. When you select this option, NT Server allocates less RAM for the file system cache so that running applications can have access to more RAM. NT Server thus favors the working set of all processes over that of the file system cache process. When this memory strategy option is selected, application memory tuning becomes much more important. When you configure applications such as SQL Server or Microsoft Exchange, you can tune them to use specified amounts of RAM for areas such as buffers for disk operations and database caches.

Comparing NT Server Memory Management Strategies

One way to illustrate the importance of selecting the correct NT Server memory strategy is to run a specific workload on a server using the Maximize

Throughput for Network Applications. Then, run that same workload on the exact server configuration, but change the memory strategy to Maximize Throughput for File Sharing. This illustration was accomplished by using Neal Nelson and Associate's Business Benchmark (NNBBM) Simulated Database Test. This stress test was run to a workload level (copy level) of 20. As the test is run, each work load level places an increasing amount of stress onto the NT Server. At load level 1, 20 users are simulated; at load level 2, 40 users are simulated; and so on up to a selected maximum of 20 copies or 400 users. At each workload level, the average amount of time required to complete the database task by all users are recorded in seconds. **Since this is a timed test, the lower the reported results, the better.** The stress test results are shown in Figure 5–3.

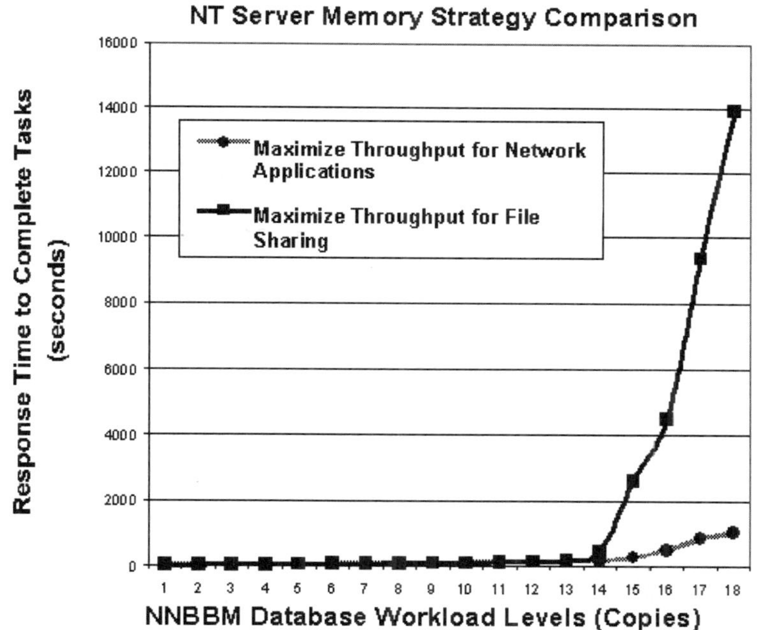

Figure 5–3 *NT Server memory strategy comparison.*

Note: Lower values on this NNBBM Database NT Server Memory Strategy Comparison are better

From this graph, we observe that under lighter loads (less than workload level 13), there is not a great performance difference between the two memory management strategies. But as the workload increases (past workload level 14), the performance difference becomes astronomical. In fact, starting at workload level 14, the server's response times difference between the server's memory management strategy tests increases from 155 percent to over 1,247 percent! By choosing the incorrect memory strategy, you may not notice a problem at first. But, when the server is under heavier loads, the difference will become apparent and the end users will think that the server has died and should be sent to the junkyard of poor performing servers.

The primary reason for the poor performance results of the Maximize Throughput for File Sharing memory strategy under heavy loads was the fact that the file system cache consumed so much of the server's memory that the database users were subsequently starved for memory. This imbalance of memory usage resulted in thrashing, but with the VMM favoring the file system cache, it was the database users' work sets that were targeted for paging to disk.

Understanding Your Environment Equals Improved Performance

Knowing what is running on your server is particularly important when tuning applications memory settings. If you allocate too much memory for each application in a multiapplication environment, there will be contention for physical memory. When this happens, the server will thrash and you will end up with one slow server!

To properly tune an application's memory usage requires a good understanding of the applications in use. Never underestimate the power of an expert or hesitate to develop a relationship with a consultant who is dedicated to a specific application environment. For example, consultants who specialize in improving the performance of specific database can easily earn their keep during a short-term engagement designed to improve the performance of your database server. Whenever using outside consultants, use the opportunity to work with them to learn how they are tuning the database. They may improve performance by making better use of the server's memory, optimizing database design, optimizing the queries, or other factors that can improve the overall server's performance for the particular application in which environment you are working.

Memory Optimization Example: Improving Microsoft Exchange Memory Usage

In the upcoming Chapter 8 case study using Microsoft Exchange, we analyze the environment very closely and determine that there were approximately 100 MBytes of RAM that went unused during the 2000 user LoadSim stress test. In a production environment, if this trend of available RAM continued, you would want to tune the application to take advantage of this extra RAM so that better performance to the end user was achieved. Plus, if you have the RAM available, why not use it to your advantage?

For the Exchange Server case study environment, the server was a dedicated Exchange electronic mail server. By dedicating the server to a single, however complex application, it makes tuning the server a little bit easier, since the only other application that we must contend with for memory is NT Server itself. Initially, using the Exchange Optimizer, Exchange was tuned to have access of all of the server's memory except for the 64 MB that we reserved for NT Server. This 64 MB of RAM was set aside as a safety zone for possible NT Server usage. However, we noticed that NT Server's file system cache (cache bytes) only used a maximum of 21 Mbytes of memory during the stress test. A high level of file system cache support was not required because Exchange caches its own disk activities. This is why setting NT Server's memory strategy to Maximize Throughput for Network Applications was important for the Exchange environment; we wanted NT Server to favor the working set of Exchange so that it was allowed to easily grow.

Tuning Microsoft's Exchange Server's Memory Usage

When the Exchange Optimizer was set to limit Exchange's memory usage to 192 MB of the available 256 MB, the Exchange registry setting HKEY_LOCAL_MACHINE\System\CurrentControlSet\Services\MsExchangeIS\ParametersSystem\MaxBuffers was set to a hexadecimal value of 0x4522. The decimal equivalent of this is 17698. This value is in pages; thus, 17698 of 4 kbyte pages equates roughly to 70 Mbytes. Thus, the maximum amount of cache that the Information Store (IS) was allowed to use was limited to 70 Mbytes. When the Perfmon logs were reviewed, the Exchange database that was most active during the stress test was the disk array that was dedicated to the Information Store. This disk array was actually one of the areas that, although providing good performance, was still a limiting factor that throttled the server's overall performance.

For example, to improve the performance of the Information Store database, we can increase the maximum, a cache area that the Exchange Information Store can use. Revisiting the Exchange Optimizer, the amount of memory Exchange allowed access was changed to 224 Mbytes. This resulted in a normalized HKEY_LOCAL_MACHINE\System\CurrentControl

Set\Services\MsExchangeIS\ParametersSystem\MaxBuffers value of 80 Mbytes. When the Exchange Optimizer was used to adjust the amount of memory Exchange has access to, it adjusted all of the internal Exchange parameters, not just the cache associated with the Information Store. This change from 192 MB to 224 MB provided Exchange access to an additional 32 MB of RAM. Unfortunately, the focus of our attention, the information stores cache size, only increased by 10 Mbytes.

Remembering that we had 100 Mbytes extra to begin with, 32 MB are now given to exchange, what shall we do with the extra 68 Mbytes? 68 Mbytes is added to the 80 Mbytes already committed to the Information Store cache. To determine the value to change the registry to, divide 68 Mbytes by 4 kbyte pages and convert to a hexadecimal value of 0x9088. This is the value then used to set the HKEY_LOCAL_MACHINE\System\CurrentControlSet\Services\MsExchnageIS\ParametersSystem\ MaxBuffers. The Information Store database cache is now increased from its initial value of 70 Mbytes to 148 Mbytes. By the way, you do not need to be a math wizard to keep all of these hexadecimal (base 16) numbers straight. Under Start|Programs|Accessories|Calculator|View|Scientfic View, you can use NT Server's built in calculator to convert between hexadecimal (base 16) and decimal (base 10) notation. Or, depending on the registry editor that you use, you can select between hexadecimal and base ten values as needed.

The Effects of Properly Tuned Exchange Server Memory

What affect did spending the time to understand the environment and tune the application have? Besides refreshing your math skills a little, the amount of RAM available once the 2000 user LoadSim stress test achieved a steady state lowered from approximately 100 Mbytes down to 4 Mbytes (what NT Server considers a minimum amount of RAM that should always be available). At no time during the stress test did the server page, thus the memory was tuned to an optimal level. The disk arrays' performance improved dramatically due to the increased IS cache size. Because of an improved cache hit rate, the Informat Store diskwork load (transfers/sec) lowered from a maximum of 110 to 86 while the maximum value of the average disk queue length lowered from 5.8 to 1.0. Success! Less time was spent waiting on data from the disk array housing the Information Store database. If these Perfmon counters quoted here appear alien to you, don't worry. In the next chapter, "NT Server and Disk Subsystem Performance," these Perfmon counters and others are explained in more depth.

It is nice to understand what happened behind the scenes on the server, but what about the true measure of performance improvement in an interactive application environment, response time? Response time to the end user improved from 0.900 seconds for NCR 4300 Exchange Server Configuration 2 to under 0.5 seconds for this optimized memory stress test configuration. Just for background information, it was the Configuration 2's disk I/O subsystem optimized configuration whose memory subsystem was tuned and retested and used as the baseline server.

In a production environment, tuning the memory subsystem to a razor thin dance line that borders paging is an aggressive strategy to follow. If you have proactively applied the tuning methodology from Chapter 2 and understand your business workload environment very well and feel comfortable with this aggressive tuning strategy, go for it! Tune your server for the utmost performance and dance that razor thin line between having enough physical memory and paging. For those who are more conservative, these same memory-tuning concepts can be implemented in a more conservative manor. Depending upon your level of risk, you can tune your application mix such that it always leaves 32 Mbytes or 64 Mbytes of RAM available on the server. This provides a safe cushion for those heavier than expected workload moments. Regardless of whether you consider yourself a renegade or a conservative, use this memory-tuning concept whenever adding more RAM to your server so that you insure it is being put to good use.

What NT Server Enterprise Edition Brings to the Table

In an effort to help escalate NT Server into the enterprise, Microsoft provided another NT Server release: NT Server 4.0 Enterprise Edition. The key differences in this edition and the Standard Edition really falls into three areas: CPUs supported out of the box, memory strategy, and additional operating features. Here we focus on the first two differences. Increasing the number of CPUs supported directly from Microsoft (versus from Microsoft through an OEM) to eight helps bring an increased processing power awareness of NT Server to a broader audience. From a memory performance perspective, Enterprise Edition allocates as much as 3 GB of memory for applications and reserves up to 1 GB for NT, which is in contrast to the 2 GB/2 GB split we reviewed earlier for NT Server 4.0 Standard Edition. This allows you to capitalize on the merits of using more RAM to avoid disk activities, which allows NT Server to reach higher performance levels than were previously possible.

Of course, the application must first be "Enterprise Edition Aware" so that it is capable of taking advantage of the additional memory space. Once properly tuned (this is completed at the application source code level), the extra memory spaces that the application takes advantage of can result in much higher levels of performance. There are always tradeoffs. For this increased performance level, you incur the risk of losing more data if the server were to crash for any number of reasons. With today's server technology now being produced with numerous high availability features and clustering technologies available, this risk can be minimized when properly architected. So, in effect, this potential data loss tradeoff can be removed by another tradeoff: cost. In a clustered environment two servers at a minimum are required, thus you can have high performance and high availability. But of course there are other tradeoffs always lurking out there somewhere.

Out of the box, NT Server Enterprise Edition does not support the 3 GB/1 GB split. You must manually edit the boot.ini file and add the /3 GB parameter to the startup line switch to take advantage of the new memory management strategy. An example boot.ini file would read: "[boot loader] timeout=30 default=multi(0)disk(0)rdisk(0)partition(2)\WINNT [operating systems] multi(0)disk(0)rdisk(0)partition(2)\WINNT= 'Windows NT Enterprise Edition 4.00' /3 GB"

Sizing the Memory Subsystem

On the down side, more and more memory is needed by NT Server and server applications. When is the last time you heard a vendor mention that their new software product uses half the RAM their previous version did? The good news is that the price of RAM has continually fallen over the last several years. With this in mind and the performance degradation that occurs when there is an insufficient amount of RAM in the server, why not just stock every server to the max? Well, memory is not that cheap yet.

When sizing the memory subsystem, follow the sizing methodology in Chapter 3 so that all of the facets surrounding your solution are taken into consideration. The size of the memory subsystem directly relates to the performance levels that you wish to achieve. The best performing NT Server solutions I have encountered are configured to avoid any paging during regular work load periods. This ensures that the server provides the maximum level of performance by keeping the CPUs fed and avoiding unnecessary disk activity by caching as much data as possible. Also remember to follow the tuning methodology after fielding your solution. By doing this, if the work load environment changes, you can tune around any server bottlenecks to avoid paging before there are any real performance problems. When sizing the memory subsystem, you want to achieve the following:

- Maximum Performance
- Minimum RAM required to meet performance goals
- Highest Density that allows for server growth
- Avoid throwing RAM away when memory requirements increase

Use Historical Performance Information Whenever Possible

Historical information is the best place to start when sizing the memory subsystem. If you are going to deploy a server in your department to support 200 users running a 50 GB Oracle database, find out if another department has implemented a similar solution. If they have, observe their end users working with their applications to determine if the response times you observe are adequate for your environment. Also, ask to review their performance logs to determine how much memory is normally being used and how much, if any, paging is occurring. Use the information you obtain to size your memory subsystem.

Vendors try their best to provide realistic information on memory requirements for servers that run their software applications. Keep in mind that they are trying to sell their product as well, thus their estimates for server resources tend to be on the skinny side to say the least (no need to scare off a potential customer). For a good starting point, be sure you take into consideration the following:

- All applications that the server is running
- NT Server's Requirements
- NT Server's file system cache use
- The number of concurrent users the server is supporting
- The amount of server resources configured (CPU, Disk, Network etc.)

Sizing memory subsystems is an additive process (ok, there are some shared structures and libraries, but let's not get too picky here). If you are running two database instances, and each instance requires 64 MB of RAM, then configure for 128 MB of RAM to avoid any memory contention. Understanding what is going to run on your server is important. Add up the minimum requirements for each server application and then add in the memory needed for NT Server's file system cache. If the application will be part of an interactive client server solution, add the amount of memory that is estimated to be required for each user.

For example, for many database environments it is typical to configure 0.250 Mbytes of RAM per concurrent user connection. Thus, for 100 concurrent users, add an additional 25 Mbytes of RAM to the server configuration. If you are conservative and want better performance, consider 0.5 MB per user. If you think the disk I/O subsystem will provide a high enough performance level for your solution, configure 0.125 Mbytes per concurrent user. Although 0.250 Mbytes is a good rule of thumb, always contact the vendor that is supplying the database for their recommendations. Vendors will be vendors, they want the sale so beware of vendors that claim a particularly low per user RAM recommendation. You may want to consider speaking to some of their current customers and see what configuration they are using for their solution. Again, we refer back to historical baselines and information.

Determine a Good Memory Size Starting Point

To get a good initial memory configuration, sum the vendor recommendations for all of the areas outlined above. For example, if you were implementing a server that was to support both a database and web server application for 60 *concurrent* database users (this implies there may be more web users connected, but of those connected web users, 60 are accessing the database too):

- All applications that the server is running
  Database Application – 16 MB
  Web Server – 16 MB
- NT Server's Requirement
  32 MB
- O/S Disk File System Cache Use
  32 MB
- The number of concurrent users the server is supporting
  60 * 0.250 MBytes of RAM for each connection

Summing these metrics together suggests a starting memory size for the server of 111 Mbytes. 111 Mbyes is not quite a power of two, thus, using a 128 Mbyte RAM configuration is the reference point.

Consider Memory Configuration

If you wish to consider an alternate view of sizing a server's memory, check out the Server Memory Assessment Engine. This is an on-line tool from Kingston Technology located at *http://www.kingston.com/servermap*. This on-line tool walks you through a questionnaire with a goal of making a memory sizing recommendation at the end. It is a helpful tool for a second or third opinion, but as before, keep in mind that Kingston is a company that specializes in selling RAM. Do not be surprised by the results. Another tool that helps size not only memory, but an entire database server is available from Compaq at *http://www.compaq*. **Review Chapter 3, "Capacity Sizing"** for techniques to determine if your server configuration will really meet you objectives.

At a minimum, regardless of the application environment, consider the following CPU/Memory ratios (Table 5–2) when configuring your server's memory for Pentium Pro class CPUs and above:

Table 5.2 CPU/Memory ratios.

Number of CPUs	Minium Amount of RAM (Mbytes
1	64
2	128
4	256
6	344
8	512

This will help to ensure that the CPUs are kept properly fed. This information is based on personal experience and industry observations.

Benchmark Extrapolations and Server Guidelines

Extrapolation from benchmarks that are similar to your environment is also a good technique to use to initially size your memory subsystem. This technique is utilized in the web server case study example in Chapter 8. The memory subsystems for most servers have some sort of memory guidelines. So, do not be too concerned with getting the number of megabytes down to a perfect science. If you determine that 120.5 Mbytes are required, the server configuration guidelines will require a 128 Mb minimum configuration.

I do not want to trivialize sizing the memory subsystem. It is always better to have a little more memory than needed, within reason. By properly sizing the memory subsystem, you avoid placing more memory in the server than required, which is wasteful and costly. In Chapter 8's file server case study, we show how saving just 64 Mbytes of RAM per server in a large NT rollout can result in significant overall savings. Stress testing your final solution, outlined in step 9 of the sizing methodology, is the best way to ensure that you have developed a solid solution that will meet your goals.

Detecting Memory Bottlenecks

Recall from Chapter 2 that it is important to consider the entire server performance picture when trying to locate an NT Server bottleneck. There can be more than one server resource area that is contributing to the throttling of the server's overall performance. Once all of the major server resource areas are evaluated, focus in on the resource that is farthest to the left in the Performance Resource Chart introduced in Chapter 2 and repeated here in Figure 5–4 for reference. This strategy will provide the greatest immediate gain to the server's overall performance. For this discussion, all other (besides memory) server resources have already been investigated and determined not be a bottleneck throttling back the server's performance. Remember to revisit the Performance Resource Chart after tuning around a memory bottleneck. Once one server resource is removed as the bottleneck, others may take its place which subsequently influences where you focus additional tuning efforts.

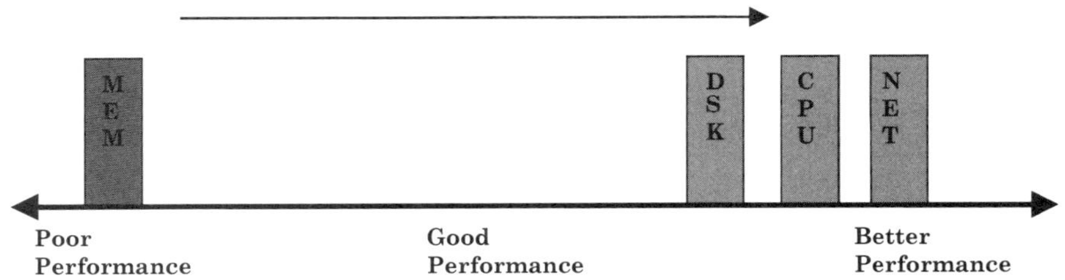

Figure 5–4 *Performance Resource Chart indicating a memory bottleneck.*

Unless you jumped right to this section of the book, it should be apparent when there is a memory bottleneck occurring when running NT Server. If all the physical memory resources are in use, as shown under Perfmon's memory object's available bytes counter as close to the NT Server minimum target of 4 MB, (similar to the SVR4 UNIX minfree/lotsfree memory thresholds), life is good. By allowing NT Server to use all the memory it can, you will be getting a return on your investment. Unfortunately, if the server begins to page excessively to the point of thrashing, you have a serious memory bottleneck. Anytime the server pages, the response time to the application or the end user is affected in some negative manor.

What to Observe in Perfmon When Diagnosing a Memory Bottleneck

A server's subsystems are all interrelated and subsequently so are the metrics to observe, even with NT Server. To determine whether your system has a memory bottleneck, use Perfmon to observe the relationship of the following metrics shown in Table 5–3.

Table 5.3 Counters to view to detect an NT Server memory bottleneck .

Object/Counter	Definition	Rule of Thumb for Bottleneck Detection
Memory: Available bytes	Available bytes displays the size of virtual memory currently on the Zeroed, Free, and Standby lists. Zeroed and Free memory is ready for use with Zeroed memory cleared to zeros. Standby memory is removed from a processor working set but is still available.	NT Server will try to keep at least 4 MB available as seen via this counter. If this value is near 4 MB and pages/sec is high, and the disk drive where the Pagefile is located is busy, there is a memory shortfall. This rule is applicable when using all NT Server memory strategies except one. NT Server lowers the amount of RAM to keep in reserve to 1 MB for the Maximize Throughput for file sharing memory strategies.

Table 5.3 Counters to view to detect an NT Server memory bottleneck *(Continued)*.

Object/Counter	Definition	Rule of Thumb for Bottleneck Detection
Memory: Pages/ sec	Pages/sec is the number of pages read from the disk or written to the disk to resolve memory references that were not in memory (RAM) at the time of reference.	This counter can be deceiving, particularly on Enterprise class systems. A high paging activity is fine (>100), unless it is accompanied by low available bytes indicator and high % Disk Time on the paging file disks.
Logical Disk: % Disk Time (for dedicated pagefile.sys disk drive)	Disk time is the percentage of elapsed time that the selected disk drive is busy servicing read or write requests.	If the % Disk Time is consistently over 10 percent, the available bytes are hovering around 4 MB, and Pages/sec is high, the Virtual Memory Manager is using the paging file significantly and the server is experiencing a memory bottleneck. Note the % Disk Time counter must point to disk drive(s) that contains paging system file(s), pagefile.sys.
Server: Pool Non-paged Failures	The number of times allocations from nonpaged pool have failed.	If this value is >1 on a regular basis, there is not enough physical memory in the server.
Server: Pool Paged Failures	The number of times allocations from paged pool has failed.	If this value is >1 on a regular basis, there is not enough physical memory in the server or the paging file is too small.

Memory Counter Relationships

When memory bottlenecks form there is a rolling snowball affect; if the problem persists, it becomes a bigger and bigger problem. When NT Server's available bytes counter lowers to the 4 MBytes level, the server is utilizing all available physical memory. To compensate for the lack of physical memory, the VMM begins to trim the working set of processes and page portions of them to the disk to make physical memory available as needed. As other processes need the paged data back in physical memory, the VMM pages the data from the Pagefile back into memory and makes room for these pages by paging other process data to disk. Pages/sec is the number of pages read from the disk or written to the disk to resolve memory references to pages that were not in memory at the time of the reference. As the VMM increases its disk activity associated with using the Pagefile, the pages/sec counter increases.

The real challenge here is to ensure that the pages/sec counter represents the disk activity associated with the VMM working with the Pagefile. The page/sec counter displays hard page faults that are not only related to the Pagefile, but to other disk operations also. Thus, to determine if the increase in pages/sec is associated with the memory shortfall noted by a low available bytes and increased pages/sec, we must determine if hard page faults being generated are associated with the disk drive where the Pagefile is located. If the disk that houses the Pagefile displays a % Disk Time over 10 percent of the time, you are starting to have a problem.

As the memory shortfall continues to get worse, the Pagefile disk is used more and more. The % disk time and the transfers/sec increase as pages are written and read to the Pagefile disk. In a worst case scenario, an NT process is not only waiting due to a lack of memory, but also on an overworked disk drive. This is exemplified when the Logical Disk objects counter Average Disk Queue Length increases beyond two on the disk drive that houses the Pagefile. When this occurs, processes begin to wait even longer to have their memory requests fulfilled since they are now waiting in line to use the Pagefile. This concept is illustrated in the Chapter 8 file server case study's configuration 1.

Memory Pool Problems

NT Server allocates pools of memory where the operating system and its component obtain data storage [*Optimizing NT Server 3.51, NT Server Resource Kit*]. To access these pools of memory, processes must enter privileged (kernel mode). These kernel mode pooled resources are divided into two "pools:" Paged Pool and Nonpaged Pool. Data residing in the Page Pool can be swapped out to the Pagefile by the VMM. Data residing in the Nonpaged Pool is not allowed to be paged to the Pagefile, as this information is deemed critical for the operation of NT Server. These are critical resources. If NT Server reports it is having a problem allocating memory for these memory resources, there is critical memory shortage. These memory pool problems are detected by checking under Perfmon's Server object: Pool Nonpaged Failures and Pool Paged Failures counters. If these counters are ever greater than one, there is a serious memory shortage that will affect NT Server operation.

Tuning Memory Resources

Insufficient memory leads to one of the most common bottlenecks you find when using NT Server. Now that we configured and sized the fastest memory subsystem, understand how NT Server uses the memory subsystem, and how to detect when memory bottlenecks are forming, let's use this information to our advantage. There are several strategies when trying to tune the memory subsystem. Some of them include:

- Controlling NT Server's memory management strategies to favor applications or the file system cache
- Optimization of Virtual Memory
- Removing unnecessary memory overhead
- Tuning of how much memory applications have access to
- Adding additional RAM

At this point, we will review a variety of practical hands-on tactics that we can use to implement these strategies.

Controlling NT Server's Memory Management Strategy

RAM is a limited resource, and NT Server lets you tune how it uses its memory subsystem. For most multiuser enterprise environments, two options for tuning NT Server's memory strategy are of particular interest: Maximize Throughput for File Sharing and Maximize Throughput for Network Applications. These options are chosen by selecting Start|Settings|Control Panel| Network|Services|Server|Properties, then selecting the optimization level. This dialog box offers five options. The selection made here can have profound effects on how the server performs, so choose wisely. The details of how these memory strategies influence NT Server's memory management are reviewed above. Here in Table 5–4, an NT Server memory management chart is presented to use as a guideline when choosing memory strategies.

Table 5.4 NT Server memory management chart.

	NT Server Memory Management Strategy	
NT Server Environment	**Maximize Throughput for File Sharing**	**Maximize Throughput for Network Applications**
Databases (Oracle, Informix, SQL Server, etc)		X
Electronic Mail Servers (Exchange, Lotus)		X
Web Servers (IIs, Site server, Netscape)		X
Web Servers and Database on the same Server		X
Dedicated File Server	X	
DHCP, WINS, or NetWare Services		X
Primary Domain Controllers and Backup Domain Controllers	X	
Any Environment that is unable to avoid thrashing including file servers (You can revert to the other memory strategy once the memory bottleneck is resolved)		X

Controlling NT Server's CPU Cache Usage

To provide the highest level of overall server performance, you want to ensure that NT Server is taking advantage of all of the server's hardware. Utilization of a CPU's second level cache is very important and was stressed in Chapter 4 "NT Server and CPU Performance." If NT Server is not taking advantage of the second level cache, it will lower your server's overall performance. Although I rarely encounter this situation, there are times in NT Server's hardware identification phase that the second level CPU cache is either not properly detected or reported by the Hardware Abstraction Layer (HAL). Contact the manufacturer of your server for any known problems in this area that might be applicable to your specific server.

To ensure that NT Server is using the second level cache correctly, you can edit the registry and force NT Server into using the correct cache size. Of course, this means that you must know which CPU technology is in your server. Telling the server it has a 1 MB second level cache when it is only 256 K in size can have less than desirable effects. To set the second level CPU cache size, use regedt32.exe or your favorite registry editor to edit the following registry key:

KEY_LOCAL_MACHINE\SYSTEM\CurrentControlSet\Control\Session Manager\Memory Management\SecondLevelDataCache.

Change the SecondLevelDataCache registry value to match the second level cache size for your server's CPU. For example, if you have a 512 K second level cache, change SecondLevelDataCache to 512 decimal (base 10) or 200 Hex (base 16). The default value is 0 which corresponds to a 256 Kbyte cache. Remember to update this value if you change CPU technologies in the future because once you manually set this value it remains set in NT's registry.

Does this change guarantee better performance? No. What it does warrant is that your server is taking full advantage of the CPU technology that is available so that you are achieving the best performance possible. I always edit this registry entry just to verify that the cache size is set correctly. It does not hurt server performance if set properly, but it will hurt performance if it is not!

Virtual Memory Optimization: Tuning the Pagefile

This is a good technique to implement that can make your life a whole lot easier for a variety of tuning and sizing tasks. The paging file system can be split up among 16 separate pagefile.sys file systems. More is better when it comes to paging files, unless you become excessive. A good rule of thumb is to split the paging file between two to four separate dedicated physical disk drives and, if possible, across different SCSI channels. This is an optimum virtual memory layout. Splitting the page files across more than four disk drives can add overhead to NT Server and actually slow down your server in some instances.

The best tactic to use when implementing multiple Pagefiles is to place them on their own identical dedicated disk drives with the Pagefile configured the same size on each disk drive. By isolating the Pagefiles on their own disk drives, you obtain two advantages. First, Pagefile access is sequential in nature. By allowing the Pagefile its own disk, there is no other outside workloads being placed on the disk that might be contrary to the sequential nature of the Pagefile workload. Secondly, when dedicated disks are used for the Pagefile, it is much easier to distinguish between a very busy server and one that is experiencing memory problems. Sharing your Pagefile disk with other applications makes it much more difficult to determine if paging activities are being caused by disk activity associated with the VMM or by your applications. When all of the Pagefiles are set to the same size, NT Server will load balance the virtual memory usage between all of the Pagefile instances. This improves performance if the server is experiencing paging activities.

What to Avoid When Optimizing the Pagefile

Another technique used when implementing multidisk Pagefile configurations is to place Pagefiles on disk arrays. (RAID Disk array technology is reviewed closely in Chapter 6.) Always avoid this. You could place your Pagefile across a RAID 5 array stripe set with parity, which can survive a single disk failure. NEVER, EVER, EVER do this. The Pagefile disk workload is write intensive. Even with write back cache enabled, RAID 5 arrays provide lower levels of write performance than their single disk counterparts. Using a RAID 5 array for a Pagefile home is like driving a racing car with its parking brake on. It will still work, but wow, will it be slow!

Placing the Pagefile on a RAID 0 array stripe set will improve the Pagefile's performance, similar to the example above when the Pagefile is individually placed on two or more separate disk drives. The technique is not recommended. If you lose one disk drive in a RAID 0 array, the entire Pagefile is lost, as a RAID 0 array cannot sustain a single drive failure. If the Pagefile was on two separate disks that are not in a RAID 0 array, there is still a Pagefile available even with the loss of one drive.

Configuring Multiple Pagefiles

To implement multiple Pagefiles, first select the disk drives that are to be dedicated to containing the Pagefiles and nothing else. Select Start|Settings|Control Panel|System|Performance. Then, select Virtual Memory and create the new paging files, one for each dedicated disk. After the new paging file systems are in place, remove the default Pagefile.sys on the root disk. Remove the root disk Pagefile by selecting the root drive, then setting the minimum and maximum Pagefile size to zero. Figure 5–5 illustrates the removal of Pagefile from the root disk drive (c: in this case).

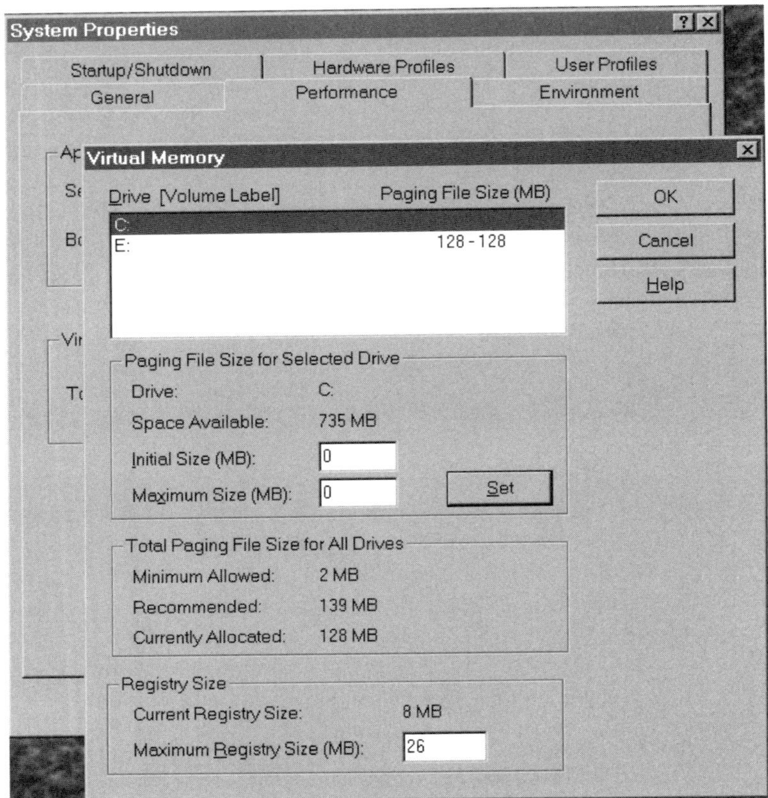

Figure 5-5 *Removing Pagefile from the root disk drive.*

This will improve your virtual memory (paging) performance. The server will be required to be rebooted before the new Pagefile design is activated.

Sizing The Pagefile

When you create the Pagefile(s), you are asked to set the initial and maximum size of the paging file. Under Perfmon, observe the Paging File: %Usage Peak parameter. To optimally use the Pagefile, set the initial and maximum size parameter to that %Usage Peak value. This limits the size of the Pagefile to exactly what is needed and can improve the time required by the VMM to locate data in the Pagefile. Although this is an optimum layout, it can limit virtual memory expansion. As corollary to this rule of thumb: at a minimum, set the paging file initial size to twice the size of physical memory and the maximum size for the Pagefile to twice the size of physical memory (to a maximum of 4 GB). This will minimize spending any resource time extending the size of the Paging file and waiting for the Paging file extension to complete. Dynamic expansion of the Pagefile can also cause fragmentation of the Pagefile on the disk drive, which lowers overall Pagefile performance. By setting the Pagefile size initially to twice the RAM configured, the amount of virtual memory that your processes can map their data to increases.

You can observe the total memory commit size (current maximum available virtual memory) that applications on your server can access by using Perfmon to look at the memory object's commit limit counter. The commit limit is defined under Perfmon as "the size (in bytes) of virtual memory that can be committed without having to extend the paging file(s). If the paging file(s) can be extended, this is a soft limit." By starting with a Pagefile two times the size of the RAM, you allow processes access to that much virtual memory immediately, even if it is not needed. Under a heavy workload surge, it is good to provide your applications room to grow so that they can accommodate the surge. Smaller Pagefiles are more efficient than larger Pagefiles. The performance hit incurred by NT Server dynamically sizing the Pagefile outweighs the benefits that a smaller Pagefile provides.

Remove Unnecessary Processes from the Server

Every byte of RAM is sacred (or at least costs money). Any processes that are not required to service your clients or manage your server should not be running on the server. Beyond knowing which processes are currently running, you need to know what the processes do. Why run a service or application in the background if you don't need it? For example, why have Remote Access Service (RAS) turned on if your NT Server does not require RAS? By turning off unnecessary background processes, you free memory resources for applications and portions of NT Server that really need the resources. Knowing your server and understanding the functions you want NT Server to perform help you tune the server. Under Task Manager|Processes, you can terminate a process by right clicking on the process and then selecting End Process (similar to the UNIX *kill* command). The NT Server Resource Kit provides a command line interface kill command version also.

Unfortunately, ending an unneeded process is only a temporary fix. If you started the process as a background service, the process will start again when you reboot the server. To avoid this situation, control how processes are started and stopped on the server. Figure 5–6 shows that from Start|Settings|Control Panel|Services you can control whether background processes start automatically, manually, or are disabled when you boot the server. Be careful which processes you kill, because some processes (such as server and workstation) are essential for NT Server operation.

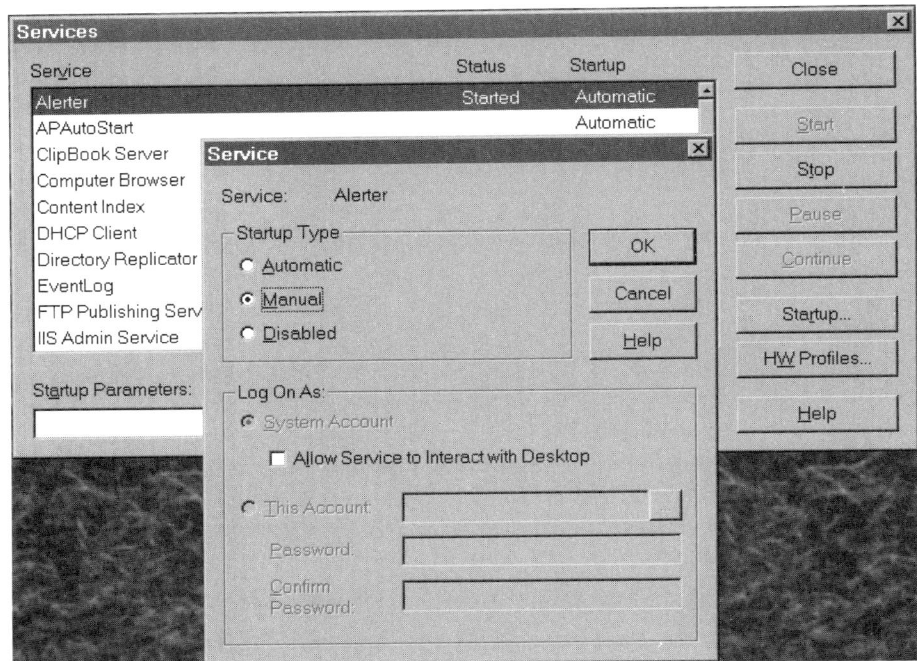

Figure 5-6 *Controlling startup of an NT Server service.*

Typically, areas to tune are found under Start|Settings|Control Panel|Services. Keep a close watch in the Services applet after installing new applications. More and more applications are slipping additional background services into this area. Here are common services that can be set to manually startup under Start|Settings|Control Panel|Services|Startup: Alerter, ClipBook, Server, Computer Browser, Messenger, Remote Access, AutoDial Manager, Server, and Telephony. NT Server can actually run with only the following two services started: workstation and server. Which services you run is a function of your environment.

Maximum Registry Size Limit

This value is set under Start|Settings|Control Panel|System|Performance|Virtual Memory. Although this tunable does not improve performance, it can limit it. Typically you would double the default value of this variable. Even though this will increase registry key size, it will not cause the system's initial request for memory to increase. It will also allow the registry more room to grow if needed, which can aid in avoiding resource limitations under NT Server. Note that the Registry Size Limit memory needs are allocated from the paged pool memory allocation that is limited to 192 MB under NT Server 4.0. You can force NT Server to recalculate its internal tuning settings, such as this one, by running "net config server \srvcomment "<text>"" from the command prompt and rebooting the server. This is a good command to run if you want the Maximum Registry Size Limit to be recalculated by NT Server again or whenever new hardware is configured into the server.

Schedule Memory Intensive Jobs During Off Peak Hours

This technique always seemed to be a bit of an easy-out strategy to alleviate memory problems, but it is effective and uses resources that may have otherwise been idle. To schedule a job during an off peak hour, use the "at" command from the command prompt. Prior to using this command, the scheduler service must be started under Start|Settings|Control Panel|Services. To look at the currently scheduled background processes, run "at.exe" at the command prompt. For a listing of the "at" command options, run "at /?" at the command prompt. If command lines make you feel uncomfortable, the NT Server Resource Kit 4.0 includes a GUI version of the at command named "winat.exe". Using either "winat.exe" or the "at.exe" commands, you can connect to and schedule background processes on local or remote NT Servers.

Control NT Kernel Paging Activities

NT will page some portions of its own kernel to disk, such as the NT Server executive system drivers, when they have not recently been in use for an extended period of time to make room in memory for other processes. This is helpful for a system with a limited RAM supply. If your server has ample RAM, for example, at least 64 MB more RAM than is normally found under Perfmon's memory object available bytes; change the following registry entry: HKEY_LOCAL_MACHINE\SYSTEM\CurrentControlSet\Control\Session Manager\ Memory Management\DisablePagingExecutive from the default value of 0 to 1. This change will force NT Server to keep the NT executive (kernel) from paging any of its executive system drivers to disk and ensure that they are immediately available if needed. Always backup and understand how to restore NT Server's registry before making any changes to it. A review of backing up and restoring the registry is provided in Appendix A.

Remove Memory Leaks

A memory leak can occur when a process allocates memory and either never returns it or continues to increase its memory usage when the server is idle. It is possible to determine if there is a memory leak occurring on the server, but it is a challenge. Using either Task Manager or Perfmon, you can detect memory leaks. What you are in search of is an application that is continually increasing its working set even when the server is idle. Under Perfmon, review Processor:

%Processor Time, and Process: Working Set. When you add the Process: Working Set counter under Perfmon's add function, select Process, Working Set, click on the first process, then press the shift key and the end key concurrently. This will select all of the current processes running on the server, then select add. Also add Process: Virtual Bytes for all processes. At this point, it is wait and see. Look for %Processor time to be quiescent and the other two selected memory counters to grow for specific processes. In this manner, you can determine if a memory leak is occurring and which process is "leaking." To make this task easier, use Perfmon's logging mode and allow Perfmon to run overnight or any other time the server is under its lowest workloads.

If you have the source code, you can use source code debuggers to troubleshoot the leak. If it is a commercial application that appears leaky, look for application patches on the software vendor's website or contact them directly.

Blank Backgrounds Are Best

Remove any backgrounds that may be in place on your server's console. This may seem trivial, but a few megabytes of RAM can help keep a busy server on the safe zone of available memory and avoid the paging performance penalty. Servers tend to sit in the designated computer room by themselves anyway.

If you really love that background wallpaper, at least find out how much memory you are donating for a pretty backdrop. Run Task Manager and look at the available bytes counter then wait a few moments for the server to settle. Once it does, write down the value, then change the background wallpaper. Again, wait a few moments for Task Manager's available memory to settle, and note the difference. Is it worth it? You be the judge. You can also use Perfmon's memory object available bytes to complete the same exercise.

The Last Resort: Purchase More RAM

Isolating the Guilt Memory Hog

If the system begins to page to an unacceptable degree, use Perfmon and Task Manager to isolate the applications or processes that are draining excessive memory and tune down the memory allocated to them (if possible). If the application source code is available, you can work with the developers to improve overall memory performance. If all of the applications operating on the server are required, adding more RAM to a server whose performance is limited by RAM resources will result in improved overall server performance.

Determining How Much Memory to Add

When all strategies to tune the memory are exhausted and you have determined that the server is paging excessively, obtain additional RAM for the server. How much RAM to add is a function of current and future system load requirements and anticipated application requirements. To avoid paging, determine how much paging your server does then add at least that amount. For example, if the Paging File object's % Usage Max counter is 20 percent and your paging file size is 1000 MB, consider adding at least 200 MB. When adding memory to the server, select the RAM sizes such that they provide the highest density while still providing the highest degree of memory interleaving for growth and performance, respectively.

Thinking Outside of the Box

Fragmented Memory

Similar to disk drives, when free memory space is contiguous, it is more efficient to work with. (Disk drive file system fragmentation is considered in Chapter 6.) Due to the high speed of memory access compared to disk drive access, memory fragmentation is less noticeable so less attention is given to it, until now. Technologies are being introduced into the NT Server marketplace to address fragmented memory. One such tool is RamCharge 2.0 from LC Technologies which is distributed by SunBelt Software (*www.sunbelt-software.com*). RamCharge is touted as a tool that runs in the background of your NT Server and actively works with NT Server's memory subsystem to improve the server's overall performance. An evaluation copy of RamCharge is available on the CD-ROM accompanying this book. The primary feature of RamCharge is that it completes timed and manual compacts of free memory. RamCharge defragments memory so that reads and writes can potentially be completed faster. RamCharge also attempts to ensure that memory is freed up consistently so that orphans and leaks do not happen as often.

This utility is not designed for a workstation desktop that is lightly loaded. This tool is designed to clean up and defragment memory on heavily used servers. If the server is not supporting heavy workloads, there really is not any need for memory to be cleaned up. To test the effectiveness of this tool, the Business Benchmark Suite for NT Server was employed again.

Test Environment

For this stress test, the entire suite of 30 tests was run on an NCR 4300 Server. The NCR 4300 was configured with 128 MB of RAM, two Pentium Pro 200 MHz/512 K CPUs, and four disk drives running NT 4 with Service Pack 3. The combination of a significant amount of memory configured on the server and a heavy varied workload employed by the benchmark provided RamCharge with a realistic environment to display its potential performance enhancements.

The benchmark stress test was first run on the NCR 4300 without the RamCharge 2.0 technology installed to develop a baseline and then run again on the exact configuration with the RamCharge installed. Installation of RamCharge is straightforward. After unzipping the RamCharge file, a pointer to the RamCharge executable is configured under the default user start up menu. There are also additional advanced user properties that were required to be configured, but the RamCharge user guide provided a friendly step-by-step guide to administer those changes. Every time the server is rebooted and logged in, RamCharge is activated. A facility was not provided to have RamCharge start automatically on server boot up alone without login intervention. This could be a bit of a hassle for servers in remote locations. Figure 5–7 shows a screenshot of the RamCharge console.

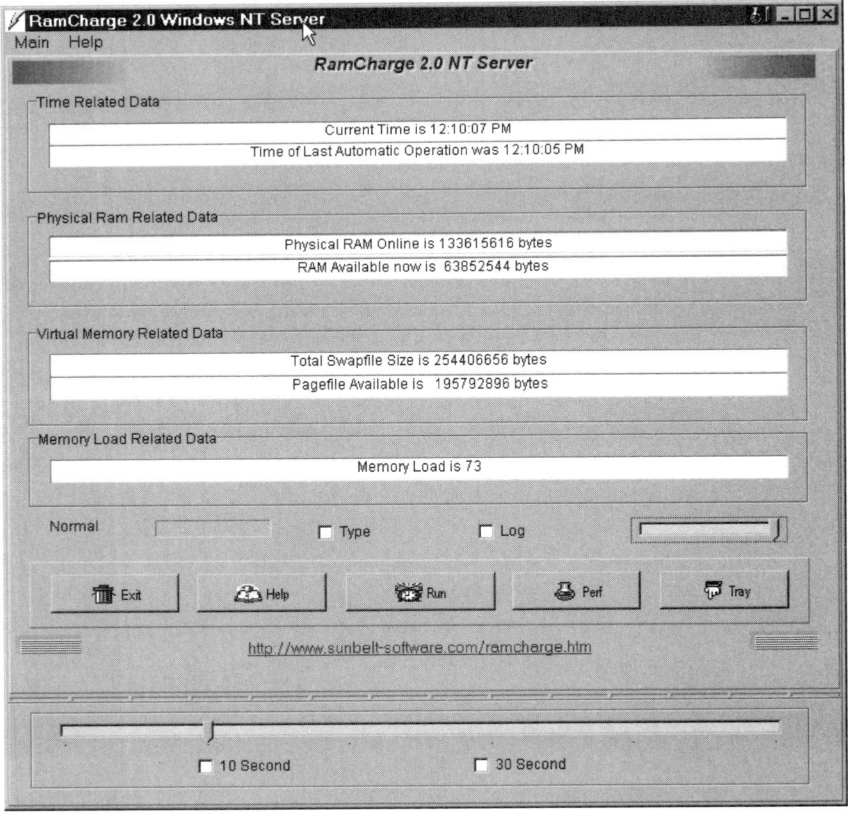

Figure 5–7 *The RamCharge console.*

Stress Test Results

For the first iteration of the stress test, the default RamCharge settings were employed. Using the default settings, the amount of performance improvement under the heavier workload factors was in the range of one and two percent, or in other words, negligible. RamCharge does provide the facilities to tune the application for your environment. In an effort to improve RamCharge's effectiveness, three settings were tuned. First, the server was allowed to sit idle for the first five minutes after it was booted. After this quiet time, all drivers and applications were loaded into memory and RamCharge was manually run in Process Level defragmentation. In this mode, RamCharge defragments memory by looking at each process's working set separately and then defragmenting memory. After this was complete, RamCharge was tuned to normal memory defragmentation mode by deselecting the type checkbox. The frequency of the normal defragmentation process was set to 15 seconds to ensure that all stress tests had the benefit of memory defragmentation. The final setting tuned was the priory level. Knowing this server would be under heavy stress, the priority slide bar was set to high. This high priority was selected to ensure that RamCharge would get a chance to run even on a heavily loaded server.

The results of the second stress test were favorable. Under the heaviest load levels of the benchmark workload levels 18 to 20, the performance improved from 7 to 20 percent on average. Reviewing the Perfmon Logs, it appeared that RamCharge's defragmentation of memory increased the amount of memory available to the file system cache and background processes.

When to Use Memory Defragmentation Tools

As with all new software technologies, it is best to install it in your environment and run a stress test against it that is representative of your workload. In this manner, you can determine if the technology provides enough of a performance boost to justify its purchase. From the stress tests run above, this technology is beneficial if your environment is one that experiences very heavy workload levels. If your server's memory environment exhibits plenty of memory (greater then 64 Mbytes available on a regular basis), a memory defragmenter will provide little overall performance gains. Conversely, if your server exhibits light paging (% Disk time on disk drive housing Pagefile in the range of one to five percent), this technology will be beneficial. If a decision needed to be made between purchasing more RAM or obtaining a memory defragmenter, a good rule of thumb is to go with the RAM. For best performance, add the RAM and the memory defragmenter.

Summary

In this chapter, a building block approach to NT Server and memory performance was utilized. Once an understanding of the base memory hardware technology that is used in modern servers was completed, we looked at how NT Server utilized the memory resources provided to it. Once these two pieces of the puzzle were covered, we looked at how to size the memory subsystem, how to detect memory bottlenecks and how to tune around them. By understanding what is happening in your environment and how NT Server provides memory management, you can maximize your tuning and sizing efforts when implementing NT Server solutions. This will ensure that NT Server provides the maximum performance for your specific environment.

SIX

NT Server and Disk Subsystem Performance

When developing an NT Server solution, the disk subsystem portion of the solution allows for the greatest amount of flexibility that you can directly influence. The disk subsystem is one area in which having an understanding from strictly an NT Server perspective is not enough. The old adage of understanding either software or hardware blurs when it comes to the disk subsystem. The variety of configurations available for the disk subsystem is numerous. To get a handle on this important topic, we will follow the data flow from the disk drive to the CPU. If you understand the flow of data through the server hardware and NT Server itself, how the disk subsystems work becomes much more apparent. With this knowledge, it is then easier to detect where bottlenecks really are and how to tune and size your NT Server solution.

We will start with a high level view of the data paths involved between getting the data from the disk drive to the CPU. Using this data path as a guide, each of the critical hardware components are reviewed from a performance perspective illustrating some of the technology's strengths and weaknesses. Once the disk subsystem hardware is discussed, we'll then investigate how NT Server takes advantage of it. After these foundations are in place, key sizing and tuning concepts that revolve around the disk subsystem are explored.

Disk Subsystem Technology: Following the Data

All that data needed for an enterprise level server is not capable of being kept in RAM, even with NT Server Enterprise Edition. A fast disk subsystem lends itself to providing significant transaction rates and excellent overall server performance. The Standard High Volume (SHV) server logical diagram that was used in earlier chapters is utilized here as our reference server architecture. Adding the primary components required in accessing the disk subsystem, we arrive at the following logical diagram (Figure 6–1).

It is important to understand the different transfer rates of each component of the server's disk subsystem. This information helps you to identify potential bottlenecks that can throttle your server's overall performance. In Figure 6–1 below, data travels from the actual disk drive to the embedded disk controller located on the disk drive unit (<10 Mbytes/sec), up the Ultra Fast/Wide SCSI channel 2 at 40 Mbytes/sec, through PCI Slot 1 on PCI Bus 1 at 133 Mbytes/sec to the Memory subsystem (533 Mbytes/sec), and then transferred to the CPU at a P6 system bus speed of 533 Mbytes/sec.

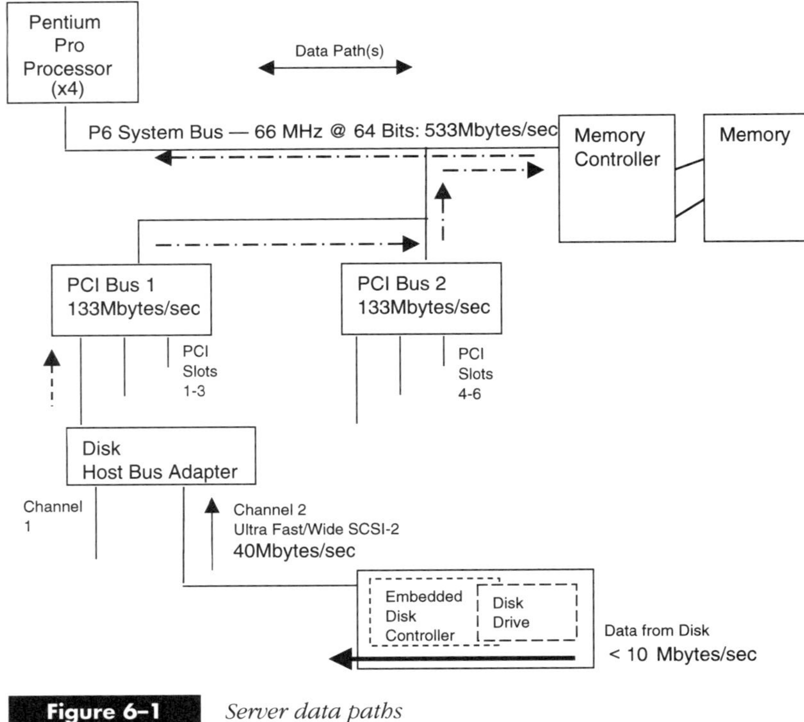

Figure 6–1 *Server data paths*

Review each link in the data path. It is the weakest link that throttles the overall disk subsystem performance.

If one component is trying to send more data than the next component can handle, there is a bottleneck. An analogy to this is a plumbing example. If the primary water pipe carrying water away from your basement is five inches in diameter and you have five two inch pipes placing water into the five inch pipe, water will be spilling out.

By completing a little mathematical word problem, you can avoid bottlenecks even before they begin. For example, placing two 3 channel Ultra Fast and Wide SCSI cards (theoretical aggregate maximum throughput of 2x[3x40 Mbytes/sec] = 240 Bytes/sec) into a single PCI bus can overwhelm the single PCI Bus data link if all of the SCSI channels were active. A single PCI bus can only support a theoretical maximum of 133 Mbytes/sec. Jamming 240 Mbytes/sec of data into it just does not work very well. If this configuration were actually implemented, you would have created a bottleneck from the start. Placing each one of the 3 channel Ultra Fast and Wide SCSI cards onto their own respective PCI bus will spread the disk I/O activities across 266 Mbytes of total aggregate PCI bus throughput.

Disk Drive Technology

The disk drive itself is the slowest link of the data path. A disk drive is a series of stacked platters (Figure 6–3) with very small heads that read and write the data to the various platters. These platters rotate or spin at very high speeds, currently up to 10,000 rpm. As disk requests come down from NT Server, the heads move accordingly over the platters to obtain the requested data. The following is an illustration of a disk drive as if you were looking at it from a bird's eye view (Figure 6–2) and from the side (Figure 6–3):

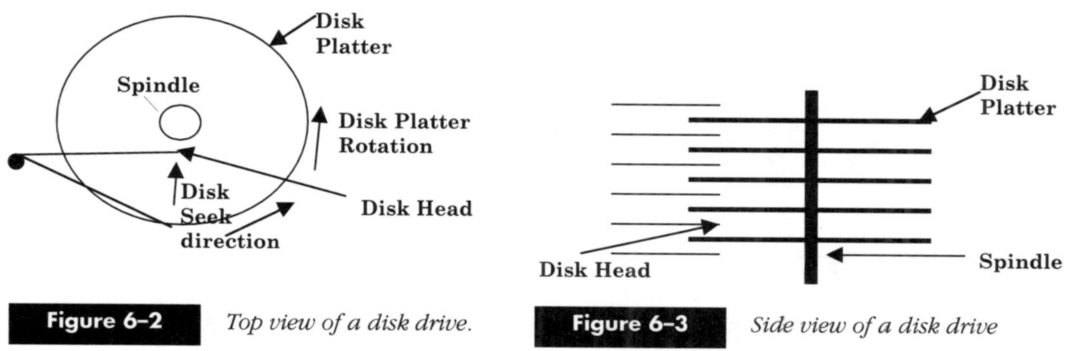

Figure 6–2 *Top view of a disk drive.*

Figure 6–3 *Side view of a disk drive*

When referring to the disk drives, there are a variety of terms describing the different disk operations. From a disk vendor perspective, one of their goals is to lower the amount of time required when retrieving data from a disk drive. Table 6.1 defines the most common terms.

Table 6.1 Disk drive technology definitions.

Disk Drive Related Term	Definition
Track	A logically defined band of data on the disk platter. Envision tracks as concentric circles on the disk platter (Figure 6-4).
Sector	A logical track is divided into smaller chucks of data referred to as sectors (Figure 6-4).
Latency	The time required for the disk platter to spin one complete revolution.
Average Latency	The time that the disk head waits for a sector to arrive as the disk platter rotates. On average, you will have to wait for approximately one half the rotational time of the drive platter for the sector to arrive.
Seek Time	The time required for the motion of the disk head as it moves to/from a particular track on the disk platter (Figure 6-4).
Average Seek Time	The time required for disk head to move to/from a particular track on the disk drive platter. On average, this will be the time it takes the disk head to travel half way across the disk platter.
Average Access Time	The average length of time it takes the disk to seek to the required track plus the amount of time it takes for the disk to spin the data under the head (Average Seek Time + Average Latency)
Transfer Rate	The speed at which the data bits are being transferred to/from the internal disk drive buffer.
NT Server Transfer Rate	The speed at which the data bits are being transferred externally from the disk drive through the SCSI data path to the server.
Disk Platter Rotation Revolutions Per Minute (RPM)	The measurement of the rotational speed of a disk drive platters on a per minute basis. How fast the disk platters spin.

Basic Disk Drive Operation

Each disk drive is a stack of disk platters that are broken into cylinders, tracks, sectors, and clusters. When the disk drive is low-level formatted, logical tracks (logical concentric circles on the disk platters used for locating data on the disk itself) are established and the disk geometry of the disk drive is determined. Low-level formatting is not normally a function available directly from NT Server but is provided by the host bus adapter vendor. For example, the low level format tool for Adaptec SCSI host bus adapters are available when a server starts by depressing "[CTRL] + a" at the same time during the server's power on self test (POST) as the Adaptec SCSI adapter is detected by the server. This type of host bus adapter tool is either started during the POST of the server or by booting the server into MS-DOS using a boot floppy and then running the host bus adapter tool. Track numbers start at 0, where track 0 is the outermost track of the disk. These outermost tracks of the disk are actually the fastest portion of the disk drive.

This is one of the reasons disk drive manufacturers generally provide throughput in ranges (for example 3-5 Mbtes/sec) when describing their products. Performance is not really affected until the available disk drive space is less than 30 percent. When 70 percent of the disk drive is used, the remaining free space is located closer to the disk's spindle at the center of the disk drive, which operates at a lower performance level. Each track is broken down into sectors, normally 512 Kbytes in size. Part of the process completed when you format a disk drive under NT Server using the "format" command or Disk Administrator is that these sectors get grouped into clusters. Clusters are referenced under NT Server as the Allocation Unit Size (ALU) for the file system. Cylinders are the vertical stacking of tracks. Figure 6–4 depicts tracks, sectors, and clusters:

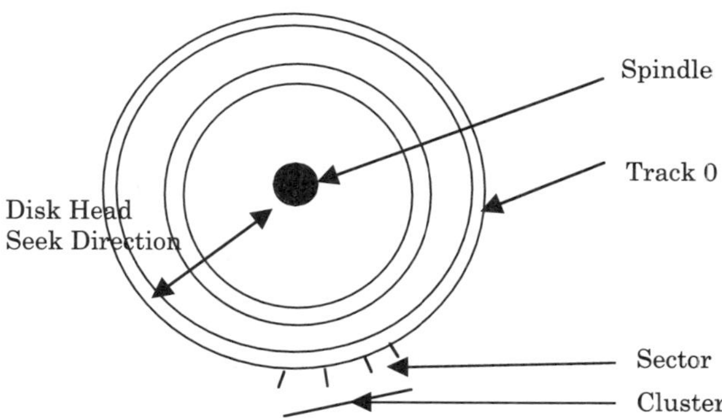

Figure 6–4 *Disk spindle, track, sector, and cluster.*

Disk Drive Performance

How do these disk drive definitions relate to overall performance? When the data requested by an NT Server process is identified on the disk drive, the disk head (which is a small transducer that reads magnetic medium) seeks to the appropriate track. The head then waits for the platter to spin until the proper sector of data is under the disk head. Once the data is under the head, the data is read. The combination of the seek and rotational time associated with obtaining the data is the access time. This data is then transferred to the embedded disk controller that is physically located on the disk drive unit. The embedded controller is the equivalent of a miniaturized computer, as it contains a small CPU and its own memory to obtain and transfer data from the physical disk drive.

The most costly portions of this process is the time it takes for the head to move to the correct track, for example, seek time and the rotation time of the disks platters (latency). Cost here is referenced in time. The longer it takes for the physical activity to be completed, the longer the process under NT Server must wait for its data. To get an understanding of what contributes to the relative time required to get data from the disk subsystem up to the PCI bus, look at the pie chart in Figure 6–5.

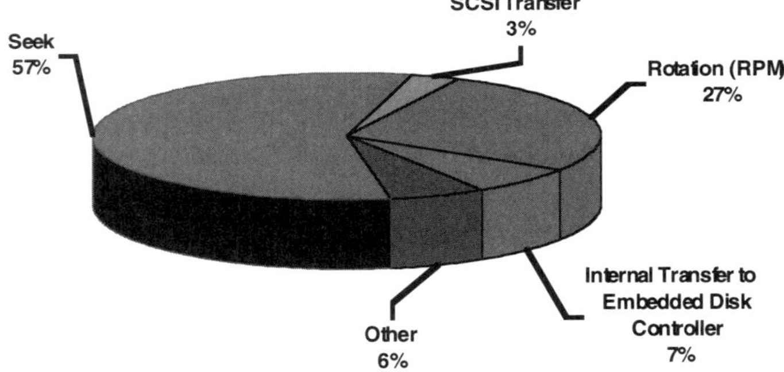

Figure 6–5 *Relative size of disk I/O time components for random disk I/O.*

Source: Page 266, Brian Wong, Configuration and Capacity Planning for Solaris Servers.

Disk Drive Selection

Now that some of the key technologies used to implement disk technology are reviewed, how do you take advantage of them? Later in this chapter, we will reference this information when explaining RAID technology and NT Server disk subsystem tuning techniques. For now, use this knowledge when selecting the disk drive technology to implement in your server. Unless you're a vendor, you will not actually be changing the internal disk characteristics. What you can do though, is select the fastest disk drive possible that fits into your budget. Table 6.2 charts some of the current disk drive technologies found after a quick check on the Internet.

Table 6.2 Disk drive technology specifications.

Brand	Capacity (GB)	Embedded Disk Controller Buffer Size	RPM	Seek Time (ms)	SCSI Type
IBM UltraStar	4.3	512 Kbytes	5400	8	Ultra SCSI
Seagate Barracuda	4.5	512 Kbytes	7200	8	Ultra SCSI
Seagate Barracuda	4.5	512 Kbytes	10,000	7.5	Ultra SCSI
Quantum Viking	4.5	512 Kbytes	7200	8	Ultra SCSI

Actual NT Server Disk Subsystem Performance

Performance information provided by vendors can be impressive. For some of the drives listed in Table 6.2, the vendor's list corresponding sustained data rates up to 20 Mbytes/sec. Unfortunately, this performance information is not measured for actual NT Server application environments, so mileage will vary. When a disk drive vendor provides a throughput measure for a specific disk drive, they typically quote the burst speed from the embedded disk controller cache to the SCSI bus. This does not take into consideration the most costly portion of the disk activity, the actual physical activities (seek and rotation) associated with obtaining data. Vendors are in business to sell disks, so this recording practice is accepted and common. Sometimes more relevant data is available. When choosing a disk drive unit or comparing them, look closely at the fine print so that you can determine what they are really reporting.

To determine a general rule of thumb about the performance that is actually provided for your environment, you can create a complete server level stress test, develop your baseline, then change a single component (disk drive or disk array) and determine what effect it has. This technique is illustrated in the Chapter 8 file server case study when one disk array is replaced by another disk array. You can also test components in your NT Server on a per-component basis in a controlled environment. There are various publicly available component-testing tools such as Intel's Galileo. More information about Galileo can be obtained by visiting their website at *http://developer.intel.com/design/servers/devtools/iometer*. The NT Server Resource Kit also contains a disk-testing tool called response probe. The NT Server Resource Kit provides a thorough explanation of the use of the response tool, but some trade magazines, such as the Windows NT Systems March 1998 issue, provide condensed instructions on its use.

Many of the disk-testing tools that exercise disk I/O do so by setting the appropriate application code flags to bypass the NT Server file system cache and test the physical disk drive directly. Although this technique is useful in pure performance testing environments, I prefer to use tools that test server components in ways that closely represent actual NT Server environments. In most environments, NT Server's file system cache is used. There are times, however, when the file system cache is either not effective because the environment is truly random in nature, or it is defeated due to the sheer size of the files being moved to and from the disk drives. In either case, the file system cache influences the overall throughput achieved. Even applications that do bypass the file system cache implement their own file caching strategies, which results in similar results.

Disk Subsystem from an Application Perspective

To determine the throughput thata single disk drive can achieve, I employed the Neal Nelson Business Benchmark suite for NT. This test suite is not publicly available, but is a commercial product. If you are interested in this product, you can contact the company directly at (312) 755-1000 (sorry, no external website URL available). Using this suite of tests, various disk loads were placed on an NCR S46 server with 128 Mbytes of RAM, two Pentium Pro CPUs, and three Ultra Fast and Wide SCSI 7200 RPM disk drives. One disk drive was configured with NT Server, one housed the Pagefile, and one drive was used as the workload target. The test suite was run up to a 20-copy workload level which corresponds to 400 users and a disk work file size of 780 Mbytes. At this heavy load, the file system cache on a 128 Mbyte server is defeated, and the actual performance of the disk drive is obtained in a simulated multiuser environment. It is important to note that this is a multiuser/threaded test which is much more realistic of an NT Server environment compared to tests that only exercise the disk subsystem under a single user/thread workload. Table 6.3 shows the results for various disk characteristic environments.

Table 6.3 Physical disk performance.

Test Characteristics using 780 Mbyte Work File	**Single 7200 RPM Fast/Wide SCSI Disk Drive Configuration** **Throughput achieved as reported by the application (Mbytes/sec)**
Sequential Reads of 1024 Byte Records	2.01
Sequential Writes of 1024 Byte Records	0.66
Sequential Reads of 8192 Byte Records	1.93
Pseudo Random Reads of 4096 Byte Records	0.61

The disk vendor rated this particular disk drive at 3.9 Mbytes/sec to 6.6 Mbytes/sec. This is substantially less than what was recorded from the disk specifications provided, but remember that this test measured the disk performance from an application, not pure hardware, perspective. Vendors are not really trying to deceive you, they are just playing the benchmark marketing game and measuring their performance from a pure hardware, not application, perspective. For example, to achieve the 3.9 Mbytes/sec to 6.6 Mbytes/sec, the vendor utilized a sector size of 2 Mbytes. Most commercial SCSI host bus adapters default to a sector size of 512 Kbytes, a big difference.

The throughput levels obtained when completing disk activities are based on your user's access patterns and application environment. How efficient the application is with its disk I/O usage and how it implements block and buffer sizes directly influences that amount of throughput possible. If an application utilizes very large block and buffer sizes, much higher throughput levels can be achieved. Table 6.3 provides good information that we will utilize later in this chapter when detecting bottlenecks, tuning, and sizing NT Server's disk subsystem. Also, be careful of single-user and multiuser environments. Multiuser environments are much more difficult to support and subsequently much more stressful on NT server's disk subsystem.

Quick Disk and SCSI Bus Sizing Example

If, for example, your environment is sequentially read intensive, a single Fast and Wide SCSI channel (40 Mbytes/sec) could support a configuration up to 15–20 Fast and Wide SCSI disk drives (30–40 Mbytes/sec aggregate). Of course, your mileage may vary, but this is a good sizing starting point. If the server application and workload mix is very efficient, this may be too many disk drives for a single SCSI channel. Conversely, if the application and workload mix is more random in nature or less efficient, additional disk drives per SCSI channel can be configured.

Disk Workload Supported

Throughput is only one measure of a disk drive performance. The number of disk I/O operations that a disk drive can support is also very important. An I/O request is a general term that refers to a read or write request. As the number of I/Os per second increases, the disk drive provides higher and higher throughput until the Logical Disk: % Disk time increases over the 60–80 percent range. % Disk time is the percentage of elapsed time that the disk drive is busy servicing read or write requests. Above 80 percent Disk time, the disk drive's response time performance can begin to degrade beyond acceptable levels. Degradation experienced is the amount of time an NT Server process must wait for the disk operation to complete.

What actually occurs is that the disk drive itself can only support a certain level of disk activity as defined by the number of I/O operations per second. When the amount of time the disk drive is busy increases, so do the I/O operations per second, and the throughput. This sounds great. Your throughput is increasing and more data is being retrieved/sent from the disk drive. Unfortunately, it takes longer to service those disk I/O requests as the disk gets busy. More work is completed (throughput), but as the disk drive's utilization increases past 80 percent, the response time back to the requested process falls off. Depending on which vendor you approach and your environment, Table 6.4 outlines the number of I/Os per second a single disk drive can support.

Table 6.4 Disk workload chart.

Disk Characteristics	4 GB Fast/Wide 7200 RPM SCSI Disk Drive Supported I/Os per second
Sequential Writes (typified by log files)	150–190
Random Read/Writes (typified by multiuser databases)	50–80
Mixed Environment Average	100

You can determine the I/Os per second by looking at Perfmon's logical disk counter: transfers/sec. To determine how long the I/O operations are taking to complete, review Average Disk sec/read, Average Disk sec/write and Average Disk transfers/sec. ***Take note that the amount of work that a single disk drive can support does not noticeably increase as disk capacity increases.***

Figure 6–6 was obtained from a server when the user load was increased in blocks of 50 users against the same disk I/O subsystem that consisted of 30 4 GB disk drives. Measurements were taken of the various disk utilization levels as the user loads increased. Note how the amount of time a process's disk request must stay in the disk queue before receiving service increased.

This graph illustrates that when the disk is under increased workload levels noted by the %Disk Time, the time disk requests must wait in the disk queue increases drastically. What was interesting in this specific NT Server environment was that the throughput provided increased along with Average Time in Queue for the disk requests. So there is a tradeoff, response time in essence degrades, but the throughput increases. What is best? It depends on your environment.

The %Disk Time counter under Perfmon can be deceiving. A high % disk time alone is not a true qualifier of an overworked disk drive in an NT Server environment. Table 6–4 also helps to provide insight into determining when a disk drive is overworked. The Perfmon data in Figure 6–7 was collected and graphed from another NT Server environment.

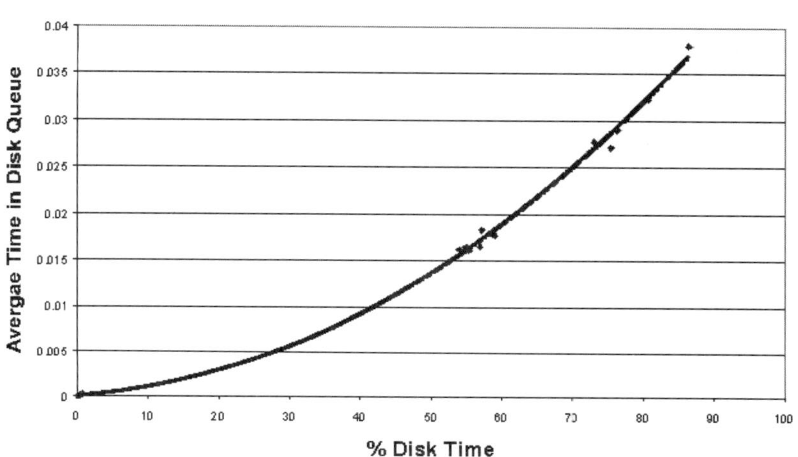

Figure 6–6 *Disk subsystem average queue time.*

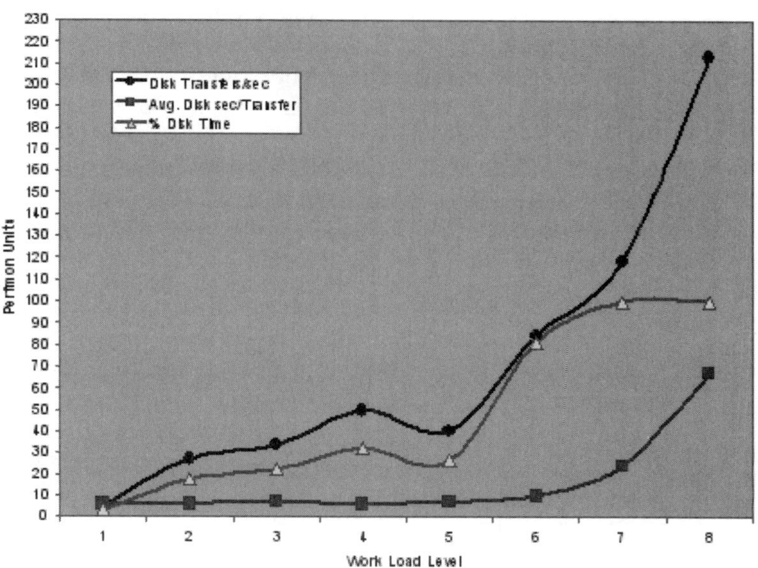

Figure 6–7 *Single disk workload graph.*

Grasping how long a millisecond is does not come easy for everyone (including me), so the Average Disk second/Transfer is scaled for this graph (Figure 6–7) by a factor of 1000. The %Disk Time counter reaches a maximum of 100 percent and plateaus. When the %Disk Time grew above 80 percent, the I/Os per second shown by Disk transfers/sec grew to 65 and the Average Disk seconds/Transfer begins to increase. The disk drive at this point began to get overloaded. The workload for this environment was random in nature; thus, a single disk drive can support roughly 50-80 I/O operations per second. When the Disk Transfers/sec are lower than 80, response time is less than a normalized 10 seconds (11 ms), which is acceptable in most environments. But, as the I/O's second (workload) increases beyond what the single disk drive can support, the response time becomes unacceptable. In fact, as the I/O workload moves past 80 I/Os per second, the disk drive saturation is so great that the response time from the disk increases six times! Imagine a process having to wait 67 normalized seconds (67 ms) for a disk access. That is an eternity from the CPU's perspective. Follow the sizing and tuning recommendations later in this chapter to avoid this overworked disk situation from happening to you.

SCSI Bus Technology from a Practical Perspective

SCSI stands for Small Computer System Interface peripheral bus and is the most common and predominant technology used to connect disk devices to servers in use today. Other technologies, once on the horizon, are now beginning to show themselves in the marketplace, but none are as prevalent as SCSI. In fact, according to Greg P Shultz's article in a recent SysAdmin column (March 1998), SCSI is predicted to be the dominant storage interface until 1999, when fibre channel should start gathering more momentum. (I will briefly touch on fiber channel later in this chapter.) SCSI buses are available in a variety of technology standards.

One of the advantages of SCSI is that the intelligence of the bus is actually spread across the peripheral devices. Each SCSI device normally has an embedded controller built into it, such as a SCSI disk drive. SCSI has various electrical standards associated with it as well as a standard protocol, which allows a host bus adapter to communicate with the devices on the bus. Intelligent SCSI devices receive SCSI commands and can disconnect from the SCSI bus while completing the requested action, such as obtaining a block of data from a disk array. In this way, other devices are not waiting to access the bus while other devices are making the necessary calculations to complete the request. Modern SCSI bus technology (past SCSI-2) allows these SCSI commands to be queued so that the embedded controller can decide on which commands to execute first for optimum performance.

As with any protocol implementation, the protocol adds some overhead to the bus for each transaction. When smaller Allocation Unit (ALU) sizes are in use by NT Server, more of the available SCSI bandwidth is used for SCSI protocol overhead. Conversely, when larger ALU sizes are implemented under NT Server, less SCSI bandwidth is sacrificed to SCSI command overhead; thus, more bandwidth is available for actual data. The larger the block size used for data transfer, the higher overall throughputs can be achieved. Due to this SCSI command protocol overhead, a general rule of thumb is not to expect more than 70-90 percent of the theoretical SCSI I/O channel bandwidth to be actually available for data. Table 6–5 charts SCSI technologies.

Table 6.5 SCSI Technology Chart.

					Maximum Bus Length (Meters)	
SCSI Interface	**Theoretical Maximum Bandwidth (Mbytes/ sec)**	***Practical Bandwidth (Mbytes/ sec)***	**Bus Width (Bits)**	**Maximum Number of SCSI Devices**	**Single Ended**	**Differential**
SCSI-1	5	*4*	8	8	6	25
Fast Narrow SCSI-2	10	*8*	8	8	6	25
Fast Wide SCSI-2	20	*16*	16	16	6	25
Ultra SCSI-3	20	*16*	8	8	1.5	25
	20	*16*	8	4	3	NA
Ultra Wide SCSI-3	40	*32*	16	16	NA	25
	40	*32*	16	8	1.5	NA
	40	*32*	16	4	3	NA
Ultra2 SCSI Fast 40	40	*32*	8	2	NA	25
	40	*32*	8	8	NA	12
Wide Ultra2 SCSI Fast 40	80	*64*	16	16	NA	12
Fibre-Channel FC-AL (SCSI_FCP)	100	*N/A*	16	126	30 Meters for Copper	2,000-10,000 Meters

Primary data from SysAdmin Journal, February 1998, Greg Shultz, p. 8

Implementing SCSI Technology

So which SCSI technology is best for you? Fortunately, SCSI technology auto negotiates the protocol and therefore the subsequent speed for devices on the SCSI bus. This is good and bad. The auto negotiation lowers the number of problems encountered when migrating or updating your disk technology. Unfortunately, you can't have it all in SCSI world. If the SCSI bus you are implementing has a combination of Fast Wide SCSI-2 devices and Ultra Wide SCSI-3 devices, you are limited to running the SCSI bus at the lowest common speed, which, in this case, would be Fast Wide SCSI-2 device. If you try to run a SCSI channel at Ultra SCSI speeds (normally set with the HBA configuration software not via NT Server) with a staggered set of disk technologies, SCSI timeouts will occur due to the variances in the impedance of the ULTRA SCSI and non Ultra SCSI devices. These SCSI timeouts are routed to either NT Server's event log or to the HBA specific monitoring software under NT Server or both.

Is there that much discrepancy between Ultra Wide SCSI-2 operating at 40 Mbytes/sec versus Fast Wide SCSI-2 operating at 20 Mbytes? The primary difference is the number of disk drives that each SCSI bus can support before becoming saturated. If you placed a single disk drive on either bus in a typical NT Server environment, you would not notice a significant performance difference. Why? As observed in Figure 6–5 "Relative Size of Disk I/O Time Components for Random Disk I/O," most of the time associated with getting data from the disk drive is due to the disk seek movements and latency times occurred from platter rotation. Initial tests show that transfers using Ultra Wide SCSI-3 are between 0.1 to 0.3 milliseconds faster than Fast Wide SCSI-2. This is not quite enough to rip out your current Fast Wide SCSI-2 investment and replace it with Ultra Wide SCSI-3. However, the price of Ultra Wide SCSI-3 is quite competitive with Fast Wide SCSI-2, so if you are planning a new disk subsystem, the slightly faster Ultra Wide SCSI-3 solution is easily justified.

What Ultra Wide SCSI-3 does bring is the capability of supporting more disk drives on a single SCSI bus than was previously possible. If you expect 2Mbytes/sec of throughput from each disk drive, then you can now configure 20 disk drives per SCSI bus channel versus a previous maximum of 10. These disk drive to SCSI bus ratios are based on the initial best-case throughput estimate of 2 Mbytes/sec. To support high numbers of disk drives on a single SCSI channel, intelligent RAID devices are required.

Determining SCSI Bus Throughput Under NT Server

How can you tell how many disk drives to configure per SCSI bus? First, understand your server environment. NT Server does not instinctively throw up a red flag and alert you to the fact that your SCSI channel is saturated. A good rule of thumb is to estimate 2 Mbytes/second for general sequential environments and 0.6 Mbyte/sec for random disk I/O based environments of throughput for each disk drive. For example, if you are implementing a single Fast Wide SCSI –2 channel that will support a random disk I/O environment, you can configure up to 27 disk drives per Fast Wide SCSI –2 channel as an NT Server initial disk subsystem sizing estimate.

How can you be sure that you have not overconfigured or underconfigured the Fast Wide SCSI channel? Proactively monitor your server's performance during regular business operations. One technique to determine the throughput of the SCSI bus under NT Server is to use Perfmon's Logical Disk object's Disk Bytes/sec counter. This counter reports the data rate in bytes that are transferred to or from the disk during write or read operations. Using Perfmon, select LogicalDisk:Disk Bytes/sec and then select all of the disk drives connected to the SCSI channel you are investigating. You will need to understand the physical hardware server connections to correlate which disk drives are on which SCSI bus. Then, sum the average, minimum, and maximum values report under Disk Bytes/sec for each of the disk drives on a particular SCSI channel by hand, or export the chart to a spread sheet file and then sum up the results. Once you get the final result, compare this value to the theoretical and practical SCSI throughput values shown in the SCSI technology chart shown in Figure 6–5. If the value of the summed Disk Bytes/sec is within 20 percent of the practical maximum throughput of the bus, consider adding another SCSI channel. If the summation values are found to be much less than the practical SCSI throughput shown in the SCSI technology chart, you have room to add more drives to the current SCSI channel.

FibreChannel

FibreChannel is an up and coming technology poised to eventually replace SCSI technology as the disk subsystem interconnect of choice. FibreChannel is based on ANSI standards similar to SCSI and is the next step in the disk I/O connectivity evolution. Parallel SCSI will eventually reach its electrical limitations, hence slowing its continued performance enhancements. Of course, every time you hear this, someone at a place like Bell Labs comes up with a creative solution to overcome accepted electrical characteristics. In lieu of this happening, FibreChannel brings new options to the disk subsystem realm.

FibreChannel's primary strength lays in the fact that it can be implemented over fiber optics and is serial in nature opposed to the parallel nature of SCSI. With the use of fiber optics, FibreChannel provides increased throughput, less distance limitations, and more topology implementation options than traditional SCSI technologies. Currently, throughput for a FibreChannel bus ranges up to 100 Mbytes/sec. When implementing FibreChannel, various topologies can be used which encompass arbitrated loop (most common), point to point, and switched implementations. Where differential SCSI is limited to 25 meters from the server to the disk drive, the fiber optic implementation of FibreChannel allows for distances up to 10,000 meters. This increased distance option allows for more flexibility in planning for disasters and overall system architectures.

Even with the new features and possibilities that FibreChannel brings, the same concepts apply that we used when reviewing SCSI technologies. The primary performance hindrance of a disk drive attached to a FibreChannel bus is still the physical disk drive limitations of the disk drive itself. With FibreChannel, more disk drives per FibreChannel bus channel can be supported due to the higher available throughput.

FibreChannel is initially being offered as a host bus adapter to attach external disk drives with little intelligence in the host bus adapter. Without any inherent intelligence, FibreChannel host bus adapters are not currently providing much in the way of hardware RAID support. This limits the current viability of this technology in the midrange NT Server space. In the higher end of the NT Server space, FibreChannel host bus adapters are more of a possibility when paired with an intelligent external disk array device. In this configuration, the intelligent external disk array device provides the hardware RAID implementation and the FibreChannel host bus adapter provides the connectivity back into the server. As the FibreChannel technology matures and more products become available, this technology will become more of a viable option in the price sensitive NT Server Super Server product space.

Host Bus Adapters

The next step in the data path is to get the requested data from the SCSI bus onto the PCI bus. The HBA performs this operation. HBAs provide a range of functions from basic SCSI connectivity to complex RAID support. There are four primary distinguishable features that separate the various HBAs available today: the number and type of SCSI channels supported, the amount of server CPU overhead introduced, RAID support level, and I/O workload supported.

The channel density that a SCSI HBA supports impacts the amount of disk devices that NT Server can support and how they are configured in the server. Today, one HBA can support from one to four onboard SCSI channels. This allows for the conservation of those precious PCI slots available on the server. Utilizing these higher densities HBAs, an SHV based server can support up to five HBAs for a total of 20 SCSI channels. Whether or not configuring that many SCSI channels in a single SHV based NT Server is a good idea is dependent upon your environment. If you do implement high numbers of HBAs in a single Intel based SHV server, you will most likely run into a shortage of interrupts. Each server vendor implements the setup of interrupts in a slightly different manner, so I will refer you to your vendor's server documentation for the steps to follow for interrupt control.

Server Interrupt Configuration Strategy

Regardless of how you set the interrupts, if you must share interrupts between devices configured in your server, try to share the interrupts between devices which use the same NT device driver. This helps to improve overall performance. The concept of plug and play PCI takes a backseat when configuring high end NT Servers that require sharable PCI interrupts to support higher number of peripheral devices. NT Server does provide a tool, Windows NT Diagnostics (found under Start|Programs|Administrative Tools|Windows NT Diagnostics) that helps to determine which interrupts are associated with which devices. There is a wealth of low level NT Server information provided by this tool. If you have not already investigated this tool, I urge you to take a moment to see what it has to offer. This tool can also be run from the command line on local or remote NT Servers and is an easy technique to get a quick inventory of an NT Server. Winmsd.exe is the command line, Windows NT Diagnostics. Run the command Winmsd.exe /? from the command line and a pop up window with available options are shown. Another, more flexible version winmsd.exe is winmsdp.exe. Figure 6–8 shows a screen shot of the interrupt information provided by Windows NT Diagnostics for a small NT Server.

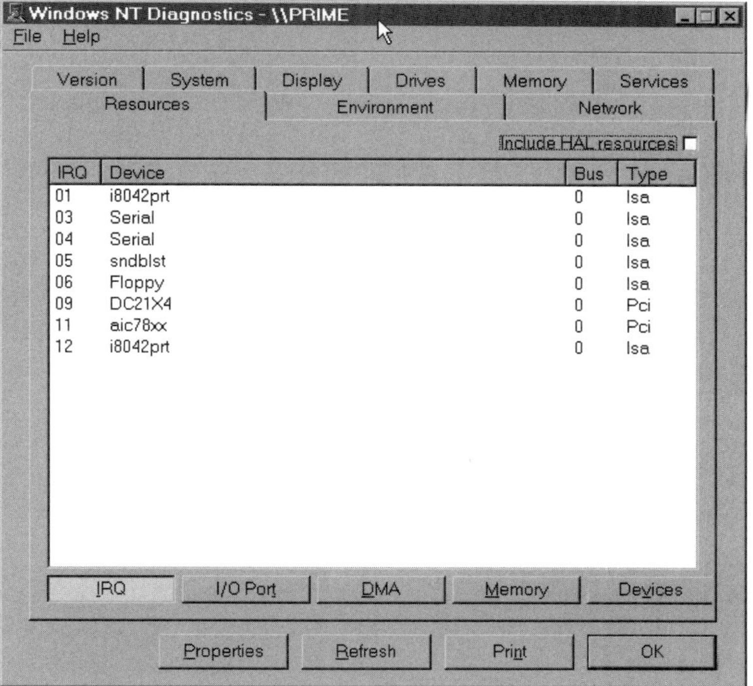

Figure 6–8 *Using Windows NT Diagnostics to determine interrupt levels for devices.*

Host Bus Adapter and CPU Power

Each HBA interrupts NT Server when an operation requires server CPU intervention. The amount of CPU cycles required varies between HBAs. The CPU time required to service an HBA is considered as the overhead the HBA places onto the server. This overhead is actually good in one sense because it is used to get data from the disk drives to the CPU so that productive work can be completed. Other I/O devices, such as network interface cards, also introduce this CPU interrupt overhead. It is important to be aware that CPU cycles are required to drive the I/O subsystem. For smaller servers that are configured with small disk subsystems, the CPU overhead introduced by the disk arrays is not significant enough to worry about. As NT Server solutions get larger and larger, the amount of CPU cycles required to drive the disk subsystem becomes more of an influencing factor. If the server application requires a great deal of computational power and there is a large amount of disk I/O activity, CPU power must be planned for to support both.

Various vendor specification sheets for four or eight CPU Pentium Pro servers state that multiple terabytes of disk can be connected to one server. One vendor stated support for 7 Terabytes. From a connectivity perspective this is possible, but the server will never be able to drive the disk subsystem if all of the disks and applications were active. Somewhere a balance must be found. If you examine the TPC-C benchmarks closely, for example, you would notice that for the larger two to four CPU NT Server benchmarks, 300 to 400 GB of disk drive space on average is configured. In these benchmark environments, vendors wish to get the highest performance rating at the lowest cost. For this reason, disks are normally not configured into the solution unless they are actually in use. If you match up the server hardware you have obtained and a benchmark that emulates your environment to published industry benchmarks, such as TPC-C, you can gather some insight into how many active disk drives can realistically be supported by your server.

These test results are subject to many factors such as NT Server version, database version, and numbers of clients, but still provide a rough estimate of the relative sizing between CPUs, SCSI channels, and disk drives in a client server database environment. Table 6.6 provides some insight to the CPU power and disk subsystem configuration used for some TPC-C benchmarks.

Table 6.6 Utilizing TPC-C results to determine relative overall server performance.

Number & Type of CPUs	Memory	Number of HBAs	Number and type of Disk Drives	Amount of Disk Space Configured (approximately)	Disk Drives per SCSI Channel
2 Pentium Pro 200 MHz/ 512 K	2 GB	5 2-Channel	79 4.3-GB 1 9.1-GB	348 GB	9
2 Pentium Pro 200 MHz/ 512 K	2 GB	6 2-Channel	79 4.3-GB 4 9.1-GB	348 GB	8
2 Pentium Pro 200 MHz/ 512 K	1 GB	4 3-Channel	72 4.3-GB 1 9.1-GB	318 GB	6
4 Pentium Pro 200 MHz/ 512 K	2 GB	3 4-Channel	114 4.3-GB	490 GB	10
8 Pentium Pro 200 MHz/ 1 MB	4 GB	2 2-Channel 7 1-Channel	2 4.3-GB 200 9.1-GB	1800 GB	20

HBA and Disk Drive Workload Sizing Example

There was more than just throughput to consider when reviewing a disk drive's performance and there is more to consider than just the number of SCSI channels that an HBA can support. When sizing the number of HBAs required, consider the theoretical I/Os per second that they can support as well. For example, if you are configuring 10 disk drives for a sequentially intensive disk subsystem environment, do the associated math. Each 7200-RPM SCSI disk drive in a sequential environment should be able to support up to 190 disk I/O operations per second and 2 Mbytes/sec of throughput. A 10 disk drive implementation would therefore require an HBA or HBAs that can support 1900 I/O's sec and 20 Mbytes/sec of aggregate throughput. To fulfill this outlined requirement, a 2 Channel Ultra Wide SCSI-3 Mylex DAC960PJ HBA could be used. A Mylex DAC960PJ HBA meets the throughput requirement (40 Mbytes/sec per channel) and allows room for growth by providing a second usable SCSI channel and has a workload rating of 2400 I/Os per second, which also provides room for growth. You can obtain this type of performance data from the server or HBA vendor's website, or by contacting them directly. The information used in this example was downloaded directly from the Mylex website (*http://www.mylex.com*).

I/O Bus Technology

From the peripheral adapter (HBA, NIC, etc.), data is passed to the Peripheral Component Interconnect (PCI) based I/O bus on its way to the system bus. The two PCI buses illustrated in the logical SHV diagram (Figure 6–1) each provide 133 Mbytes/sec (32 bit bus operating at 33 Mhz) of burst bandwidth and 80 Mbytes of sustained throughput. A PCI slot is not the same as a PCI bus. This distinction is often not clear in vendor literature, particularly for smaller 2 CPU servers. If there are two distinct peer PCI buses, 266 Mbytes/sec of aggregate I/O throughput is available to the server. The number of PCI slots per PCI bus is based on the number of electrical loads the PCI bus can support. On average, between three to five PCI slots are available per PCI bus. Occasionally, the PCI devices connected to a specific PCI bus are somewhat hidden, as they are connected to the PCI bus via a direct connection on the motherboard, not through a PCI slot.

To increase the number of PCI slots available on a single PCI bus, vendors can implement a PCI bridge. What a PCI bridge provides is an electrical extension of a single PCI bus. This increases the number of PCI slots available, but does not increase the bandwidth provided. On a single PCI bus based server that utilizes a PCI bridge to extend the PCI bus, the I/O throughput is still limited to 133 Mbytes/sec.

I/O Bus Importance

As larger NT Server solutions are developed to support higher numbers of concurrent users, the I/O bus is a common physical server resource that becomes saturated. To overcome the basic SHV limitation of only providing two peer PCI buses, higher end NT Servers are now available which provide more than two peer PCI I/O buses. Depending on the vendor, up to 4 peer PCI bus servers are now available which provide 532 Mbytes/sec of aggregate I/O throughput. With additional peer PCI buses, more PCI slots also become available. For example, the NCR 4380 supports 14 PCI slots spread across 4 peer PCI buses.

Placing 10 Quad Ultra Wide SCSI-3 bus adapters across the 4 peer PCI buses in an NCR 4380 provides for 400 Mbytes/sec of available SCSI throughput. This 400Mbytes/sec of potential SCSI throughput feeds 532Mbytes/sec of total aggregate I/O subsystem throughput, thus no I/O bottlenecks for this portion of the data path. These super NT Servers are configurable up to 8 Pentium Pro CPUs. Although CPUs are normally the centers of attention, it is the increased I/O throughput that provides the real advantage for databases and other I/O intense server applications. Vendors currently shipping their own 8 CPU NT Server designs that support 4 peer PCI buses are Axil Computer Corporation (*http://www.Axil.com*), a division of Hyundai, and NCR Corporation based in Dayton, OH (*http://www.NCR.com*).

I/O Bus Selection

From a legacy perspective, Intel-based servers have supported numerous system bus and I/O bus technologies throughout the years. Some environments still require the use of legacy peripheral adapters such as those based on Industry Standard Architecture (ISA, 8 Mbytes/sec), Extended Industry Standard Architecture (EISA, 33 Mbytes/sec), and Micro Channel (MCA, 80 Mbytes/sec) I/O busses. EISA and ISA bus support is still designed into many PCI based servers today. The SHV based server provides a bridge to an EISA I/O bus, which provides several slots for EISA/ISA based I/O cards. Micro Channel based servers are still available from a handful of vendors, but are rarely being produced with the most recent Intel or DEC CPU architectures that are supported by NT Server.

Avoid using any legacy bus based I/O cards. Unless you have no other choice for your environments, legacy based I/O cards (ISA, EISA, and MCA) should never be used in your enterprise class NT Servers. These older I/O cards do not provide nearly the same level of performance of modern 32 bit PCI cards that support bus mastering, direct DMA support, and PCI burst speed (133 Mbytes/sec) support.

Next Generation PCI I/O Bus

The current PCI bus employs a 32-bit data path operating at 33 MHz. The next generation PCI bus is based on a 64-bit data path operating at 66 MHz and supports the ability to hot swap PCI adapter cards. To accommodate this next generation of I/O bus, both NT Server and the server hardware must be capable of taking advantage of the new I/O design. NT Server 5.0 will support the next generation I/O bus and there will most likely be a service pack update for NT Server 4.0 to support it as well. This, of course, is subject to change by Microsoft. What if Microsoft does not support the new I/O bus technology in previous versions of NT Server? There will have to be enough vital Microsoft customers clamoring for support of the new I/O bus technology if they are to influence Microsoft's decision. From a server hardware perspective, current servers that support 32-bit PCI I/O bus will require a motherboard swap out or an incredibly creative solution (or kludgey, depending how you look at it) to support the forthcoming 64-bit PCI bus.

Next Generation Server I/O Technology: Intelligent I/O Initiative (I_2O)

There are two primary, limiting factors when working with I/O operations besides the physical device. Software is actually the first area that slows down I/O operations. There are many operating system layers and device driver layers that slow down I/O operations before they ever reach the actual hardware. Secondly, even with bus mastering technology which allows PCI devices to detach from the bus to perform operations, peripheral devices still rely on a high number of CPU interrupts to complete the requested I/O tasks. This software and hardware combination lowers the overall scalability of the server.

To overcome the current server limitations, an Intelligent I/O Initiative (I_2O) special interest group was formed. Although the I_2O standard is not fully completed, many vendors are already endorsing it. What I_2O technology does is attempt to improve overall I/O performance. The first major change is in the operating system software architecture. In the I_2O software architecture, the driver is split. The Operating System Module portion of the driver handles I/O interaction with the operating system, thereby controlling I/O subsystem access to the CPU. The Hardware Device Module is the other part of the I_2O subsystem that manages how hardware controllers interact with I_2O-compatible I/O devices to gain access to I/O services. The goal of this new design is to lower the overhead associated with I/O operations traversing the operating system hierarchy to the device and standardize device driver development and management.

Another benefit of I_2O technology is the advent of truly intelligent peripherals. These I_2O based peripheral devices will be able to operate without constantly interrupting the CPU for their operations. Many of these devices will include their own CPU and memory subsystems, which offload the actual device activities from the server's CPU. This can improve the performance of the peripheral card, lower the traffic on the system bus, and lower the amount of CPU power required for I/O operations. It allows the server's CPU to focus its attention on more productive application and user related tasks and improves overall server throughput by lowering system bus contention. I_2O Disk I/O devices will still need to interrupt the CPU, not for their internal operations, but when the requested data is available for transfer up the data path.

NT Server 4.0 will not currently take advantage of I_2O technology unless either Microsoft or other vendors implement the new software architecture to interact with the I_2O ready devices. Until a service pack or the next release of NT Server arrives, this technology is only on the horizon. The server itself must also be aware of the I_2O technology and be equipped with an intelligent PCI based I_2O device. Most of the top tier vendors have already pledged their support to this new technology. From a hardware perspective, for the server to be I_2O ready, the server's BIOS must be ready to handle the new peripheral devices or be capable of being upgraded when the technology is available. For the NT Server marketplace, I_2O technology will only be on the horizon until the combination of NT Server, server hardware, peripheral intelligent I_2O aware devices and their associated drivers become available. Why be concerned with this technology? When obtaining new servers, you should ensure that they support I_2O technology either now or in the future. Adding I_2O technology to currently deployed servers shows the promise of improving their I/O subsystem and overall performance levels.

The Server's System Bus

The system bus is the final data highway that leads to both the memory and CPU subsystems. The SHV based reference server's system bus is 64 bits wide and supports a bandwidth of 533 Mbytes/sec. (The system bus was reviewed in detail in Chapter 4.) It should be very clear that the server's system bus is the backbone of any NT Server. It is startling when the system bus is referred to as the PCI bus—it makes one wonder what they are referring to.

Next Generation Server System Bus

The next generation of standard high volume server bus is currently being touted as operating at 100 MHz. This technology utilized in conjunction with a new generation of CPUs and memory technology will improve overall NT Server technology performance. A new system bus for the server's motherboard is not a trivial plug in upgrade. For a server to be upgraded to the new system bus, the server's motherboard would be required to be completely replaced and the power and cooling system will need to be capable of accommodating the new electrical loads. By the time the motherboard is replaced, it might be less expensive to purchase a new server with the latest technology and just re-deploy the older technology.

Redundant Array of Inexpensive Disks (RAID)

It should be obvious from following the data path through an SHV based server that a single disk drive cannot provide enough performance capacity to meet the performance requirements of an enterprise NT Server or even begin to tax the server's I/O subsystem. RAID allows for the grouping of multiple smaller, or inexpensive, disk drives into larger logical disk devices. Adding RAID technology to your server's disk I/O subsystem is becoming a more common choice for enterprise servers to increase performance, disk management, and availability. RAID is a particularly excellent choice if multiple disk drives are available and it is not possible to break up the data files across separate disk drives to balance the use of the disk subsystem. Implementing a RAID array, you can place data files onto a single logical drive under NT Server that takes advantage of the multiple drives that compose the actual RAID array. NT Server allows for the use of both software and hardware based RAID solutions.

The following outlines the performance and fault tolerance tradeoffs of the various RAID levels.

RAID 0–Disk Striping

RAID level 0 stripes the disk activity across two or more disk drives. This logical layout provides the advantages of better performance for read, write, random, and sequential environments. RAID 0 also provides direct disk capacity improvement. When two disk drives are configured in a RAID 0 array, the total available disk space is the sum of the capacity of each individual disk drive in the array. If three 9 GB disk drives are configured as a RAID 0 array, there is 27 GB of user available data space.

For optimum performance and efficient capacity usage, the disk drives used in the array should always have the same performance characteristics and capacity. When a RAID 0 array is implemented, the average seek time required to access the data is lowered when compared to that of a single disk drive. This is one of the ways in which a RAID 0 or any of the RAID levels improves performance. The tradeoff for using RAID 0 is it provides no fault tolerance. If you lose one drive in your RAID 0 disk array, you will lose the data for the entire array. In a RAID 0 environment, increasing the number of drives in the array improves the overall I/O performance.

RAID 1–Disk Mirroring

RAID level 1 mirrors the disk activity across two or more disk drives. This logical layout provides for better read performance, especially in multiuser environments, but lower performance in write intensive environments. When data is read from a RAID 1 mirror, it does not matter which disk drive in the array provides the data; each individual drive can perform simultaneous read operations, thus the read operations are typically dispatched across the different drives in the array. Once the data is provided by any disk drive in the array, the host bus adapter considers it valid and continues on.

Writing to the RAID 1 array works slightly differently. Each write must be sent to each drive in the RAID 1 mirror so that all data is kept identical. Because of this, the HBA must wait until all drives in the array acknowledge a successful write before moving on. This contributes to lower write performance when compared to a single disk drive configuration.

RAID level 1 provides complete data redundancy, even if you are using only two disks. The tradeoff for this high level of fault tolerance is that the capacity of a RAID 1 two-disk mirror is lowered by 50 percent. For example, if you have two 9 GB disk drives in a RAID 1 mirror, there are only 9 GBytes of storage space available to NT Server.

RAID Levels 2, 3, 4, and others

These RAID levels are not commonly used in general computing environments so they are not addressed here. If you are curious, seek a more in-depth understanding of RAID technology, or are just looking for some trivia facts, search the web for "RAID technology." You can also visit the web pages of one of the many hardware based RAID manufacturers such as Adaptec, AMI, DPT, Mylex, or Symbios (just to name a few) for a complete definition of all of these RAID levels. The RAID Advisory Board also keeps a website located at *http://www.raid-advisory.com/*. As you peruse these different websites you may find it interesting how each site interprets RAID technology just a little differently, each adding their own spin.

RAID 5–Disk Striping with Parity

RAID level 5 stripes the disk activity data and calculated parity data across three or more disk drives in a rotating fashion. When data is written to a RAID 5 array, the data is broken up and written to all of the disk drives in the array. For each write, the parity information must be generated and updated. This is accomplished by determining which data bits were changed by the write operation to the other disks in the array and then completing a logical XOR operation with this information. This parity data is then written to the RAID 5 array.

In RAID 5, the parity information is rotated between all of the disk drives in the disk array. For example, if there are three disk drives in logical RAID 5 array E: composed of disk 1, disk 2, and disk 3, as the first set of data is written to the array it is placed onto disk 1 and disk 2, while the parity information is written to disk 3. Subsequently, when the second set of data is written to the RAID 5 array E:, data is written to disk 1 and disk 3 and the parity information is written to disk 2, and so on, in a rotating order. In this manner, parity information is spread across all of the disk drives in the RAID 5 array. To lower the confusion level with this concept, refer to Figure 6–9, which shows data placement in RAID 5 array.

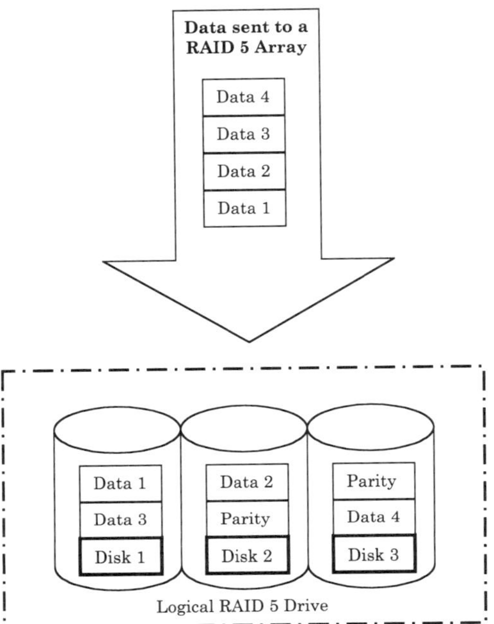

Figure 6–9 *Writing data to a RAID 5 array.*

If one drive was to fail, there is enough parity information available on the surviving disk drives in the RAID 5 array to continue disk operations and rebuild the failed disk drive's data when the failed disk drive is replaced with a working disk drive. If the server is experiencing its regular workload during a reconstruction of a failed drive from the parity located on the other disk drives in the array, the performance provided by the RAID 5 array to server is lowered. Under normal RAID 5 operations, for every write, there are four disk transfers (I/O's). Each write is actually composed of read data, read parity, calculate parity by logically XORing read information, write data, and then write parity information. Not surprising, write operations take longer to complete in a RAID 5 array than any other RAID configuration due to this read/compare/write characteristic.

On the bright side, when data is read from a RAID 5 array the performance provided is very similar to that of a RAID 0 stripe set. Data is spread across the drives in the RAID 5 array so you glean the advantage of having multiple disks service your requests at the same time.

RAID level 5 provides data redundancy, allowing for the loss of one of the arrays member disk drives without the loss of any data. If two drives in the same RAID 5 array fail, all data in that array is lost. Of course, that is what good backup strategies are for. The tradeoff for this redundancy is that the capacity of a RAID 5 stripe with parity is lowered by a factor of 1/(size of the one disk drive members). For example, if you have three 9 GB disk drives in a RAID 5 array, there is 18 GB of usable storage space. If there were 10 9-GB disk drives in a RAID 5 array there would be 81 GB of usable disk space, a capacity loss of only 1/9. In RAID 5 environments, increasing the number of drives in the array improves the random read I/O performance.

RAID 10: Combining Raid 1 Mirroring and RAID 0 Stripes (1+0)

RAID 10 stripes data across two or more drives then mirrors that logical drive set with another stripe set for fault tolerance. This logical layout provides better overall performance than a direct implementation of RAID 1. The tradeoff for this performance improvement and high level of fault tolerance is that the capacity of a RAID 10 mirror is lowered by 50 percent, just as it is for a direct RAID 1 mirror implementation. For example, if you have two 9 GB disk drives in a RAID 0 stripe that are mirrored to another two 9 GB disk drives in a RAID 0 stripe, there is only 18 GB of usable storage space. This RAID configuration provides for excellent performance in all disk environments and complete fault tolerance. It is, however, the most costly RAID implementation in cost per megabyte.

Just a Bunch of Disks (JBOD)

JBOD borders on a trivia fact, but is referenced in some RAID literature so I will mention it here. Depending on the vendor, JBOD is referred to in many different contexts. Someone must have become tired of referring to a single disk drive operating on its own without the influence of any RAID level, thus the phrase JBOD, or just a bunch of disks. In any case, now you can sound extra technical when referring to any single stand-alone disk drive not associated with any RAID levels.

Implementing Software Based RAID With NT Server

You can use NT Server to implement RAID levels 0 or 1 without any concern of a significant performance overhead penalty. NT Server refers to RAID 0 as a stripe set, RAID 1 as a mirror set, and RAID 5 as a stripe set with parity. Do not use NT Server to implement a software based RAID 5 solution unless there is a significant amount of server CPU capacity available that can be allotted for calculating the parity calculations required for RAID 5. To implement RAID level 0,1, or 5 under NT Server, use the Disk Administrator found under Start|Programs|Administrative Tools|Disk Administrator. The steps to configure one of the supported NT Server software based RAID levels is omitted here since NT Server actually provides good step-by-step instructions under the Disk Administrator Help menu option.

A good rule of thumb is to implement all RAID arrays, especially RAID 5, using hardware based RAID solutions. Hardware based RAID solutions offload the RAID calculations from the server CPU to a CPU on the RAID Host Bus Adapter and does not occupy any precious RAM on the server like software RAID implementations do. Hardware based RAID solutions also shield NT Server from problems in the underlying array disk drives. NT Server does provide a solid and cost effective RAID solution for smaller NT Server environments.

Other Benefits of Hardware Based RAID

When a RAID 1 mirror is implemented under NT server and the primary disk drive fails, what happens when the server reboots? It doesn't. First, the failed drive must be replaced with the new disk drive. Then you must utilize an NT Server boot diskette so that you can tell NT Server to boot from the second disk drive in the RAID 1 mirror. Hopefully, you created this diskette and tested its functionality before there was a problem. Once the NT Server is back on its feet, you can use NT Server's disk administration to recreate the mirrors on the new disk drive. This process unfortunately requires a server reboot. This is an inconvenient process, but still quite functional.

Use of a hardware based RAID controller avoids this problem. The hardware based RAID controller shields NT Server from disk problems that are covered by the various RAID levels. In generic terms, when a disk drive fails in hardware based RAID implementation, the following sequence of events occur:

- One disk drive fails if the RAID 1 mirror fails
- The fault indicator light above the drive is displayed
- A hardware RAID controller provided service running under NT Server detects the disk problem and sends the alert to the event log and console (if not another alternate mechanisms as well)
- At this point, someone hopefully notices the problem
- The old disk drive is removed
- If the drive is hot pluggable, the hardware raid controller shields NT Server from the fact that one of its drives was just removed, thus a server reboot is not required
- A new drive is inserted to replace the failed drive
- Either the drive begins an automatic rebuild or the hardware RAID vendor supplies a tool to initiate the rebuilding of the new drive from the mirrored information of the old drive

Is a hardware based RAID host bus adapter the best option for you? It depends on the performance level required and budget available. With many of the components of entry level NT Servers commoditized, a hardware based RAID solution is a sound investment. I prefer to use hardware RAID controllers on all enterprise class NT Servers.

Tuning Flexibility When Utilizing Hardware Based RAID Solutions

Another advantage when using a hardware-based RAID solution is the increased overall performance that it can provide, particularly on servers that are CPU bound. Besides offloading server CPU and memory resources to the RAID HBA, read and write performance of the array can be improved through the use of another level of cache (fast RAM) on the RAID HBA. The advantages of an extra layer of cache vary for each server environment. The advantages of having a RAID host bus adapter level cache is that it allows the algorithms in the hardware based RAID more flexibility when working with the arrays it is controlling. Some hardware based RAID solutions provide a tunable read ahead caching algorithm that can complement NT Server's file system cache.

Where hardware based RAID caches exhibit higher levels of added value is when they are used in conjunction with RAID 5 implementations. Caches on RAID HBA's are normally set to a write through mode by default, which allows data to pass directly through the cache. This does not significantly provide any performance improvements. Cache selected for write through operations is the default setting in place by most vendors to ensure data integrity in the face of a power outage. If the RAID HBA does not include a battery backup for the cache and power is lost to the server, there is a potential for data loss. If the cache is supported by a battery backup system on the RAID HBA, you can set the cache for write back functionality with confidence.

The write back cache setting is configured on most NT Servers by booting from an MS-DOS diskette and running the particular vendor's RAID setup tools. Write-back cache signals back to the requesting process that the data is committed to the disk drive once it is resident in the hardware based RAID HBA cache, before the data is physically committed to the disk drive. When this occurs, the NT Server process reaps the benefit of writing data to a faster cache holding area. The RAID HBA can then calculate the required parity and commit the data to the RAID 5 array as needed. As long as the write-back cache is activated, the caching RAID controller helps compensate for the inherent disk write overhead associated with implementing a RAID 5 solution.

RAID Performance Under NT Server

How do you decide which RAID level provides the highest performance levels? It depends on your environment, your budget, and the level of fault tolerance required. As more and more disk drives are in use, the probability that one might fail actually increases. Windows NT Magazine ran a good article in October of 1997 on RAID performance under windows NT Server titled "Optimizing Exchange to Scale on NT by Joel Sloss: Side Bar RAID Performance Under NT." The results of this exhaustive series of tests are shown in Figure 6–10.

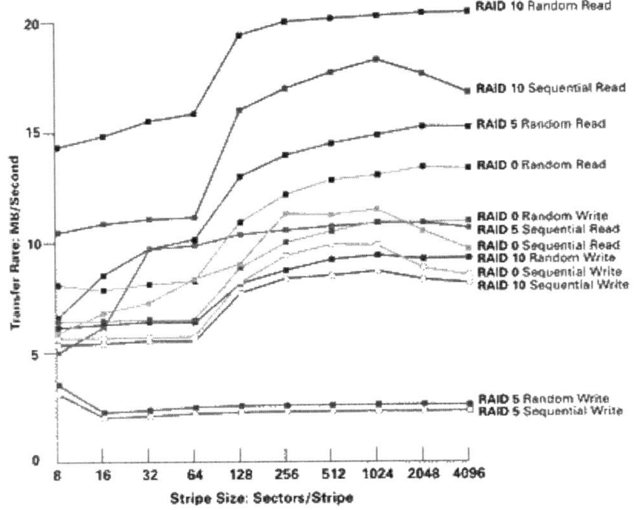

Figure 6–10 *Relative RAID performance chart.*

This test series was run on a Tricord NT Server that used eight disk drives for each RAID array test. You can utilize this graph to help determine the relative performance impact implementing different RAID levels in your NT Server might have, as well as the affect that different RAID stripe sizes can have on your RAID performance. RAID stripe sizes are reviewed in the next section, RAID Stripes. To read this graph, compare the performance results for similar stripe size settings. If you were curious of what relative performance difference there would be between implementing a RAID 5 array and a RAID 0 array for a random read environment using a stripe size of 64 sectors/stripe, you would notice that the performance difference is negligible. If, however, you compared a RAID 5 array and a RAID 0 array in a random write environment at the 64-sectors/stripe size, you would see a huge difference of over 5

Mbytes/sec. As always, how any disk subsystem solution performs will vary with the NT Server environment it is operating in, but using test results such as these, you can gain insight as to how to initially configure your server and help in planning for future disk subsystem growth.

Optimizing RAID Stripes

When data is written to a RAID array, for example, a RAID 0 array composed of four disk drives, the data is broken into chunks and these chunks of data are placed onto each drive in the array. The size of this logical, continuous chunk of data placed on each drive in the array is referred to as the stripe size. The stripe width is the number of disk drives in the array. There will be no test on this later, but try to keep stripe size (chunk) and stripe width straight in your mind. In a RAID 5 array, the stripe width is one less then the number of drives in the array, since one drive is logically used for parity.

The optimum stripe size (chunk) is a function of the server application in use. Ideally, we would want the typical I/O size to be the same as the stripe width times the stripe size (chunk). So to determine the optimum stripe size (chunk), divide the typical I/O size by the stripe width.

When optimum stripe size (chunk) is found, use this data to low level format hardware based RAID solution with the tools provided by the RAID vendor. The hardware based RAID technology can provide the highest level of performance through the efficient use of writes and reads. If the data is much larger than the optimum stripe size, more writes are required. If the data is smaller than optimum stripe size, then the reads are less efficient due to the fact the unused portion of the stripe size goes unused. You can determine what size I/O operations are occurring in your server by separating disk activities across as many individual disk devices as needed to focus in on the different disk activities that are occurring. Next, use Perfmon to monitor the Logical Disk object's counter average disk bytes/write and average disk reads/ write. These counters will show the average number of bytes transferred to the disk during write and read operations.

Stripe Size Optimization Short Cut

Ok, determining the optimum stripe size (chunk) is time consuming, but can be worth the effort. Looking at the relative RAID performance in Figure 6–10, when the stripe size was set from 64 sectors/stripe to 128 sectors/stripe, there is a significant performance increase across most the different RAID configurations and disk loads. At the point where the stripe size (chuck) closely matched the applications I/O characteristics, the best performance is achieved. If you are not interested in this level of tuning, try to at least determine if the general disk characteristics are either sequential or random in nature. In general, larger stripe sizes provide better performance for large sequential data transfers, while smaller random data transfers benefit from smaller stripe sizes (chunks).

Figure 6–10 can be a challenge to decipher, so a condensed reference chart (Table 6–7) was compiled. This performance guide shows the relative performance ratings when comparing the various RAID options using a sector/stripe size of 128 KB. Use this guide when selecting the appropriate performance level that matches your server's disk I/O characteristics and overall disk subsystem goals.

Table 6.7 Condensed version of the relative RAID performance chart.

Raid Level	Random Read	Random Write	Sequential Read	Sequential Write
Stripe (0)	3rd	1st	3rd	1st
Mirror (1)	4th	3rd	4th	3rd
Stripe w/parity (5)	2nd	4th	2nd	4th
Mirrored Stripe Set (10)	1st	1st	1st	2nd

Scaling RAID Arrays

Now that the respective performance levels of the various RAID levels are outlined, how well does NT Server take advantage of RAID arrays when comparing them from the perspective of increasing the number of disk drives in an array? NT Server will in fact take advantage of additional drives in RAID arrays. To characterize what performance levels you could expect, I ran a series of disk subsystems tests using the Neal Nelson Business Benchmark Suite of NT Server tests. The server used for this disk test was an NCR 4300 with two Pentium Pro 200 MHz/512 K cache CPUs, 128 Mbytes of RAM, and two internal 7200 RPM Fast and Wide SCSI disk drives configured on a single SCSI channel. Sizing the server in this manner ensured that there was enough horsepower to drive the disk-intensive test and inhibit NT Server's file system cache from growing beyond 128 Mbytes in size. As in previous tests performed in this book using this test suite, the disk subsystem tests were configured to run to a 20 copy workload test that generates a 780 Mbytes work file. The combination of this large work file size and relatively small amount of RAM configured in the server ensured that the test suite would defeat NT Server's file system cache and that actual physical level disk drive activity would occur.

For disk test 1, a single 7200 RPM Fast and Wide SCSI disk drive was configured on its own SCSI channel. For disk test 2, a 10 disk (7200 RPM, FW SCSI) Symbios Logic Series 3 intelligent external RAID array with 16 Mbytes on board cache was configured as a single RAID 5 array. From NT Server's perspective, this 10-disk array appeared as one logical disk device that provided 36 Gbytes of available storage. The external disk array was attached to the server via an Adaptec 2940 Ultra Fast Wide differential SCSI adapter. Both disks were formatted under NT Server with an NTFS file system and an ALU size of 64 Kbytes. This ALU option is not available under the Disk Administrator and must be completed from the command line. The command used to format the drives as described was "c: >format F: /fs:ntfs /a:64k." Formatting drives from the command line is also a great way to format multiple drives simultaneously by running the format command from multiple command prompt windows. Table 6.8 outlines these disk results.

Table 6.8 NT Server RAID Disk Performance Results.

Test Characteristics using a 780 Mbyte Work File	Percent (%) Improvement	10 Disk RAID 5 Array	Single Disk
		Physical Disk Throughput (Mbytes/sec)	
Sequential Reads of 1024 Byte Records	310.9	6.25	2.01
Sequential Writes of 1024 Byte Records	407.5	2.69	0.66
Sequential Reads of 8192 Byte Records	481.8	9.30	1.93
Sequential Writes of 8192 Byte Records	191.5	2.92	1.67
Pseudo Random Reads of 4096 Byte Records	790.1	4.82	0.61

There are performance improvements across the board. As is typical for a RAID 5 environment, the greatest gains came from the random read environment, while the slightest performance improvement resulted from the write intensive test. This is not an earth-shattering discovery, but is very useful when sizing an NT Server disk I/O subsystem. With this information in hand, a general idea of what you might experience when implementing larger disk arrays is now available.

Using Perfmon to Investigate the Disk Array Scaling

From an NT Server perspective, the highest throughput measured under Perfmon for this test by the Logical Disk: Disk Bytes/sec counter was 9.59 Mbytes/sec, which is very close to what the test suite application reported for the Sequential Reads of 8192 Byte Records test. From an I/O workload perspective, Perfmon reported that the maximum Transfers/sec was 690. For RAID 5 arrays, the Transfers/sec reported is not directly representative of the actual workload the disk array is experiencing. To determine RAID 5 Stripe with Parity I/Os per second, use this formula: (Disk Reads/sec + 4x[Disk Writes/sec] / (number of drives in this RAID 5 array). For this sequential read environment, the I/Os per second for each disk drive in the array works out to (690+4[40])/10=85 I/Os per second.

The RAID 5 array was composed of 10 disk drives. From NT Server's perspective, the RAID array appears only as a single, logical device which is now capable of supporting a higher number of concurrent I/O requests because of the multiple drive configuration. There were no other devices connected to the SCSI channel containing the RAID 5 Array. From the provided information and understanding of the configuration, you can conclude that the 20 Mbytes/sec SCSI bus was not near saturation and the disk array could support a slightly increased workload. Each disk in the disk array can support approximately 100 to 190 I/O operations on their own in a sequential read intensive workload environment.

How NT Server Uses the Disk Subsystem

NT Server implements several techniques to improve overall I/O performance when working with the disk subsystem: file system caching, disk read ahead, and lazy writes, lazy commits. NT Server's I/O Manager manages all requests of the disk subsystem. The process that NT Server actually utilizes when interacting with the physical device is quite complex, in fact, entire books are dedicated to the topic. For an in-depth review of the I/O Manager, peruse *Windows NT File System Internals* by Rajeev Nagar. For this discussion, I will focus on some of the performance aspects of NT Server's I/O process.

Caching Read Requests

Unless a process specifically requests that the file system cache should not be used to obtain data from the disk subsystem, the I/O manager passes the request for data to the Cache Manager. When the Cache Manager obtains the request, it first checks the file system cache that resides in physical memory (RAM) to see if the requested data is available there. In Chapter 5, the file system cache was investigated in depth. If the data is found in the file system cache, it is returned to the requesting process. This is the best way to implement disk I/O: Avoid physical disk activity completely. By avoiding actual physical disk drive activity, the data is presented to the requesting process faster and overall server performance increases. In testing where the file system cache is effective, applications can achieve over 100 Mbytes/sec of throughput. Having a server application that takes advantage of a properly tuned NT Server results in a night and day difference in overall performance.

If the data is not found in the file system cache, it is read from the physical disk drive itself. To increase the chances that the next request for data from the process is found in the file system cache, the Cache Manager employs a disk read ahead caching technique. Statistically, there is a good chance that the next piece of data requested by the process will be close to the last. This concept is referred to as locality of reference. To capitalize on this, the Cache Manager reads ahead on the disk drive and obtains slightly more data than required, in the hopes that the next data requested will already be in the file system cache. Depending on the data access patterns of the process, the read ahead functionality can operate in the forward or reverse direction of the file data.

Caching Write Requests

When data is written to the disk subsystem, the I/O Manager again invokes the Cache Manager unless otherwise requested to do so. The Cache Manager will place the data into the file system cache and report back to the process that the data write is complete. This is a lazy write. By somewhat falsely reporting back to the process that the data is committed to disk, the process can trot off on its merry way faster than if it had to wait on the actual physical disk I/O. Again referencing Table 6.3, the throughput recorded when completing an actual sequential write to the disk drive was 0.66 Mbytes/sec compared to 40 Mbytes/sec when the data could be cached (not shown in the chart, but recorded during the same test suite). There is a tradeoff for this performance enhancement. If the server suddenly lost power, data could be lost. The NTFS file system does utilize techniques to compensate for potential data inconsistencies that could occur due to a power loss. Data that has not actually been committed to the disk drives still resides in the file system cache; this is one of the reasons it is recommended to use the shutdown command to turn off an NT Server as opposed to just shutting off the power.

At some point the data destined for the disk subsystem must be moved to the actual physical disk drives. The Cache Manager has a timer that controls the flushing of data destined for the disk drive from the file system cache. Once every one to three seconds the Cache Manager schedules a scan through the cache to find candidates that should be flushed to the disk subsystem. This scan is adaptive and will flush up to one-fourth of cache at a time.[1] After four scans or earlier (if all the writeable data is flushed), all data destined for the physical disk will have actually been written. By waiting an adaptive period of time (perhaps when the server workload is lighter) before flushing the cache, more data is written to the disk at one time. This technique is NT Server's lazy commit. Lazy commit improves the disk subsystem's efficiency and helps write the data in a more contiguous fashion onto the physical disk.

Similar to the UNIX sync command that forces a flush of the disk buffers to disk, Mark Russinovish developed a tool under NT Server named "NTSync.exe" to accomplish this same task. When you run "NTSync" from the command line, the file system cache is immediately flushed. This freeware tool is available from *http://www.Ntinternals.com*. There is no reason why you have to use this tool as NT Server's file system cache flushing algorithm works fine. If, however, you are working with some very important data and you want to make sure the data is committed to the actual physical disk, such as making sure a few hundred pages of a book you are working on are committed to physical disk, it is a helpful tool.

NT Server Device Drivers

A device driver is a specialized piece of code that allows NT Server and the specific hardware device to communicate, such as a SCSI host bus adapter. Device drivers are pieces of software that are commonly overlooked but have a great impact on the performance that is obtained by peripheral devices attached to the server.

There are several steps inside of NT Server in which the SCSI driver code must traverse. Each one of these code path steps adds a certain amount of overhead to the I/O data path. Why is this important? The more steps that the code path must take, the slower the access is to an external device. As NT Server matures, so do the crucial device drivers that drive the disk subsystems. NT Server has a very defined structure for device driver developers to follow. For people not writing the device drive code, but just implementing solutions with them, it is imperative to keep abreast of the latest driver technologies. Other operating systems such as Linux, publicly distribute their source code in the hopes that if something looks inefficient someone will take the time to improve it. For Linux, this process works surprisingly well. Information on Linux is available on a variety of websites throughout the Internet. A good place to start is *http://www.linux.org*.

In the NT Server realm, you are dependent on the independent vendor for device driver updates and improvements. From a performance perspective,

1. Paraphrased from *NT File System Internals*, p. 353

vendors are always working to make their device drivers more efficient and faster. More efficient refers to the amount of overhead added to the servers CPUs to drive the external device. The more efficient the device driver is, the more work it can complete with the least amount of direct CPU cycles. From a speed perspective, when code paths are lowered, improved efficiency is achieved which leads to obtaining data from the external device in less time.

It does not matter how fast the external device is, if the device driver is not written well, access to the peripheral device will be limited. One way to guarantee your device driver runs as fast as possible is to ensure that the device driver in use is the latest and greatest from the vendor's device manufactured. Some smart devices such as hardware RAID host bus adapters also have their own BIOS or firmware. If a peripheral device does have its own firmware, then it may also require periodic updates. There is nothing wrong with the device drivers provided on the NT Server CD-ROM, but if the manufacture date of the CD-ROM is six months old, the device drivers it contains may have undergone two new iterations in that time span.

Updated NT Server Device Drivers Can Equal Better Performance

Once NT Server is installed, the device drivers are normally forgotten about. If the server runs reliably, who cares? If you want the best performing server you should care. With a multitude of vendors producing devices for servers, it may be time consuming to check all of the vendors websites on a regular basis to download new device drive releases. Fortunately, web technologies are moving fast, and browsers such as Netscape can automatically check websites for you and alert you of changes. NT Magazine recently ran an evaluation of SCSI host bus adapters comparing their performance. (You always want to choose the fastest and most reliable devices for your server.) Evaluations like the one NT Magazine completed help to provide insight on the differences that a new device drive can make. Table 6.9 is a chart of their results.

Table 6.9 NT Server device driver comparison

SCSI Host Bus Adapter	Device Driver Version	Bench32 Disk Mark Score	% Improvement
Adaptec AHA-2940U	Default NT CD-ROM Driver	150	N/A
Adaptec AHA-2940U	Latest Driver from vendor	161	+7.33%
Mylex/Bus Logic Flash-Point LT	Default NT CD-ROM Driver	162	

Table 6.9 NT Server device driver comparison *(Continued)*

SCSI Host Bus Adapter	Device Driver Version	Bench32 Disk Mark Score	% Improvement
Mylex/Bus Logic Flash-Point LT	Latest Driver from vendor	167	+3.09%
Qlogic ALQ-1949	Default NT CD-ROM Driver	171	
Qlogic ALQ-1949	Latest Driver from vendor	175	+2.34%
Symbios Logic SYM8751SP	Default NT CD-ROM Driver	145	
Symbios Logic SYM8751SP	Latest Driver from vendor	176	+21.38%

(Windows NT Magazine, January 1998, page 190 by Sean Daily)

As shown in these results, updating your device driver influences the performance that you can achieve. The larger the NT Server solution that you deploy, the bigger impact on your server's overall performance drivers have. Some vendors develop specialized drivers for their benchmark tests, which they subsequently allow limited public access to. In particular, some vendors have developed what is referred to as monolithic SCSI drivers. These monolithic drivers can provide higher levels of SCSI performance, yet utilize lower amounts of the server's CPU. To obtain these monolithic SCSI drives, contact your SCSI host bus adapter, or server vendor for availability.

As with any new technology, test the new device driver in a controlled environment to ensure there aren't any problems with the revision of the devices you have deployed before fielding the new drivers. I personally have experienced huge performance improvements in disk I/O subsystems when updating a device's firmware and device drivers.

Sizing NT Server's Disk I/O Subsystem

Throughout this chapter, references to sizing the I/O subsystem for an NT Server solution are intertwined in the various sections presented. In this sizing section, the focus is on the two most common areas of concern that I have encountered when sizing the disk I/O subsystem:

- Disk Storage Capacity versus Disk Performance Capacity
- The Number of Disk Drives per SCSI Bus

Disk Storage Capacity versus Disk Performance Capacity

There is an important distinction between providing enough disk storage capacity for your requirements and providing enough disk performance capacity. We will focus on this topic, but when sizing the disk subsystem also consider the following selection factors:

1. Cost
2. Amount of Usable Disk Space Required
3. Performance
4. Fault Tolerance Level Required
5. Available Memory
6. Data Path Sanity Check

   These are not the only factors involved when sizing and selecting your disk subsystem. However, they do cover the major areas of concern. As with all methodologies presented in this book, use them as a guide, not gospel. If you have more criteria you want to add, go for it and have fun!

   Let's look at each of these storage selection factors a little closer.

1. Cost

   If the initial hardware cost is the only factor, then the highest density disk drives will provide the most effective cost solution. A few years ago this was not true. But today with the commoditization of entry level and PC's NT servers, one 9 GB disk drive is less expensive than two 4 GB disk drives. Making the decision totally on cost is sometimes the only option. However, if you want a good long-term solution that meets your performance and management objectives, choosing the minimum number of disk drives based on cost alone will rarely meet your needs.

2. Amount of Usable Disk Space Required

   Perhaps cost is not the driving factor. If this is the case, let's look at the other disk storage selection factors. The amount of usable disk space required. This becomes a factor for two reasons. First, if you only have five disk bays available in your server and require more, an external array solution is required which adds to your cost considerations. Secondly, the higher the disk drive density, the more data that is lost to fault tolerance RAID features. If you have a RAID 5 array and implement it with four 9-GB disk drives, you would lose 9 GB of disk space to parity storage versus only 4 GB of storage space lost if you implemented a 7 4-GB disk array. When working with RAID devices, remember to complete the math equation for the RAID levels chosen to ensure that you end up with the amount of usable disk space you desire.

3. Performance
   The next factor to consider is performance. **Always note that the workload level in I/O's per second and throughput that the disk subsystem will be required to support is separate from storage capacity.** Plain and simple, the more disks and SCSI buses that are implemented provide for more disk subsystem performance. This is a true statement up to the point when either the aggregate throughput of the I/O buses are overwhelmed or there is not enough CPU horsepower to drive the extensive disk arrays and the application at the same time.

   Remember that overall server performance will not improve unless the disk subsystem is the bottleneck throttling the server's overall performance. Even though a disk drive's capacity increases, its relative performance stays about the same. This statement is applicable for disk drives in the same vendor drive family, (for example, they operate at the same RPM levels, seek times, etc.). A 9 GB 7200 RPM Ultra Fast Wide SCSI disk drive provides roughly the same level of performance as a 4 GB 7200RPM Ultra Fast Wide SCSI disk drive. For example in a random environment, either drive will still only support an approximate random application workload of 100 I/Os per second and a throughput level of 0.6 Mbytes/sec. Higher performance levels are possible if the file system cache is avoided and very large block sizes are used when working with the disk drives.
4. Fault Tolerance
   Choose the appropriate RAID that will provide the level of data protection you require. It is easier to configure and manage an NT Server that has one large single RAID 5 disk array than some combination of RAID levels. This premise aligns with obtaining the highest density drives and placing them into a RAID 5 array. If, however, some of your data is truly critical and the workload disk characteristics are varied, having additional disk drives not only provides more fault tolerance options, but tuning options as well. If seven 4 GB disk drives were selected (let's leave the usable disk space requirement out of this for a moment) and you had a requirement to house particularly important data that could survive a dual disk drive crash, you have options. With the seven 4 GB disk drives, you could implement two RAID 1 mirrors consisting of two disk drives each, and a RAID 5 array with the other three disk drives. In this manner, the critical data placed on the RAID 1 mirror could withstand a dual drive failure. Using a combination of RAID levels to implement the fault tolerance required can help lower the cost of your disk subsystem solution by not having to group all noncritical with critical data.
5. Available Memory
   With NT Server's dynamically sized file system cache, the addition of physical memory to the server can improve your disk subsystem performance. When more disk operations are cached, the disk I/Os per sec

that actually make to the disk subsystem are lowered. If this occurs, fewer disk drives are required to meet the work load (I/Os per second) requirement since there are less I/Os per second to support. Higher throughputs are also achieved when disk requests are fulfilled in cache.

There is no steadfast rule of thumb on disk storage to available memory ratios that always work. For this decision, your environment really dictates what is best. As a starting point, configure your server with the amount of memory outlined in Chapter 5. Then observe the Logical Disk: Transfers/sec and Memory: Cache Bytes counters to determine if adding more memory is helping. If the Logical Disk: Transfers/sec go down while the Memory: Cache Bytes goes up without a memory bottleneck forming when more memory is added to the server, the additional RAM is beneficial in relieving some of the disk I/O workload. Of course, this is only a valid observation if the workload placed onto the server is similar before and after the additional RAM is added. Cache memory placed onto hardware based RAID solutions can also increase the amount of work a disk subsystem can withstand.

6. Data Path Sanity Check
   Configuring huge data paths that overwhelm the SCSI channel, HBA, or I/O channel is not desirable. After developing the disk drive or array solution, follow the data path. Utilize the performance charts in this chapter to aide in making an initial sanity check that none of the data paths are overloaded before you field the solution.

Disk Subsystem Sizing Example

To illustrate the difference between storage and performance capacity, let's walk through an example and then use the disk storage selection factors above to help in making the selection. If you wanted to deploy a generic application that required 27 Gbytes of usable disk space, how should you purchase your disk drives? Before we make a decision, let's consider three options to meet this basic disk storage requirement.

- Option 1: obtain four 9 GB disk drives
- Option 2: obtain seven 4 GB disk drives
- Option 3: obtain 15 2 GB disk drives

Which option you select directly influences how you answer the disk storage selection factors. Let's add some requirements information based on the disk storage selection factors and make a selection.

1. Cost
   A consideration, but it is more important to provide a solution that works well.
2. Amount of usable disk space required
   Stays the same at 27 Gbytes.

3. Performance
   Limited Perfmon log information is available from another server running this generic application, but supporting only one half of the projected load for this server. The old server supported 300 Transfers/sec (I/Os per second) on a sustained basis. Throughput information is not available at this time. With almost a doubled projected workload, the new server's I/O subsystem will need to support at least 500 I/Os sec.
4. Fault tolerance level required
   The data is important but not critical. Continued operation after losing a single drive is acceptable.
5. Available Memory
   There are two Pentium II 300 MHZ/512 K cache CPUs configured with 256 MB of RAM.
6. Data Path Sanity Check
   Single Fast and Wide SCSI-2 channel (20 Mbytes/sec) and hardware based RAID controller are supplied which supports over 500 I/Os per second. The server has a single PCI bus.

And The Solution Is....

Based on the above information each option is revisited. Option 1: Using four 9 GB RAID 5 solution will meet the available disk space requirement of 27 GB, but will have trouble meeting the 500 I/Os per second requirement. Option 3: Using 15 2 GB disk drives meets both the usable disk space and performance requirements, but is deemed too costly. Option 2: Using seven 4 GB disk drives fulfills both the usable disk space and performance requirements. Option 2 is neither the most expensive nor cheapest, but is a solution that meets the requirements and provides more tuning and availability options for the future.

The current memory configuration looks as if it is large enough to feed the CPUs and dynamical buffer data headed to the disk. It will be watched closely. A single Fast and Wide SCSI-2 channel provides enough bandwidth to support a seven disk RAID 5 array, with room to grow. A RAID disk controller is selected to offload parity calculations from the two server CPUs and is reported by the vendor to support more than 500 I/Os per second requirement.

Detecting Disk I/O Bottlenecks

Recall from Chapter 2 that it is important to consider the entire server performance picture when trying to locate an NT Server bottleneck. There can be more than one server resource area that is contributing to the throttling of the server's overall performance. Once all of the major server resource areas are evaluated, focus in on the resource that is farthest to the left in the Performance Resource Chart introduced in Chapter 1 and repeated here in Figure 6–11 for reference. This strategy will provide the greatest immediate gain to the server's overall performance.

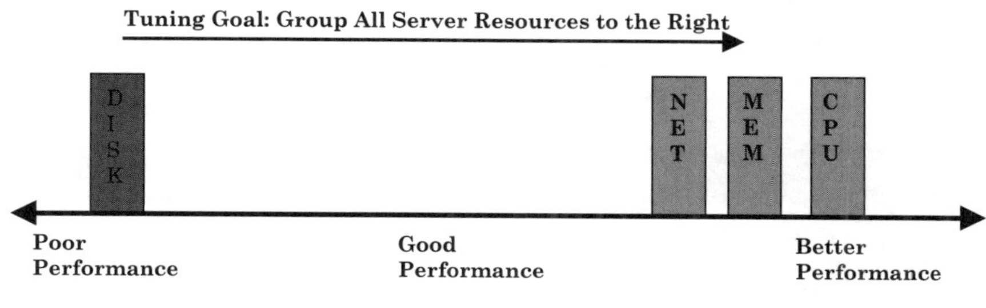

Figure 6–11 *Performance Resource Chart depicting a disk resource bottleneck.*

When a disk drive is unable to keep pace with the requested workload, the response time that the disk drive provides begins to degrade when it becomes overworked. If the requested workload increases to an even higher degree, then the disk drive is capable of servicing; the disk I/O requests begin to backup. When this occurs, disk queues form. When disk queues form, the NT process that requested a disk I/O operation must wait in line for service from the disk drive. When was the last time you enjoyed waiting in line? This worst case disk I/O queuing is easier to detect than the slowing of disk response times. Table 6.10 outlines the counters to observer when sleuthing for disk bottlenecks.

Table 6.10 Primary counters for disk bottleneck detection .

Object Counter	Definition	Rule of Thumb for Bottleneck Detection
Logical Disk: % Disk Time	% Disk time is the percentage of elapsed time that the selected disk drive is busy servicing read or write requests.	If this value increases above 60-80%, then the response time from the disk drive may become unacceptable. This is the red flag to begin investigating the other disk counters listed below.
Logical Disk: Average Disk Queue Length	Average Disk Queue Length is the average number of both read and write requests that queued for the selected logical disk during the sample interval.	If this value is greater than two for a single disk drive and the % Disk Time is high for a sustained period of time, the selected disk drive is becoming a bottleneck. This value is an average calculated during the Perfmon sample period. Use this counter to determine if there is a disk bottleneck and the Current Disk Queue Length counter to understand the actual workload distribution.

Table 6.10 Primary counters for disk bottleneck detection *(Continued)*.

Object Counter	Definition	Rule of Thumb for Bottleneck Detection
Logical Disk: Current Disk Queue Length	Current Disk Queue Length is the number of requests outstanding on the disk at the time the performance data is collected.	If this value is greater than 2 for a single disk drive over a sustained period of time and the % Disk Time is high, the selected disk drive is becoming a bottleneck. This value is instantaneous. Collect granular statistics over time to ensure that there is a sustained problem, not an instantaneous workload increase.
Logical Disk: Disk Transfers/sec	Disk Transfers/sec is the rate of read and write operations on the disk. This counter provides a good indication of the workload level the disk drive is supporting.	If this value rises consistently above 80 for a single physical disk drive, observe if the Average Disk sec/Transfer counter is reporting values higher than your baseline or what you consider acceptable. If it is, then the disk drive is slowing down the overall server's performance.
Logical Disk: Average Disk sec/Transfer	Average disk sec/Transfer is the time in seconds of the average disk transfer.	When the Transfers/sec counter is consistently above 80 for a single disk drive or the %Disk time is above the 60–80 percent range, the Average Disk sec/Transfer should be observed to determine if it is rising above your baseline. A value greater than 0.3 seconds indicates that the selected disk drive's response time is uncommonly slow.
Logical Disk: Disk Bytes/sec	Disk Bytes/sec is the rate bytes are transferred to or from the disk during write or read operations.	Sum this counter's value for each disk drive attached to the same SCSI channel and compare it to 80 percent of the theoretical throughput for SCSI technology in use. If the summed Disk/bytes per second is close to this 80 percent value, it is the SCSI bus itself that is becoming the disk subsystems bottleneck. Use this data and some math to review the complete disk subsystem data path.

Detecting the Obvious Disk Subsystem Bottleneck

Trying to observe an inordinate amount of disk counters at the same time may become confusing. The two most important counters to keep an eye on are: Logical Disk: % Disk Time and Average Disk Queue Length. Whenever the %Disk Time raises above 60 to 80 percent, the selected disk drive is earning its keep by working hard. Once this counter moves into this range, it is like a flashing red light indicating more disk problems may be occurring and should be investigated. If this high %Disk Time is associated with an Average Disk Queue Length greater than two, the disk has become a bottleneck. To investigate if the queue length is not being affected by only spikes of heavy disk workload activity, observe the Current Disk Queue Length counter by changing the Perfmon sampling period to a finer granularity to glean a better understanding of the workload patterns.

Determining the Disk Queue Length for a Disk Array

When determining the Average Disk Queue Length for a disk array, values greater than two for the entire disk array is acceptable. A disk array is composed of multiple disk drives that can support concurrent disk operations. To determine if the disk array's queue length is above the acceptable level of two outstanding requests per disk drive, divide the Average Disk Queue length by the number of disk drives in the array. For example, if you had a 10-disk RAID 0 array, and the reported Average Disk Queue Length was 11, the normalized Disk Queue Length would be one. One outstanding disk queue operation per disk drive is acceptable. However, if the reported average Disk Queue length is 24, the normalized disk queue length would be greater than two per drive, which is unacceptable. Without knowing exactly what is configured in your server, the values reported by Perfmon are practically useless.

Detecting the Not So Obvious Slow Disk

The %Disk Time climbing into the 60 to 80 percent range is a good indicator to begin an investigation into other areas of disk performance. Even if the disk queue is not greater than two, the disk drive could still be hindering overall server performance. There can be times when the %Disk Time is actually at 100 percent, but the disk queue is not greater than two; subsequently, there is not a definitive disk bottleneck. Figure 6–12 is an example where a 10 disk RAID 5 array is experiencing 100 percent Disk Time, but the disk queue is not yet indicating a sustained bottleneck (a sustained value above 20):

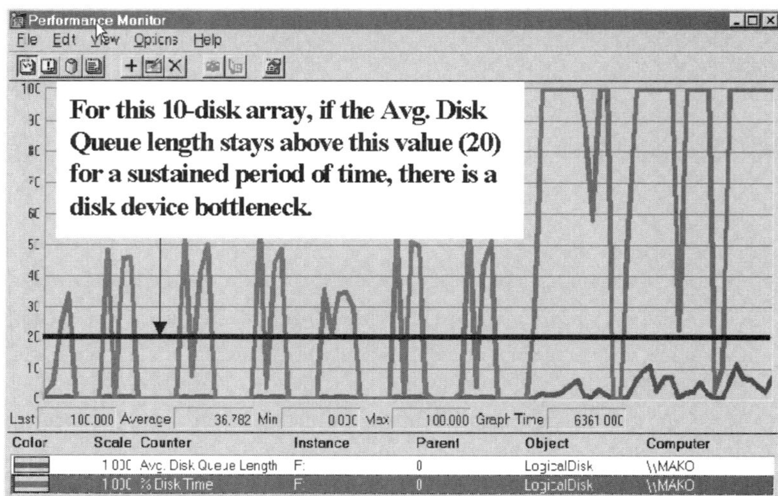

Figure 6–12 *100% Disk Time but no bottleneck.*

When this condition occurs, the disk drive is working hard and you are obtaining a good return on your disk investment. However, it can also indicate the performance levels being provided, although not a bottleneck, are becoming increasingly slower. If you see this type of condition occurring, review the Transfers/sec counter, which indicates the disk I/O per second workload that the disk device is experiencing. As illustrated earlier in this chapter, if the per disk I/Os per second are in the range of 80–100 and rising in a random environment, review the Average Disk sec/Transfer. This counter will show how long the disk device is taking to service both read and write requests. If this value steadily rises above your baseline, or what you consider acceptable, it is a prelude to a disk bottleneck occurrence. As a general rule of thumb, if this value rises above 30 milliseconds, you should consider some of the tuning methods outlined in the next section. This concept of slow disk response times was also illustrated in the Electronic Mail Case Study in Chapter 8. In the case study, it was the disk write times that were getting slower. For the case study environment, some of the write intensive log file activity was relocated from the RAID 5 array to a RAID 1 array to alleviate the situation. By proactively managing a performance slowdown, you can tune around it before it ever becomes an actual bottleneck.

Remember the Data Path

If the disk drive is not a bottleneck or even experiencing high workload levels, but the disk subsystem feels sluggish from your application perspective, what could be wrong? Before even configuring your server, follow the disk sizing guidelines presented in this chapter, but remember that computer performance is part art as well (there, I slid it into this chapter, too). Occasionally, sum up the Disk Bytes/sec value of all of the logical disk devices on a particular SCSI chain as well as the Transfers/sec. Once you have this information in hand, work from the beginning of the I/O data path (the disk drive), then continue working your way up through the SCSI channel, and start doing your math.

If the summation of the Disk Bytes/sec is closing in on 80 percent of the theoretical bandwidth of the SCSI technology in use, the SCSI bus itself may be slowing down the disk subsystem operations. To solve this, either less work must traverse the SCSI channel or another SCSI channel must be added. To lower the workload on the specific disk subsystem in question, additional physical memory or SCSI channels can be added to the server. If a new SCSI channel and perhaps disks are added to the server, the workload should be evenly spread across the new hardware. Also, compare the summation values of the Transfers/sec counter of all of the SCSI channel devices feeding the HBA. Is the HBA rated to support such a workload? To remove such a bottleneck, an HBA with increased workload capacity could be used or additional HBAs can be implemented, again distributing the disk I/O workload across the new hardware.

Calculating I/Os per second for RAID Devices

Calculating the I/Os per second for a single disk drive is straightforward, review the transfers/sec counter. When determining the I/Os per second for RAID array, Perfmon's Logical Disk only reports on the logical drive, not each individual disk in the array. To determine the I/Os per second for each drive in the array, use the following guidelines:

- RAID 0 Stripe I/Os per second equals:

  (Disk Transfers/sec) / (number of drives in this RAID 0 array)

- RAID 1 Mirror I/Os per second equals:

  (Disk reads/sec + 2x(Disk Writes/sec) / (number of drives in this RAID 1 array)

- RAID 5 Stripe with Parity I/O's per second equals:

  (Disk Reads/sec + 4x(Disk Writes/sec) / (number of drives in this RAID 5 array)

In RAID 5 arrays, each write consists of: Read data block, read parity block, write data block, write parity block, and so on, for each single write operation.

Tuning Disk Resources

Now that we have all of this wonderful information on how the servers disk subsystem operates, how do we make it go faster or, at least, become more efficient? Properly armed with an understanding of how NT Server and the server hardware works is actually the first step in tuning the disk subsystem. The primary strategies to implement when tuning the disk subsystem are

1. Evenly distribute the disk workloads
2. Appropriately size and tune the server's memory subsystem
3. Lower the overhead associated with the disk operations
4. Try to improve the disk operations efficiency
5. Understand the workload characteristics and implement RAID technology accordingly

General NT Server Tuning Considerations and Recommendations

Evenly Distribute File System Activity

Review the Perfmon logs regularly to insure that you have evenly distributed the workload across the entire disk subsystem. If %Disk Time or Disk Transfers/sec approach the thresholds mentioned above, consider spreading the data of the affected logical drives to other physical devices that are in less demand. A common source of contention is having all applications loaded and running on the root NT Server disk. The root disk is where WinNT (%SystemRoot%) resides, most commonly "C:". The root disk can quickly become a bottleneck.

To distribute the disk subsystem workload, you need to understand where the workload is emanating from. When you know where the workload is emanating from, you can work with the particular application generating the workload and tune it to place its data or logs in another location. A tool that is helpful in determining what processes are accessing which disk subsystems on your server is ntfilmon.exe. This tool is freeware and is available at *http://www.ntinternals.com*. Figure 6–13 dipicts a short output from ntfilemon.exe that you might expect.

Another tool that can aid in determining which processes are using which logical disk is Nthandle.exe. NTHandle is a utility that displays information about open handles (files) for any process in the system. This tool is also by Mark Russinovich and is available from *http://www.NTinternals.com*. Use this tool in conjunction with nfilemon.exe to help in understanding where to distribute the disk I/O workload among the entire disk subsystem.

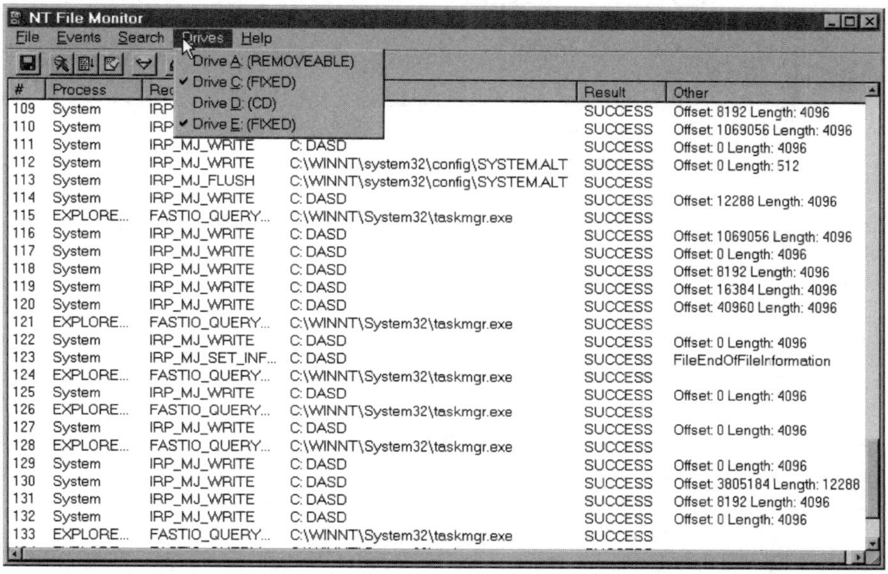

NT File Monitor

File Events Search Drives Help

Drive A: (REMOVEABLE)
✔ Drive C: (FIXED)
Drive D: (CD)
✔ Drive E: (FIXED)

#	Process	Rec		Result	Other
109	System	IRP		SUCCESS	Offset: 8192 Length: 4096
110	System	IRP		SUCCESS	Offset: 1069056 Length: 4096
111	System	IRP_MJ_WRITE	C: DASD	SUCCESS	Offset: 0 Length: 4096
112	System	IRP_MJ_WRITE	C:\WINNT\system32\config\SYSTEM.ALT	SUCCESS	Offset: 0 Length: 512
113	System	IRP_MJ_FLUSH	C:\WINNT\system32\config\SYSTEM.ALT	SUCCESS	
114	System	IRP_MJ_WRITE	C: DASD	SUCCESS	Offset: 12288 Length: 4096
115	EXPLORE...	FASTIO_QUERY...	C:\WINNT\System32\taskmgr.exe	SUCCESS	
116	System	IRP_MJ_WRITE	C: DASD	SUCCESS	Offset: 1069056 Length: 4096
117	System	IRP_MJ_WRITE	C: DASD	SUCCESS	Offset: 0 Length: 4096
118	System	IRP_MJ_WRITE	C: DASD	SUCCESS	Offset: 8192 Length: 4096
119	System	IRP_MJ_WRITE	C: DASD	SUCCESS	Offset: 16384 Length: 4096
120	System	IRP_MJ_WRITE	C: DASD	SUCCESS	Offset: 40960 Length: 4096
121	EXPLORE...	FASTIO_QUERY...	C:\WINNT\System32\taskmgr.exe	SUCCESS	
122	System	IRP_MJ_WRITE	C: DASD	SUCCESS	Offset: 0 Length: 4096
123	System	IRP_MJ_SET_INF...	C: DASD	SUCCESS	FileEndOfFileInformation
124	EXPLORE...	FASTIO_QUERY...	C:\WINNT\System32\taskmgr.exe	SUCCESS	
125	System	IRP_MJ_WRITE	C: DASD	SUCCESS	Offset: 0 Length: 4096
126	EXPLORE...	FASTIO_QUERY...	C:\WINNT\System32\taskmgr.exe	SUCCESS	
127	System	IRP_MJ_WRITE	C: DASD	SUCCESS	Offset: 0 Length: 4096
128	EXPLORE...	FASTIO_QUERY...	C:\WINNT\System32\taskmgr.exe	SUCCESS	
129	System	IRP_MJ_WRITE	C: DASD	SUCCESS	Offset: 0 Length: 4096
130	System	IRP_MJ_WRITE	C: DASD	SUCCESS	Offset: 3805184 Length: 12288
131	System	IRP_MJ_WRITE	C: DASD	SUCCESS	Offset: 8192 Length: 4096
132	System	IRP_MJ_WRITE	C: DASD	SUCCESS	Offset: 0 Length: 4096
133	EXPLORE...	FASTIO_QUERY...	C:\WINNT\System32\taskmgr.exe	SUCCESS	

Figure 6–13 *Using ntfilmon.exe to determine disk activity and the guilty processes.*

Tuning NT Server File System Cache Usage

The most common way to control how NT Server uses the available RAM for disk caching purposes is outlined in Chapter 5's "Tuning Memory Resources: Selecting NT Server Memory Strategy" options. In particular, the selection of either option 1; Maximize Throughput for File Sharing, or option 2; Maximize Throughput for Network Applications, drastically affects your server's disk I/O performance. Although it depends on your environment, adding additional RAM will improve the disk I/O performance.

If the server is functioning as a file server and option 1 is chosen, nothing more than a reboot of the server is required to take advantage of the additional RAM. If option 2 is selected, just rebooting the server will improve some disk I/O performance as more RAM is available for NT Server's dynamic cache management, but tuning any applications that can be adjusted internally should be revisited. For example, Microsoft Exchange allows the amount of memory allowed for use to be easily set via the Exchange Optimizer Program. So if more memory is added to the server, tune the applications accordingly to take full advantage of your investment.

Control Access to Network Shared Disk Subsystem Resources

It is normal to find disk resources shared to the network under NT Server. If a specific popular network disk subsystem resource becomes a bottleneck, but it is not currently possible to tune around the bottleneck, what can you do? One technique is to control the number of concurrent users who access the disk resource until the bottleneck can be removed. To control the concurrent user access for a specific shared resource, use the following command from the NT command prompt: "c: > net share SharedDiskResource=F:\Directory-Shared /users:40 /remark: "For a limited time only 40 concurrent users can use this resource." Now that the shared resource access is limited, let's not allow people to tie up this popular shared resource. To control the amount of time a shared resource connection can set idle before disconnecting the user, use the following command from the command prompt: "c:>net config server /autodisconnect:5." The net config server command sets the maximum number of minutes a user session can be inactive before it is disconnected. The default value for this command is 15 minutes. Also, this command is immediate and permanent. To change this value, you will need to rerun this command. For information on the status of a network share, perhaps to determined sessions timed out, run the following command from the command prompt "c:>net statistics server | more."

Low Level Format Disk Drives Before You Format Them Under NT Server

When using a SCSI disk drive on a different SCSI host bus adapter, always use the host bus adapter's provided tools to low level format the disk drive before attempting to format the drive under NT Server. The geometric translation combination in use varies between each host bus adapter and disk combination. When SCSI disk drives are placed onto a new host bus adapter, you want to ensure the correct translation information is being used. Low level formatting the disk drive with the tools that the host bus adapter vendor provides confirms that the translation in use is correct. This will provide the proper functionality, reported capacity, and performance achieved when using the disk drive with NT Server.

Allocate Only One Logical Drive per Physical Drive

A technique that helps isolate disk performance problems and improves disk drive performance is to format only one logical drive per physical drive. This technique can lower the amount of head movement (seek) over the disk drive. For example, if you have three disk drives, create only three logical drives, C, D, and E.

To illustrate the goal behind this tuning technique, consider a single disk drive formatted with two logical NTFS file systems E: and D:. Suppose application 1 has data files on E:, and application 2 has data files on D:. When application 1 requires data, the disk head moves to the E: partition to locate the data. For this example (see Figure 6–14), the data is on the outside edge of the platter. If the data for application 2, which is on D:, is on the inside edge of the drive platter, there is a significant amount of head movement which results in additional time added to accessing the disk data.

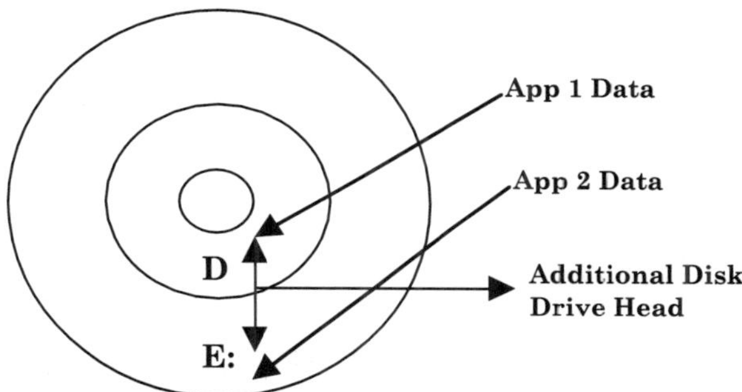

Figure 6–14 *Data on a platter.*

With seek time being the costliest portion of a disk operation, it makes sense to attempt to lower it. If only a single NTFS file system is placed on the entire drive, the data has a better chance of being written together instead of forcing it to different areas of the disk based on logical partitioning. Seek time has a greater chance of being lowered when data being read is grouped closer to one another. Lowering the disk drive's seek times significantly improves overall disk drive response time. The concept of seek times was explored in the disk drive technology and SCSI technology sections of this chapter.

Select the Appropriate Allocation Unit Size (ALU)

Consider matching the file system ALU to the block size of the application you are using. If SQL Server is using a 4 KB block size, when you format a file system on a new disk drive launch Disk Administrator, create the partition, commit the partition changes, select Format, and then set the ALU to 4096 bytes. Matching the file system block sizes to the server's workload characteristics can improve the efficiency of the disk transfers when you use the application. For more ALU size options, use the format command from the command prompt in exchange for the Disk Administrator tool. An example use of the format command used from the command line to set up an NTFS file system with a 64 Kbyte file system is: "format h: /FS: NTFS /A:64K." For all of the format command options, type "format /?" at the command prompt.

The NTFS file system uses clusters as the fundamental unit of disk allocation. A cluster is composed of disk sectors. When using the format command or the Disk Administrator, cluster sizes are referred to as Allocation Unit Size (ALU). In the NTFS file system, the default ALU depends on the volume size. Utilizing format command from the command line to format your NTFS volume, you can specify any ALU. The default cluster sizes for the NTFS file system are shown in Table 6.11.

Table 6.11 Automatic NT Server format options default ALUs.

Partition size	Sectors per ALU (cluster)	Default ALU (cluster) size
512 MB or less	1	512 bytes
513 MB–1024 MB (1 GB)	2	1 K
1025 MB–2048 MB (2 GB)	4	2 K
2049 MB–4096 MB (4 GB)	8	4 K
4097 MB–8192 MB (8 GB)	16	8 K
8193 MB–16,384 MB (16 GB)	32	16 K
16,385 MB–32,768 MB (32 GB)	64	32 K
> 32, 768 MB	128	64 K

This technique of setting the proper ALU is implemented when tuning the server (see Chapter 8's: file server case study). There is always a tradeoff somewhere when tuning your server. There is some loss of available capacity when using the larger ALUs. Unless you are really low on disk space or value every byte of possible storage, the slightly lower capacity sizes associated with larger ALUs is a nonissue.

To determine the size of your server's disk I/O operations, consider reading the friendly manuals provided by the vendor or complete research on the operation of the application. Sizes of disk I/O operations and workload characteristics can also be determined by using Perfmon. Observe the Logical Disk counters: %Disk Read Time, %Disk Write Time, Average Disk Bytes/read, and Average Disk Bytes/write.

File System Related Tuning

Select the appropriate file system to meet the solution requirements. Which file system to choose has traditionally been a heavily debated topic. For this topic, I will stray from performance for a moment. Under NT Server, there are two file system options: NTFS or FAT. If security is a consideration at all, there is only one choice, NTFS. If FAT file systems are in operation, try to limit their use to disk drives or partitions smaller than 500 GB. For smaller file system sizes that are characterized by many small files, FAT can actually outperform NTFS. FAT file systems are more apt to become fragmented in a shorter period of time and begin to degrade in overall performance for larger file system sizes. Thus, for all file systems larger then 500 GB, use NTFS.

Disable Short Name Generation

Disabling short name generation on an NTFS partition can increase directory performance significantly if a high number on non-8.3 filenames are in use (for example, long file names). This is becoming increasingly common as legacy clients and applications are updated. NT Server must calculate the short 8.3 compliant filename every time a long NT Server file name is used. This increases CPU overhead and causes additional writes to the disk subsystem. To disable short name generation, use REGEDIT32.exe to set the registry DWORD value to 1 in the following Registry location: HKEY_LOCAL_ MACHINE\SYSTEM\CurentControlSet\Control\Filesystem\NtfsDisable8dot3nameCreation. It is very important to remember that this will cause problems if legacy 16 bit MS-DOS and MS-Windows based applications are still in use on the NT Server you use this technique.

Disabling Last Access Updates

Another registry tunable that can improve file system performance by lowering file system overhead is located in: HKEY_LOCAL_MACHINE\SYSTEM\CurrentControlSet\Control\FileSystemNtfsDisableLastAccessUpdate. Changing the default REG_DWORD value of this key from 0 to 1 will stop NT from updating the last access time/date stamp on directories as directory trees are traversed.

Defragmenting NTFS

Like any other file system, NTFS can become fragmented over time on heavily used disks. There are commercial products available to defragment disk drives which can improve performance of the file system. Current lists of defragment utilities are available at *http://www.microsoft.com/infosource.* Some of these disk fragmentation tools market that they not only defragment the file system, but also place files not touched for longer periods of time together on slower areas of the disk drive. Conversely marketed is that they group recently used files together on faster areas, or more commonly traveled areas of the disk. These techniques, if successful, will improve disk access time by lowering the time for seek operations and freeing up contiguous areas of disk for NT Server's use. If these defragmentation tools are in use in your server, you may not want to utilize the "Disabling Last Access Updates" tuning technique mentioned above. Using this tuning technique may conflict with the defragmentation tools operations.

Currently there isn't an industry standard benchmark to be utilized when reviewing these disk defragmentation tools. The performance gains achieved will vary greatly from one environment to another. Custom server baseline tests, such as the ones mentioned in Chapter 2, are helpful in determining the value that these disk defragmentation tools have in your environment. Your Perfmon baseline is also a helpful tool when evaluating the effectiveness of disk defragmentation. Compare the Perfmon counter Average Disk Second/Transfer before and after the disks are defragmented under similar workloads (same time of day during, similar workloads activity, etc.) to help determine if they are providing a beneficial service.

To lessen the impact of fragmentation and take advantage of the physical characteristics of disk drives without a defragmentation tool, try to keep file systems at a capacity lower than 60-80 percent. This will allow NTFS to compensate for fragmentation by taking less time to find additional free space when needed.

An evaluation copy of Diskeeper by Executive Software is included in this book's CD-ROM for you to take a test drive with to determine if this technology is helpful in your environment. This tool is also available for download from *http://www.sunbelt-software.com*.

Avoid Compression

When NT Server's file system compression is activated, it taxes all of the server's resources. The CPU is needed to make the calculation, which requires memory, and during this period the process is waiting for the disk I/O to complete. Unless absolutely necessary, do not use disk compression. If you must use disk compression, relegate its use to archiving less frequently used data.

SCSI Channel, Disk Subsystem, and Host Bus Adapter Tuning Considerations

Group Similar Physical Devices on the Same SCSI Channels

To maximize the performance and efficiency of your SCSI channels, group similar external devices on the same SCSI bus. By placing an active CD-ROM on the same SCSI bus as a 10 Disk RAID 0 array, the CD-ROM can effectively slow down access to the faster disk array. When SCSI commands are sent to request data from the CD-ROM, which is a slower device than a disk drive, the other devices on the SCSI bus must wait until the CD-ROM (or another slower device) transfer is complete before transferring the data associated with the other devices. A good rule of thumb to follow is to place CD-ROMs on their own SCSI channel, place each tape unit on its own SCSI channel, and group disk drives with similar features (size, rpm, throughput) on their own SCSI channels. Also, avoid configuring SCSI devices using different levels of SCSI standards on the same SCSI channel, as they will be limited to running at the speed of the slowest SCSI standard on the particular SCSI channel. For example, operating Fast and Wide SCSI-2 (20 Mbytes/sec) and Ultra Fast and Wide SCSI-3 (40 Mbytes/sec) on the same SCSI channel limits the SCSI channel to the slower Fast and Wide SCSI-3 speed.

SCSI Command Queuing

Some drivers for SCSI adapters have registry settings for SCSI command queuing. By increasing this value, you can improve the performance of the attached disk subsystem. When this value is increased, more SCSI commands can be in the disk device queue. This technique is particularly helpful in disk array environments. Due to the multiple disk drive nature of disk arrays, they are capable of coalescing multiple SCSI requests in the most efficient manner to achieve higher levels of performance. Use this technique cautiously and test your performance before and after editing the registry values. For most large disk array (>10 disks) environments, doubling the default value for the driver improves disk performance. Contact the disk adapter vendor for assistance in finding the SCSI command queuing entry in the registry. For example, Symbios SCSI adapters (whose default is 32) SCSI command queue entry is located in the following location: HKey_Local_Machine\System\CurrentControlSet\Services\symc8xx\Parameters\Device\NumberOfRequests (REG_DWORD 32).

Monolithic SCSI Drivers

In an effort to improve SCSI host bus adapter performance, some vendors have implemented what is referred to as monolithic device drivers. These specialized drivers appear to have been born out of necessity to improve NT Server's performance for the TPC-C benchmark. Monolithic device drivers incorporate the NT Server SCSI port driver and miniport driver into one large, monolithic driver. These monolithic device drivers lower the amount of code path steps required that disk I/O request must traverse. The benefits of these drivers are twofold. First, these drivers tend to improve the disk I/O performance on heavily utilized disk subsystems. Secondly, they require less CPU cycles when implementing the actual disk I/O activity, which is particularly beneficial in a CPU intensive server environment. Vendors such as Compaq, Dell, NCR, and others offer the monolithic device drivers for some of the SCSI host bus adapters that they use. Check the respective server or host bus adapter vendor's website or contact them directly for information on how to obtain this technology.

Properly Configure the Host Bus Adapter (HBA)

The host bus adapter setup determines what performance level the SCSI channels connected to it will operate at. Because technology moves so fast, an HBA that may be rated for Ultra Fast and Wide SCSI speeds does not guarantee that it is configured for it. As the server boots, or using the tools provided by the host bus adapter vendor, be sure that the SCSI channel speeds are set to operate at the desired performance level. Some of the HBA settings to double-check and enable are: SCSI bus speed, tagged command queuing, disconnect, and wide transfers. You have an investment in the technology for your server; make sure you get to use it.

Update Host Bus Adapter Device Drivers and BIOS (Firmware)

This is one of the easiest techniques to implement to improve disk I/O performance. Manufacturers of disk drive adapters are constantly working on removing bugs and improving the performance of respective disk adapters. Typically, the latest drivers are available from the manufacturer's website. Even before installing NT Server for the first time, check to see that it is the latest, best performing stable disk adapter device driver available. Check your manufacturer's website periodically. It is amazing how much performance you can obtain through the use of improved device drivers. Also, don't forget to keep the embedded HBA BIOS levels current too.

RAID Tuning Considerations

RAID Array Background Services

When NT server utilizes a disk array, either through software or hardware implementation, the data consistency of the actual array is not checked. Parity or mirrored operations are completed, but the health of the disk array itself is not checked during regular disk I/O operations. Either through hardware implementation or NT background services, vendors commonly implement routines to periodically check the disk array's health. This is an important activity that should occur on a regular basis.

For example, the SMART-2 Array HBAs from Compaq default to checking the disk array's health every hour. On very busy servers, consider lowering the frequency of these health checks or postponing them to periods of lower workloads. By controlling the frequency of disk array health checks, you control the overhead that detracts from the array performance but still ensures the health of the array. Array checking techniques differ between vendors, so you'll want to look at the vendor's documentation closely on this one.

Tuning RAID Controller Cache

If there is a built-in cache on the RAID host bus adapter and a battery backup unit, the general rule of thumb is to configure it for the write back caching turned on. The default setting for most adapter caches is write through. Having the write back cache enabled is particularly helpful in write intensive environments implemented with RAID Level 5 disk arrays where there are pauses between periods of heavy disk activity. When your environment is characterized by heavy disk write activity followed by a lull, the write back cache takes advantage of this workload slowdown to write the cache data to disk.

There are, however, some instances when write back cache is not as helpful. One such instance is when log files are continuously being written to. When data is constantly being written to a disk array, the write back cache's effectiveness is diminished because it does not get a chance to take advantage of a workload slowdown window in which to flush its cache. For these continuous activity environments, enabling the write through cache can provide a higher level of performance. Many hardware RAID vendors allow you to selectively control how the cache is used on the various arrays under its control. For example, perhaps you have a RAID 1-mirror configured for the application logs and a RAID 5 array configured for a transaction based database. You can set write through caching for the RAID 1 mirror and write back caching for RAID 5 array. Customizing your cache settings to match the workload's characteristics helps to improve the performance of the overall disk subsystem. This technique can be quite effective but is application-dependent. This technique should always be tested for the specific application and RAID technology in use before fielding.

Setting RAID Stripe Sizes

Ideally, you want the typical server application I/O size to be the same as the stripe size on the RAID array. This concept was investigated earlier in this chapter under RAID Stripes. For now, use this condensed version as a reminder. Depending on the hardware RAID implementation, there are numerous options available for setting up the RAID array stripe sizes. When you do set the arrays stripe size, the array will require a new low level format using the hardware RAID vendor's tools. Stripe size is not the same as ALU, which can be set under NT Server with the format command. If you implement software based RAID arrays using NT Server, stripe size cannot be tuned.

Short of tuning the RAID array stripe sizes, you should consider at least setting it according to your general disk subsystem workload characteristics. In general, larger stripe sizes provide better performance for large sequential data transfers, while smaller random data transfers benefit from smaller stripe sizes (chunks).

Group Similar Disk Drives into the Same Array for the Best Capacity and Performance

It is tempting to build a disk array from different disk drive makes and models. Whatever is lying around the office or lab will do, right? If you place a lower capacity disk drive into an array with a higher capacity disk drive, you lower the array's overall capacity. For example, placing a 2 GB disk drive into a RAID 0 (stripe) array with four other 4 GB disk drives limits the overall array capacity to 5 x 2 GB=10 GB, not 4x4 GB+2 GB=18 GB. This same concept is true for performance. Grouping one older 5400-RPM drive into the same array as 10,000-RPM disk drives lowers the overall performance of the array.

Use More than One RAID Level in Your Solution: Group Similar Disk Characteristic Work Loads

You can group all of your disks into one large array and let the server applications have at it. With fast enough hardware in large enough quantities, this tactic actually can provide acceptable performance. Unfortunately, implementing this tactic can become expensive and may not meet other requirements, such as the required fault tolerance levels. To properly lay out the disk subsystem, you need to understand the technology you are implementing (hardware and software) and the server disk subsystem workload characteristics.

Either through reading those famous manuals (RTFM) that come with software products or by using Perfmon and ntfilmon.exe (*http://www.NTinternals.com*), try to determine the characteristics of the disk I/O activities occurring on your server. Determine which applications exhibit sequential activities, random activities, and are read or write intensive. A little research before you begin provides insight on how the server applications do or do not behave, whichever is the case.

Once a server is fielded, user access patterns influence which areas of the disk subsystem are used more heavily than others. To help to determine what disk resources are under siege, use the Perfmon counters listed above in Figure 6–10: Primary Counters for Disk Bottleneck Detection to determine which disk resources are being used heavier than others. For an even more granular view of what is going on in your disk subsystem, review the Perfmon counters in Table 6.12.

It is sometimes helpful to draw a logical picture of the server's disk subsystem or build a table of the disk usage for each resource. With this data, you can then determine how and where to rearrange or add additional disk subsystem hardware.

Once you have determined the characteristics of your disk activities, group similar activities on the same disk drives or arrays. This is a corollary rule to Evenly Distribute File System Activity. For example, place sequential write intensive log files on a separate disk drive and file system rather than on

Table 6.12 Perfmon counters.

Object: Counter	Definition	Rule of Thumb for Bottleneck Detection
Logical Disk: % Disk Write Time	Disk write time is the percentage of elapsed time that the selected disk drive is busy servicing write requests.	This counter becomes crucial in determining disk I/O characteristics which directly influences how to lay out and sizing of the Disk I/O system.
Logical Disk: % Disk Read Time	Disk read time is the percentage of elapsed time that the selected disk drive is busy servicing read requests.	This counter becomes crucial in determining disk I/O characteristics which directly influences how to lay out and sizing of the Disk I/O system.
Logical Disk: Disk Read bytes/sec; Disk write bytes/sec	Disk Read (or Write) is the rate bytes are transferred from (or to) the disk during read (or write) operations.	These counters help provide insight on the amount of throughput being used for either read or write operations. This data is helpful in spreading disk subsystem activity across multiple host bus adapters, SCSI channels, disk drives, and RAID levels.

a general user database area characterized by a random read intensive workload. Once the workload characteristics are evenly distributed, group disk activities across the disk subsystems utilizing the various RAID levels based on the performance guidelines provided in the next section. For example, to improve the performance of sequentially write intensive logs files, place them onto RAID 0, 1, or 0+1 arrays and avoid RAID 5. For a predominantly random environment that is read intensive, RAID 0 and 5 are good selections. The more clearly you understand your server's environment, the better tuned your NT Server will be.

Data Placement and RAID Selection

With the information presented above fresh in your mind, you are in an educated position to make decisions on which RAID level or combination of RAID levels to implement, where to add disk drives, and perhaps where to take them away. In the Chapter 8 Electronic Mail case study, the disk subsystem workload characteristics for Microsoft Exchange were reviewed very closely. Repeated here in Table 6.13 is a high performance and availability example of distributing the disk workload among various RAID levels to meet the performance and availability objectives.

Table 6.13 Distributing Disk Subsystem Workloads Across Multiple RAID Array .

Logical Disk Assignment	SCSI Bus	Physical Disk Arrangement	Motivation behind data placement and RAID selection	Microsoft Exchange File Location
C:	1	2 Disk RAID 1 Mirror	Critical resource if NT Server does not boot, the server is useless. A RAID 1 mirror allows for loss of drive without loss in operation.	NT Operating System and Exchange Binaries
E:	1	2 Disk RAID 1 Mirror	Log data is sequential and write intensive. RAID 1 does not provide the best performance, but it provides much better write performance than RAID 5 and still provides increased data availability.	Information Store Logs
F:	1	2 Disk RAID 1 Mirror	Same as above	Directory Service Logs
D:	2	1 Disk NO RAID, JBOD	NT Server paging activities sequential in nature, good write and read performance required. This drive is not as critical as other data drives, but provides good performance and overall value.	NT Paging file Note: Dedicated single drive used. Heavy paging not in design plan.
G:	2	2 Disk RAID 1 Mirror	General read/write database characteristic workload. This is deemed critical for Exchange operation. Same motivation as the other RAID 1 implementations above.	Message Transfer Agent
I:	2	3 Disk RAID 5 Array	Random read/write database characteristic workload. Provides excellent read performance with cost effective fault tolerance.	Directory Service

Table 6.13 Distributing Disk Subsystem Workloads Across Multiple RAID Array *(Continued)*.

Logical Disk Assignment	SCSI Bus	Physical Disk Arrangement	Motivation behind data placement and RAID selection	Microsoft Exchange File Location
E:	3 (External Array)	10 Disk RAID 5 Array	Intense Random read/write database characteristic workload. Heaviest used disk subsystem in case study environment. RAID 5 composed of a large number of disk drives provides excellent random read performance and a sound level of fault tolerance.	Private Information Store
E:	3 (External Array)	3 Disk RAID 5 Array	Potential intense random read/write database characteristic workload. RAID 5 provides excellent random read performance and a sound level of fault tolerance.	Public Information Store (if used)

Disk Capacity Storage and Disk Capacity Performance

This concept is reviewed in-depth throughout this chapter. Because it is so important but commonly misunderstood, I'll review the condensed version again.

Should you choose three 9 GB disk drives in a RAID 5 array which provides 18 GB of usable storage to meet an 18 GB disk requirement or six 4 GB disk drives in a RAID 5 array that provides 20 GB of usable storage? Both solutions meet the 18 GB of usable disk space storage requirement, but the three 9 GB solution provides a lower level of performance. Which to choose depends on the level of performance required and economics of your situation.

If economics is a greater concern than disk performance scalability, the three 9 GB disk drives meet the requirements. Alternatively, if performance is the more important factor, choose the six 4 GB or 12 2 GB disk drive solution. Mileage may vary for every environment, but in general the addition of disk drives (spindles) can greatly improve your disk subsystem throughput performance and supported I/Os per second. The three 9 GB disk drive solution can support approximately 300 I/Os per second and a sustained physical drive sequential read throughput of 6 Mbytes/sec. The six 4 GB disk drive solution, supports 600 I/Os per second and a sustained physical drive sequential read throughput of 12 Mbytes/sec. This comparison is based on using the same family (SCSI connection, RPM level, etc.) disk drives at different capacities.

Additional Disk Subsystem Hardware—The Last Resort

As with any resource that has become a bottleneck, additional resources can normally be added if all other efforts to improve performance do not meet your requirements, or if you just need more disk storage capacity. Always select the fastest components that have a positive life cycle (remember VESA versus PCI years back).

For the disk subsystem, this would involve selecting the fastest available disk drives and disk adapter technology available for insertion into the fastest I/O bus available. For example, if there was a need to add three additional disk drives, selecting a PCI based SCSI-3 Ultra Fast/Wide Disk Adapter and SCSI-3 Ultra Fast/Wide Disk Drives rotating at 10,000 rpms would be a good place to start.

Thinking Outside of the Box

RAM Disks

No matter how well you sized and tuned your NT Server disk subsystem, the disk subsystem is still composed of physical devices that are slow when compared to RAM. There may be times, regardless of how well you have load balanced and tuned your disk subsystem, when "hot spots" still exist. "Hot spots" are defined here as areas of the disk subsystem that application(s) consistently request services from which greatly impact the application's performance. Consider another technique to alleviate hot spot situations; try implementing RAM disks.

RAM disk technology is available in two forms. The first RAM disk form is also referred to as solid state disk drives. These types of devices look similar to normal disk drives, but are composed of nonvolatile or battery backed RAM that appears to the NT Server as a regular disk drive. These solid state disks connect to an NT Server over a SCSI connection, but are much faster than traditional disk drives. The second type of RAM disk is software based which allows you to configure part of NT Server's memory subsystem to appear as a disk drive. This is what we will investigate here.

RAM disk support is not native to NT Server, so I obtained a RAM disk package from EEC systems (*http://www.eecsys.com*) named SuperDisk-NT. An evaluation copy of this software is included in the CD-ROM that accompanies this book and is also available from *http://www.SunBelt-Software.com*. This software actually provides two RAM disk options. The first option is a traditional RAM disk in which you can allocate some of NT Server's main memory to act as a disk drive. The second option allows for a disk drive backed RAM Disk implementation—in other words, the RAM Disk is mirrored to a physical disk drive.

Installing the SuperDisk-NT product is similar to installing other NT Server applications. To configure the RAM disk, you bring up the super disk configuration tool and set the RAM disk size as needed then reboot the server. Server RAM designated for the RAM drive is removed from use by NT Server's Virtual Memory Manager. For example, if you created a 200 MB RAM disk on a server that is configured with 1 GB of RAM, only 800 Mbytes would be available to normal NT Server RAM operations. Once the server is rebooted, another drive letter—S: is now available to use as needed (your RAM disk). Files can now be placed into this area either manually or via a start up script. When applications that use these files are launched, they will operate at much higher performance levels while interacting with the RAM disk subsystem. This is a great way to speed up your disk subsystem, but there is a draw back. Files on the RAM disk should not be critical. If the files are critical they probably should not be on a RAM disk, but if you do wish to keep them, you must copy them to a normal disk drive before powering down NT Server. As with all tuning, there are tradeoffs for improved performance. When power is removed from the server, any files located in the RAM disk area are lost. If the system crashes, you will also lose the data on the RAM disk.

Another option available by SuperDisk-NT is to provide a normal disk drive to back up RAM disk operations. This option provides higher performance levels by using the normal (nondisk drive backed) RAM disk, but then saves the data written to the RAM disk in a lazy write mode process. This lazy write mode of operation periodically saves the data from the RAM disk to a designated NT Server partition (this same lazy write concept was reviewed earlier in this chapter). The goal of this combination is to provide improved performance through the use of a RAM disk and nonvolatile data storage. Using this technique, data is not lost when NT Server is powered down. When NT Server is booted, a SuperDisk-NT driver again creates the RAM disk, but then populates it with the data from the RAM drive backup partition.

RAM Disk Performance

So, how much performance improvement might you expect when using RAM disk technology? To address this question, the Neal Nelson Business Benchmark for NT was again employed. Test 18: Sequential Reads of 1024 Kbyte Records from NT Files and Test 19: Sequential Writes of 1024 Kbyte Records to NT Files were selected and executed at the 20-copy workload level. A 20-copy workload level exercises the disk subsystem under a load of 400 simulated users using a combined work file size of 700 Mbytes. An NCR 4300 configured with NT Server 4.0 (Service Pack 3), 1 GB of RAM, 3 Ultra Fast/Wide SCSI 10,000 rpm disk drives, and 4 Pentium Pro 200MHz/512 K cache CPUs was the system under test.

To accommodate the 700 GB benchmark work file, an 800 GB RAM disk was created using SuperDisk-NT. So that the relative performance level provided by a RAM disk could be more easily related to, this same benchmark was also run against a single Ultra Fast/Wide SCSI 10,000 rpm disk drive. Table 6.14 reports the benchmark results:

Table 6.14 RAM Disk benchmark results

	Ultra Fast/Wide SCSI 10,000 rpm disk drive (Mbytes/sec)	Disk Backed RAM Disk (Mbytes/sec)	RAM Disk Only (Mbytes/sec)
Test 18 Sequential 1 KB reads	2.3	18.6	23.5
Test 19 Sequential 1 KB writes	0.76	11.59	15.7

RAM Disk Performance Results

Performance improvements provided by the RAM disk are dramatic! What is more important than the specific throughput values reported are the relative performance differences between using the RAM disk and a traditional disk drive. For the read intensive environment, the RAM disk provides over 10 times the performance of a normal disk drive and over 15 times the performance in a write intensive environment. Even when the RAM disk data is backed by a normal disk drive, the performance improvement is drastic. With this information, you are now aware of the relative disk subsystem performance that a RAM disk can provide. You can make your own decision of whether the additional cost of the extra RAM for use as a RAM disk is justified by the increase in performance.

Using a RAM disk to improve disk subsystem performance is not a replacement for utilizing sound tuning and sizing techniques for the rest of your disk subsystem. It does, however, provide a strong ally to add to your arsenal of tuning techniques. The benchmark used in this test is a particularly intense multiuser benchmark. The performance you achieve is influenced by the various elements of your specific environment such as: user workloads, application in use, CPU performance, type of memory, and memory bandwidth (system bus) of your server.

Other Possibilities for RAM Disk Technology

Now that you are familiar with some of the positive and negative aspects of using a RAM disk product like SuperDisk-NT, there are numerous areas you may consider when implementing this technology to improve the disk subsystem performance of your NT Server solution. The most common justification for using a RAM disk is to remove disk subsystem hot spots, but don't let this one example limit your imagination. Other areas where you might employ RAM disk technology are:

- TEMP directory/file system replacement

  This technique is similar to what is done in some UNIX implementations such as Solaris. Use a RAM disk to replace the TEMP directory. Some applications use the TEMP directory to store frequently accessed, but temporary files, thus a potential hot spot.

- Database Enhancements

  If you have a database and enough memory, it is possible to place the entire database on a SuperDisk-NT partition. If you don't have a lot of memory, but the index to your database can be separated from the rest of the database, you could place it on RAM Disk mirrored to a disk drive.

- Web Site Enhancements

  If your server is hosting a web site, you can improve the access speed of your web pages by placing the web site, or frequently accessed web pages, on RAM Disk mirrored to a disk drive.

- Pagefile replacement

  Even if your NT Server is not paging heavily, small areas of the Pagefile are commonly accessed on a regular basis. For some environments, replacing the Pagefile with a disk backed RAM disk solution can improve end user response times.

You may think of even more options. Deciding when it is best to implement these options is based on your environment and requirements.

Summary

By reviewing each link in the disk subsystem data path, it is the weakest link that throttles the overall disk subsystem performance. In this chapter, the importance of understanding the entire path that the disk subsystem data follows was closely examined in conjunction with reviewing how NT Server tries to maximize the performance of the disk subsystem. With this information it becomes easier to identify potential bottlenecks that can throttle your server's overall performance. Building upon this foundation, specific practical examples of how to tune and size the disk subsystem were provided to help you get the maximum performance from NT Server's flexible disk subsystem.

SEVEN

NT Server and Network Performance

The network subsystem is the superhighway for end users to access your NT Server solution. When an end user is working with an application, it is easy for someone to state that the "the server is slow," since it is a physical object that people can easily relate to. It could of course be a slow client, an ill-behaved application, or that nebulous network stuff which is more difficult to associate an actual object to. When you log into an NT Server client system, you are actually logging into the network, a network that is backed by NT Servers and perhaps other servers as well. In this chapter, we focus on network performance from the perspective of NT Server. The entire network architecture in place has a large impact on the overall network performance of NT Server. Because of this fact, the technologies that are implemented to achieve the network architecture will be referenced as needed.

In this chapter, the focus is on network performance from NT Server's perspective when connected via a local area network (LAN) environment. We will start by reviewing the performance of network technologies that are normally found in NT Server environments, then move on to how NT Server utilizes the network. As in previous chapters, once this foundation is in place, we will explore sizing issues, then detecting network bottlenecks, and finally focus on the tuning of NT Server to obtain the maximum performance possible in a networked environment.

Different network technologies exhibit different performance characteristics when under load. I am not advocating one technology over another. It is, however, of paramount importance to understand the performance characteristics of the network technology that is implemented with your NT Server solution so that you can take advantage of positive characteristics and understand its potential pitfalls so that bottlenecks are avoided. This important fact is applicable to any networked LAN or WAN based environment. To illustrate this principle, several common networking technologies are used here as practical examples. Besides NT Server itself, the network technologies concentrated on are Ethernet (10BaseT), Fast Ethernet (100BaseT) and TCP/IP. The same concepts that are illustrated using these technologies can be extrapolated from for use in your environment. Of course, that might require obtaining a good reference book on the technology you are implementing.

Similar to following the data path technique utilized in Chapter 6, we will again follow the general network data path of information through the network and NT Server. Some references are made to networking hardware devices as it pertains to getting data to and from the server. These references are not intended to be a comprehensive overview of all available networking device technologies.

Relative Network Throughputs

To provide a basis for network subsystem performance, let's first review what is theoretically possible when networking an NT Server. Table 7.1 summarizes the relative theoretical network throughputs and the basic protocol characteristics of a wide range of network technologies. The common bits/sec notation is provided as well as the bytes/sec equivalent (8 bits are in one byte).

Table 7.1 Relative theoretical network throughput and media access characteristics.

LAN Network	Throughput Megabits/sec	Throughput Megabytes/sec	Topology Media Access (Protocol Characteristics)
Ethernet (10BaseT)	10	1.25	CSMA/CD
Token Ring (16 MB Ring)	16	2	Token Passing
Ethernet (100BaseT)	100	12.5	CSMA/CD
FDDI	100	12.5	Token Passing

Table 7.1 Relative theoretical network throughput and media access characteristics.

WAN Network Technology	Throughput Megabits/sec	Throughput Megabytes/sec	Topology—Media Access
Dedicated PPP/SLIP	modem (up to 56 Kbit/s)	0.007	Point to Point
PPP ISDN	128 Kbit/s	0.016	Point to Point
T1	1.544	0.193	Point to Point
T3	44	5.5	Point to Point
ATM	155	19.3	Point to Point

(The WAN technology information provided is for reference to illustrate the throughput disparity between common LAN and WAN technologies.)

Realistic Network Throughput Under NT Server

Realistic network throughput is a bold statement since every environment is different, thus mileage always varies. In general, the most common misapprehension when configuring the network subsystem is a misunderstanding of the actual throughput that the network can provide and the load characteristics of the network protocol in use. Just because one network technology implementation states a certain level performance can be achieved does not mean that level is actually achieved when working in NT Server based application environments.

There are two key pieces of information presented above to consider when configuring the server's network subsystem. First, the theoretical throughputs of all of the various networks are typically referred to in bits/sec, not bytes/sec. Mixing up bits/sec and bytes/sec is a common slip, so always keep this in mind when determining the aggregate network requirements of the client.

Secondly, consider the Topology—media access method or protocol characteristic of each type of network technology that you are implementing with NT Server. Each network type displays different response time characteristics under higher utilization levels. The amount of work each specific network technology can support is based on its characteristics under load. For example, the deterministic nature of token passing network technologies such as Token Ring and FDDI are capable of supporting much higher network utilization levels before slower response times are exhibited to the end users when compared to a shared or collision based technology such as Ethernet. To illustrate a specific network characteristic example, we will look closer at Ethernet.

Shared Ethernet Characteristics

Ethernet is one of the most popular and easiest network technologies to deploy with NT Server. Pick up a trade magazine and look for an advertisement for an entry level NT Server and you will find an Ethernet based Network Interface Card (NIC) bundled with the package. Ethernet 10BaseT (IEEE 802.3) and Fast Ethernet 100BaseT (IEEE 802.3U) technologies are based on the Carrier Sense Multiple Access/Collision Detection (CSMA/CD) protocol to carry the actual electrical signals across the physical wire (medium). This fancy terminology states that Ethernet and Fast Ethernet are shared bus technologies.

In Ethernet environments, all devices on the same network segment (collision domain) have equal access to the entire network segment and all stations on this network segment are considered as peers (multiple access). Before transmission, a network station is required to listen to the network (carrier sense) to determine if anyone is using the network segment. If no network station is sending data over the network segment, data is sent over the network. Using this technique, only one station at a time can transmit data over this shared bus network segment. If another network station on the same network segment sent data at that same moment in time as another network station, there is a network segment collision. The data sent from both stations is assumed lost. Each station will detect the collision (collision detection), wait for a random period of time, and then repeat the process to resend the same data.

10BaseT Ethernet Performance

When the workload on the network increases, collisions occur and the station must wait for the shared Ethernet network segment to be calm before sending any data. Each time this occurs, it slows down the response time back to the NT Server process that is requesting use of the network or an end user trying to get to the server.

In an Ethernet environment, as the average network utilization increases above 20 percent, a network general expert sniffer will generate a network usage alert event that the network is becoming a potential bottleneck. This is a little conservative for me, but it will catch my attention to take a closer look at the network. At which % utilization Ethernet performance degrades depends on your environment and the published reference you use. It is generally accepted that when Ethernet network utilization rises above the 50-70 percent range, response times increase dramatically due to the associated network congestion bogging down the shared bus environment.

Some level of overhead is added to every packet of data that is placed onto the network by the protocols in use. When data is sent from an NT Server over the network, various protocols, such as the physical Ethernet and TCP/IP protocols, add certain amounts of overhead to each packet of information that heads out onto the network. This overhead takes up some of the available bandwidth on the network. Sending a smaller piece of information over the network takes up the same amount of protocol overhead as sending a larger piece of data. Thus, sending many smaller pieces of data over the network is less efficient than sending data in larger sizes.

Because of Ethernet's (10BaseT) loading characteristics and protocol overhead, expecting to get a full 10 Mbits/sec (1.25 Mbytes/sec) of throughput in conjunction with acceptable end user response times is unrealistic. Depending on the network characteristics that your NT Server is a part of, throughput achieved for a multiple client Ethernet network falls into the range of 5–7 Mbits/sec (0.6–0.8 Mbytes/sec).

100BaseT Fast Ethernet Performance

To improve the performance of 10BaseT Ethernet, 100BaseTX Fast Ethernet was developed. Electrically, Fast Ethernet and Ethernet operate at the same speed; however, Fast Ethernet increases the amount of bandwidth available by a factor of 10. An analogy to this is a highway. If 10BaseT Ethernet is a two-lane highway, Fast Ethernet is a 20-lane highway. Cars still operate at the local speed limit, but in a Fast Ethernet environment, many more cars can travel at the same time.

The Fast Ethernet protocol is also based on CSMA/CD. Hence, it exhibits similar network loading characteristics to Ethernet. Depending on the network characteristics that your NT Server is a part of, the realistic throughput that can be achieved for multiple client Fast Ethernet network segment ranges from of 50–70 Mbits/sec (6–8 Mbytes/sec).

Switched and Full Duplex Fast Ethernet

Networking technology moves just as fast, if not faster, than the rest of the information technology world. In an effort to improve the performance of the Ethernet protocol, shared media Ethernet has given way to switched Ethernet and full duplexing technologies. As outlined above, Ethernet's original design was based on a shared bus topology that is commonly implemented by using a shared Ethernet hub. With the advent of an Ethernet switch, an existing network is dynamically divided as needed into multiple parallel networks. Now, instead of implementing Ethernet with a shared Ethernet hub, an Ethernet switch can be used.

In a switched Ethernet environment, the Ethernet switch allows two or more pairs of network nodes to communicate together while other network nodes are also communicating at the same time. Depending on the number of network connections or ports that an Ethernet switch has available, multiple Ethernet connections can occur in parallel on the same Ethernet network segment without affecting the other stations on the network segment. Consider the following NT Server environment (Figure 7–1):

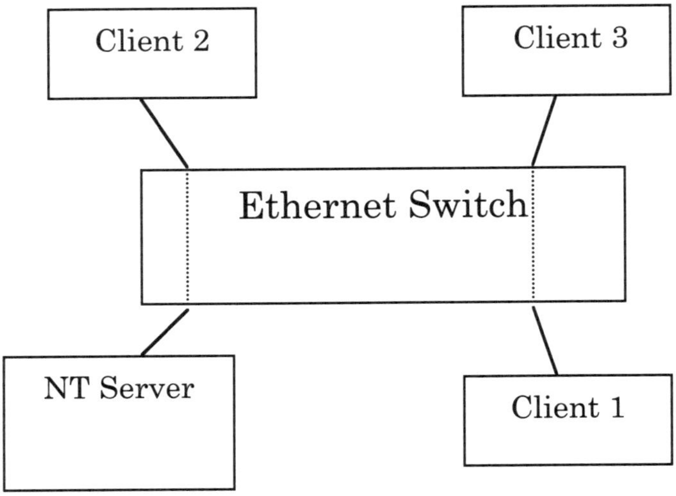

Figure 7-1 *Switched Ethernet environment.*

In this Ethernet switch based implementation, data is passed between NT Server and Client 2. While this is occurring, data is being passed between Client 1 and Client 3 at the same time, or in parallel. In an Ethernet switch environment, the switch manages the electrical interfaces that allow simultaneous transmission between multiple nodes, which eliminates collisions. When two clients want to access the same network station, such as if client 1 and client 2 wanted to access NT Server simultaneously, essentially the traditional Ethernet CSMA/CD still applies once the buffers in the switch are exhausted.

Under half duplex communications, data is only transmitted in a single direction at a time. Full duplex Ethernet technology is an enhancement that allows simultaneous two-way transmission between nodes while eliminating collisions. Full duplex transmission increases performance and efficiency by doubling the theoretical bandwidth of 10BaseT to 20 Mbits/sec or 200 Mbits/sec for 100BaseT.

For information on shared Ethernet and switched Ethernet environments, the Tolly Group produces extensive white papers analyzing network technologies from a network centric perspective. One such paper that was sponsored by Compaq provided an in-depth analysis of shared and switched Ethernet technology. This white paper, titled "Building Efficient Networks Using Switched 10 Mbit/s and Share 100 Mbit/s Ethernet" dated November 1997, can be downloaded from *http://www.tolly.com*.

Other Network Technologies

Beware of the network technology-of-the-week. When new technologies are implemented, they bring new functionality, flexibility, and sometimes improved performance to your NT Server solution. As new technologies are brought to market, they need to be supported in the NT Server framework, especially in how they utilize NT Server and how NT Server communicates to them through device drivers. Maturity of the device drivers and how well they handle the multiuser workloads of a server environment are very important.

Every environment is different. To understand how NT Server operates with different networking technologies, Buzz Payne of Cisco completed an exhaustive network test suite. This test suite involved two testing scenarios, a file transfer throughput test and a mixed traffic throughput test. The file transfer test consisted of transferring larger 10 Mbyte files to and from the server. The mixed data traffic consisted of the following data mix: 10 percent database transactions, 10 percent file transfers, 40 percent HTML text data, and 40 percent HTML graphics. Both tests were run in a switched Ethernet environment operating in *full duplex mode*. The Chariot software tool set was utilized to generate and measure the network workloads. More information on this tool is available from *http://www.ganymedsefotware.com*. Table 7.2 shows the results of this testing.

Table 7.2 Relative throughput levels of network technologies running under NT Server.

Network Technology	File Transfer Throughput (Mbits/sec)	Traffic Mix Throughput (Mbits/sec)
100BaseTX (Switched Full Duplex Ethernet)	128.9	72.2
FDDI	88.1	48.8
ATM	79.2	63.5

Each of these network technologies was tested in the same exact manner. These are the throughput levels achieved from a server perspective and measured by the clients in a switched network environment using TCP/IP as the network protocol. Under different conditions, the performance ratings may be different. What is important to recognize here is that every network technology requires an understanding of how it works and in which environment it works best.

Gigabit Ethernet

Gigabit Ethernet technology is the next step in improving Ethernet network performance. As of this book's publication, the total Gigabit Ethernet standard was not fully complete, although products are already emerging. As the name states, Gigabit Ethernet operates at a throughput of 1 Gigabits/sec (1000 Mbits/sec) and utilizes the same general protocol as Ethernet. In a test reported in the January 12, 1998 issue of Internet Week (*http://www.inter-netwk.com*), a Gigabit Ethernet adapter was tested running under NT Server 4 on a Digital Alpha Server 533 using a 64 bit PCI bus implementation. Internet Week reported throughput levels of 237 Megabits/sec (29.6 Mbytes/sec) using a single Gigabit Ethernet adapter in their test environment.

Even as a brand new technology, Gigabit Ethernet shows promise. As NT Server continues to mature, the combination of device drivers capable of better handling multiuser environments and the I20 I/O technology subsystem (reviewed in Chapter 6) , provides a good mix to continue improving the network performance that an NT Server solution will be capable of providing. One Gigabit/sec is approximately equivalent to 125 Mbytes/sec. Remembering that when configuring an NT Server the throughput of each link in the server's hardware data path should be considered; a Gigabit Ethernet adapter running at its theoretical speed could easily consume an entire 32 bit PCI bus (133 Mbytes/sec) on its own!

Understand the Network Architecture that Your NT Server Operates In

What may appear to be a performance problem blamed on the poor unsuspecting server could actually be caused by the network hardware and data workload patterns used to implement your network architecture. When implementing switching technology to get data to your NT Server, avoid potential bottlenecks from occurring outside of your server in the network. Look closely at the data flows of the network and aggregate throughput of the switch being employed. If your environment is such that many of the clients utilize peer to peer networking, an Ethernet switch is an excellent choice since it will be able to take advantage of the multiple parallel Ethernet communication paths which a switch provides.

When Is an Ethernet Switch Really Almost a Shared Ethernet Hub

If the network environment is one in which the clients rarely utilize peer to peer networking but rely primarily on the NT Server, ensure to do your data path link math. If you utilize a switch that has ten 10Mbit/sec ports which connects 9 clients and one NT server, there may be a problem. In a worst case scenario, each of the clients is active at the same time. This would generate a theoretical throughput of 90Mbits/sec. 90 Mbits/sec of data driving into an NT Server that only has a 10Mbit/sec-network connection switched or not creates a network bottleneck before the data ever reaches the NT Server.

For this specific environment, the benefits of the switch are not truly being realized and it is in essence acting like a shared media hub. To avoid this scenario, you must understand the network traffic flows. If, after reviewing the networking data, you see the NT Server is the center of attention, consider employing an Ethernet switch that encompasses nine 10Mbit/sec ports and one or two 100Mbits/sec connections. Using a switch with this combination, the 90Mbits/sec of worst case client workload can be better served as the data is placed onto a larger 100Mbit/sec data path into the NT Server.

NT Server Networking Performance Considerations

Many of the factors influencing the network subsystem performance of NT Server have already been reviewed throughout this book. Applications, CPU, memory, disk subsystem, and the performance of NT Server itself all influence how well the network subsystem operates. Taking a queue from Chapter 6, "NT Server and Disk System Performance," let's continue to follow the data path of network traffic as a client accesses data from an NT Server. For this example, shown in Figure 7–2, the client is an NT Workstation and the server is based on NT Server.

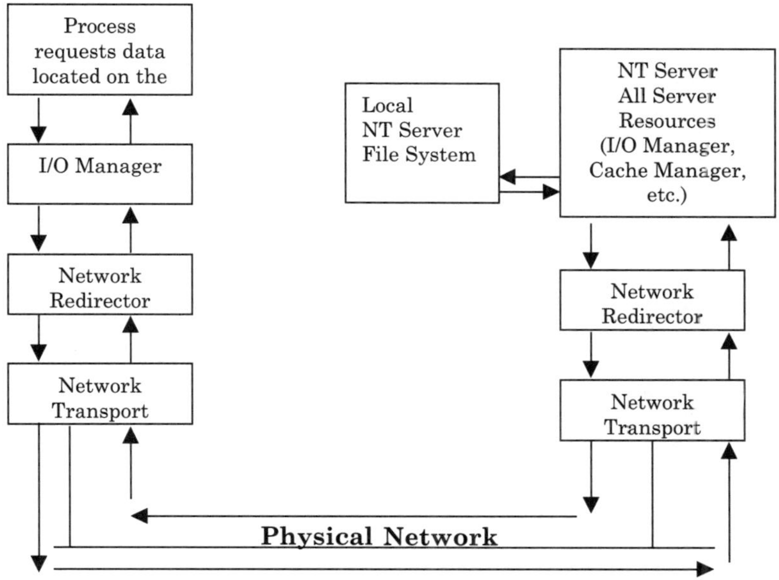

Figure 7–2 *Obtaining data from an NT Server.*

Figure 7–2 is a simplification of the data path followed when an NT Workstation process requests data from a shared resource on an NT Server, but it suffices to point out the primary data paths involved around NT Server's performance considerations.

Once the data request is made by the client process, the client's I/O manager realizes that the requested data is not located on the local disk subsystem and sends the data requests to the network redirector for service. The network redirector in turn sends the request across the network using a network transport. The network redirector must be able to access the remote server's resource using some type of client software. Under NT Server or Workstation, the client software that handles the client portion of this client server connection is the workstation service. (A service under NT Server or Workstation is an application/process running in the background.) The data utilizes a network transport such as TCP/IP over the physical network (Ethernet in this example) to NT Server.

The networking software component on NT Server checks the first network transport bound to the network interface card and then continues through the list of available transports until a match is found or an error is generated. Once the correct network transport is located, it is utilized to get the data to the server's redirector. Under NT Server (or Workstation), the network software component that accepts data from the client side workstation service is the server service. This is the same server service component that allows NT Server to share data across the network as well as accept client requests. The client request for data is then passed to NT Server's I/O manager which, working with NT Server's other components, obtains the data from the disk subsystem attached to the server. The data is then returned using the same data path to the client making the request.

From a performance perspective the physical network technology is already closely discussed. But what of the other components of the data path? From the perspective of the client application requesting data from the shared resource, perhaps a word processing file that resides on the server, it is not concerned where the file is located, the requesting process just considers it a file. From NT Server's perspective, the I/O manager takes advantage of the Cache Manager in the same general manner outlined here and in Chapter 8. If multiple clients are requesting the same data from the server, this data will quickly be cached in the file system cache on the server. As the requested data is cached, the response time provided back to the clients is greatly improved because the amount of disk I/O required is lowered. *The file system cache is an important fact to consider when sizing the memory subsystem for both disk and network subsystem performance.*

This example illustrates the importance of understanding the network data flow and what NT Server is doing with the request. In some aspects, NT Server handles a request for data on a networked resource similarly as if it was requested by a locally running server. The same techniques outlined in

Chapter 5 (memory) and Chapter 6 (disk) for monitoring and tuning memory and disk resources also apply in the networked environment.

NT Server Network Performance and the CPU

An NT Server utilizes a network interface card (NIC) to physically attach itself to the network. As network data in the form of packets arrive, they are passed up the server's data path. For this to occur, the NIC must interrupt the server's CPU and request service. This is an interrupt request (IRQ). When a hardware device interrupts the processor, the server's CPU interrupt handler may elect to execute the majority of its work in a deferred procedure call (DPC). This is typical of network device drivers that adhere to the NT Server miniport device driver specification. DPCs run at lower priority than interrupts, permitting new interrupts to occur while DPCs are being executed. The server's CPUs are assigned to handle interrupts for a particular network interface during initialization. More powerful CPUs are capable of handling higher numbers of IRQs, which results in fewer DPCs occurring and subsequently supporting higher network load levels and better response time to the end user.

In a multiple CPU NT Server environment that is characterized with high amounts of network activity, one of the CPUs can become overloaded servicing network-generated interrupt requests. The catalysts for a single CPU bottleneck in a multiple CPU based server is due to the fact that a single CPU is assigned to handle interrupts for a particular NIC at boot time. The other CPUs in the server are not assigned to handle interrupts directly from the specific NIC, but do provide a supporting role servicing DPCs. If the network traffic is intense and multiple CPUs are available, additional NICs can be added to take advantage of the other CPUs in the server. The addition of multiple NICs spreads out the network interrupt servicing between the CPUs. When NT Server is rebooted after adding additional NICs, the interrupt handling for the different NICs are spread across the server's CPUs. In this manner, more network-intensive workloads can be supported. Figure 7–3 depicts a Perfmon screen shot from an NT Server involved in an increasingly intense network environment that is composed of four Pentium Pro CPUs and four 100BaseT NICs.

Each individual CPU's interrupt processor time is shown in this graph. If it is a little difficult to distinguish between each of the CPU's usage levels in the graph, this is because the interrupts generated from the network load of the four NICs are distributed among the four CPUs. Although this distribution is not perfect, it is a significant improvement over a single CPU server implementation. If a single CPU based server were supporting this level of network workload, over 34 percent of the CPU's activities would revolve around servicing low-level interrupts. This particular server also supported a CPU intensive server application. With a combination of these two workloads, the server would have quickly developed a CPU bottleneck in a single CPU environment. Once the CPU became the bottleneck, it would slow further network operations.

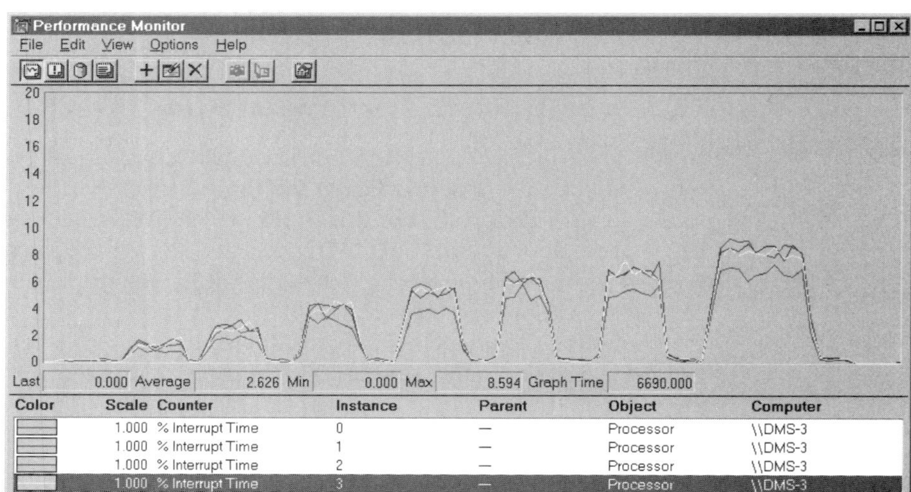

Figure 7-3 *Four NICs interrupt workload balanced across four CPUs.*

When to Use Multiple NICs

Whenever an NT Server is supporting an intensive network workload, the server is a candidate to support multiple CPUs and NICs. NT Server supports multiple NIC cards attached to the same logical network segment or subnet. I refer to a logical network segment as networked computers in the same collision domain. When multiple NICs are used on the same network segment, response time can be improved as the CPU workload is spread across the CPUs in the server; consequently, each NIC can be provided with better service. Multiple NICs servicing the same network segment does not improve network performance if the network segment itself is saturated (50–70 percent utilization).

When the network segment itself is saturated, distributing client workload between separate network segments can provide better performance. For this type of implementation, each NIC being used under NT Server must be assigned a different network segment or collision domain. Multiple NICs still take advantage of the multiple CPUs while each network segment's utilization level is lowered as fewer clients are connected to each network segment.

It Takes Two to Tango

Up to this point various links in the data path have been reviewed except one, the client. NT Server supports a plethora of networking protocols and clients running various operating systems. True performance in an interactive user application is measured by the perceived response time that the end user experiences. Many of the concepts investigated in this book can be applied directly to detecting and tuning client computer bottlenecks as well, regardless of the operating system. Obviously, it is easier to apply the concepts covered if the client computer is running NT Workstation or Server, but even if the operating system in use is different, the biggest change is the tools that are utilized for collection of the pertinent data. One suggestion when working with the performance of client systems: closely investigate the application design and the client's video display card. The combination of a well designed front-end application and a fast video display card greatly influence an end user's perceived response time.

Next Generation Server Networking: $I_2 0$

With all of the overhead introduced by the network protocols in current use (the extensive code path that many device drivers must follow, CPU interrupts overhead generated by NIC cards), a new technique to implement server networking is on the horizon to address these issues. The same Intelligent I/O Initiative ($I_2 0$) technology reviewed in Chapter 6 will also influence network performance of future NT Servers.

$I_2 0$ technology allows the CPU overhead traditionally handled by the server's CPUs to be offloaded to more intelligent $I_2 0$ based NICs. $I_2 0$ based intelligent devices utilize their own CPUs to offload low level I/O handling and create a secondary PCI bus to move I/O activity off the primary PCI bus. This hardware technology in conjunction with the $I_2 0$ split driver architecture allows for the design of more efficient network device drivers. With less data traversing the system bus and more of the server's CPU power available for the applications, NT Servers have the potential of drastically improving their overall performance. Although not fully supported today, new server technology should be obtained so that it can be upgraded in both hardware and software to take advantage of the emerging $I_2 0$ technology.

Sizing the NT Server Network Subsystem

How Many Users

A classic question when sizing an NT Server network subsystem is, "How many concurrent users or clients can a single network segment support?" Each client that is logged into a server consumes some level of server resources. But it is the clients who are concurrently making requests of the server that are the primary focus when sizing the network subsystem. This is an important distinction. Supporting 500 users sounds much more impressive than stating 50 concurrent users can be supported. The total number of users impacts the sizing of other server resources, such as required user disk space, more so than it affects sizing the network subsystem.

A simplified rule of thumb to determine the number of concurrent clients to connect per network segment is to ascertain what the least acceptable throughput for each concurrent network client is, then divide that amount into the selected network throughput. For example, if each client should have no less then 1.5 Mbits/sec of available bandwidth, and the network supports 100 Mbits/sec, the segment could possibly support 66 clients. Unfortunately, this simple calculation does not take into account the network media characteristics, but it does provide a starting point for the maximum amount of clients per network segment.

Obtain The Basic Requirements

As with any sizing exercise, the type of workload the server must support is very important. How a user is defined varies greatly from one environment to the next. Once the type of network workload is determined, the throughput level and response time provided to the end users are the next pieces of the puzzle that must be defined. User workload information is many times available as historical information from server log files currently supporting similar workloads. Under NT Server, information such as bytes/sec and total user connections can be obtained under Perfmon's Server object. The bytes/sec counter displays all network traffic occurring on the NT Server (including the additional bytes added by the network protocols). Dividing the bytes/sec by the theoretical network bandwidth for the networking technology in use provides the %utilization of the network. The Logon Total is a helpful counter to determine the total number of users who have logged into the server since the last reboot. An even more helpful counter is Server Sessions. The Server Sessions counters provide a count of the number of active sessions or concurrent users on the server. Reviewing the %utilization and Server sessions over time you can conclude how much bandwidth is required to support a specific number of concurrent users. If only 20 percent of an Ethernet based network is utilized when supporting 25 users, the current network technology in place has room to grow or plenty of headroom to support potential surges in network traffic.

Applications such as Microsoft Exchange, SQL Server, and others add extensible counters to Perfmon. These application specific counters are very helpful in determining the historical information under NT Server. For network subsystem sizing, these extensible application counters help to identify more exact information on each application's workload than NT Server's default Perfmon tool can provide by itself.

Industry Benchmarks Are Your Next Best Friend

Using a combination of historical information and your own stress tests (as outlined in Chapter 2) are excellent methods to use when initially sizing your network subsystem. Unfortunately, what can you do if none of the options stated are available? Hopefully, some type of background information on what the server will be used for will be available. Try to match this background information against the various Industry Benchmarks (Chapter 2) available, then extrapolate from them for your environment.

To determine the initial network subsystem requirements for Chapter 8's File Server case study, we found the Ziff Davis NetBench as a relevant industry benchmark. For the File Server case study example, it was determined that the server will be placed into the current network architecture via a 100BaseT-switch up-link. PC Magazine's NetBench results implied that a file server with two 100BaseT network interface cards could support a throughput of up to 60 Mbites/sec while servicing 20 concurrent clients. This indicates that each network adapter was only able to support approximately 30 Mbites/sec and 10 concurrent clients. This extrapolation provided an excellent place to start. Refer back to Chapter 8's File Server case study for an example of sizing the network in conjunction with a stress test, and Chapter 8's Web Server case study for sizing the network requirements without the benefit of a stress test.

Vendor websites for NCR, Microsoft, HP, Compaq, and other vendors that manufacture NT Servers are good places to search for industry benchmarks to use in your sizing efforts. One site that gathers multiple benchmark results together in one place is the IDEAS International site located at *http://www.ideasinternational.com/benchmark/bench.html.*

Server Network Card Selections

The type and number of network cards required for a server is obviously dependent on the network architecture the server will be deployed into. Once the other basic requirements such as throughput and number of network segments are determined, keep in mind that NT Server can support multiple network interface cards. 100BaseT Ethernet cards are now available in single, dual, and quad channel configurations. The largest benefit from the use of higher density channel NICs is the conservation of PCI slots on the server. In real world testing, a quad Pentium Pro NCR 4300 server easily supports four 100BaseT NICs. Under Perfmon, each NIC supported a separate network segment while the bytes/sec being driven from the server on a per NIC basis was 4 Mbytes/sec (32 Mbits/sec) for a combined aggregate throughput of 16 Mbytes/sec (128 Mbits/sec). Even at this level of performance, the NT Server's network subsystem had room to grow.

Detecting NT Server Network Bottlenecks

Always Consider the Big Picture

Before looking at an NT Server specific network related counter, let's step back and consider a broader view of the NT Server solution in place. Why? The Perfmon counters that we review to help in detecting a network bottleneck are not as distinctive as the other Perfmon counters used for detecting other bottlenecks in the server that we covered in previous chapters. When you look at disk usage, the data paths involved are internal to the server (clustering is another discussion). For network environments, the data paths outside of your server influence the end users perception of the server's performance.

When detecting network bottlenecks, it is of the utmost importance to understand the network architecture that your NT Server is part of to help in deciding that the network is a bottleneck. Stop here and read that last sentence a few more times; it is that important. When detecting network bottlenecks, a reverse detection strategy is prudent. Instead of sleuthing out a network bottleneck directly by looking at NT Server's network related Perfmon counters (later in this chapter), first look at the other server resources. Are they acting as bottlenecks? This reverse detection strategy is a process of elimination. If all of the other server resources are not bottlenecks, and the server's application response times to the end users has seen better days, look closely at the server's network subsystem.

When reviewing the network subsystem, a close understanding of which network technology is in use and its characteristics must be known when sleuthing out NT Server network bottlenecks. NT Server is sometimes deceiving in what it reports.

Big Picture Network Bottleneck Detection Example: Follow the Network Data Flow

Consider if an NT Server is connected to a Fast Ethernet network via a network hub that was recently replaced for service; users begin reporting slow response times a few weeks later when the end of the month reports are due. Under Perfmon, you observe that the Network Interface object counter, Current Bandwidth, is reporting that the network interface card is operating at 100 Mbits/sec (12.5 Mbytes/sec) and that the network interface bytes/sec is operating at 6.5 Mbits/sec (0.813 Mbytes/sec). This Perfmon data is illustrated in Figure 7–4.

The obvious reaction would be that there is plenty of bandwidth available, as less than 6.5 percent of the network is utilized. So let's look for the bottleneck elsewhere. Employing the reverse detection strategy, you use the

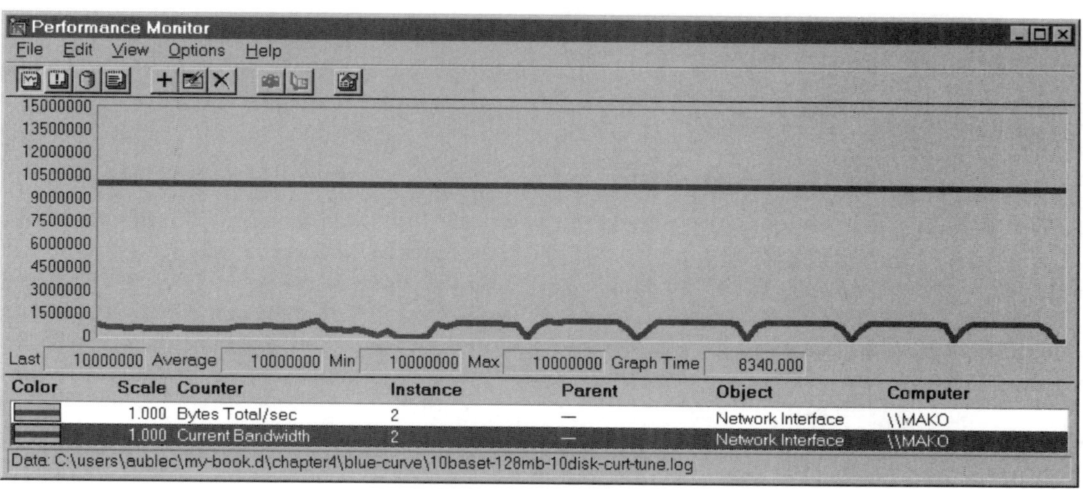

Figure 7–4 *Network utilization from a big picture perspective.*

methodologies and techniques outlined throughout this book to check all the server resources and find them well within acceptable limits. Now what?

If all of the server resources are operating normally and the applications are running normally, follow the data flow out to the server's network connection. From the Perfmon data shown in Figure 7–4, it does appear that the bytes/sec counter flattens out during each network surge, which is indicative of something holding back its performance since more than 6.5 Mbits/sec should be achievable in a 100BaseT networking environment. Even though the Current Bandwidth counter indicated a 100BaseT connection, the network interface card in auto sensing mode provided false information; this server was actually connected to a 10BaseT hub.

This discovery was made when following the data from the server to its first stop, the new network hub. As the hub was examined, even though it looked like the old network hub, it was mistakenly replaced with a 10BaseT hub. Because of this, the network segment the server was attached to was running at 10 Megabits/sec (1.25 Mbytes/sec). Now compare this newly acquired knowledge about the network architecture with the network interface average bytes/sec counter that reported 6.5 Mbits/sec (0.813 Mbytes/sec). It can now be determined from the information provided here and the Ethernet characteristics reviewed in the beginning of the chapter that it was indeed a network bottleneck. The 10BaseT Ethernet based network was near its saturation level by trying to operate at an average utilization level of 65 percent. If you were curious, this problem was removed by replacing the 10BaseT Ethernet hub with a 100BaseT implementation and rebooting NT Server once the new network connections were in place. This is a good example why NICs should be set to a specific setting. If the NIC was set to 100BaseT and a 10BaseT hub replaced the 100BaseT hub, the NIC would not have worked, thus avoiding any problems to begin with.

How Bad Is Bad?

In the example above, a 100BaseT hub was accidentally replaced by a 10BaseT hub used by the client systems to access the NT Server. When the network is the resource throttling the overall perceived NT Server performance, what type of effects might the end users experience? The throughput and response times provided would obviously lower considerably. To find out just how much, the 100BaseT-shared Ethernet hub was replaced with a 10BaseT hub in Configuration 4 of Chapter 8's File Server case study. No other changes were made. The File Server stress test user loads introduced using the Bluecurve stress-testing tool were also identical. Figure 7–5 and 7–6 show the associated throughputs and average response times experienced before and after the slower hub was introduced.

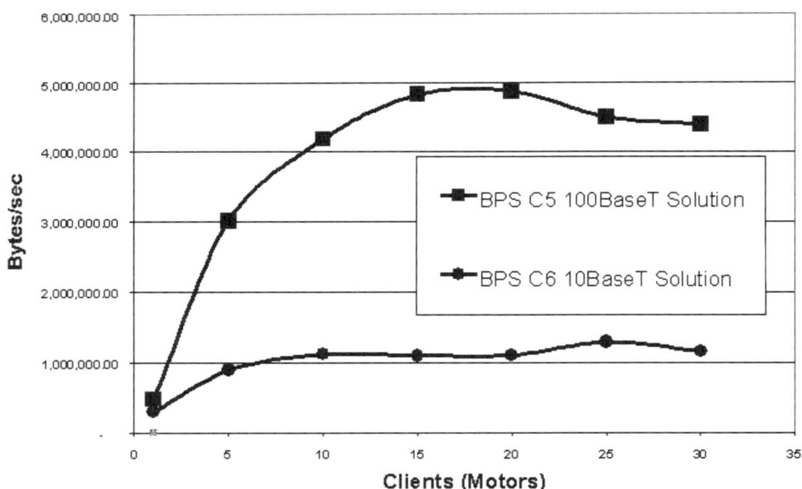

Figure 7–5 *Average network response time when comparing 100BaseT Network versus 10BaseT Network.*

(Note: The average response time is measured in bytes/sec.The higher the values, the better the results.)

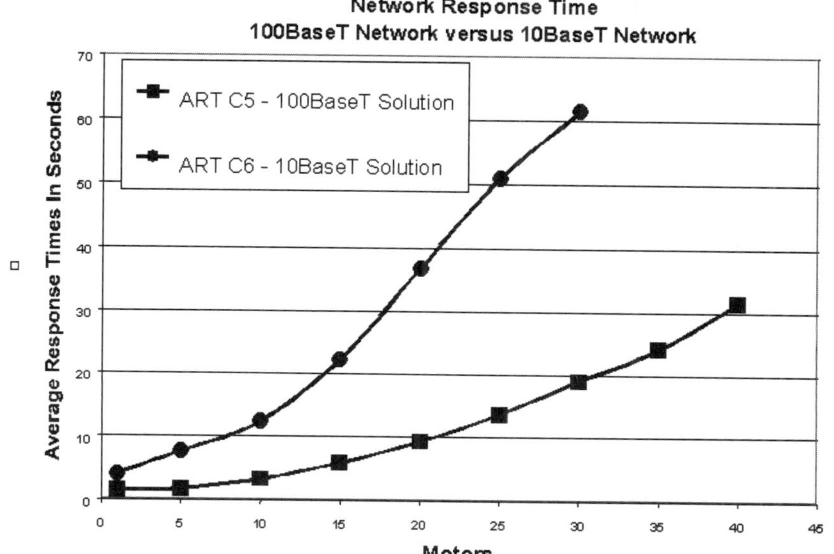

Figure 7–6 *Average network throughput when comparing 100BaseT and 10BaseT Networks.*

(Note: The network throughput is measured in seconds. The lower the values, the better the results.)

It is amazing the effect one slow performance link in the network data path can make!

Never Quit

What if the problem is not as obvious as an incorrectly installed network hub? With the information provided in this book, you can help prove that the NT Server is not the bottleneck. A detailed answer on network troubleshooting is outside of the scope of this book's focus of NT Server tuning and sizing. In general, however, continue to follow the data path through the network all the way to the client experiencing the poor response times. Once at the client, utilize the same strategies and techniques used throughout this book to sleuth out client and network bottlenecks, although the actual tools you use may be different.

These troubleshooting roads actually lead back to Chapter 2's recommendation of creating a prototype of your NT Solution and developing a baseline of it in a controlled environment before deployment. With a sound baseline to use as a frame of reference, it becomes easier to detect server, network, or application bottlenecks.

General NT Server Network Bottleneck Detection Strategy

Recall from Chapter 2 that it is important to consider the entire server performance picture when trying to locate any NT Server bottlenecks. There can be more than one server resource area that is contributing to the throttling of the server's overall performance. Once all of the major server resource areas are evaluated, focus in on the resource that is farthest to the left in the Performance Resource Chart introduced in Chapter 2 and repeated here in Figure 7–7 for reference. This strategy will provide the greatest immediate gain to the servers overall performance.

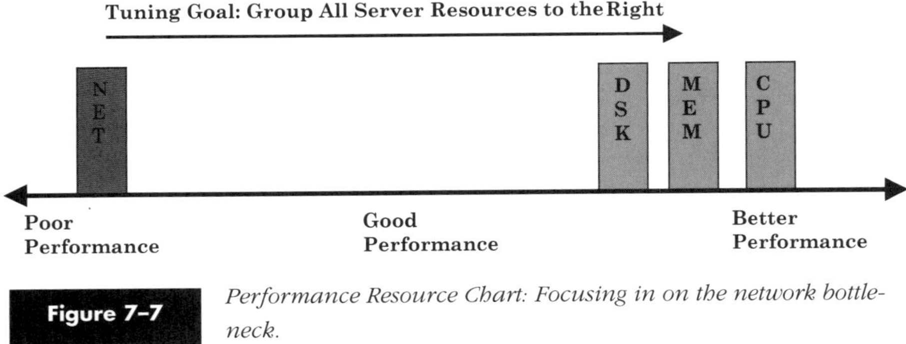

Figure 7–7 *Performance Resource Chart: Focusing in on the network bottleneck.*

Focusing in on Specific NT Server Network Bottlenecks

Ok, you know your environment, understand the network technologies in use, and employ the reverse bottleneck detection strategy. What indicators does NT Server itself provide that a network bottleneck may be forming? Listed in Table 7.3 are the primary Perfmon objects and counters to consider when investigating an NT Server bottleneck.

Table 7.3 Network focused Perfmon counters to use in network bottleneck detection.

Object/Counter	Definition	Rule of Thumb for Bottleneck Detection
Network Interface: Output Queue Length	Output Queue Length is the length of the output packet queue (in packets).	If this value is >3 for sustained periods of time (>15 minutes), the selected network interface instance is becoming a network bottleneck. Note that this value is not valid in SMP environments as of NT 4 SP3. Look for future service packs to fix this abnormality.
Network Interface: Bytes Total/sec	Bytes total per second is the rate that bytes are sent and received on the selected network interface, including framing characters.	This value is directly related to the network architecture in use. If the value of bytes total/sec for the network instance is close to the maximum transfer rates of your network, and the Output Queue Length is >3, you have a network bottleneck.
Network Interface: Current Bandwidth	Current Bandwidth is an estimate of the interface's current bandwidth in bits per second.	For interfaces that do not vary in bandwidth or for those where no accurate estimation can be made, this value is the nominal bandwidth reported by NT Server. Use this information in conjunction with the Bytes Total/sec counter to determine the network utilization levels.
Network Segment: %Network Utilization	Percentage of network bandwidth in use on this network segment.	The network architecture in use determines the acceptable level of % Utilization. For Ethernet based network segments, if this value is consistently above 50-70 percent range, the network segment is becoming a bottleneck and is increasing the response times to everyone using the network.
Network Interface: Packets Outbound and Received Errors	Packets Outbound Errors/ Received is the number of outbound packets that could not be transmitted/ processed because of network errors.	If this value is >1, the selected network interface is experiencing network problems that are causing the network to slow and potentially become a bottleneck. This problem could be emanating from any NIC or network device connected to the network segment.
Redirector: Current Commands	Current Commands counts the number of requests to the Redirector that are currently queued for service.	If this number is much larger than the number of network adapter cards installed in the computer, then the network(s) and/or the server(s) being accessed are seriously bottlenecked.

Table 7.3 Network focused Perfmon counters to use in network bottleneck detection.

Object/Counter	Definition	Rule of Thumb for Bottleneck Detection
Server:Work Item Shortage	The number of times STATUS_DATA_NOT_ACCEPTED was returned at receive indication time.	This indicates that NT Server has not allocated sufficient initworkitems or maxworkitems which are causing network limitations.

Adding Networking Related Counters to Perfmon

As a reminder, both the Network Interface and Network Segment objects are not installed under the default NT Server installation. To add these Perfmon objects, follow these steps:

1. Add the SNMP Agent service under Start|Settings|Control Panel|Network|Services|Add select SNMP Service. Adding this service installs the network interface segment object to Perfmon.
2. Add the Network Tools and Agent under Start|Settings|Control Panel|Network|Services|Add select Network Tools and Agent. This will install the network segment object to Perfmon, network monitor agent, and the real time Network Monitor based application.

After these services are added, NT Server is required to be rebooted before any changes will take affect.

Performance Drain: Network Segment Object

The Network Segment is the only Perfmon object that may significantly affect your server's performance in a negative manor. Collecting data using this object places the selected network interface card into promiscuous mode. This will add additional overhead to your server above and beyond the standard Perfmon application. In promiscuous mode, the selected NT Server NIC grabs (reads) every network packet traversing the network segment that it encounters even if it is not addressed to the server itself. This is less of a concern in a switched Ethernet environment. If the NT Server is attached to the network via a switched Ethernet port, the designated NIC in promiscuous mode still reads every packet on the network subnet. However, the network traffic headed to an address other than the server itself will never pass by the promiscuous NIC due to the parallel nature of the switch.

Single CPU NT Server Network Subsystem Bottleneck Detection

If NT Server data headed for the network must wait in line to traverse the network, the network has become a bottleneck throttling the server's performance. A good counter to check for a network queue backup is the Network Interface object's Output Queue Length counter. The Output Queue Length counter displays if there are any outbound network packets backing up in the selected NIC's queue. If this value is greater than three over an extended period of time, there is a bottleneck associated with the network. This counter is only relevant in single CPU NT Server implementations. In NT Servers with greater then one CPU, this counter does not provide reliable information. As of NT 4.0 Service Pack 3 this "feature" has not been fixed.

Multiple CPU NT Server Network Subsystem Bottleneck Detection

NT Server does not currently (as of NT Server 4 SP3) provide a clear mechanism for the detection of network bottlenecks. However, with the combination of several Perfmon counters and an understanding of the networking architecture in use (the theme of this chapter), network subsystem bottlenecks can be detected. If the %Network Utilization counter indicates that more than 50-70 percent of an Ethernet network segment is being utilized for a sustained period of time, the network has become a bottleneck. It is normal for an occasional large file transfer to send a spike into the %network utilization counter. An occasional spike of intense network traffic is not a good indicator of network bottleneck, as it will only affect the network's overall performance for a very short period of time. Of course, if the network traffic spikes occur during an important network videoconference with your most important customer, you may want to track down the prankster or change the network architecture in place.

If the %Network Utilization counter is not enabled, determine the %utilization of the network architecture in use by dividing the bytes total/sec counter by the current bandwidth counter. Once you obtain the %utilization, follow the loading characteristics for the network technology in use by your NT Server to determine what level of utilization is acceptable.

Extreme Network Bottleneck Detection and Errors

Determining if the network utilization levels for a specific network technology are causing a network bottleneck is a sound concept to take advantage of to determine if the network subsystem is becoming a bottleneck. Under extreme circumstances, when the network subsystem is truly under siege, by which time end users will be storming the computer room gates, there are some red flag counters to keep a close watch on. If the Redirector: Current Commands counter is greater than the number of NIC cards in the server, or Server: Work Item Shortage counters is greater than a one, the network has become a serious bottleneck. When errors on a network segment occur in such a manner that when the data that arrives to NT Server is unusable, precious network bandwidth is being wasted and response times may be suffering. Monitor Network Interface: Packets Outbound and Received Errors to determine if there are problems with the network segment connecting NT Server to the outside world. In the Electronic Mail Server case study in Chapter 8, errors were found occurring during the initial stress tests. These network errors were isolated using a Network General Sniffer (*http://www.networkgeneral.com*). A network sniffer is a network specific troubleshooting tool. The network errors were eventually tracked to malfunctioning NICs.

Tuning Network Resources

Now that we can sleuth whether or not the network is becoming a bottleneck or already is, here are several strategies to consider when tuning the network:

- Distribute the network load supported under NT Server network
- Directly tune various components of NT Server to improve performance
- Remove unnecessary data from the network as it pertains to NT Server
- Adjust the system architecture to control network traffic flows
- Select a different networking technology with higher bandwidth

From the strategies defined above, we will now focus on tactics to implement them that relate directly to NT Server's perspective of the network.

Distributing NT Server Network Load

Balance NT Server Network Loads

Balance your network load by distributing the more heavily used network segments between two or more NICs. Even though network segmentation can involve some new cabling (physical) and subnetting (logical addressing), it is a proven technique to optimize your server's network I/O.

To accomplish this, a tool generically referred to as a network sniffer becomes helpful in analyzing the network traffic associated with NT Server. There are software and hardware based sniffers available for this task. Fortunately, NT Server 4 provides a limited functionality network sniffer that is an excellent addition to the growing NT Server tool set. The Network Monitor tool is installed under NT Server when the Network Tools and Agent are installed. This procedure is outlined earlier in this chapter. Start the network monitor by selecting the Start | Programs | Administrative Tools | Network Monitor. Activate the Network Monitor by selecting Capture | Start. Once activated, the Network Monitor tool provides a large amount of data in the default configuration view. Figure 7–8 depicts a screen shot of the Network Monitor Tool.

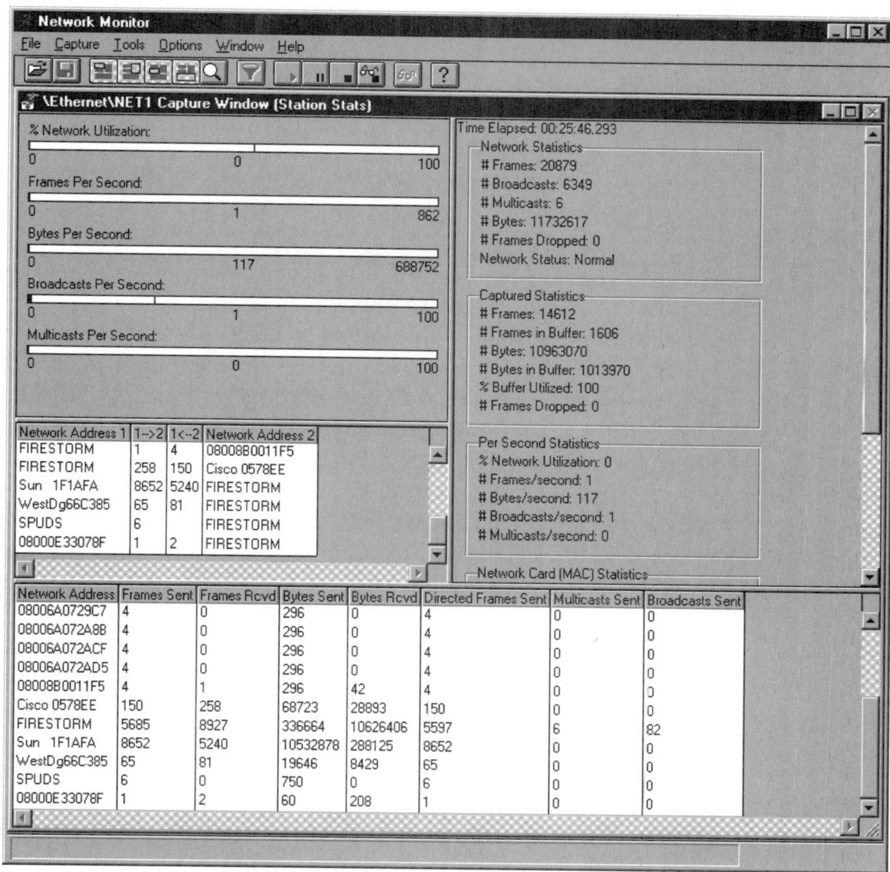

Figure 7–8 *Using Network Monitor to isolate network intensive clients.*

As shown in Figure 7–8, this tool can be used to quickly isolate that unruly power user or users. In this Network Monitor screen shot, the top three network stations are a Sun system (server), Firestorm (an NT Server), and a Cisco network device (router). Data from each capture can be saved over time to help in developing a network traffic baseline. Once you determine which users are slowing the network down for everyone, connect an additional NIC to your NT Server and reconfigure your network to support another network segment. This will lower the amount of traffic on the first

NIC and allow the interrupts from both NIC workloads to be spread across multiple NT Server CPUs (if needed). This will improve the overall response times that the end users are experiencing if the network is indeed the bottleneck throttling NT Server's performance.

The Network Monitor is not a fully functional network sniffer as found in tools dedicated to this function, but it does provide some packet drill down capabilities. Install and investigate this tool. You may find it a helpful ally to have.

Tuning NT Server's Network Subsystem Directly

Available Network Protocols/Redirectors

Another technique that can help you optimize your NT Server's network subsystem performance is to bind only protocols and redirectors (server components other than NT Server "server service") that your network is actually using to your network adapter. Binding is a technique NT Server utilizes to establish a communications channel between the protocol driver (TCP/IP, IPX, etc) and the NIC itself. Under Start|Settings|Control Panel|Network Protocol, check which protocols (TCP/IP, NetBEUI, etc) are currently installed. Also under Control Panel|Network |Services, check which redirectors (RIP for NwLink, RPC support for Banyan, etc.) are installed. Removing unnecessary protocols and redirectors lowers the amount of memory that NT Server requires for network I/O (which can then be used for other tasks) and ensures that your network is not generating any unnecessary traffic, such as unwanted broadcasts.

Network Binding Selection Order

If more than one network protocol or redirector is in use, tune the binding search order by placing the protocol/redirector most commonly used on the top of the bindings list under Start|Settings|Control Panel|Network |Bindings. All network calls are routed to the protocol/redirector first on the list, then NT waits for a response before submitting to the next protocol/redirector.

Multiple NICs Provide CPU Advantages

Slow network response can on occasion be contributed to an overworked CPU. NT Server can support multiple NICs on the same network segment. This technique is referred to as multihoming. To alleviate slow response time contributed to an overworked CPU, add an additional CPU and NIC. Splitting the network into multiple segments, the network load can be distributed across the multiple NICs and CPUs. This distributes the interrupts required for servicing the NICs across the CPUs and frees up the CPU cycles to work on other tasks besides low level networking I/O.

Tuning Multihomed Computers

When a multihomed computer is connected to two different networks using NetBIOS over TCP/IP, a connection delay can occur. This problem occurs when more than one path to the destination computer exists, and the redirector selects the less optimal path. This can cause packets sent to a directly connected subnet to be routed internally to the destination, causing a delay.

To work around this problem, a new version of the redirector and the NetBT transport are provided with NT Server 4.0 Service Pack 3. After updating NT Server 4 with Service Pack 3, the registry must be edited to force NT Server to have the redirector connect using the first successful call to the destination; thus ignoring the transport binding order when establishing a NetBIOS connection. Use regedt32.exe or your favorite registry editor to add the "'IgnoreBindingOrder'" key of data type REG_DWORD with a value of 1 to the HKEY_LOCAL_MACHINE\System\CurrentControlSet\Services\Rdr\Parameters registry location. [This information obtained and paraphrased from the Microsoft Knowledge base website found under *http://www.microsoft.com*.]

Permanently Cache MAC Addresses

A MAC address is a unique address that a manufacturer burns into a NIC, such as a 100BaseT Ethernet card. TCP/IP uses arp broadcasts over the network to associate an IP address with a physical layer MAC address. To lower the number of broadcasts and time it requires to obtain MAC addresses, you can permanently (until next reboot unless a startup script is used) place the associated MAC/IP address pair into memory. Use the following command sequence from the command prompt to implement: "arp -s 137.111.141.101 01-01-01-12-s3-44." This feature is particularly helpful when accessing a commonly networked system that uses a static IP address. This is not a suggested technique when the networked system uses dynamic IP addressing (DHCP).

Controlling Network Users Timeout Period

There are only so many resources allocated for network connections, so if a user strolled away from their desk to enjoy a sunny day, disconnect them. This frees up resources for active uses. The command "net config server" lists the NT Server's current settings. Running the command "net config server / AUTODISCONNECT: 10" sets the automatic disconnect time (idle session time) to 10 minutes. This command is run from the NT Server command line and is permanent until it is run again.

Network Interface Card (NIC) Tuning

In some cases it is possible to tune a NIC itself. Some NICs allow the maximum number of receive lists the driver allocates for receive frames which can improve the NICs performance. For example, the registry entry to add for a Compaq Netelligent 10/100TX NIC is MaxReceives. This key is a REG_DWORD and values are placed into it in hex. The Compaq website, *http://www.compaq.com*, suggested increasing the MaxReceives counters for this NIC to 500 (a hex value of 0x1F4). Place this registry value into the following location:

HKEY_LOCAL_MACHINE\SYSTEM\CurrentControlSet\Services\cpqnf3(#)\Parameters

Avoid Automatic Network Interface Card Settings

Setting the NIC properly is an area that is commonly taken for granted. Even though various standards defining the physical and logical specifications of network communications exist, some compatibility issues show up when you are not looking. Set your NT Server's NIC and any other network devices your server may communicate with to the best possible network speed setting available. For example, if full duplex 100BaseTX is available and the other network devices support this setting, choose it. Only as a last resort select auto sensing. This does incur more work, but it can be well worth the effort.

Tuning Interrupt and Deferred Procedure Calls (DPCs)

Each network request received over the network generates an interrupt to the processor requesting service. If the processor does not find the request urgent enough (a high enough interrupt level), it will defer the request. This deferred interrupt request becomes a Deferred Procedure Call (DPC). As more and more requests come into the server, the number of interrupts and DPCs increase. When an interrupt is sent to a particular CPU and it gets deferred, additional server overhead is incurred if this DPC is shipped off to another CPU in the server. This can be costly from a performance perspective. To stop this from happening, set the following registry value to: HKEY_LOCAL_MACHINE\System\CurrentControlSet\Services\NDIS\Parameters\ProcessorAffinityMask to 0. This will force the CPU that handled the interrupt initially to also handle any subsequently associated DPCs that are generated. This tuning can improve the CPU's service of interrupts and DPCs generated by the NICs.

Removing Unnecessary NT Server Data from the Network

Controlling Network Traffic Patterns

If you can lower the amount of unnecessary network traffic traversing the network, the overall network %utilization is lowered and more bandwidth is available. Controlling all user network traffic flow is unrealistic. You can, however, control some aspects of it. In an NT Server environment, there is a large amount of network traffic generated around the network that borders on excessive to meet NT Server's objectives.

The Browser Service provides a list of available network resources. A master browser collects and maintains a list of available network resources and assigns backup browsers to take its place in case it fails. When a backup browser computer is booted, it exchanges network resource lists with the master to ensure that if the need arises, the backup browser can seamlessly take over the master browser responsibilities. If a backup browser is unable to locate the master browser, it will force an election on the network, between all available backup browsers, which contributes to even more network traffic. By controlling the number of computers that can become backup browsers on your NT Server network, you can control the potential network surges of information associated with the browser process described. Various Microsoft client systems can become master browsers such as NT Server, NT Workstation, Windows for Workgroups, and Windows 95, to name a few. For the non-Microsoft world, such as UNIX based computers, the browser network overhead is a nonissue (unless they are running an NT Server emulation application such as SAMBA).

In NT Server, you can control if it can become a master, backup, or will not participate in the browser games by editing the following registry entry with regedt32.exe or your favorite registry editor: HKEY_LOCAL_MACHINE\System\CurrentControlSet\Services\browser\paramters\MaintainServerList. The possible entries are yes, no, and auto. A yes entry indicates the server will be a backup browser. A no entry indicates that this server will not participate in the browser game. The auto entry, which is the default, forces the server to ask the master browser to decide if this server can be a backup browser. How you make your selection depends on your environment requirements.

SNMP Agent Control

Simple Network Management Protocol (SNMP) agents can be a source of major performance problems for both the server and the network if not properly configured. Many networks today are managed using SNMP technology. If the network management station that is requesting SNMP event information from an NT Server (or any station on the network for that matter) is configured incorrectly, overhead is created on NT Server and the network. For example, if a Network Management station requests event information every 15 seconds instead of every 15 minutes, ensure that this level of granularity is truly required.

Under NT Server, investigate if the SNMP.EXE process is consuming large amounts of CPU time via Task Manager or Perfmon to recognize runaway SNMP services. To tune around this problem, a two-phase approach should be taken in concert. First, work with the network management team to ensure that the SNMP polling periods are set correctly. Secondly, under NT Server, you can view the SNMP agent setup information under the Start|Settings|Control Panel|Network|Services|SNMP Service.

Tune System Architecture to Control Network Traffic Flows

NT Server Needs the Network

An NT Server based network under NT Server 4.0 is composed of various NT Server services. These NT Server services encompass such roles as PDC, BDC, WINS, DNS, Server Service, etc. The distribution of these various NT Server services influence the end users perceived response time and overall network performance. The topic of NT Server architectures is one that is very dependent on your needs and requirements. Although not addressed in this book, it is important to remember that there are many areas that affect end users perceived performance in addition to the NT Server portion of the solution. When tuning or developing an NT Server solutions, insure each portion of the "big picture" data path is considered that extends from the client system, network architecture, applications, and NT Server itself.

The techniques and methodologies encompassed throughout this book can be applied to help manage and develop the overall NT architecture in place. More references are required to develop a sound and efficient NT Server architecture. The NT Server Resource Kit is a good place to start for information on this topic.

Select a Different Networking Technology with Higher Bandwidth

NIC Selections

Select only stable PCI based NICs for your server. Although it may be tempting to use a NIC based on EISA, ISA, or MCA because the available PCI slots are dwindling, avoid the temptation if the best performance is a consideration. The relative performance difference between an EISA and PCI based NICs were tested separately using a file transfer intensive environment, in the same NT Server. Table 7.4 illustrates the drastic performance differences between a generic PCI and EISA based adapter.

Table 7.4 PCI and EISA performance differences.

Network Technology (Switched Full Duplex Ethernet)	File Transfer Throughput (Mbits/sec)
PCI 100BaseTX	131.0
EISA 100baseTX	9.61

Performance levels achieved always vary based on the workload. But even with a fairly large deviation, which technology would you choose based on these test results?

Faster NICs—The Last Resort

When all of the networking components in and around your NT Server solution are running at their optimum level, but more network performance is required, consider implementing a different network technology. In this chapter Ethernet technologies are the reference network technology, but do not let this limit the possibilities. Other network technologies provide different workload characteristics that may prove beneficial for your environment.

Thinking Outside of the Box

Advanced Tuning: NT Server Interrupt Control Managers

When an NT Server is configured with more than two CPUs, NT Server's interrupt allocation algorithm is not always optimal. Tools are now becoming available in the marketplace to control which CPUs in the server control which interrupts generated from the server's various peripheral components. One such tool now available is the SMP Utilization Manager from NCR (*http://www.ncr.com*). Using these classes of tools allows for more flexibility in tuning how NT Server resources are utilized.

Figure 7–9 shows a screen shot of the NCR SMP Utilization Manager controlling which CPUs a specific NIC (E100B) will be limited to.

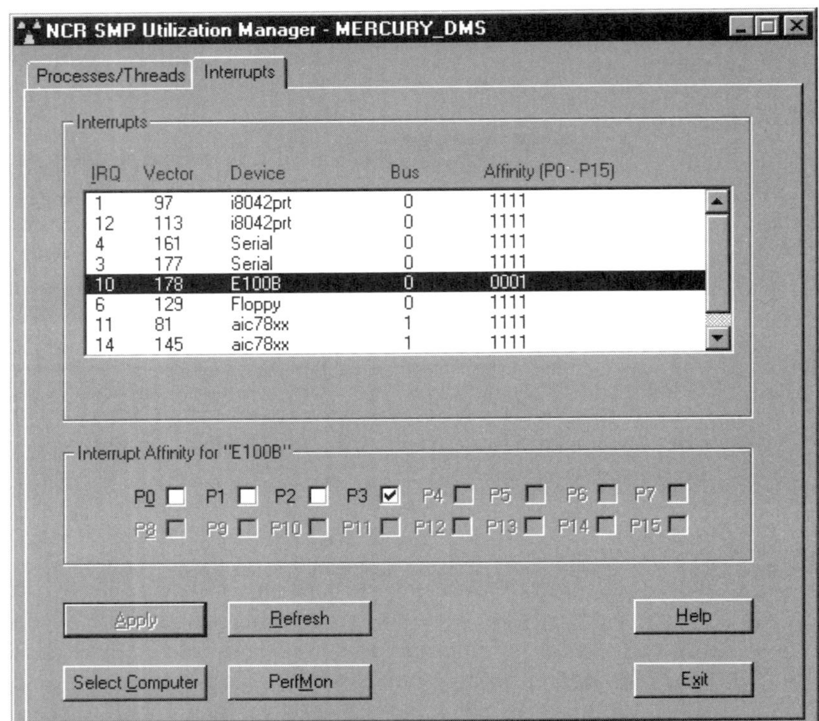

Figure 7–9 *Controlling CPU Interrupt Handling.*

Summary

This chapter emphasized the importance of understanding all of the NT Server resources covered throughout this book and the characteristics of the network technologies in use. Focusing in on a single Perfmon network counter alone does not provide much in the way of assistance when trying to tune and size NT Server's network subsystem. Several examples were used to illustrate the importance of understanding the correlation between both low level network characteristics and the NT Server architecture in place to understand what was actually occurring. Armed with this knowledge, the ability to size NT Server network solutions, detect NT Server network bottlenecks, and tune around network subsystem bottlenecks becomes much more apparent.

E I G H T

Putting Theory into Practice: Sizing and Tuning Case Studies

Putting It All Together

You can have the best strategies and methodologies, but if you cannot implement them in a timely manner, what good are they? In Chapters 2 and 3, tuning and sizing methodologies and strategies are introduced to use as a foundation when developing optimized NT Server based solutions. Chapters 4 through 7 investigate tuning and sizing techniques for each of NT Server's major resources. In this chapter, these methodologies and techniques are followed as we work through various case studies implementing NT Server solutions. While these case studies are designed to be realistic, more importantly they give real world practical examples of implementing the methodologies presented.

These case studies may or may not fit your environment exactly, which is ok. Why? The goal here is to gain valuable insight into tuning and sizing of NT Server and to improve your understanding of the methodologies used. It does not matter if the NT Server solution you are developing is based on Microsoft Exchange Server, Oracle, SQL, or a File Server. Once you understand the concepts behind the methodology, you can use them to your advantage whenever you tune and size any type of NT Server solution—even as technology changes. Do not get bogged down in the very small details. Even if your configuration solutions are 1 MB to the left or right, following a sound methodology will get you to a solution that is in the ballpark, which can then be tuned into a very good fit.

Three case studies are presented in this chapter. The first case study centers on sizing, stress testing, and tuning an electronic mail solution based on Microsoft Exchange supporting 2000 users. The second case study focuses on sizing, stress testing, and tuning of a large File Server solution. The final case study encompasses the sizing and initial tuning of a combination web and file server. Each case study provides the specific steps required to size and tune each solution.

Case Study: Microsoft Exchange—Electronic Mail Server

THE ENVIRONMENT

Acme Rockets decided to move out of the dark ages and begin moving toward a paperless office. Their first step is to begin using electronic mail internally and externally with select vendors and colleagues. They are hoping to field an electronic mail solution that will support 1000 concurrent electronic mail users today and over 2000 concurrent users within six months. Acme Rockets expects astronomical growth when their new product takes off. They typically work in a host based text environment but are expecting to begin using more client server based applications. Everyone in the company is expected to begin using e-mail as the primary means of communicating message traffic. The company founder enjoys seeing his employees, so all electronic mail users are located at the company campus and have LAN connectivity.

Now that the general environment is in place, let's walk through the sizing methodology introduced in Chapter 3, "Capacity Sizing" to determine a server solution for Acme Rockets. For reference, the sizing methodology is provided here again.

1. Define objective(s)
2. Understand requirements needed to meet your objective
3. Determine loading characteristics
4. Determine performance requirements
5. Understand future business requirements
6. Understand future server architectures
7. Configure the server
8. Stress test and validate the server configuration
9. Proactively follow the tuning methodology during validations testing
10. Deploy the server into production
11. Proactively follow the tuning methodology after the server is deployed

Some of the gory details associated with obtaining the actual information are circumvented for brevity. Keep in mind that there is more to a complete electronic mail solution than just the server. Some of the other considerations include domain or directory service structure, site design, site connectors, etc. However, the focus here is on applying the sizing and tuning methodologies to determining a realistic initial server solution. Secondly, key information on the tuning and sizing of Microsoft Exchange Server solutions is investigated.

Applying the Sizing Methodology

1. Define Objective(s)

Develop a scalable electronic mail solution. Scalability is used in the context here that once the server is deployed, it will be capable of supporting increasing electronic mail workloads. This server will be dedicated to supporting electronic mail exclusively. Dedicating the server to a single task, such as an electronic mail server, has several advantages. This server is required to support a high workload level. With a heavy (greater than 500) user workload, it is important that the server provides a high level of availability and performance. If these goals are not achieved, a large number of end users will be adversely affected. By dedicating the server to one application, administration and performance management is less challenging, since only the electronic mail application and the operating system are competing for the server's resources. An electronic mail server that supports a high number of users is a complex NT Server solution to keep properly tuned and maintained even without the addition of other applications operating on the server concurrently. By dedicating the server to one task, there is less chance that there will be any interoperability concerns with other applications running concurrently on the server. Also, the historical performance logs will be easier to extrapolate from for future sizing requirements since no other application loads will have influenced the Perfmon log information.

2. Understand Requirements Needed to Meet Your Objective

To meet this electronic mail requirement, Microsoft Exchange is selected. The mail server will be the primary message server. The electronic mail client software selected to connect to the mail server is the Microsoft Exchange client. Acme Rockets expects higher than normal availability requirements, but economics are a consideration. From a storage perspective, they expect that the end users will keep their e-mail locally on their client systems. They plan to provide each end user with an initial mailbox size on the electronic post office of 10 MBytes. Acme Rockets considers this a reasonable estimate for their initial field trials, but also expects to limit the mailbox size by setting corporate policy. Fortunately, Acme Rockets is aware that a corporate policy alone may not fully control mailbox size growth, so they are also planning budgetary dollars required to obtain additional disk storage for the anticipated mailbox size growth.

3. Determine Loading Characteristics

The total number of users to initially support is 1000, growing to 2000 within six months. With the excitement of the new solution, the expected initial concurrency rate is 1000 users. After surveying Acme Rockets executives and associates who currently have external e-mail accounts, the average mail recipient rate is 100 messages per day and average message sent mail rate of 25 per day. The typical work environment is eight hours. Unfortunately, there is not any historical server performance information to work from to help in determining the transaction rates or disk characteristics (read/write/random/sequential, etc.).

4. Determine Performance Requirements

Being an impatient bunch, Acme Rockets expects nothing less than a subsecond average response time when interacting with their e-mail environment. This level of performance is expected to be sustained even when all 1000 users are concurrently using the mail server.

5. Understand Future Business Requirements

Acme Rockets is expecting astronomical growth and plan on doubling the size of the company in six months. If the business goals are achieved as planned, continued future growth is expected. This would require supporting 2000 concurrent users with subsecond response times. Over the long term, more concurrent users are expected every year.

6. Understand Future Server Architectures

Acme Rockets loves technology but prefers not to completely replace their server for at least three years. With this in mind, they have decided to proceed with a standards based server architecture that can support the planned increased capacity. When running Microsoft Exchange, disk I/O and memory subsystems are the most heavily stressed portions of the server. A server that can support significant I/O and larger RAM configurations are to be key discriminators when selecting the server.

7. Configure the Server

Acme Rockets is rushing to complete this project as soon as possible. Enough information is presented in steps 1 through 6 to initially size the server. But before we begin the configuration phase, let us review the primary application that will be used on the server, Microsoft Exchange. Understanding the general application characteristics influences the server configuration.

Application Characteristics Review

Microsoft Exchange environments are characterized by the following resource usage activity: Memory: Active, Processor: Medium, Disk: Active, and Network: Medium. Exchange is a complex application sitting on top of its own database. In high (>500) user environments, typical Exchange environments exhibit high transaction rates due to the electronic messages being read into and out of the underlying Microsoft Joint Engine Technology (JET) database engine which Exchange is based on. Many generic techniques and recommendations for tuning of database environments can be applicable when sizing Microsoft Exchange Server.

Configuring a server to support Microsoft Exchange is similar to that of a database, and based on the information provided from steps 1 through 6, the following initial configuration is developed. When putting together the initial sizing configuration, each server resource is reviewed.

Review Each Server Resource

DISK I/O REQUIREMENTS

Disk Storage Capacity Considerations and Requirements

NT Server O/S: 124 MB

NT Server Pagefile: 256 MB (RAM) times two equals 512 MB of available disk space for NT's Pagefile

Application executable/binaries Exchange: 250 MB

Private Information Store (User Space): 1000 users at 10 MB per user for their post office box equals 10 GB of available disk space

MTA Logs & DSA Logs Estimate: 1000 users at 2 MB per user equals 2 GB of available log disk space

Exchange Directory Estimate: 1000 users at 0.8 MB per user equals 800 MB of available directory disk space

Total minimum disk capacity required: 13.2 GB

Relevant Industry Benchmark: SPECint95

Future Relevant Industry Benchmarks: LoadSim results reported by companies such as Compaq (http://www.compaq.com), HP (http://www.hp.com), NCR (http://www.NCR.com), Microsoft (http://www.microsoft.com), etc.

These results are found by searching each company's website under the keyword "LoadSim" or "benchmarks." The LoadSim stress-testing tool is covered in depth later in this chapter. For now, LoadSim is a tool produced by Microsoft designed to stress test Microsoft Exchange based solutions.

Disk Availability Considerations and Requirements

The server selected to support this exchange environment is the NCR 4300. This server supports 12 internal disk drives that can be split across 2 Ultra Fast and Wide (UF/W) SCSI buses. With economics and availability a concern, Acme Rockets decides to implement six 4 GB disk drives in a RAID 5 striped array with parity array (Redundant Arrays of Inexpensive Disks are investigated in Chapter 6) for the Exchange databases, files, and logs. RAID 5 is selected because of its ability provide a higher level of disk fault tolerance than separately configured disk drives and its capability to sustain a single disk drive failure. NT Server and the Exchange binaries are placed onto a separate 4 GB disk drive. This provides 20 GB of usable data storage for Exchange. The single 4 GB disk drive provides ample room for NT Server files, Exchange files, the Pagefile, and a fair amount of room for growth.

Disk Performance Considerations and Requirements

Just because there is sufficient disk capacity (storage space) does not indicate that the performance level will be met. The more disk drives and SCSI buses configured, the higher the performance provided by the disk subsystem. The six-disk RAID 5 array provides a higher level of availability, excellent read performance, but poor write performance. Acme Rockets hopes that a six disk RAID 5 array will provide sufficient disk I/O performance. A hardware based RAID HBA is selected to provide improved disk management features and to improve the RAID 5 write performance by providing battery supported write back cache. The RAID controller shipped with the NCR 4300 is the Mylex 960 PG with 16 MB of battery protected onboard cache. The benefits of hardware based RAID HBAs, RAID 5 technology, and various other discussions on disk performance are investigated in Chapter 6, "NT Server and Disk Subsystem Performance."

CPU Requirements

NT Minimum: Intel 80486/66

Microsoft Recommendation to support 250 Medium Exchange Users: Intel Pentium 90 MHz CPU

The CPU(s) will need to support potentially high transaction rates when 1000 concurrent users are connected to the server and drive a significant level of I/O (disk and network). The minimum CPU technology required for NT is not relevant here. Obtaining a modern server based on the older 80486 CPU technology is just not realistic. This reference to old 80486 technology that is provided here is done so to illustrate how new technology commonly outpaces vendor reported sizing information.

An extrapolation from the Microsoft planning recommendation that a single Pentium 90 can support 250 medium users is possible. SPECint95, which measures the relative performance of CPU technology, rates the Pentium 120 (Pentium 90 is so old the SPECint95 results were not easily available) at 3.7. We will need to support 1000 concurrent users or four times the Microsoft recommendation, which indicates a Specint95 CPU performance level of 14.8 is needed. To support this level of CPU performance, two Pentium Pro 200 MHz/512 K cache CPUs are configured. The Specint95 rating for a Pentium Pro 200 MHz/512 K cache CPU is 8.58. By the time this book is published, more LoadSim results should be available for larger server configurations by a variety of vendors as noted above. By defaulting back to a core technology benchmark such as SPECint95, a good extrapolation can still be made. If LoadSim results are not available for the current CPU technology available, this technique of extrapolating between a core benchmark that is normally published with the introduction of new CPU technology and an application specific recommendation such as LoadSim is a viable alternative.

These types of direct CPU extrapolations are a bit of a reach from a purely scientific view of the world, but remember that sizing is part art. The goal here is to create a good starting point when configuring a server to meet the sizing requirements. From a technology perspective, there are only two current Intel CPU choices available: Pentium II Slot 1 and Pentium Pro. The Pentium II Slot 1 architecture is a slightly faster CPU than the Pentium Pro for some environments that do not rely heavily on Level 2 CPU caches. CPU caches are reviewed closely in Chapter 4. The Pentium II Slot 1 server architecture supports a maximum of 2 CPUs in a single server. Acme Rockets strategy outlines that they expect to grow rapidly and support all users from a single server. Part of their strategy to host all of the mail users on a single server is to lower long-term system administration costs through the use of fewer NT Servers. Reviewing both the current customer strategy and current available technology, starting with two Pentium Pro CPUs provides a valid initial configuration starting point. This will allow for the future addition of a greater number of CPUs (up to eight) in the NCR 4300 if required.

The possibility of eight CPUs may contradict conventional wisdom, but I am aware of at least three vendors (Axil, HP, and NCR) that will be publishing benchmarks of very high (greater than 14,000 users) using 8 CPU technology.

Memory Requirements

NT Server O/S: 32 MB
NT Server O/S Disk buffers: 32 MB
Exchange Application Executable space: 24 MB
Exchange Application dataspace (buffers, etc.): 168 MB
Relevant Industry Benchmark: Loadsim as reviewed earlier

To provide subsecond response times, the server will need a sufficient amount of memory to ensure that any paging to disk or general disk access is kept to a minimum. Providing NT Server with an extra 32 MB of RAM will lower the possibility of any NT Server O/S disk access overhead through the use of NT's dynamic file system/disk cache buffering. The Exchange application has its own cache management scheme. Without any historical data or Industry Benchmarks to extrapolate from, we look to how the server can be configured. Future growth is a concern; thus, the use of higher density memory modules is prudent. The selected server supports DIMM memory, which can be configured in 128 MB increments. Based on these facts, the initial configuration selected is 256 MB of 60ns four way interleaved RAM. This will allow the server's memory subsystem to be expanded to a maximum of 8 GB.

NETWORK I/O REQUIREMENTS

Relevant Industry Benchmark: Loadsim as reviewed earlier

The server will be placed into the current network architecture via a 100BaseT-shared hub. Two factors will dictate the amount of network bandwidth required to support the end users: user concurrency rate and size of messages. The characteristics of the 1000 users greatly influence the amount of network bandwidth required. If large attachments and high concurrency rates become common, more network bandwidth will be required. How much network bandwidth will be required is an unknown quantity at this time. The current architecture dictates that a single 100BaseT-network card will be configured into the server. If this proves to be insufficient, the network architecture will be revisited. Internet connectivity is provided through Acme Rockets current network infrastructure.

Hardware Configuration and Tuning

NCR 4300

SCSI CD-ROM

> Installed on the internal motherboard Ultra Fast and Wide SCSI adapter channel 1

Floppy Disk Drive

20/40 GB DLT Drive

> Installed on the internal motherboard Ultra Fast and Wide SCSI adapter channel 2
>
> DLT Drives can support 3 Mbytes/sec of compressed theoretical throughput. Other high speed options are available, but Acme Rockets currently has a large inventory of DLT based tapes which they would like to leverage.

2 Pentium Pro 200 MHz/512 K cache CPUs

> Up to six more CPUs can be added to this configuration if needed

256 MB of DIMM RAM

> Initially configuring the server with this amount of RAM still allows for additional RAM modules to be added for a total of 8 GB.

1 Intel EthernetPro 100B 100BaseTX NIC
Installed in PCI Bus 1
1 4 GB Disk Drive for NT Server, Paging File, Microsoft Exchange Application Binaries
6 4 GB Seagate Cheetah Ultra Fast/Wide SCSI disk drives
Configured as a RAID 5 array
This array contains the six primary Exchange components: Public Information Store, Private Information Store, Information Store Logs, Directory Service Logs, Directory Service, and Message Transfer Agent
1 Mylex 960PG 2 Channel Ultra Fast and Wide SCSI-2 PCI RAID adapter with 16 MB of battery backed onboard cache
Installed in PCI Bus 2

Software Configuration and Tuning

SOFTWARE VERSIONS

NT Server 4.0
Service Pack 3 (available via Technet CD-ROMS, or over the web from *http://www.microsoft.com*)
Microsoft Exchange Version 5.0

Initial Tuning

To allow Exchange more room in memory to manage its own memory space, the NT Server memory strategy is set to Maximize Throughput for Network Applications.

The NT Server memory strategy is set under Start|Settings|Control Panel|Network|Services. Select Server, then click Properties. Select memory strategy: Maximize Throughput for Network Applications.

Once the server hardware, operating system, and Exchange are installed, Microsoft Exchange Server Performance Optimizer Wizard is run. This wizard is the server optimization's tool that autotunes many of Microsoft Exchange's settings and is included with Exchange. Based on the server configuration, the Exchange Optimizer makes recommendations concerning Exchange Server file locations, memory usage, and various other system parameters that affect the performance of the Exchange Server. Always run the Performance Wizard when you install Exchange Server and whenever you change your server configuration. For the initial server configuration, the following settings were input to the Exchange Optimizer:

- How many users you expect to host on this server: more than 500 users
- How many users will be in your organization: 1000-9999 users in organization

- For what type of server will this server be configured: Private Store, Public Store, MultiServer
- Limit Exchange Memory usage to: 192 MB
- Microsoft File Locations: All Exchange database files located on the RAID 5 array

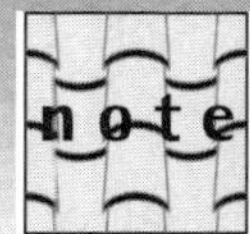

It is important to point out that Exchange is given access to all of the available memory except 64 MBytes. 64 Mbytes are kept in reserve for the NT Server operating system functions and general file system disk buffering. If other applications are in use besides Exchange, revisit the memory allocation strategy. Overconfiguring memory allocation can cause immediate performance problems.

It always makes one wonder what "auto tune" products really do. The Exchange Server Performance Optimizer Wizard configures a set of parameters relating to the server resources based on how you respond to the Exchange Optimizer's questionnaire. The Exchange Optimizer tunes the Exchange internal database parameters, which is heavily influenced on the amount of RAM you allot to Exchange and the estimated user load. Exchange parameters are stored in the Exchange registry application hive. This hive is located in: HKEY_LOCAL_MCHINE\System\CurrentControlSet\Control\ServicesMSExchangeDS, MSExchangeIS, MSExchangeMTA, and MSExchangeSA. Two of the most influential parameters tuned by the optimizer are the directory and information store cache sizes. Typical Exchange parameters tuned by the Exchange Optimizer are shown in Table 8.1.

Table 8.1 Typical Exchange parameters.

Exchange Configuration Parameter
# of information store buffers
# of directory buffers
Minimum # of information store threads
Maximum # of information store threads
# of directory threads
Maximum # of cached categorizations
Maximum # of cached restrictions
# of private information store send threads
# of private information store delivery threads
# of public information store send threads
# of public information store delivery threads
# of information store gateway in threads

Table 8.1 Typical Exchange parameters. (Continued)

Exchange Configuration Parameter
# of information store gateway out threads
# of information store users
# of concurrent connections to LAN-MTAs
# of concurrent connections to RAS LAN-MTAs
# of LAN-MTAs
# of X.400 gateways
# of API MA threads
# of XAPI MT threads
# of XAPI MT queue threads
ds_read cache latency (secs)
# of dispatcher threads
# of transfer threads
# of kernel threads
# of submit/deliver threads
# of RAS LAN-MTAs
# of database data buffers per object
# of database file handles
# of database file count delete threshold
# of database file size delete threshold

The optimizer also recommends locations for the various exchange database files. It is my experience that for most environments, Exchange Optimizer does an excellent job of improving the overall performance of Exchange Server. I have read this fact in a variety of sources, but I am always hesitant to use auto tune products. After working extensively with Exchange, I have no hesitation in recommending the Exchange Optimizer as an excellent tool to use when you understand what it does.

There is an improtant drawback to the Exchange Optimizer that you should be aware of. The Exchange Optimizer has an "I am the center of the universe attitude." The optimizer will not take into consideration any other applications that may be running on the server. Other applications have CPU, network, memory, and disk requirements that tax the server which can quickly become resource bottlenecks if not properly tuned. For large-scale servers supporting greater than 500 users, I recommended dedicating the server to only running one mail/groupware application for peak performance and ease of administration.

Server Architecture Relationship Check

Now that we have created an initial server configuration, let's make a common sense review of the configuration from the perspective of the overall server architecture in place. Two Pentium Pro 200 MHz/512 K CPUs should be capable of supporting the processing requirements of the expected load and have sufficient resources to drive the 2 Ultra Fast/Wide SCSI SCSI channels and single 100BaseTX network interface. The 256 MB of RAM appears sufficient to keep the CPUs fed, applications in memory, and provide enough memory for the application space to buffer I/O activities.

There are two peer PCI buses in a 2–4 CPU based NCR 4300 server (in an NCR 4300 with greater than four CPUs, four PCI buses are available). A quick basic math check of the I/O subsystem indicates that the I/O subsystem is required to support 2 Ultra Fast and Wide SCSI buses (80 Mbytes/sec) and a single 100 Mbit/sec network connection. Two Peer PCI buses provide an aggregate I/O bandwidth of 266 Mbytes/sec which is more than sufficient to support the current configuration. Why complete this common sense check? I have encountered locations that size servers in interesting fashions such as a 4 CPU configuration with 128 Mbytes of RAM. They then wonder why the server performance is so poor. This common sense check is intended to avoid questionable server architecture configurations. At least start out on the right foot.

Future Business and Server Architectures Check Review

From steps 5 and 6 of the sizing methodology, the server is based on current industry standards and market trends. This level of Super Server still has a significant amount of additional resources available if needed. CPUs are upgradeable up to a total of eight, memory up to 8 GB, and two additional peer PCI buses for a total of four provide a clear in box scalability path. This is in line with Acme Rockets strategy of future in-box growth.

8. Stress Test and Validate the Server Configuration

Congratulations! We now have a solid configuration that will run Microsoft Exchange and should support the required number of users (and provide subsecond performance). The key word here is should. To ensure that this configuration will support our objective, we will stress test the server before it enters production. To accomplish this stress test, Microsoft distributes (on the Exchange CD-ROM) a helpful stress-testing tool: LoadSim.

LoadSim is a tool used for simulating a client user load on an Exchange Server. Its purpose is to enable a single Windows NT machine—called a LoadSim client—to simulate multiple Microsoft Exchange client users from a single NT Server client computer. The operation of the LoadSim users is governed by a LoadSim profile. This profile controls factors such as how long a LoadSim "day" is, how many e-mail messages to send in a day's time, how many times to open and read existing e-mail, whether to use distribution lists, whether to use public folders, etc. LoadSim emulates actual Microsoft exchange/outlook clients. Although custom profiles are configurable, the Heavy LoadSim Canonical Profile is a very close fit to the information obtained from Acme Rockets in step 3. Table 8.2 outlines the various LoadSim Canonical Profiles.

Table 8.2 LoadSim Canconical Profile.

LoadSim USER ATTRIBUTE	ATTRIBUTE DETAIL	LIGHT	MEDIUM	*HEAVY*
TEST DURATION	Length of a day (hours)	8	8	8
READING MAIL	New mail (times/day)	12	12	12
	Existing mail (times/day)	5	15	20
AFTER READING MAIL	% of Reply	5%	7%	15%
	% of Reply All	3%	5%	7%
	% of Forward	5%	7%	7%
	% of Move	20%	20%	20%
	% of Copy	0%	0%	0%
	% of Delete	40%	40%	40%
	% of Do nothing	27%	21%	11%
DISTRIBUTION LISTS	Minimum size	2	2	2
	Maximum size	20	20	20
	Average size	10	10	10
	Distribution Lists per site	30	30	30
	Cover 100% of users (no overlap)	Yes	Yes	Yes
ATTACHMENTS	% to Run/Load Mail Attachment (if one exists)	25%	25%	25%
INBOX SIZE	Inbox Size Limit (# messages)	20	125	250
SENDING MAIL	New mail (times/day)	2	4	6
	Save a copy in Sent Mail Folder?	Yes	Yes	Yes
	Number of random recipients	3	3	3
	% of time to add a Distribution List	30%	30%	30%

Table 8.2 LoadSim Canconical Profile. (Continued)

LoadSim USER ATTRIBUTE	ATTRIBUTE DETAIL	LIGHT	MEDIUM	*HEAVY*
	Message Priority	Normal	Normal	Normal
	Delivery Receipt?	No	No	No
	Read Receipt?	No	No	No
NEW MAIL MESSAGE CONTENT Text-only, no attachment	1K body (ups1K.msg)	Weight 90	Weight 60	Weight 50
	2K body (ups2K.msg)	0	16	10
	4K body (ups4K.msg)	0	4	5
NEW MAIL MESSAGE CONTENT 1K mail body, with attachment	10K attachment (ups10Kat.msg)	10	5	10
	Embedded bitmap object (upsBMobj.msg)	0	2	5
	Word attachment (upsWDatt.msg)	0	2	5
	Excel attachment (upsXLatt.msg)	0	4	5
	Embedded Excel object (upsXLobj.msg)	0	2	10
SCHEDULE+ CHANGES	Changes per day	1	5	10
	Update Free/Busy information?	No	No	No
	Average Schedule File Size	22K	22K	22K
PUBLIC FOLDERS	Folder activity	None	None	None
CALCULATED DAILY LOAD (based on these defaults)	TOTAL MAIL RECEIVED PER DAY	22.94	66.30	118.89
CALCULATED DAILY LOAD (based on these defaults)	TOTAL MAIL SENT PER DAY	4.70	14.18	30.67
	Mail sent as New mail	12.00	4.00	6.00
	Mail sent as a Reply	1.05	3.76	13.03
	Mail sent as a Reply to All	0.60	2.67	5.82
	Mail sent as a Forward	1.05	3.76	5.82
CALCULATED DAILY LOAD	AVG. # RECIPIENTS FOR EACH MESSAGE	4.88	4.68	3.88

STRESS TEST CONFIGURATION

To generate the load on the Exchange Server, five client systems were configured on the same 100 Mbit/sec-shared fast Ethernet network as the Exchange server. The stress test configuration is outlined in Figure 8–1.

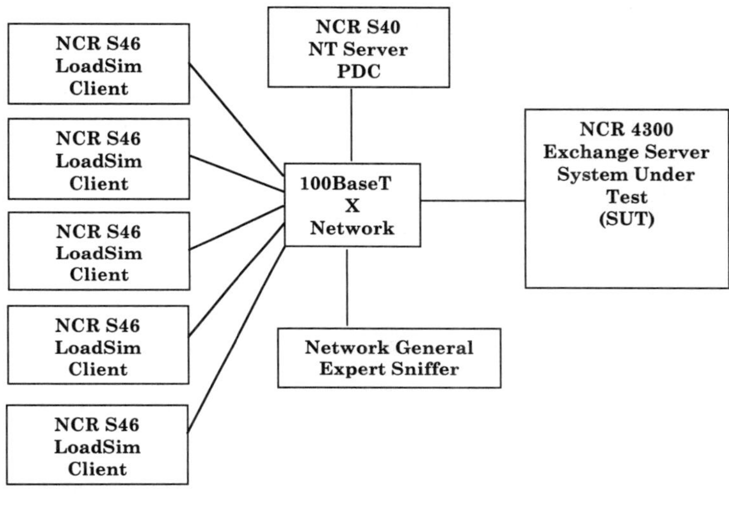

Figure 8–1 *Stress test environment.*

The performance of the LoadSim client generators and Ethernet based network was monitored at all times to ensure that they were not a source of any bottlenecks during the stress test. This step is critical during stress testing to ensure that the stress is correctly being placed on the system under test (SUT). Each client was configured with two disk drives, two Pentium Pro CPUs, and 512 MB of RAM. A Network General Expert Sniffer was used to ensure that there were not any significant amounts of network errors and that the network capacity was not exceeded.

STRESS TEST RESULTS

Once the stress test environment was in place, the Exchange Server Configuration 1 was stress tested at the 500, 1000, and 2000 user levels. While the stress test was run, the tuning methodology was followed. NT Server's Performance monitor's (Perfmon) logging mode was enabled during all of the tests. The following (Table 8.3) are the initial LoadSim results. *Lower LoadSim scores indicate better Exchange Server performance as perceived by the end user.*

The LoadSim Score represents a weighted average of the 95th percentile Exchange client response time (in milliseconds) for the various Exchange

Table 8.3 LoadSim results for Exchange Server under test configuration 1

Number of Heavy LoadSim Users	95th Percentile response time score (seconds)
500	0.470
1000	0.613
2000	1.200

tasks defined in the LoadSim Canonical Profile table above. The READ task is the task weighted highest, accounting for over half of the score. Table 8.4 shows an example of a LoadSim results file.

Table 8.4 Example LoadSim detailed results file.

Category	Weight	Hits	95th Percentile (milliseconds)
SEND	1	2512	729
Subweight	10	733	2000
Subweight	5	509	2203
Subweight	50	1270	328
READ	10	26297	594
REPLY	1	2636	218
REPLY ALL	1	1232	234
FORWARD	1	1698	297
MOVE	1	5178	203
DELETE	2	10590	187
SUBMIT	0	8078	172
RESOLVE NAME	0	4218	47
LOAD IMSG	0	2522	1719
DELIVER	0	24234	125
Weighted Avg	17	89195	470

The reason for this weighting distribution is that different client tasks (READ, BROWSE, DELETE, SEND, etc.) are perceived differently by the user. Acme Rockets decided that the acceptable response time for their environment is subsecond, when all 1000 users are accessing the server. The

Microsoft-recommended maximum for the MAPI protocol used by the LoadSim clients is also subsecond response time (<1000 ms). The MAPI protocol was the protocol used for this stress test. A *lower LoadSim Score indicates better Exchange Server performance.*

INITIAL EXCHANGE SERVER CONFIGURATION RESULTS SUMMARY

This Exchange Server Under Test configuration will indeed support 1000 heavy LoadSim users, meeting Acme Rocket's short term objectives. We have now validated the initial configuration solution. At this point, we could closely evaluate the Perfmon logs from the stress tests and generate some theoretical longer-term capacity sizing analysis from the current data. But, what about the requirement to support 2000 users with subsecond response times in six months?

9. Proactively Follow the Tuning Methodology During Validation Testing

Throughout the stress and validation testing, the tuning methodology is employed to aid in locating and tuning around the server's bottlenecks.

PLANNING AHEAD: SOLVING THE PERFORMANCE BOTTLENECK

It is not difficult to stress test your server before placing it into production. However, it is resource intensive and can be time consuming. Since the stress testing lab is already set up, which is half of the battle, let's utilize the tuning methodology in an effort to determine why the current Exchange server configuration will not meet Acme Rocket's long term performance requirements. We will refer to the first configuration that was tested as Exchange Server Configuration 1.

For quick reference, here is a summary of the tuning methodology introduced in Chapter 2.

1. Always have a backup of the system, files, and registry before making any changes

It is also a good idea to document exactly how you set up the server in the unlikely event that the server is required to be restored from backup information but is not successful and you must rebuild the server from scratch

2. Monitor your server and develop a baseline
3. Proactively monitor your server
4. Determine what resource is acting like or becoming a bottleneck
5. Try a single change at a time, when possible, and carefully document all change(s)
6. Benchmark your system to determine if the change(s) is helpful
7. Return to step 3

Reviewing the tuning methodology from Chapter 2, we are currently at step 4, "Determine what resource is acting like or becoming a bottleneck." Just adding another server resource such as two additional CPUs will not greatly improve the situation if the CPUs are not the bottlenecks throttling the server's overall performance. To help in determining where the bottlenecks are, we'll use the .pmw files from Chapter 2 in conjunction with the log file generated for the 2000 user stress test.

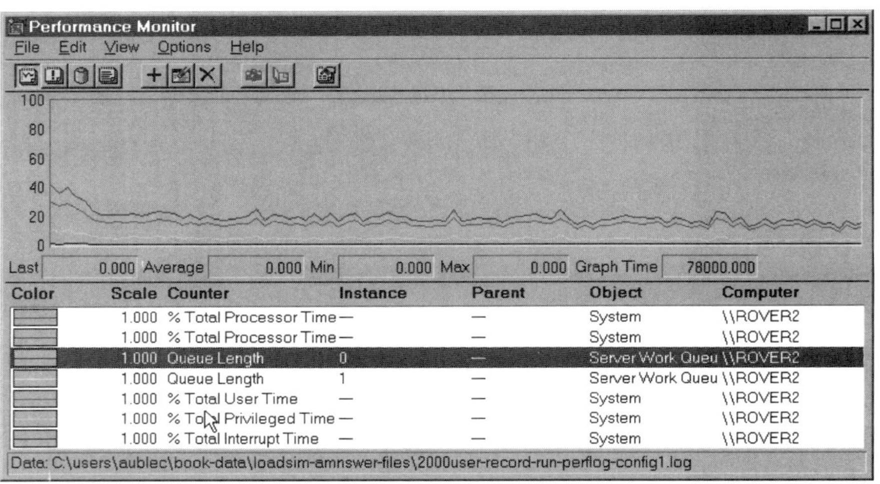

Figure 8–2 *cpu-resources.pmw for Exchange Server Configuration 1*

Figure 8–2 shows that the average CPU usage is hovering around 20 percent with the CPU's queue length at zero. From Chapter 4, "NT Server and CPU Performance," the CPU becomes a bottleneck when it sustains a %utilization over 90 percent and the Queue Length is greater than two times the number of CPUs in the server. Obviously the CPUs are not the bottleneck, but it is important to note from a processor sizing perspective that there is plenty of room to grow. This CPU usage is for both CPUs. Thus, a single CPU would show a usage level of 40 percent. At first glance, it appears that we overconfigured the CPU power. However, this does not take into account possible surges that may be produced when Acme Rockets is approaching a due date on a project. Configuring enough CPU capacity to support surges in the workload is an important consideration when fielding a server that is considered critical.

Figure 8–3 focuses on physical memory (RAM) usage. There is currently no shortage of memory. In fact, there are still approximately 100 Mbytes of available memory that can be used by the application. This fact is determined by looking at the available bytes counter's minimum amount of RAM that was

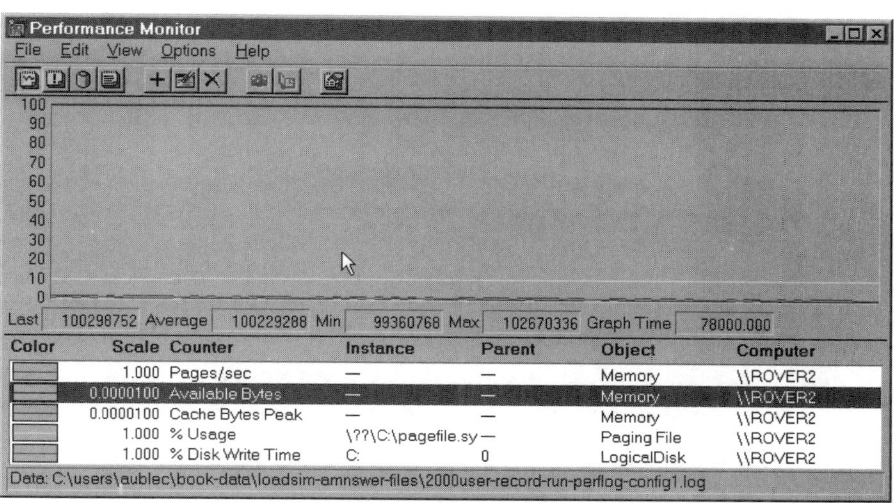

Figure 8–3 *Memory-resources.pmw for Exchange Server Configuration 1*

still available on the server when the stress test was at a steady state. In Chapter 5, this key fact is utilized when completing some advanced Exchange Memory Tuning. If you missed that tuning discussion, refer back to it after completing this exchange case study. (See "Case Study: Microsoft Exchange—Electronic Mail Server" on page 304.)

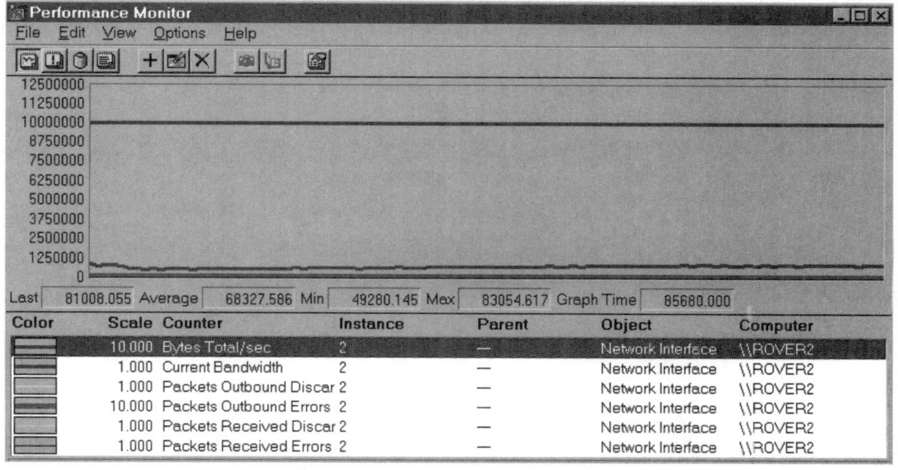

Figure 8–4 *Network-resources.pmw for Exchange Server Configuration 1*

Figure 8–4 focuses on network usage. Even with 1000 concurrent users, the network overhead from the client server based Exchange server environment was minimal. Only 664,432 bits/sec of the available 100 Mbits of theoretical throughput were ever in use. There is a significant amount of network capacity available for future growth. Note that as of NT 4 Service Pack 3, the Output Queue Length counter does not report valid information for SMP based NT Server environments. Perhaps this limitation will be addressed in future Service Packs or NT Server releases.

STRESS TEST BONUS: DETECTING SOLUTION ERRORS BEFORE DEPLOYMENT

Even though the primary objective of this stress test exercise is to insure that the server can support the projected workload at a specified performance level, there are other benefits to stress testing the solution before deployment. In particular, the Perfmon Network Performance Chart in Figure 8–4 shows a high rate of packet output errors. This particular server never exhibited any network problems while under lighter loads in previous environments, but it did suffer then while placed under heavy loads during the stress test. Using a Network General Expert Sniffer, we were able to isolate the network problem to a set of faulty network interface cards on both the server and one of the clients. The network interface cards were replaced and the stress test was successfully rerun. Debugging this network error in production would have been significantly more difficult.

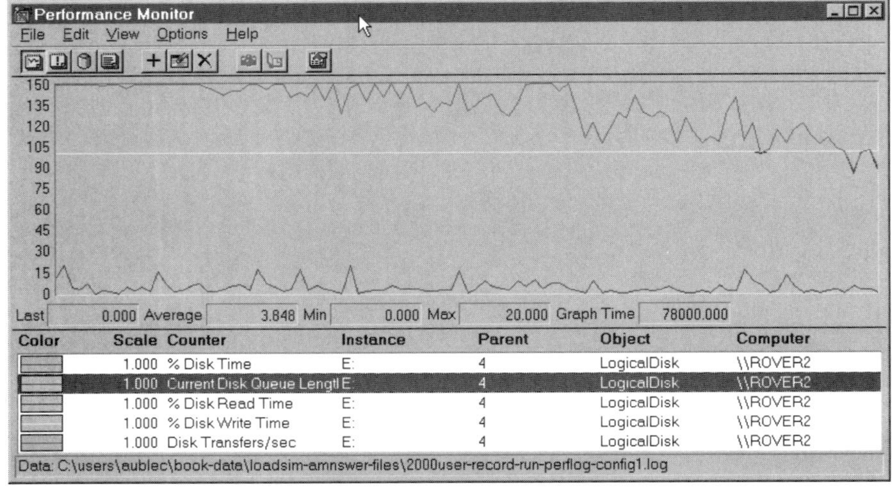

Figure 8–5 *Disk-resources.pmw for Exchange Server Configuration 1.*

Figure 8–5 shows the disk I/O usage when stress testing the Exchange Server Configuration 1. Reviewing this report and the other associated Perfmon Charts, the bottleneck is discovered. The values for the Perfmon disk resource chart were off the scale. To compensate for this, the Perfmon scale is increased to 150. (Perfmon chart scales are adjusted under the chart menu item.) When the % Disk Time is very high (>60–80%) and the Current Disk Queue Length is greater than the array normalized value of 2, there is a disk I/O bottleneck. Logical Disk E: is a disk array comprised of six 4 GB disk drives, thus the Current Disk Queue Length normalized array data is calculated by dividing the number of disk drives (six) into the values reported by Perfmon. The disk queue length was commonly over three for each drive in the array. This indicates that the disk array (E) is not servicing all of the disk requests in a timely manner. To expand upon the disk bottleneck analysis, all of the logical disk counters are shown in the following Perfmon disk report log (Figure 8–6).

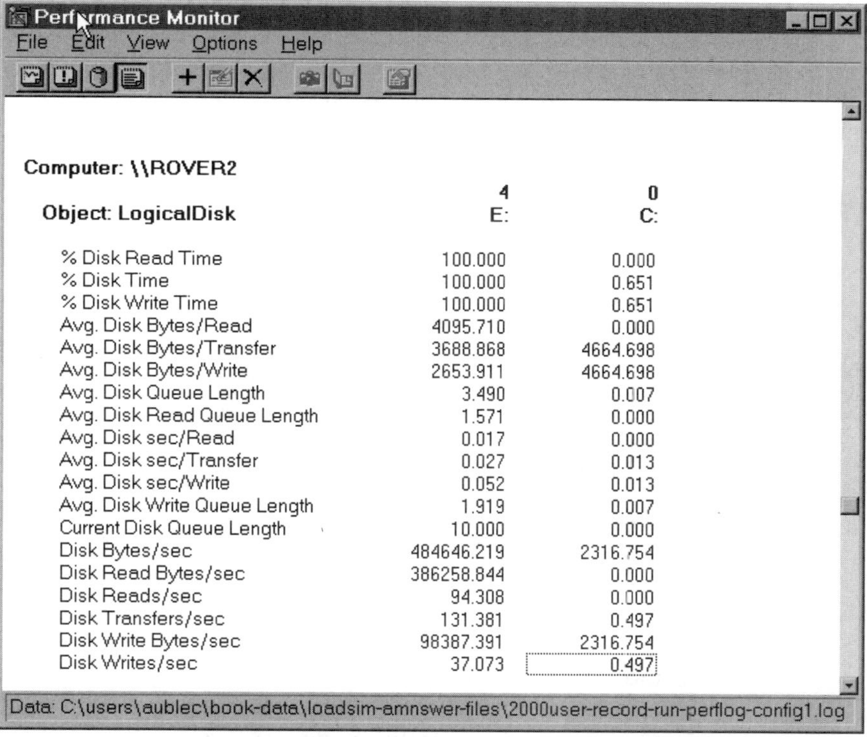
Performance Monitor

File Edit View Options Help

Computer: \\ROVER2

Object: LogicalDisk	4 E:	0 C:
% Disk Read Time	100.000	0.000
% Disk Time	100.000	0.651
% Disk Write Time	100.000	0.651
Avg. Disk Bytes/Read	4095.710	0.000
Avg. Disk Bytes/Transfer	3688.868	4664.698
Avg. Disk Bytes/Write	2653.911	4664.698
Avg. Disk Queue Length	3.490	0.007
Avg. Disk Read Queue Length	1.571	0.000
Avg. Disk sec/Read	0.017	0.000
Avg. Disk sec/Transfer	0.027	0.013
Avg. Disk sec/Write	0.052	0.013
Avg. Disk Write Queue Length	1.919	0.007
Current Disk Queue Length	10.000	0.000
Disk Bytes/sec	484646.219	2316.754
Disk Read Bytes/sec	386258.844	0.000
Disk Reads/sec	94.308	0.000
Disk Transfers/sec	131.381	0.497
Disk Write Bytes/sec	98387.391	2316.754
Disk Writes/sec	37.073	0.497

Data: C:\users\aublec\book-data\loadsim-amnswer-files\2000user-record-run-perflog-config1.log

Figure 8–6 *Complete disk usage for Exchange Server Configuration 1.*

There is a plethora of good information shown in this Perfmon log view snapshot. I mention snapshot here because this only provides a single point in time, but is useful for this analysis study since it is representative of the steady state achieved during the stress test. Reviewing the Perfmon Chart view is helpful in determining when a snapshot is taken and the relationship between the counters. This snapshot was taken when the test achieved a steady state, or constant load level with all users active. This information is very useful in characterizing the disk I/O subsystem under load. Once you understand how the disk I/O is being used, you can begin to intelligently tune the disk subsystem. More information on detecting and tuning disk subsystem bottlenecks are covered in Chapter 6, "NT Server and Disk Subsystem Performance."

UNDERSTANDING THE DISK CHARACTERISTICS

A flag that all areas of disk performance should be investigated is when both the %Disk Time is very high and the Current Queue Length is increasing. When the % disk time is high, (> 60–80 percent), disk response times begin to suffer. For example, the time for read transactions is 0.017 seconds. This may sound fast, until you compare it to a disk read response time from the root disk of 0.012 seconds, 40 percent faster! Similarly, the write response time is 0.055 sec. This write time is 300 percent slower than a corresponding read operation. Poor write performance is partially contributed to the use of the RAID 5 array, less effective use of the disk buffers by the Exchange application for write operations, and having mixed disk I/O operations occurring on the same disk array.

We also see that this disk environment is characterized as both a significant read and write environment shown by the 100 percent disk read and write times. This characterization makes sense for this user workload environment, since many users will be sending messages (writing to disk) and reading messages (reading from disk) throughout the day. This information is instrumental for tuning around this bottleneck.

EXCHANGE DISK CHARACTERIZATION

Located on the Microsoft website is a paper, "Planning your implementation of Microsoft Exchange Server." Aparaphrase from this paper states, "Microsoft Exchange Server database is structured to first write from memory (RAM) to a fast, sequentially organized transaction log file and not directly to the Information Store. Later, when there is less disk activity, they will write from memory to the actual Information Store. This is done primarily for performance reasons because data can be written to the transaction log file very quickly. However, it is also helpful in crash recovery scenarios because the database files can be fully recovered from these logs." Armed with the above information provided from Microsoft and the analysis of the Perfmon logs, a strategy to tune around the disk I/O bottleneck can now be developed and deployed.

STRATEGY FOR TUNING AROUND THE PRIMARY EXCHANGE SERVER BOTTLENECK

From a tuning methodology perspective, the current Performance Resource Chart looks like this:

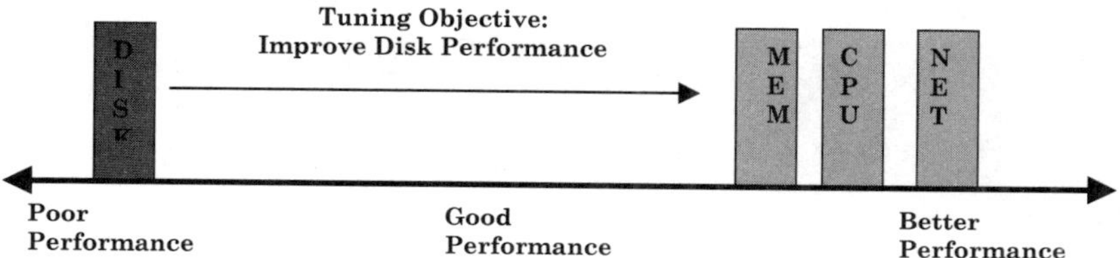

Figure 8–7 *Performance Resource Chart for Tuning Exchange*

To improve the server's performance we must tune around the disk I/O bottleneck. Adding or tuning any other resources besides the bottlenecked resource will provide little, if any, overall performance improvement. Reviewing the information presented above, there are several tactics which are implemented. From a performance perspective, RAID 5 is up to four times slower when completing write operations when compared to read operations. In this Exchange environment, we observed that our disk write response times are roughly three times slower than our disk read response times. The first order of business is to move the write intensive transaction logs away from the RAID 5 array, which currently houses all of the Exchange components. This will provide three benefits:

1. Lower the disk activity on the RAID 5 array—this should yield better response times for disk access
2. Improve disk write times for the transaction logs
3. Drastically improve the availability of the server

The third benefit may not be as obvious as the other two. The availability of the server will be improved by not having all of the Exchange Server transaction logs on the same array as the user's data. If both the user data and transaction logs are placed on the same array and there is a multiple disk drive failure (greater than two disk drives), ALL data is lost. In contrast, if only the user data is on the RAID 5 array and there is a multiple disk failure, then the recent user data can be recovered from the transaction logs.

TUNING TACTICS: IMPLEMENTING THE DISK I/O TUNING STRATEGY

The Exchange Optimizer provides a friendly interface to recognize and move the Exchange data files. The six primary Exchange data files and their functions are outlined in Table 8.5.

Table 8.5 • Exchange database component descriptions.

Exchange Database Components	Exchange Database Component Descriptions and Characterizations
Private Information Store	This component is a database, which maintains all messages in users' mailboxes, enforces storage limits, and delivers messages to users on the same server. Disk workload is characterized as random in nature.
Public Information Store	This component is a database that maintains information stored in public folders and replicates public folders as required. Disk workload is characterized as random in nature.
Information Store Logs	This component records all information store transactions. Disk workload is characterized as sequential in nature.
Directory Service Logs	This component records all information store transactions. Disk workload is characterized as sequential in nature.
Directory Service	This component is an implementation of the directory services standard that is defined by the ISO X.500 specification. The directory store maintains information about an organization's recipients, servers, and messaging infrastructure. This component is automatically replicated to all servers in the organization and is used by the other three core components to map addresses and route messages. Disk workload is characterized as random in nature.
Message Transfer Agent	This component is responsible for moving messages between Information Stores, connectors, and third-party gateways. It is the service that performs the actual routing, submission, and delivery of messages. Disk workload is characterized as random in nature.

With this disk characteristic knowledge, Acme added an additional five disk drives to the Exchange Server, for a total of twelve. All of the disks were first low level formatted with the Mylex RAID host bus adapter SCSI tools since they had never been used with this SCSI host bus adapter model before. An NTFS file system with an ALU size of 2 Kbytes was placed on each logical drive. The addition of more disk drives was inevitable for Acme Rockets. Once the additional 1000 concurrent users are supported, the additional disk storage capacity will be utilized.

Now that the hardware is completely configured, the Exchange Optimizer is run for a second time. With the addition of the new disk drives, the Exchange Optimizer recommended a new exchange file distribution. Even though the optimizer does a good job suggesting exchange file locations, it also provides a mechanism to manually override the recommendations. The new disk I/O layout outlined in Table 8.6 is a combination of the optimizer's recommendations and Perfmon information gathered from the first stress test.

Table 8.6 Exchange Server Configuration 2 performance enhanced disk I/O layout table.

Logical Disk Assignment	Physical Disk Arrangement	SCSI Bus	Microsoft Exchange File Location
C:	JBOD	1	NT Operating System, Exchange Binaries, and NT Paging file *Note: If the amount of RAM available in the server was not plentiful, not placing the pagefile on its own dedicated disk drive(s) is acceptable.*
G:	JBOD	1	Information Store Logs
H:	JBOD	1	Directory Service Logs
I:	3 Disk RAID 5 Array	1	Directory Service, Message Transfer Agent
E:	6 Disk RAID 5 Array	2	Private Information Store
E:	Same as above	2	Public Information Store *Note: The Public Information Store is not used for this solution. If it were actively used, it would not be recommended to be located on the same disk array as the Information Store.*

JBOD, an acronym for "just a bunch of disks," indicates that the physical disk represents a single non-RAID configured disk drive. Note that the NT Server Paging file for this environment is on the same drive as the NT operating system file. This arrangement is not recommended unless the server paging activities are anything but negligible.

STRESS TEST 2: DID OUR EFFORTS TO TUNE EXCHANGE HELP?

The Exchange Server is tuned to remove the current disk I/O bottleneck. But can you be sure it was removed? Again, as before, the same LoadSim stress test was run. Table 8.7 lists the LoadSim results for the second stress test. *(Note: Lower LoadSim scores indicate better Exchange Server performance as perceived by the end user.)*

Table 8.7 LoadSim results.

Number of Heavy LoadSim Users	Exchange Server Configuration 1	Exchange Server Configuration 2 (Improved Disk I/O Distribution)
	95th Percentile response time score (seconds)	
500	0.470	0.334
1000	0.613	0.513
2000	1.200	0.900

Success! Configuration 2 will meet Acme Rockets' longer term goal to support 2000 concurrent users with subsecond response times. Even though the overall performance goals are met, proactive sizing and tuning should always be an on-going strategy. Reviewing the Perfmon logs from the second stress test provides insight into why the overall performance was improved and where future bottlenecks may develop. When one bottleneck is removed, there is always the potential danger that another bottleneck may form. This is a natural progression due to the fact that other resources begin to perform closer to their optimal levels when other resources are not constraining them.

ANALYZING STRESS TEST 2

CPU USAGE

CPU usage increased slightly from an average utilization of 18 percent and maximum utilization of 40 percent for configuration 1 to an average utilization of 22 percent and maximum utilization of 60 percent for configuration 2. This increase is contributed to improved access to the data, which lowered the overall idle CPU time.

MEMORY USAGE

Memory usage was similar for both configurations. With 96 Mbytes of available RAM, increasing the amount memory provided to the Exchange application should be revisited. With a large amount of free memory still available, more memory can be allocated to some of Exchange's database buffers by re-running Exchange's Performance Optimizer from the command line using perfwiz –v, or by directly editing the Exchange registry hives. (Advanced tuning of Exchange's memory usage through the use of the registry is covered in Chapter 5, "NT Server and Memory Performance," page 165) This will result in improved response times to the end users.

DISK I/O USAGE

Disk I/O usage improved drastically. As mentioned earlier, data is first written to the Exchange transaction logs before being committed to the primary data store. Reviewing the average time in seconds to a write data to the Information Store logs (Avg. Disk sec/Write), there is a drastic improvement from the Configuration 1 average time of 0.054 to the configuration 2 average time of 0.006. Understanding the disk characteristics of the application under load and its data placement strategy is very helpful when trying to redistribute disk I/O use effectively.

The Information Store database, which resided on the six 4 GB disk RAID 5 array still needs improvement. From configuration 1 to configuration 2, disk response times improved and disk queue length was shortened in half, but the disk array was still 100 percent busy servicing requests. The Exchange Server release used for this case study was version 5.0, which limits the Information Store Database size to 16 GB. To alleviate some of the disk contention, smaller disks could be used to create the RAID 5-disk array in conjunction with increasing the buffers allocated to the Exchange application. Exchange 5.5 is now available which supports a theoretical unlimited Information Store database size.

With larger Information Store database sizes available, disk arrays providing a good combination of disk capacity and disk quantities can be used to remove this future disk I/O bottleneck. It should be noted again that, even with the Information Store Logs essentially on their own disk array performing at higher than suggested workload levels, the Acme Rocket's performance requirements are still achieved.

NETWORK I/O

As expected, the network I/O load stayed close to its same level of utilization. This is not currently (or for the foreseeable future) considered a bottleneck.

THINKING OUTSIDE THE BOX: MORE TUNING OPTIONS

There are always more tuning techniques and options available. As operating systems become more popular, more and more applications and tools are created for them. This has been the case with NT Server. As NT Server continues to mature, more and more tools have become available. Keeping an open mind on tuning techniques, a new tool was evaluated to see if it might help improve Acme Rockets' long term sizing strategy to get the most out of their current server hardware investment. Keeping all hardware and tuning efforts exactly the same as configuration 2, a new software tool named AutoPilot was employed to determine if it would help the performance of the Exchange Application Server environment.

AutoPilot is a software product from MCSB Technology (*http://www.mcsb.com*) promoted to "improve the performance of any NT Server by measuring and adjusting application workloads to ensure optimal use of the underlying system components." Once AutoPilot is installed in the typical NT point, click, and reboot fashion, the application is automatically started each time the server is booted. In the evaluation version of the software, there were not any configurable options. AutoPilot is designed in this manner as it uses algorithms that dynamically tune NT Server on the fly. However, some folks (like myself) tend to head off to the registry to gain insight into the products in use, just for fun.

AutoPilot Technology Reviewed

From the AutoPilot literature provided by MCSB Technology CTO Kitrick Sheets, there are essentially three components of AutoPilot that work together trying to improve system performance. The first is the performance module (or p-modules) that are responsible for watching specific behaviors in the system (for example, affinity, bus utilization, etc.) and reporting their findings to the second component, the metaalgorithm module. The metaalgorithm module is the component that absorbs input provided by the p-modules and builds a consolidated picture of performance related thread selection options. Using the input from the p-modules, the metaalgorithm module determines which thread should be selected in order to provide optimal performance based on overall workload conditions. The third component of AutoPilot works to improve overall system performance of the environmental modules. These modules monitor environmental conditions across all applications (for example, file cache usage, or application memory usage) and manipulate global system parameters in an attempt to create an environment that supports higher performance. Consider the environmental modules as components that try to relieve pressure on global resources that may be constraining overall system performance. The environmental modules allow the p-modules and metaalgorithm to try to improve and effectively manage application workload to increase system performance.

AutoPilot Tuning Results

So how did the addition of the AutoPilot software to Exchange Configuration 2 fare? Table 8.8 outlines the results from all three of the stress tests.

Table 8.8 AutoPilot stress test results.

Number of Heavy LoadSim Users	Exchange Server Configuration 1	Exchange Server Configuration 2 (Improved Disk I/O Distribution)	Exchange Server Configuration 3 (AutoPilot S/W Addition)
	95th Percentile response time score (seconds)		
500	0.470	0.334	0.258
1000	0.613	0.513	0.323
2000	1.200	0.900	0.700

The response times to the end users improved across the board with the greatest gains appearing when the Exchange Server Configuration 3 was under the greatest loads. Comparing the Perfmon logs from stress tests 2 and 3, the most obvious effect adding the AutoPilot software had was increasing the amount of memory the server used during the stress test from 158 Mbytes to 173 Mbytes. Increasing the amount of memory in use by the server increased the average CPU usage by 5 percent to 27 percent, and improved the disk I/O usage again by caching more disk requests, which resulted in slightly lowering the disk queue length.

The AutoPilot software performance technology looks promising. But like any new technology, always test it in your environment before fielding to ensure that it performs as advertised. For this heavily loaded Exchange environment, AutoPilot improved the performance capacity of Exchange Server Configuration 2. Before adding any server software package, I suggest that a server baseline stress test be completed in a before and after fashion prior to deploying the server into production (like our Exchange Configurations 2 and 3).

10. Deploy the Server into Production

Now that the NT Server configuration and solution is tested and verified to meet Acme Rockets' requirements, the server is fielded with confidence that it will successfully complete the job.

11. Proactively Follow the Tuning Methodology After the Server Is Deployed

Following a strucured sizing methodology and stress testing the server configuration before production deployment builds confidence in the solution, but end users can always change their work habits. Continuing to follow the tuning methodology after the server is deployed helps to proactively plan and tune around future performance hurdles.

Key Observations for Tuning and Sizing Microsoft Exchange Server Application

EXCHANGE SERVER SIZING REFERENCE CHART

Even though every environment is different, Table 8.9 provides excellent sizing guidelines on which to base your initial server configurations.

Table 8.9 Exchange Server configuration chart.

Concurrent Exchange Users	Pentium Pro 200 MHz/512 K Class CPU	RAM (MB)	Number of SCSI Disk Drives	Network Interface Card
<= 1,000	1-2	128	7	10BaseTX
<= 2,000	2-3	256	12	100BaseTX
<= 4,000	2-4	512-1 GB	18	(1-2) 100BaseTX
<= 10,000	4 (1 MB cache CPUs)	2-3 GB	24	(1-2) 100BaseTX, FDDI

EXCHANGER SERVER RESOURCE USAGE

CPU Usage

The CPU resource is typically not the bottleneck in Microsoft Exchange environments. As larger and larger I/O subsystems are required to support the concurrent user loads, ensure there is enough CPU processing power to drive the disk, network, and application needs.

Memory Usage

The most important fact to consider when reviewing the amount of RAM to use is allocating sufficient RAM to ensure that the server does not page during normal operation. To provide high levels of performance, enough RAM is required to be configured such that most Exchange and NT Server activities are cached in RAM. This results in improved overall performance.

The Exchange Performance Optimizer Application is the easiest technique to allocate memory to Exchange. If, under Perfmon's memory object's available memory counter, there is significant amounts of RAM available, reallocate surplus RAM to Exchange via the Exchange Performance Optimizer, perfwiz command, or by editing the Exchange registry directly. *It is very important to leave memory set aside for NT Server itself. Overallocation of memory to Exchange results in performance degradation.*

Network I/O

The network server resource is typically not a bottleneck in most exchange environments. NT Server will support multiple network interface cards if the need does arise.

Disk Subsystem

This is the typical bottleneck for most Exchange Server environments. Allocate sufficient numbers of disk drives and SCSI buses to support not only the capacity requirements, but also the performance requirements. At a minimum, understand the disk subsystem characteristics outlined in Table 8.5 (Exchange Database Component Descriptions) presented earlier in this case study. The Exchange Performance Optimizer provides a friendly interface to move the various Exchange components around the disk subsystem. The key disk subsystem strategy to consider is ensuring that random and sequential disk components are placed on physically different disk drives/arrays. In the case of Exchange, this implies that the Information Stores are placed on separate physical disks than the transaction logs. A good disk I/O design is shown in Table 8.6 (Exchange Server Configuration 2 performance enhanced disk I/O layout). A higher availability Exchange disk subsystem designed for an enterprise class server that still keeps an eye on performance is outlined here in Table 8.10.

Table 8.10 Enterprise Class Exchange Server high availability and performance enterprise disk subsystem design.

Logical Disk Assignment	SCSI Bus	Physical Disk Arrangement	Microsoft Exchange File Location
C:	1	2 Disk RAID 1 Mirror	NT Operating System and Exchange Binaries
E:	1	2 Disk RAID 1 Mirror	Information Store Logs
F:	1	2 Disk RAID 1 Mirror	Directory Service Logs
D:	2	1 Disk JBOD	NT Paging file
G:	2	2 Disk RAID 1 Mirror	Message Transfer Agent
I:	2	3 Disk RAID 5 Array	Directory Service
E:	3 (External Array)	10 Disk RAID 5 Array	Private Information Store
E:	3 (External Array)	5 Disk RAID 5 Array	Public Information Store (if used)

USING THE EXCHANGE PERFORMANCE OPTIMIZER

This is a friendly and useful tool for tuning Exchange. Always rerun this tool if server hardware components have been added or removed to ensure that the tuning settings are set appropriately to take advantage of the resources available. The Optimizer does not take into consideration other applications that may reside on the server; manual intervention for those environments are required.

Case Study: File Server

THE ENVIRONMENT

Acme Rockets' decision to move out of the dark ages and begin moving toward a paperless office created a need to share electronic documents between co-workers and backup essential electronic documents on a regular basis. To accomplish this, Acme Rockets decided to deploy file servers throughout their enterprise. They are deploying the file servers throughout their architecture relatively close to each work group. There are 1000 workgroups that need to be supported. By deploying each server in close proximity to the working group, they hope to reduce the volume of network traffic traversing their primary network backbones. What is not known is how many concurrent Acme users a file server and a 100BaseTX Ethernet network segment can support. Peer-to-peer network sharing is removed as a possible consideration in favor of centralized workgroup file servers which control an entire workgroup's backup and sharing requirements. With a combination of developers, rocket scientists, and documentation control personnel working together in teams, the File Server is expected to support sharing and backing up of compressed and uncompressed data, text, and images. All of the primary workstations are Windows NT workstations. Economics are a concern, as always. Acme is hoping to get the most out of their file servers while implementing them with the least amount of hardware as possible.

Now that the general environment is in place, let's walk through the sizing methodology to determine a File Server solution for Acme Rockets. As in the first case study, some of the gory details associated with obtaining the actual information are circumvented for brevity. The focus here is on applying the sizing methodology and determining a solid initial server configuration. Secondly, key information on the tuning and sizing of File Server solutions is investigated for future sizing and tuning.

1. Define Objective(s)

Develop a File Server solution that will support Acme Rockets' mixed application workgroup sharing and backup environment. They are trying to keep to a minimum the amount of server hardware required to support each workgroup.

2. Understand Requirements Needed to Meet Your Objective

To meet this requirement, Microsoft NT Server is selected as the network operating system. No surprise here, this book's focus is NT Server. The workgroup file servers will be the primary backup and data-sharing servers for critical documents. Acme Rockets expects basic availability requirements, but economics are a consideration. They plan to provide each end user with a backup and sharing area on their workgroup File Server of approximately

60 Mbytes. An in-house-developed application works in conjunction with standard NT Server shares for backing up and restoring files.

3. Determine Loading Characteristics

The total number of users to initially support is based on the various workgroup sizes. Typical workgroups encompass 130 end users. Always under a tight schedule, Acme Rockets expects that of the 130 users on rotating 24 hour shifts, each file server will be required to support a concurrency rate somewhere between 15–20 percent. This indicates that a workgroup File Server will be required to support between 19 and 26 concurrent File Server end users.

4. Determine Performance Requirements

The files backed up and shared are typically comprised of various sizes and formats. On average, they expect to backup, restore, and share (read/write) transaction response times to be less than 20 seconds. This 20 second transaction response time is required to be sustained when there are 25 concurrent users. Note that this may seem like a high response time value, but it is acceptable for Acme's environment as they do not expect to use the file servers for truly interactive applications.

5. Understand Future Business Requirements

As the workgroups develop and expand various projects, Acme Rockets expects to add more personnel to each workgroup. As this occurs, the same 15–20 percent concurrency rate is expected as concurrent users accessing the File Server increases.

6. Understand Future Server Architectures

Acme Rockets continues to love technology, but would prefer not to completely replace their server for at least three years (current company policy). With this in mind, they have decided to proceed with a standards based server architecture that can support the planned increased capacity. In a file server environment, disk and network subsystems are typically the most heavily stressed portions of the server. Thus, a server that can support a fair amount of disk and network I/O is considered optimal.

7. Configure the Server

Just like other businesses, Acme Rockets is rushing to complete this project as soon as possible. Even though this project is rushed, they still plan to stress test the server before deployment due in part to the large 1000 unit rollout. Enough information is presented in steps 1 through 6 to initially size the server. But before we begin the configuration phase, let us review the primary application that will be used on the server.

Application Characteristics Review

Most file server environments are characterized by the following resource usage activity: Memory: Medium to Heavy, Processor: Light, Disk: Active, and Network: Active. The two key areas of concern are disk I/O and network I/O usage patterns.

Review Each Server Resource

DISK I/O REQUIREMENTS

Disk Storage Capacity Considerations and Requirements

NT Server O/S: 124 MB

NT Server Pagefile: RAM x 2

Acme Customer Application executable/binaries: 50 MB

User Backup Space: 130 users at 60 MB per user for backup space equate to 7.8 GB of available disk space

Total Minimum Disk Space required: 8.122 GB

Relevant Industry Benchmark: None were applicable for this size disk capacity requirement

Disk Availability Considerations and Requirements

The server selected to support this exchange environment is an NCR S46. This server supports six internal disk drives, which can be split across two SCSI buses. With economics and availability a concern, Acme Rockets decides to implement three 4 GB disk drives in a RAID 5 array for the User Backup Space, place NT Server on a separate single 4 GB disk drive, and place the NT Server Pagefile on its own dedicated disk drive.

Disk Performance Considerations and Requirements

Not knowing how the server will respond under load, the paging file is placed on a separate dedicated disk. The dedicated 4 GB disk drive can be added to RAID 5 Striped array with parity if additional storage is needed and paging activities do not become a concern. The Pagefile would then be moved back to the dedicated NT Server operating system disk drive. The three 4 GB based RAID 5 disk array provides 8 GB of fault tolerant usable data storage for backup user space. The single 4 GB disk drive provides ample room for NT Server files, the custom Acme Application files, and a fair amount of room for growth. The RAID controller shipped with this server is the Mylex 960PL with 4 MB of on board battery backed cache. The onboard RAID cache helps to improve the write performance of the RAID 5 array.

CPU Requirements:
NT Minimum: Intel 80486/66
Relevant Industry Benchmark: Ziff Davis NetBench

From an application perspective, where the primary application is NT Server networking, there is a relatively low processing power requirement required for sharing, copying, and reading the varied file workloads. The primary processing required is for driving a significant level of disk and network I/O. The minimum CPU technology required for NT is not relevant here. Obtaining a modern server based on the older 80486 CPU technology is not realistic.

The relevant industry benchmark for this environment, NetBench, measures how well a file server handles typical office productivity application file I/O requests workloads by stressing the file server with various client types. Although Acme Rockets is a custom environment, NetBench provides a good general File Server characterization which is applicable in helping develop an initial server configuration. In Chapter 3's explanation of NetBench, one of PC Magazine's lab NetBench results was described and is used here.

The top performing servers from the NetBench tests provided a maximum network I/O throughput of just over 60 Megabits/sec. Supported throughput began to fall when more than 20 concurrent clients were requesting service. These departmental servers were configured roughly the same with a single Pentium Pro or Pentium II CPU, 128 MB of RAM, two 10/100 network interface cards, and two 4 GB hard disks in a RAID Level 1 mirrored configuration. The total network load for each benchmark test was a 60-node network divided into two identical 30 client segments.

This NetBench environment is close enough to our environments to extrapolate some key configuration information. This benchmark indicates that 1 Pentium Pro class CPU is sufficient to sustain a relatively high network throughput topping out at 20 clients. This is close to the 25 concurrent user load, which is Acme Rockets' goal. For the initial CPU configuration, a single Pentium Pro 200 MHz/512 K cache will be utilized.

Memory Requirements:
NT Server O/S: 32 MB
NT Server O/S Disk buffers: 32 MB
Relevant Industry Benchmark: Ziff Davis NetBench

The server will require a sufficient amount of memory so that most general disk accesses are buffered by NT Server's dynamic file system cache. The additional 32 MB of RAM will provide available memory for the dynamic disk cache buffers. The NetBench results presented above indicates that at least 128 MBytes of RAM are required to support 20 concurrent clients. Without the corresponding Perfmon log results to review, there is no way of knowing if all of the 128 Mbytes of RAM were helpful. Acme Rockets decides to initially configure the File Server with just 64 Mbytes of RAM. They hope that this amount of RAM will be sufficient so that they can keep costs down. This File Server solution will be fielded across workgroups. Just in case the initial File Server RAM configuration is not sufficient, they understand the NCR S46 can be upgraded to a maximum 4 Gbytes of RAM.

NETWORK I/O REQUIREMENTS

Relevant Industry Benchmark: Ziff Davis NetBench

The server will be placed into the current network architecture via a 100BaseT-switch up-link. PC Magazine's NetBench results imply that a file server with two 100BaseTX network interface cards can support a throughput up to 60 Mbytes/sec while servicing 20 clients. This indicates that each network adapter was only able to support approximately 30 Mbytes/sec and 10 clients. Note that this information is pertinent to the Ziff Davis NetBench benchmark and the server utilized in the benchmark example. This does not indicate that every environment is limited to supporting this number of clients.

Each of Acme Rockets' workgroups currently share a single subnet. To support two or more subnets, changes in the network architecture are required. Acme Rockets is reviewing their network architecture to determine the best way to support multiple subnets in one workgroup. Items that they may change in their network architecture could include additional NICs for the server, additional interfaces for their routers, or switched support for VLAN technology, just to name a few. Until then, they hope to make due by configuring the File Server with only one 100BaseTX Ethernet card.

Initial Hardware Configuration and Tuning

Initial hardware tuning considerations revolve around the I/O subsystem. The network and disk I/O adapters are placed into different PCI buses to avoid any possible contention. The DLT Tape Drive and CD-ROM drives are placed onto the internal Adaptec SCSI adapter channels to avoid contention with the faster disk drive unit SCSI buses.

NCR S46

SCSI CD-ROM

  Installed on the internal motherboard Ultra Fast and Wide SCSI-2 adapter channel 1

Floppy Disk Drive

20/40 GB DLT Drive

  Installed on the internal motherboard Ultra Fast and Wide SCSI-2 adapter channel 2

  (Acme Rockets still has that surplus of DLT Tape Units)

1 Pentium Pro 200 MHz/512 K cache CPUs

64 MB of 60ns SIMM RAM

1 Intel EthernetPro 100B 100BaseTX NIC

  Installed in PCI Bus 1

1 4 GB Fast and Wide 7200 RPM SCSI Disk Drive for NT Server, Acme backup Application
1 4 GB Fast and Wide 7200 RPM SCSI Disk Drive for the Paging File
3 4 GB Fast and Wide 7200 RPM SCSI Disk Drives for End User Backups
1 Mylex 960Pl 2 Channel Fast and Wide SCSI PCI RAID adapter with 4 MB of onboard cache Installed in PCI Bus 2

Initial Software Configuration and Tuning

SOFTWARE VERSIONS

NT Server 4.0
Service Pack 3

Initial Tuning

No special software tuning considerations are put into place at this time. Acme Rockets feels NT Server's default installation will provide adequate performance to meet their requirements. By default, NT Server's Memory Strategy is set to Maximize Throughput for File Sharing. A single large NTFS volume is created across the three 4 GB RAID 5 disk array. On this array, each user is given a shared folder for their data. The root disk drive will use NTFS due to its security attributes.

Server Architecture Relationship Check

Now that we have created an initial server configuration, let's make a common sense review of the configuration from the perspective of the overall server architecture in place. Having a relevant industry benchmark (PC Magazine's NetBench results) available for reference is helpful when completing the Server Architecture Check. The NetBench results influence the configuration and provide a third party stress test that showed how well a similar configuration performed. One Pentium Pro 200 MHz/512 K CPU should be capable of supporting the processing requirements of the expected load and have sufficient resources to concurrently drive the 2 Fast/Wide SCSI SCSI disk channels and single 100BaseTX network interface. 64 MB of RAM appears sufficient to keep the CPU fed, and provide enough memory for the application space to buffer I/O activities. Based on the NetBench results, the amount of RAM may need to be increased and will be watched closely. There are two peer PCI buses in an NCR S46 server. A quick basic math check of the I/O subsystem indicates that the I/O subsystem is required to support 2 Fast and Wide SCSI buses (40 Mbytes/sec) and a single 100 Mbit network connection. Two Peer PCI buses provide an aggregate I/O bandwidth of 266 Mbytes/sec, which is more than sufficient to support the current configuration requirements.

Future Business and Server Architectures Check Review

From steps 5 and 6 of the sizing methodology, we see that the server is based on current industry standards and market trends. This level of File Server still has significant amount of additional resources available if needed. CPUs can be expanded up to four, memory up to 4 GB, and four additional PCI slots are available. Do not confuse PCI slots and PCI buses as was pointed out in Chapter 6. When additional users are added to the Acme Rockets workgroups, there will not be a sufficient amount of internal disk space available to support this future requirement. Thus, the only out of box scaling that may be required is the addition of an external disk array(s). Except for the use of an external disk array in the future, this File Server configuration is in line with Acme Rockets' strategy of growth.

8. Stress Test and Validate The Server Configuration

Congratulations! We now have a File Server configuration that can be placed into production which might support the required number of users while providing 20 second response time performance for file sharing and backup. Based on the NetBench results, a second NIC may need to be added. Acme Rockets is currently planning for this infrastructure possibility.

Curious as to what performance levels the current File Server configuration will be able to support, Acme Rockets decides to stress test their File Server configuration prior to deployment. They have four objectives to achieve when running this stress test:

1. How many concurrent users will a single File Server Support and still provide better than a 20 second response time?
2. How many concurrent File Server Users will the 100BaseTX Ethernet segment support?
3. What types of throughput can they expect for future planning?
4. What resources may need to be upgraded in the future?

DEVELOPING THE STRESS AND VALIDATION TESTS

Various scripting tools are available for developing a baseline for tuning or for stress test sizing as shown in Chapter 2. Here I selected a third party product from Blue Curve technologies. Blue Curve has a variety of tool classes. To emulate this end user environment and stress test the File Server solution, Blue Curve's (*http://www.bluecurve.com*) Dynameasure product was employed. Dynameasure is an active measurement technology which measures end-to-end system performance from the application layer by applying controlled stress to the system using actual client/server hardware and software components. This product allows for in-depth capacity and performance analysis of NT Server environments.

An evaluation copy of this product is on the CD-ROM included with this book so that you can experience first-hand stress testing of NT Server solutions in your environment. Use this case study as an example of how to use Blue Curve's Dynameasure product to your advantage when implementing the tuning and sizing methodologies. The details on using the actual Blue Curve Dynameasure product are left to the Blue Curve documentation.

STRESS TEST DEVELOPMENT

From the information gathered from Acme Rockets in steps 1 through 6, we need to develop a stress test series that encompasses sharing, copying, and backing up of compressed and uncompressed data, text, and images for at least 25 concurrent users. Dynameasure has a variety of built-in stress tests that are available or you can develop custom stress tests. Reviewing the File Server stress tests included in Dynameasure yielded a test suite that closely resembled Acme Rockets' environment. This file server suite is named "Copy All Bi-directional" and encompasses the following activities between the File Server and client workstations: bidirectional copy of compressed and uncompressed data, text, and image files from the clients to the server.

The breakdown of the file operations is shown in Table 8.11.

Table 8.11 File Server stress test characteristics.

Transaction Name	Copy Direction	File Name	File Size (Kbytes)	Transaction Weight (%)
1001	Client to Server	Cpydsk_uncp_data_ctos	10000	6.25
1002	Client to Server	Cpydsk_uncp_text_ctos	1000	6.25
1003	Client to Server	Cpydsk_uncp_image_ctos	10000	6.25
1004	Client to Server	Cpydsk_uncp_binary_ctos	1000	6.25
1005	Client to Server	Cpydsk_cmpr_data_ctos	10000	6.25
1006	Client to Server	Cpydsk_cmpr_text_ctos	1000	6.25
1007	Client to Server	Cpydsk_cmpr_image_ctos	10000	6.25
1008	Client to Server	Cpydsk_cmpr_binary_ctos	1000	6.25
1009	Server to Client	Cpydsk_uncp_data_stoc	10000	6.25
1010	Server to Client	Cpydsk_uncp_text_stoc	1000	6.25
1011	Server to Client	Cpydsk_uncp_image_stoc	1000	6.25
1012	Server to Client	Cpydsk_uncp_binary_stoc	1000	6.25
1013	Server to Client	Cpydsk_cmpr_data_stoc	1000	6.25

Table 8.11 File Server stress test characteristics. (Continued)

Transaction Name	Copy Direction	File Name	File Size (Kbytes)	Transaction Weight (%)
1014	Server to Client	Cpydsk_cmpr_text_stoc	1000	6.25
1015	Server to Client	Cpydsk_cmpr_image_stoc	1000	6.25
1016	Server to Client	Cpydsk_cmpr_binary_stoc	1000	6.25

The Copy All Bidirectional workload is configured in the following manner for the Acme Rocket environment:

- Data set size set to 0.1—this corresponds to working data set size of 59.8 Mbytes for each end user emulated
- Think time set to 5 seconds—this relates to the time each emulated end user waits before starting a transaction

STRESS TEST ENVIRONMENT

To generate the load on the File Server, three client computers were configured on the same 100 Mbit/sec shared Ethernet network as the File Server. The stress test configuration is illustrated in Figure 8–8.

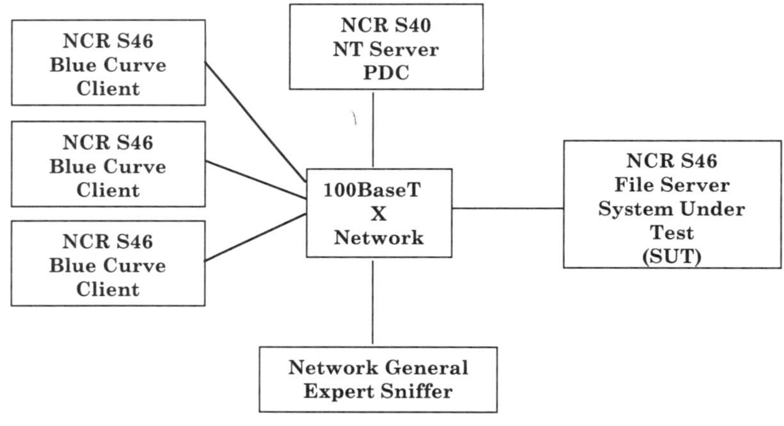

Figure 8–8 *File Server stress test environment.*

The performance of the Blue Curve client generators and Ethernet based network was monitored at all times to ensure that they were not the source of any bottlenecks during the stress test. This step is critical during stress testing to ensure that the stress is correctly being placed on the system under test (SUT). Each client was configured with two disk drives, two Pentium Pro

CPUs, and 512 MB of RAM. A Network General Expert Sniffer was used to ensure that there were not any significant amounts of network errors and that the network capacity was not exceeded.

FILE SERVER STRESS TEST RESULTS: BASELINE CONFIGURATION—FILE SERVER CONFIGURATION 1

Once the stress test environment was configured, the initial File Server configuration was tested at the 1, 5, 10, 15, 20, 25, and 30 motor levels. Blue Curve refers to their emulated clients as "motors," where each motor represents a single client/user. While the stress test was run, the tuning methodology was followed. NT Server's Performance Monitor's logging mode was enabled during all of the tests.

Blue Curve provides two primary measurements: Throughput and Average Response Time (ART). This information provides insight into what the end user can expect to experience (ART) and what type of throughput the server is providing each of the client's workstations. Figures 8–9 and 8–10 show the initial Blue Curve results.

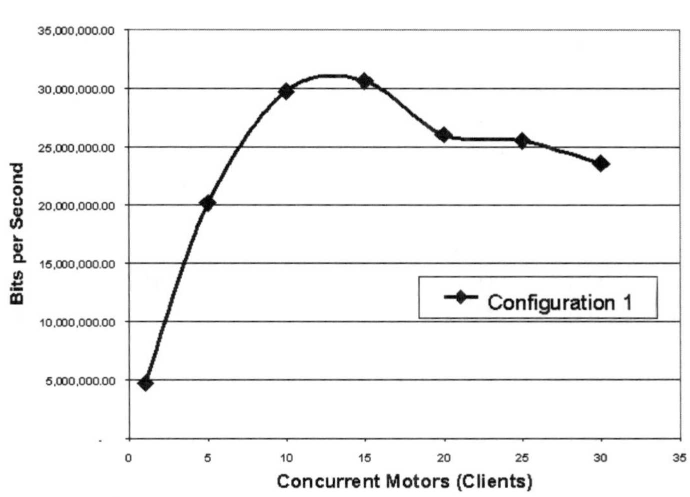

Figure 8–9 *File Server configuration 1 stress test throughput results. (For all throughput graphs, such as the one above, higher throughput values are better.)*

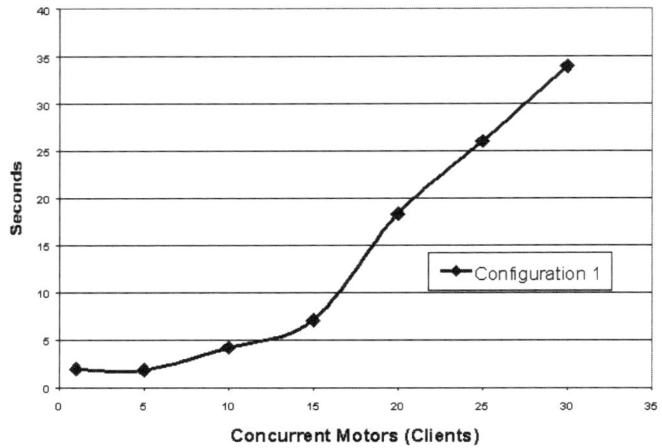

Figure 8–10 *File Server configuration 1 stress test ART results (For all Average Response Time (ART) graphs, lower response time values are better.)*

BASELINE FILE SERVER CONFIGURATION 1 RESULTS SUMMARY

Acme Rockets' performance goal of supporting 25 concurrent users while providing a response time less then 20 seconds is not met with the current NT File Server configuration. With the current configuration, when 25 concurrent users are accessing the file server, the average response time is 26 seconds. From the throughput graph, there is a definite bottleneck occurring just past the 15 concurrent user's mark.

We have now, unfortunately, invalidated the initial configuration solution. This leads us to either quit now and go home, or try to determine what bottleneck is throttling the File Server solution from meeting Acme Rockets' performance goals. Surprisingly, we'll try to remove the server bottleneck.

9. Proactively Follow the Tuning Methodology During Validation and Stress Testing

We will utilize the tuning methodology to determine why the current File Server configuration will not meet Acme Rocket's short-term performance requirements. The first configuration that was tested is referenced as Baseline File Server Configuration 1.

FINDING THE PERFORMANCE BOTTLENECK

Reviewing The tuning methodology from Chapter 2, we are currently at step 4, "Determine what resource is acting like or becoming a bottleneck." To help in determining where the bottlenecks are, we'll again use the .pmw files from Chapter 2 in conjunction with the Perfmon log file generated for the 30 motor/client user stress test.

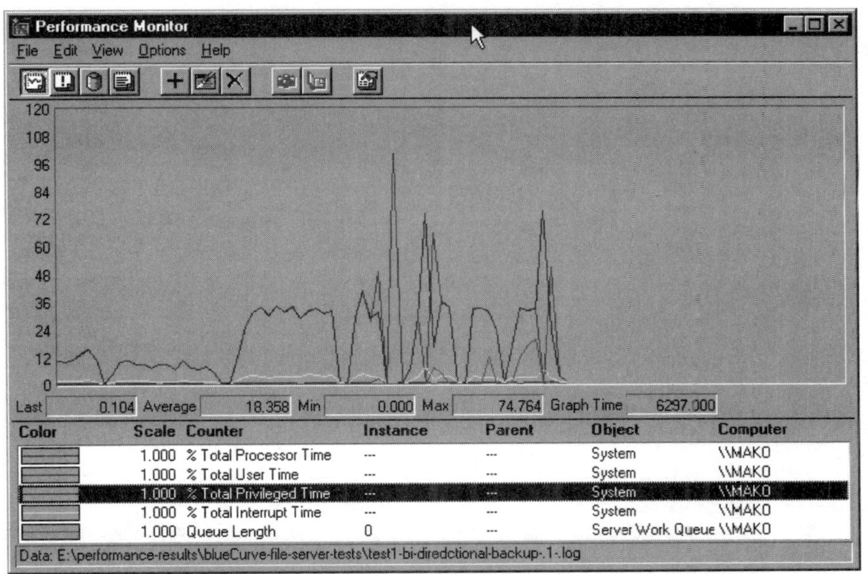

Figure 8–11 *cpu-resources.pmw for File Server Configuration 1.*

CPU usage is not a bottleneck in Figure 8–11, in fact, on a server that should be very busy, the CPU is relatively quiet. There are some process backups in the CPU queue, but this can be contributed to the fact that the CPU is almost stalling while it is waiting for data to move and manipulate. CPU stalling is typified by relative low CPU usage levels (< 60%) with a small increase in the CPU work queue. We'll watch CPU usage closely. If we are successful in removing the bottlenecks caused by other server resources, CPU usage may begin to increase as it begins to move larger amounts of data.

Network resources are not taxed at all in Figure 8–12. Although there are a few spikes of intense network traffic, the average traffic is using less than half of the theoretically available network bandwidth. This fact in conjunction with no network errors leads us to remove the network as a current possible source of the server's bottleneck.

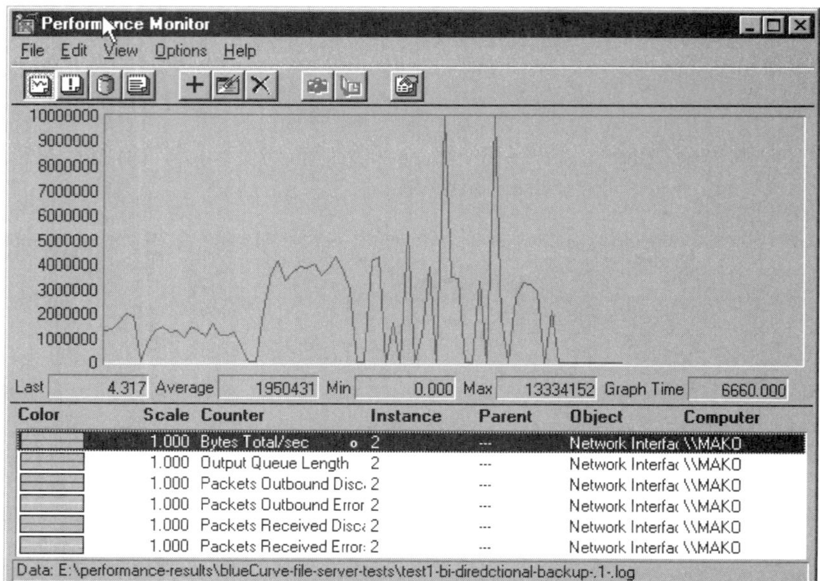

Figure 8–12 *network-resources.pmw for File Server Configuration 1.*

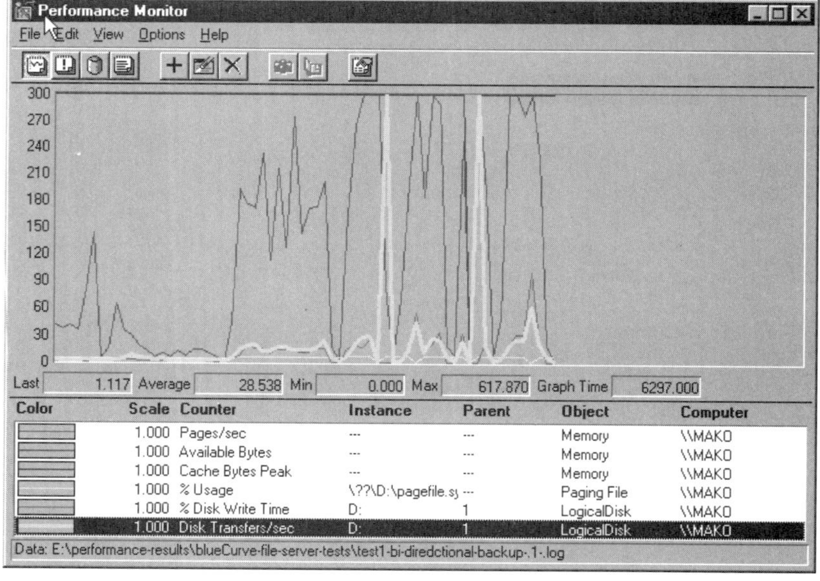

Figure 8–13 *memory-resources.pmw for File Server Configuration 1.*

Welcome to a memory bottleneck! The high Memory:Pages/sec in Figure 8–13 is not actually a good indicator of a memory shortage for heavily used file servers since a vast majority of the paging is due to soft page faults, or in other words bringing data into memory to send across the network. Remember this is the real world, but for the Microsoft exams, pages/sec is an indicator of RAM resource contention on small servers.

The default memory strategy for this File Server is Maximize Throughput for File Sharing. NT Server followed this strategy and used every possible extra scrap of memory for dynamic file buffering, which is exactly what we wanted. The amount of available memory during heavy stress periods (there is a small pause between each stress test user level which accounts for the drastic up and down graphs) is well below the NT Server memory available target level of 1 MByte for servers using this memory strategy.

The paging file was placed on a dedicated physical disk drive, logical drive D: This drive had a very high %disk time usage, but more importantly the disk transfers per second were at times up to three times higher than a single disk can comfortably handle. (The Transfers/sec or I/Os per second disk drives can support under NT Server are reviewed in Chapter 6.) This resulted in an extremely high disk queue. Thus, NT Server did page furiously when under heavy loads as seen by reviewing the disk drive activity that housed the paging file and the lower than targeted available memory.

Paging activities are typically sequential in nature. Depending on the source of your information, a 7200 RPM Fast and Wide SCSI disk drive can sustain approximately 100 to 150 I/Os per second (disk transfers per second) in a sequential environment. At peak loads the disk transfers/sec for drive D: were over 600! Watching the Paging File:%Usage, very little of the actual paging file was utilized. This indicates that adding another small increment of RAM would improve the overall performance of the server by allowing the File Server to greatly reduce that amount of its very slow paging activities. It is very, very important to note that locating this memory bottleneck and estimating that only a small amount of additional memory would improve the overall server performance would be more difficult to determine if the paging file was placed on a disk drive that shared other active file sets.

Memory is not the only bottleneck occurring in this File Server configuration stress test as shown in Figure 8–14. Logical drive E: is a three disk RAID 5 array which holds all of the file sets for Acme Rockets' end users. The two biggest areas of concern here are the transfers/sec and the disk queue size. This type of multiuser File Server environment is typically slightly more random in nature then sequential. In environments characterized by random disk I/O activity, again depending on the source of your information, a 7200 RPM Fast and Wide SCSI disk drive can sustain approximately 55 to 100 I/Os per second (disk transfers per second). This three disk array in a random read characterized environment can support between 165 to 300 I/Os per second.

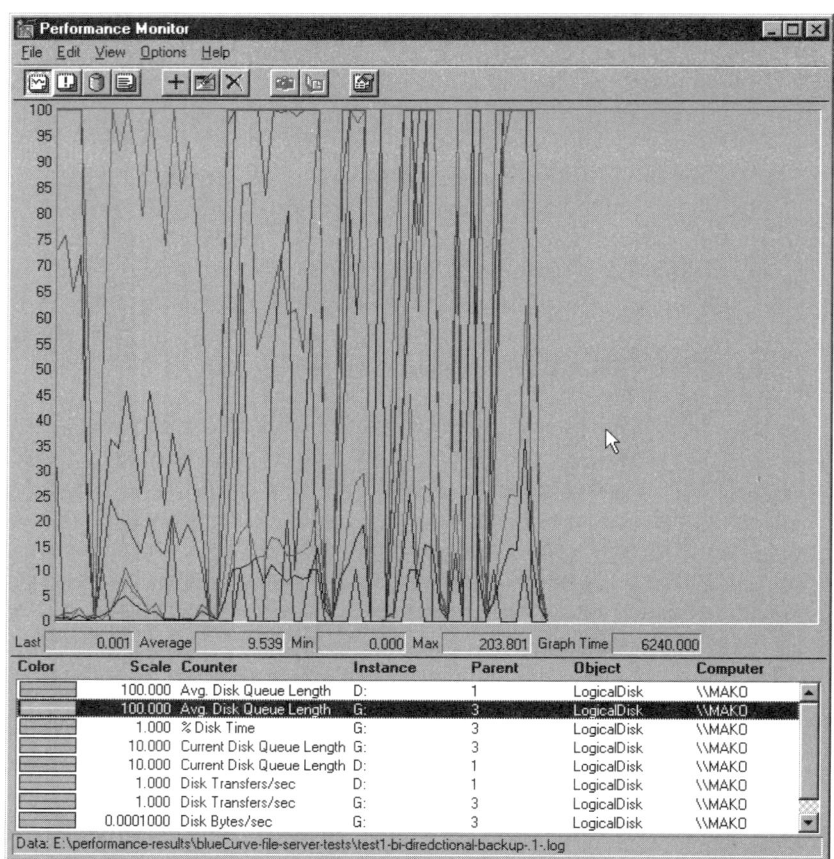

Figure 8–14 *disk-resources.pmw for File Server Configuration 1.*

This threshold is being greatly surpassed, even before extrapolating the exact RAID 5 workload calculations described in Chapter 6.

When the disk array is unable to sustain the amount of disk I/Os requested of it, the disk queues begin to increase. Both the average Disk Queue Length and Current Queue Length counters are good gauges to employ when determining disk queue build up. When these counters are used to measure the queues of disk arrays, take the reported disk queue value and divide it by the number of disk drives in the array. For example, if logical drive E: was composed of 3 physical drives and the Average Disk Queue Length was reported at 9.5, this would yield a normalized disk queue length of 3.3 for each drive in the array. Average disk queue lengths in the range of 1–2 are generally acceptable, but when they reach a maximum value of 203 for the array or over 60 per disk drive in the array which is shown above, there is no question that the disk subsystem is a bottleneck.

To remove this disk I/O bottleneck, there are three techniques to implement: improve the disk I/O buffering through the addition of RAM, add additional capacity to the disk I/O subsystem via additional disk drives and SCSI channels, or tune the NTFS file system layout.

Tuning Around the File Server Bottleneck

Decision time! Figure 8–15 illustrates the current bottleneck dilemma.

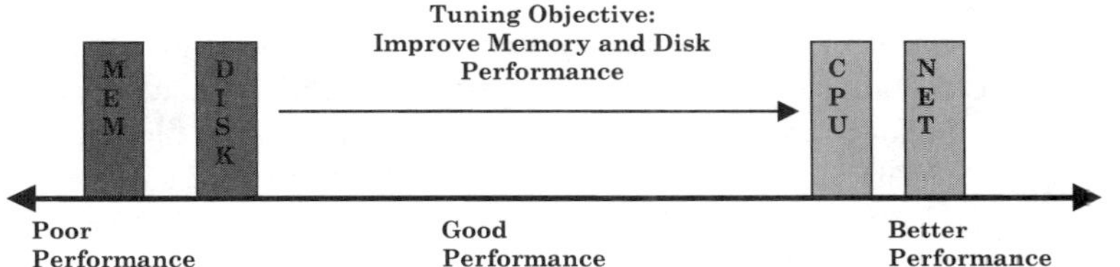

Figure 8–15 *Performance Resource Chart depiciting two file server bottlenecks.*

Which resource should be tuned to yield the greatest immediate performance gain? Adding additional memory will provide for the largest immediate gain by improving NT Server's File System cache and lowering the amount of paging activity. But in lieu of adding any hardware, the folks at Acme would like to consider if there is any tuning that can be completed on the server at no cost. The tuning strategy is still linked to the performance resource chart above which indicates that the memory and disk I/O performance will need to be improved before any real overall performance gains are achieved.

NO COST NT SERVER TUNING

With this strategy of "no cost tuning" in mind, two areas will be tuned: memory and disk I/O. To tune the memory subsystem, the following actions are taken:

- Check the primary NT Server memory strategy. The current memory strategy is already set correctly to Maximizing Memory for File Sharing.
- A quick look under Task Manager shows numerous processes that are not really needed for a File Server only environment. With this in mind, various unneeded services are removed from the NT Server start-up sequence. Services are removed from the NT boot process by setting them to start manually under the Start|Settings|Control Panel|Services icon. The services turned off are: FTP Publishing Service, Gopher Publishing Service, Messenger, Alerter, RPC Service, Spooler and World Wide Web Publishing.
- Another unneeded background processes is also removed. Again using Task Manager, a process that was unexpectedly started is located: find-

fast.exe. The findfast program was installed when the Office 97 Suite was installed. Findfast is removed by removing it from NT Server start-up folder.

Now that some memory is freed up when the server is rebooted, let's turn our attention to improving the disk subsystem performance. From the Acme Rocket sizing environment information, we notice that there are no workstations running legacy Windows or DOS PC operating systems and that all applications support long file names. This allows us to confidently turn off NT Server's legacy habit of writing both long and short filenames to the disk. Ensure you back up the registry and understand how to restore selected hives before attempting any registry tuning. A registry backup and restore refresher is located in Appendix A. To disable short file name generation, use REGEDIT32.exe to set the registry DWORD value to 1 in the following Registry location: HKEY_LOCAL_MACHINE\SYSTEM\CurentControlSet\Control\Filesystem\NtfsDisable8dot3nameCreation. Disabling short name generation on an NTFS partition can increase directory performance significantly if a high number of non 8.3 filenames are in use, which is exactly what happens when all of the client workstations generate long file names and have no need for the short file name format.

The above tuning recommendations will cause headaches for any end user that uses a workstation that does not support long file names.

With a high number of concurrent users traversing directory tree structures on the File Server, another NT Registry value that should be tuned is: HKEY_LOCAL_MACHINE\SYSTEM\CurrentControlSet\Control\FileSystemNtfs-DisableLastAccessUpdate. By changing the default REG_DWORD value of this key from 0 to 1, you improve file system performance by lowering the file system overhead associated with updating the last access time/date stamp on directories as directory trees are traversed. The file actually updated is still properly time stamped.

The last item to tune on the File Server is the size of the Allocation Unit Size (ALU) used when creating the NTFS file system on the RAID 5-striped disk array with parity. Reviewing the Perfmon log counter Logical Disk: Average Disk bytes/Write, we see that the average size of data written to the disk array is close to 64 Kbytes. To improve the efficiency of each disk write, the ALU size is set to 64K. This is accomplished by backing up the data on the disk array, then formatting the disk array from the NT command line using the following command "format g: /F:NTFS /A:64k", then restoring the data back to the array.

FILE SERVER RESULTS FOR CONFIGURATION 2: NT SERVER OPERATING SYSTEM TUNING ONLY

Ideally, we would like to only make one tuning change at a time. This is very important if you do not have the time or tools to test the tuning changes made before production, since tuning efforts occasionally backfire. If a server is going directly into production without the benefit of being stress tested first and having the results compared against a baseline, only make one change at a time. In this way, in the highly unlikely event that your tuning events are not successful, it is relatively easy to return the server back to its stable pre-tuned state. Fortunately, for this tuning effort, we will rerun the same File Server Stress Test to determine if our tuning efforts are successful. Figure 8–16 shows the Blue Curve stress test results comparing File Server Configuration 1 (the baseline) to File Server Configuration 2 (Internal NT Server Tuning Only).

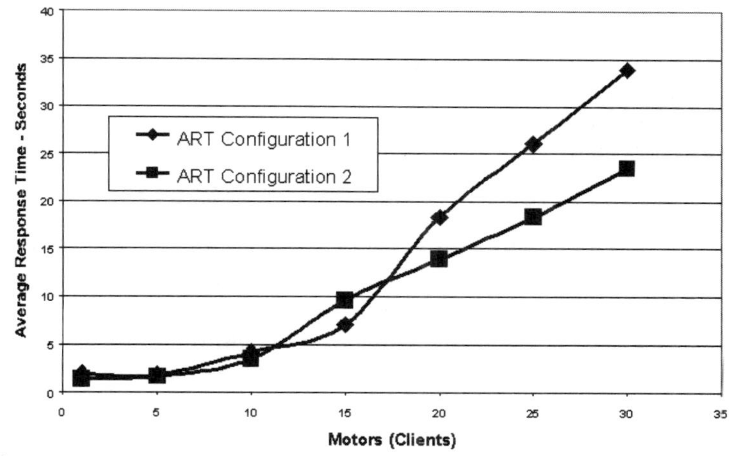

Figure 8–16 *File Server Stress Test Configuration 1 vs. Configuration 2 (Note: Lower values are better in the Average Response Time Graphs – ART)*

ONE-SIZE-FITS-ALL SOLUTIONS PROVIDE AVERAGE RESULTS

Our tuning efforts have had a profound affect! At the 25 concurrent user level, the tuned File Server provides an average response time of 18 seconds versus 26 seconds for the default NT Server installation used for File Server Configuration 1! This is over a 32 percent improvement in response time! NT Server out-of-the-box provided a nice, easy-to-use one-size-fits-all solution which provided average performance levels. But, with a little bit of analysis of Acme Rockets' environment in conjunction with some analysis of the Perfmon log files, the NT based File Server can be tuned for a significant performance advantage. The whopping cost to Acme for this tuning? Zero! Well, actually, a fair amount of thought and some time ensuring that the tuning was successful should be counted. Acme Rockets now has a File Server configuration that will support a 20 second response time when 25 concurrent users are accessing the File Server. This tuning improvement also improves future additions to the server as well.

ECONOMIC BENEFITS FROM TUNING NT SERVER

Meeting Acme Rockets' performance goals without adding additional hardware has an economic impact. Think, for example, if 64 Mbytes of additional RAM was required for each server before deployment to achieve the desired performance levels (if NT Server tuning was not completed). RAM prices are volatile and have been lowering in price over the last few years. With this basic premise, estimate that 64 Mbytes of RAM would cost Acme Rockets $500.00. This results in an extra $500,000.00 in savings when you consider that they are rolling out 1000 File Servers. Quite a savings!

Figure 8–17 shows the throughput results comparing the baseline File Server Configuration 1 (C1) and internally tuned File Server Configuration 2 (C2)

The tuning efforts completed on Configuration 2 have helped extend the throughput level peak and sustain throughput levels that the File Server is capable of handling. More obvious than the ART chart is the knee in the curve which begins to occur on the throughput chart at the 15 user level. 33 Mbits per second is a fair throughput level to achieve in a 100 Mbit/sec Ethernet environment, but there is still a resource that is acting as a bottleneck. This bottleneck is continuing to throttle the server's overall performance.

CONTINUED PLANNING FOR THE FUTURE

Running stress test to determine if your tuning efforts are effective is an iterative process that can continue on for a significant amount of time. Typically, this is an exercise of diminishing returns until you reach a point that you either:

- no longer are obtaining significant performance improvements
- you have configured a well balanced solution and have obtained the best performance possible out of the server
- you throw the server out the window, piece by piece

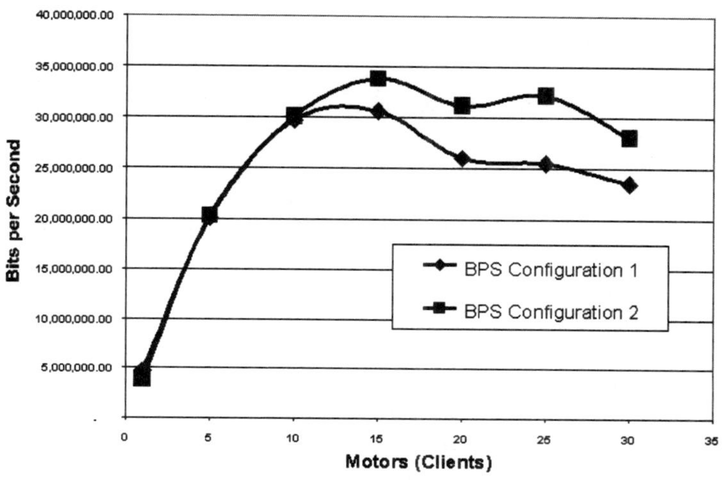

Figure 8–17 *Comparing C1 and C2.*

Fortunately, we have not quite entered any of these areas, yet.

Acme Rockets is still planning for astronomical growth, thus they expect to continually add additional associates to each of their work groups over time. What will happen to the server as the concurrent user levels increase? Where should they add additional capacity to the File Server in the future? How much capacity is required to sustain their performance goals? To answer these questions and help in planning for the future, we'll need to determine where the bottlenecks are occurring and remove them. As you proceed through the tuning process, it is interesting to find which resources can become a bottleneck as other resource bottlenecks are removed.

FILE SERVER CONFIGURATION 3: ADDING MEMORY TO TUNE AROUND THE SERVER BOTTLENECK

Reviewing the Perfmon logs from stress testing File Server Configuration 2, there is no indication of a bottleneck forming in the network or CPU subsystems. Paging is still excessive, noted by the combination of low available memory, very high logical Disk:Transfers/sec levels on the dedicated Pagefile disk, and particularly high Memory:Pages/sec. Paging to disk will ultimately always slow any type of server activity. Removing the memory bottleneck will provide the next greatest gain in performance and is the easiest to implement. First, we must determine how much memory is required to significantly lower the amount of paging occurring in the File Server.

A good starting point to determine the amount of RAM that should be added is found by reviewing the Paging File: %Usage counter. For File Server Configuration 1, the maximum amount of the Paging file used is 7 percent. Multiplying this value by the size of the paging file, which was set at 512 MBytes, yields approximately 36 MBytes. Adding a 36 Mbyte chunk of memory is unrealistic in today's modern servers due to vendor configuration guidelines. Keeping in consideration the long term potential that more memory may be required, another 64 MB SIMM set is added to the server configuration which will allow for the most efficient use of the available SIMM sockets on the server's memory board. Thus, another 64 Mbytes of RAM are added for a total of 128 Mbytes. Adding this memory should lower the amount of paging occurring on the server and improve some of the disk performance by buffering a larger amount of the disk read activities. The initial NT Server internal tuning was successful in improving performance, so those tuning efforts are left in place on the File Server for stress test 3. Figures 8–18 and 8–19 show the results of adding an additional 64 Mbytes of RAM to the File Server (File Server Configuration 3)

So what did purchasing 64 Mbytes of RAM really buy you? Reviewing Figure 8–18, we get support for an additional 10 concurrent users. The File Server can now support just over 30 concurrent users while providing a 20

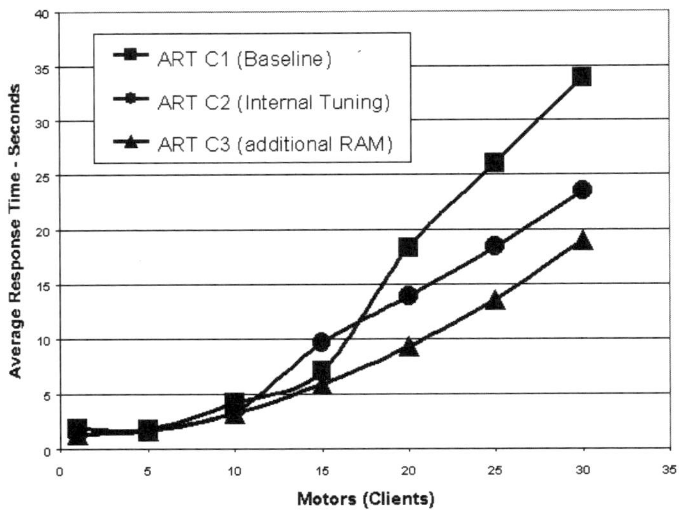

Figure 8–18 *File Server Configuration 3 average response time results. (Lower values for ART are better)*

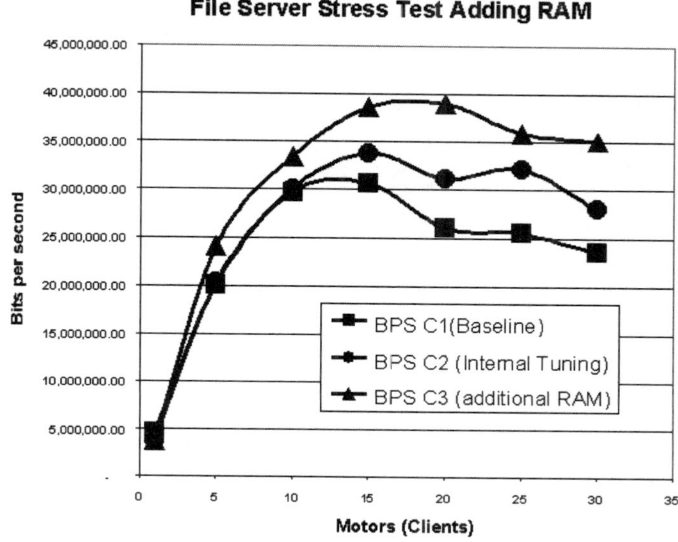

Figure 8–19 *File Server Configuration 3 Throughput results.*

second response time. Adding the additional RAM improved the overall performance of the File Server, but the Blue Curve throughput graphs still indicates a bottleneck above 20 users. This bottleneck could be acceptable if, as in the case of Acme Rockets, a 20 second response time is acceptable when 30 concurrent users are accessing the File Server.

Adding the additional RAM removed the memory bottleneck. To make sure the memory bottleneck was removed and determine where the bottleneck is that is still throttling back the server resource (as shown in the Blue Curve throughput graph, Figure 8–19) we review each server resource again.

CPU usage has increased and leveled out considerably (see Figure 8–20 and 8–21) even under the higher load levels. This is contributed to several observations: The CPU is not the bottleneck and less CPU usage is required since the amount of paging is lowered considerably. CPU usage actually begins to lower at the heavier load levels as other server resources increasingly become greater bottlenecks which forces the CPU to wait on data to process.

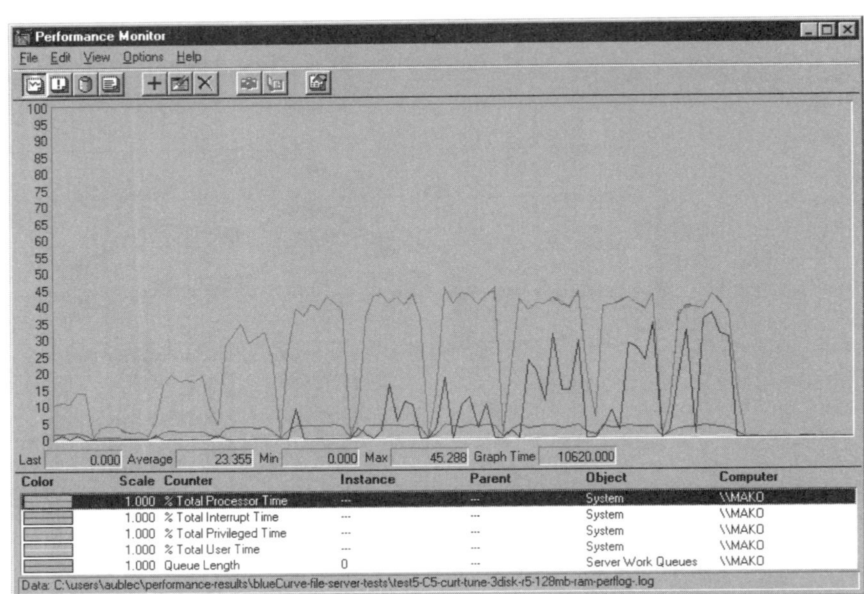

Figure 8–20 *CPU usage for File Server Configuration 3 (additional RAM added)*

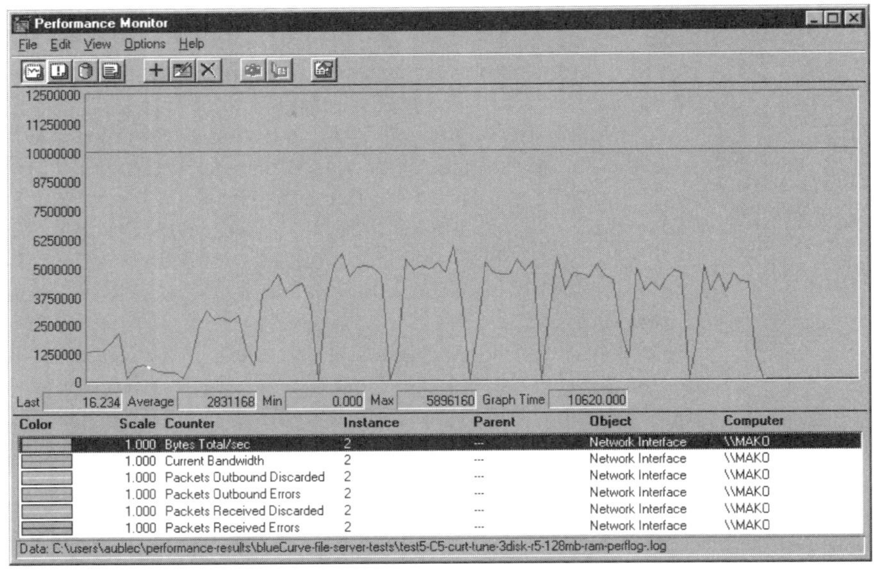

Figure 8–21 *Network usage for File Server Configuration 3 (additional RAM added).*

The network still is not experiencing any errors. Changing the Perfmon's chart view to a scale factor of 125 and the scale of the counters to one, the amount of network utilized becomes more apparent. Here the network usage peaks at 58 Mbits/sec. Similar to the CPU graph, the network usage actually begins lowering under the heaviest loads which is an indication that there is another server resource throttling the server. From a network perspective, this 100BaseT subnet still has additional capacity available, but is closing in the available network bandwidth that is usable. Recall from Chapter 7 that for an Ethernet environment, when the %Utilization (available bandwidth/(bytes total/sec of bandwidth used)) rises consistently into the 50–70 percent range, a network bottleneck is forming.

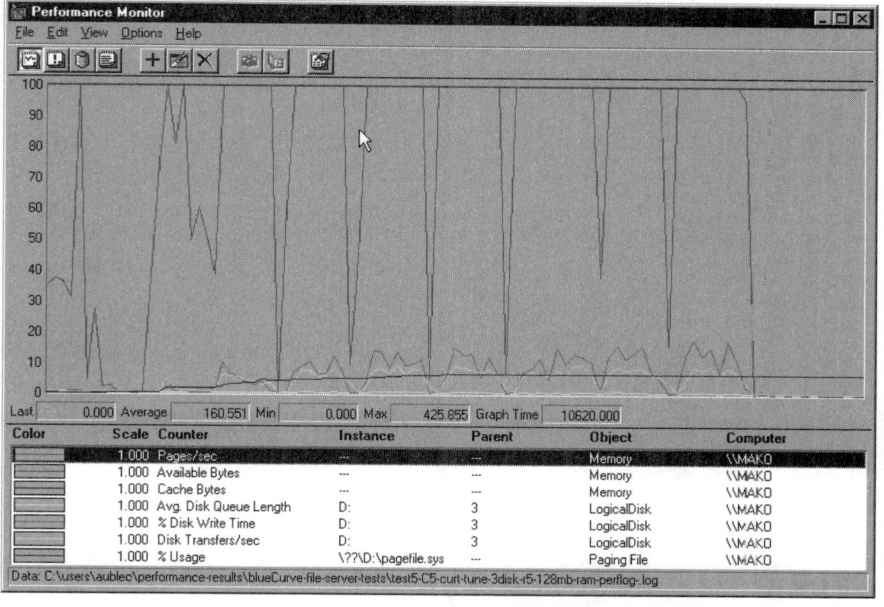

Figure 8–22 *Memory usage for File Server Configuration 3 (additional RAM added).*

In Figure 8–22 the Memory Subsystem is removed as the primary bottleneck in the File Server. All of the key indicators that there was a bottleneck are drastically lowered. The rate at which the paging file is in use is lowered significantly. Paging File Disk Transfers/sec lowered from a maximum of over 600 to a maximum of 9. With the amount of paging activity lowered tremendously and the amount of RAM used for caching disk activity increased from 56 Mbytes to 120 Mbtyes, the overall response time to the end user improved. This observation is from the Blue Curve ART graph for File Server Configuration 3.

The average pages/sec value lowered slightly from 205 to 160. Even though there is not any excessive paging occurring in File Server Configuration 3, the pages/sec is still relatively high. Again, these soft page faults are occurring as the File Server is bringing data from disk into memory, not paging parts of process's working sets out of memory to make more physical memory available. Since the page file is on its own dedicated disk which is not experiencing a heavy load, we can be sure the high pages/sec value is not associated with any memory shortages.

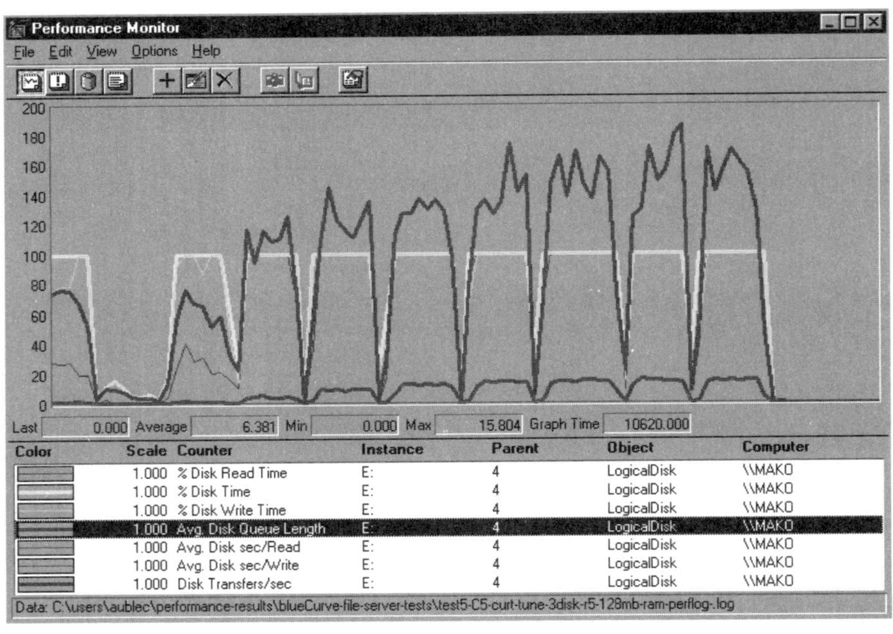

Figure 8–23 *Disk I/O usage for File Server Configuration 3 (additional RAM added).*

Even with the improved disk buffering provided by the additional RAM, the disk I/O subsystem is still a bottleneck that is throttling back the File Server's performance (see Figure 8–23). The Logical Disk: Disk bytes/sec counter indicates that the three 4 GB based RAID 5 disk array is providing close to 5 Mbytes/sec throughput, but this is still not adequate for a balanced configuration under this workload. The Average Disk Queue Length ranges from 6 to a maximum of 15. Dividing the number of disk drives in the RAID 5 array from these values shows the normalized disk queue time actually ranging from 2 to over 5. Any normalized disk queue length values greater than the 1–2 range indicates that other portions of the server are sitting around for an unacceptable amount of time waiting service from the disk I/O subsystem.

Developing a Balanced File Server Solution

At this point, the disk subsystem is the primary bottleneck throttling back the overall File Server performance. Viewing the current Performance Resource Chart perspective (Figure 8–24), we notice that the Memory subsystem was moved significantly to the right of the graph, which is good, but the disk I/O has not shifted enough.

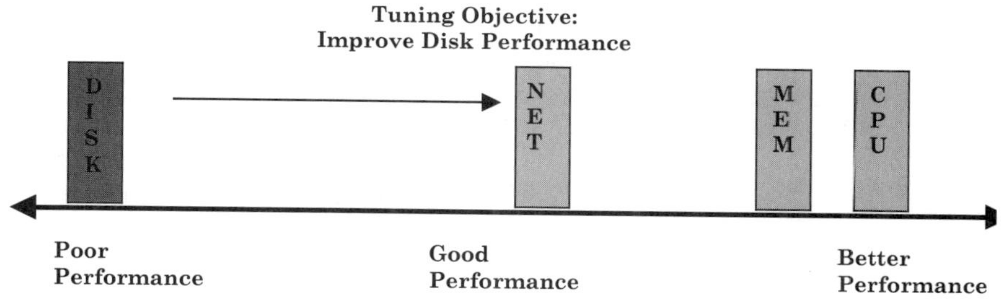

Figure 8–24 *Performance Resource Chart for File Server Configuration 3.*

To remove the disk bottleneck, additional disk subsystem capacity needs to be added to the file server. This server has room for six total disk drives. One disk drive is currently used for the NT Server operating system, the second is in use as the paging file, and three of the drives compose the RAID 5 disk array where the end users work areas are located. There is one open slot available on the S46, but adding one drive to the RAID 5 array for a total of four would not improve the disk I/O throughput enough to remove the disk I/O bottleneck.

If the same amount of actual disk space is needed to be kept the same, the three internal 4 GB disk drives could be replaced by six 2 GB disk drives in an external disk array cabinet. This would increase the disk throughput performance. Acme Rockets is a forward thinking company and is planning to expand the workgroup sizes that each file server will support. When this occurs, more actual disk capacity (disk space) will be required.

To accommodate the need for additional disk subsystem throughput and disk capacity, an external ten-disk array is added to the configuration. The current RAID 5 array was composed of three disk drives. During the last stress test, logical drive E: associated with the RAID 5 array exhibited an Average Disk Queue Length of over 16. Dividing 16 by the three disk drives in the RAID 5 array indicates that each drive had at least five or more outstanding disk requests waiting for service. From Chapter 6, "NT Server and Disk Subsystem Performance," we l[illegible]ever the sustained Average Disk Queue Length is greater th[illegible]disk is a bottleneck. Adding a 10-disk RAID 5 array to the se[illegible]eriencing the same workload level should lower the Average Dis[illegible]ueue Length to less than two for each member of the RAID 5 array. Th[illegible] disk array added is an intelligent NCR/Symbios Logic 6210 Series 3 array populated with ten 7200 RPM 4 GB fast and wide SCSI disk drives. The disk array is attached to the server via an Adaptec 2944-W fast and wide differential SCSI adapter via external differential SCSI cable. Acme is considering redeploying the internal three disk drives composing the internal RAID 5 array to other servers in their enterprise if the external disk array is successful in removing the disk I/O bottleneck.

The external disk array is first properly tuned for Acme Rockets' environment. The disk array is low level formatted as one large RAID 5 array with the disk array manager software supplied by NCR and then formatted with an NTFS file system under NT Server. With the work characterization staying the same, the same ALU tuning is applicable. Thus, the new external disk array is formatted from command line "format g: /F:NTFS /a:64k" indicating a 64K ALU block size. After formatting the external array with NTFS, there is 36 GB of usable disk storage available on the external array for end user storage requirements.

FILE SERVER CONFIGURATION 4: EXTERNAL DISK ARRAY STRESS TEST RESULTS

Blue Curve is again employed to stress test File Server Configuration 4, which is the same as Configuration 3, except for replacing the internal three disk RAID 5 array with an external 10 disk RAID 5 array. Here we tune only one aspect of the server at a time and stress the server with the same exact workload. This technique allows us to see exactly what effect our specific tuning efforts are having. The results are dramatic. In fact, they were so good (see Figure 8–25), the level of stress (number of concurrent users) was increased to see how well the single CPU File Server could perform.

File Server Configuration 4 (Figure 8–26) can support 50 concurrent users while meeting Acme Rockets' performance requirement of 20-second average response times. The sustained throughput provided by the File Server over a single 100BaseTX Ethernet subnet is close to 60 Mbits/sec. Reviewing the performance logs for this stress test indicates that the Logical Disk: Average Queue Lengths average was four with a maximum of 13. Dividing the number of disk drives in the RAID 5 array from these values shows the normalized disk queue time is less than one for each disk drive in the array. With the disk queue size significantly lower, the response and throughput provided to the end user is greatly improved. The external disk array provided over 7.5 Mbytes of disk I/O throughput while supporting 279 transfers/sec. The external disk array was, however, 100 percent busy according to the %disk

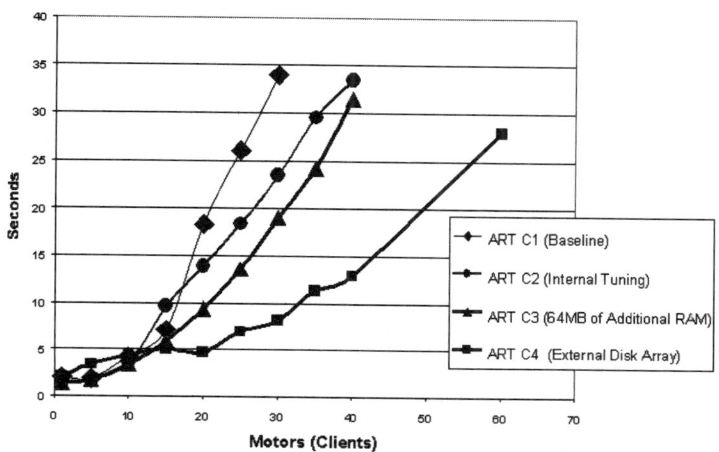

Figure 8–25 *File Server Configuration 4 average response time results.*

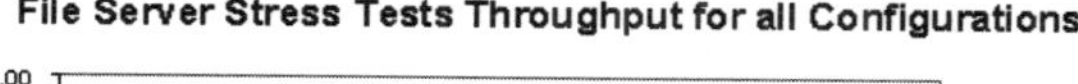

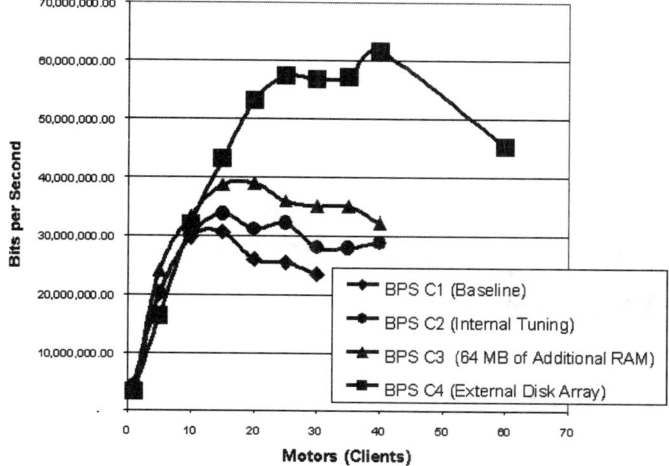

Figure 8–26 *File Server Configuration 4 throughput results.*

time Perfmon counter. This indicates that even better disk subsystem performance can be achieved distributing end users across an additional external disk arrays if a higher performance was required.

With the addition of the external disk array, File Server Configuration 4 provides a solid, well balanced solution that Acme Rockets can plan accordingly for and grow into. As a quick review, Configuration 4 encompassed

- NCR S46
  - 1 Pentium Pro 200 MHz/5125K CPU
  - 128 Mbytes of RAM
  - 1 Internal PCI Mylex 960PL RAID Controller w/4 MB of cache
  - 1 Adaptec 2944W External Fast/Wide SCSI-2 Differential Adapter
  - 1 Internal Fast/Wide SCSI-2 Disk Drive for NT Server Operating System
  - 1 Internal Fast/Wide SCSI-2 Disk Drive dedicated for the paging file
  - NT 4.0 with Service Pack 4
  - Tuned NT Internal Parameters
- 1 NCR 6210 External Disk Array
  - 10 Internal Fast/Wide SCSI-2 Disk Drives
  - 16 Mbytes of cache

The ending Performance Resource Chart of the File Server Performance is shown in Figure 8–27.

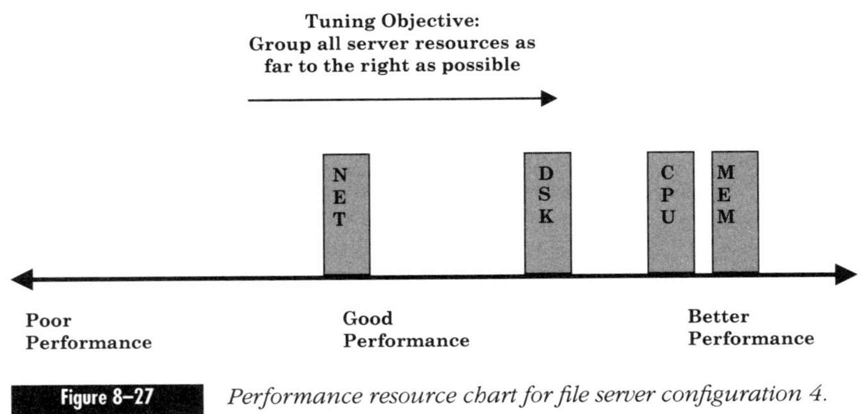

Figure 8–27 *Performance resource chart for file server configuration 4.*

10. Deploy the Server into Production

Now that the NT Server configuration and solution is tested and verified to meet Acme Rockets' requirements, the server is fielded with confidence that it will complete the job and provide an excellent performing solution.

11. Proactively follow the Tuning Methodology After the Server Is Deployed

Following a sound sizing methodology and stress testing the server configuration before production deployment builds confidence in the solution, but end users can always change their work habits. Continuing to proactively monitor the File Server's performance enables you to stay ahead of tuning and sizing challenges.

Future Considerations

Reviewing the Perfmon logs for File Server Configuration 4, this configuration provides a well-balanced solution. The next major tuning and sizing effort required to support additional concurrent file server users is the addition of another network interface card for the File Server, additional disk array capacity, second CPU and an additional memory. Wow, just about everything! Part of this plan is already underway, due to the fact that Acme Rockets has already begun planning to someday subnet and/or create a switched network environment. This is a good long term strategy that will not be needed until it is required to support over 50 concurrent users or improved response times is required.

File Server Case Study Lessons Learned and Summary

It is amazing now much performance improvement occurs when the proper resources are sized and tuned, and the correct additional server resources are added as needed. Applying a structured methodology and properly sleuthing out the true bottleneck that is throttling server performance are the real keys to providing great performing servers that can scale.

File Server Configuration 2 internal (NT Tuning only) actually exceeds Acme Rockets' performance objective and provides some breathing room for possible concurrent user surge protection. File Server Configuration 2 also provides for some future growth. Using PC Magazine's NetBench results as a reference for the initial sizing worked out well. Additional stress testing provided information that will be used for future server capacity sizing and planning projects.

If we stropped stress testing at File Server Configuration 3, we would not have met all of Acme Rockets' original objectives. Acme Rockets had four objectives to achieve when running the stress tests, which were all successfully completed through additional tuning and stress testing. Table 8–12 summarizes these objectives.

Table 8.12 Summary of Acme Rockets' objectives.

Base Line Configuration: NCR S46 1 Pentium Pro 200 MHz/512 K 64 MB RAM 1 F/W SCSI Disk Drive for NT 1 F/W SCSI Disk Drives for NT Paging File 3 F/W SCSI Disk Drive for RAID 5 Array 1 Mylex 960PL PCI RAID Adapter w/4 MB cache	**Configuration 1** **Base Line Configuration**	**Configuration 2** **NT Server Operating System Specific Tuning**	**Configuration 3** **64 MB of RAM added**	**Configuration 4** **Internal three 4 GB disk RAID 5 disk drive array replaced by ten 4 GB disk drive external disk array**
How many concurrent users will a single CPU File Server support and still provide better than a 20 second response time in the Acme Rockets environment?	20 Concurrent Users	26 Concurrent Users	32 Concurrent Users	50 Concurrent Users
How many concurrent File Server Users will the 100BaseTX Ethernet segment support?	20 Concurrent Users	26 Concurrent Users	32 Concurrent Users	50 Concurrent Users
What type of throughput was achieved on a single Fast Ethernet Subnet while meeting the acceptable Average Response Times?	26 Mbits/sec	32 Mbits/sec	35 Mbits/sec	61 Mbits/sec
What resources may need to be upgraded in the future? This is next step in the tuning and sizing process.	Next Step: Proper Tuning (Configuration 2)	Next Step: Add Memory (Configuration 3)	Next Step Add Disk (Configuration 4)	Next Step(s) 1 - Network, 2 - Disk, 3- CPU, 4 - Memory, (Configuration X)

Case Study: Microsoft Internet Information Server (IIS)—Intranet and Internet World Wide Web Server

THE ENVIRONMENT

Acme Rockets continues to race into the future. Now that they work in an office environment based heavily on electronic documents, they are in a sharing mood. Acme Rockets decided to field a World Wide Web Server to provide documents to their partnering corporations across their internal private network that connects the partnering companies, an intranet if you will. In the future, they also plan to allow a portion of their website to be available across the Internet. Using the World Wide Web is a relatively new technology for Acme Rockets, so initially they plan only to publish static documents and information on their website. In the future, they expect to provide more dynamic based information. Microsoft IIS is chosen as the Web Server software portion of the Web Server solution.

Document sizes range in size from 10 Kbytes to multiple compressed megabytes. How often the web server is access is expected to range from 100,000 to 8,000,000 hits per day. Availability is a priority. Initially, performance is less of a consideration. The only performance concern is that each Web client request is responded to.

Acme Rockets' schedule is very aggressive. These aggressive schedules dictate that there is not enough time to properly stress test or validate the final server configuration. They are hoping to quickly develop a server configuration capable of providing the expected performance levels, begin development, and field their solution immediately. Part of the decision not to stress test the Web Server solution is based on available stress testing tools for Web based solutions. Several companies produce tools for testing web server solutions that can be customized for a variety of scenarios. Unfortunately, these tools require a fair amount of custom development to be completed for specific environments. This customization is too time consuming for Acme Rockets at this time. Hopefully, vendors specializing in testing technology will introduce fast and friendly Web Server stress testing technology in the near future.

Now that the general environment is in place, let's walk through the sizing methodology to determine a server solution for Acme Rockets.

1. Define Objective(s)

Develop a World Wide Web Server solution which provides a mostly static environment today, but allows for support of more dynamic content in the future.

2. Understand Requirements Needed to Meet Your Objective

To meet this requirement, Microsoft Internet Information Server (IIS) is selected. Acme Rockets expects a high level of availability. The data shared on this server is already backed by Acme Rockets' high speed backup File Servers based in each of their workgroups. From a storage perspective, they expect that the Web Server Content (HTML documents) will encompass approximately 200 MBytes and the documents they wish to share will encompass 6 GBytes.

3. Determine Loading Characteristics

One of the driving forces behind fielding a Web based solution for Acme Rockets was the high level of demand voiced by their many partners for information. Based on this potential demand, Acme Rockets expects between 100,000 and 8 million hits on their web site per eight hour day. This is much higher than the average website experiences, but the folks at Acme Rockets think of themselves as above average. Most of these hits are expected for browsing through the information on their HTML based pages. They expect approximately 30 users to concurrently download published Acme Rocket documents at any one time. Eventually, they expect to post data on their website from sources other than Acme Rockets. At this time the size of the HTML based pages that will be served range from 5 Kbytes to 25 Kbytes. The non-HTML files that are to be shared typically range in size from 0.5 Mbytes to 10 Mbytes in size.

4. Determine Performance Requirements

Without control of many of the end users environments, Acme Rockets' only performance requirement is that the Web Server is capable of supporting the planned maximum 8 million hits per day and 30 concurrent users downloading shared documents at any one time. A web hit or operation is not the same as a complete web page. Web pages are normally generated by numerous web hits.

5. Understand Future Business Requirements

Acme Rockets continues to expect astronomical growth, as they plan on doubling the size of the company in six months. As this occurs, more and more data will be required to be shared. As more data is shared supporting a larger audience, the reality of a mostly static web page environment will become unrealistic. Support for and increased amount of dynamic page generation becomes more important.

6. Understand Future Server Architectures

Acme Rockets loves technology and continues to prefer not to completely replace their server for at least three years. With this in mind, they have decided to proceed with a standards based server architecture that can support the planned increased capacity. When running a Web Server with Microsoft IIS, network, CPU, and memory subsystems are the most heavily stressed portions of the server. With this in mind, a server that can support significant network I/O, increased amount of processing power, and larger RAM configurations are the key discriminators when selecting the server. Other high availability factors continue to influence the final decision.

7. Configure the Server

Acme Rockets is rushing to complete this project as soon as possible. Enough information is presented in steps 1 through 6 to initially size and tune the server.

Application Characteristics Review

Web Server environments are characterized by the following resource usage activity: Network: High, Memory: Active, Processor: Active, and Disk: Medium.

Configuring an NT Server as a Web Server is similar to that of configuring both an application and a file server at the same time. Just as is done for any server that supports multiple applications, size each function that is supported by the Server and then add up the associated resources. For this environment, the two primary functions are Web Server and File Server. The Web Server portion responds to hypertext transport protocol (http) requests. For Acme Rockets' environment, their requests are either fulfilled by static or dynamic Hypertext Markup Language (HTML) documents. From these HTML based documents, or pages, there are two primary actions: searches or file downloads. If a search for information on the website is requested, a search engine is invoked (such as Microsoft Index Server, Excite, Netscape, etc.) which can consume significant amounts of CPU and memory resources. If a file download is requested, the Web Server invokes use of the File Transport Protocol (FTP) to download the actual file to the web client.

Microsoft IIS is a web server engine that provides services for both the Web (http) and File (ftp) operations and supports various technologies for the generation of dynamic web pages. Search engines are typically another separate application that is invoked by links from the HTML pages. Even though search engines are linked to the web server software in use, they run in their own application space. This becomes more important when monitoring the Web Server site's performance.

Reviewing Each Server Resource

DISK I/O REQUIREMENTS

DISK STORAGE CAPACITY CONSIDERATIONS AND REQUIREMENTS

NT Server O/S: 124 MB
NT Server Pagefile: RAM (512 Mbytes) x 2
Application executable/binaries IIS: 25 MB
Web/HTML Pages: 200 MB
Acme Shareable Documents: 6 GB
Total Minimum Disk Space required: 7.35 GB
Relevant Industry Benchmarks: SPECweb96
Other relevant resources: Tuning and Sizing NT Server's File Server Case Study

DISK PERFORMANCE CONSIDERATIONS AND REQUIREMENTS

Understanding the disk subsystem characteristics is essential when sizing or tuning. From an end user workload perspective, Acme Rockets' Web environment is almost completely a read only environment. Acme Rockets' WWW servers disk I/O is characterized by a two types of read intensive workloads: Web Server based HTML pages provided under the hypertext transfer protocol (http) and downloading of shareable documents using the file transfer protocol (FTP) protocol. Each WWW page is transferred to the requesting web client via http. These pages are of various sizes and contain anything from text, graphics, audio, or video. Due to the wide variety of file sizes and randomness associated with serving these web pages, they should be placed onto their own dedicated disk array. Use this same strategy for files that are downloaded via FTP. The various document files downloaded via FTP are typically much larger than HTML web pages. Providing the FTP transferred files with their own disk array formatted and with a larger ALU size provides improved disk subsystem performance.

How many disk drives are required to support the projected web based (HTML) workload? From a Web Server perspective, reference the SPECweb96 results for the NCR 4300 shown in Chapter 3, which reports the 2 CPU NCR 4300 supporting just over 1100 web operations/second. Acme Rockets' Web Server workload is projected to be 277 connections or operations per second. This is calculated by normalizing the daily eight hour maximum hit rate into seconds. Matching this requirement with the NCR 4300 SPECweb96 results, to support 277 connections/sec, approximately one-fourth of the benchmarked 4300's overall disk performance capacity is required. The NCR 4300 benchmark was supported by the use of five 4.3 GB disk drives in an external disk array placed on a single F/W SCSI channel. Using only one-fourth of the 4300 array used for web content indicates that one or two disk drives will support the projected I/O load associated with 277 connections/second.

To provide a generally high level of performance, plan to cache a lions share of the web document pages to improve performance. This will lower the disk I/O performance required. Even if the files are cached, they must still be initially brought in from the disk array. A single disk drive which supports between 55 and 100 disk I/Os per second in a random environment should be sufficient to support the web pages. Use of RAID 1 Mirrored Array for the web document pages will provide a fault resistant data store RAID 1 Mirrored Arrays provide slightly improved read performance. (RAID arrays are reviewed in depth in Chapter 6, "NT Server and Disk Subsystem Performance.")

Microsoft IIS generates log files of the activity occurring on the Web Server. The log file is sequential in nature and can generate large log files under heavy loads, depending on the log level settings. Because of this, the log file is provided a dedicated physical disk drive. The location that the log file reside can be changed under Microsoft Internet Information Server|Internet Service Manager|WWW Service|Properties|Log File|Properties. The default location for the log file is C:\winnt\System32\LogFiles. Also, regardless of performance concerns, keeping the log file located on the %SystemRoot% disk on a very active server, can fill the disk surprisingly fast.

Supporting Acme Rockets' worst case requirement of 30 concurrent end users downloading multiple shareable documents is more of a configuration challenge than the Web Server pages themselves. When trying to size any server, it is always helpful if some types of published performance results are available to compare or extrapolate from in order to obtain some initial sizing information. For Acme Rockets' requirement, the stress test results from the File Server Case Study are quite helpful. From this case study, File Server Configuration 3 delivers a sustained 35 Mbits per second under a load of 32 simultaneously users downloading various documents. File Server Configuration 3 supports this workload by using the combination of 120 Mbytes of RAM for dynamic file system disk caching, and placing all of the user data across a three disk RAID 5 array composed of 4 GB disk drives. Note that we know that 120 Mbytes are used for NT Server file system caching by reviewing the Perfmon log counter Memory: Cache Bytes maximum use values exhibited during the stress test. Choosing a RAID 5 array configuration provides fault tolerance and excellent performance in a random read only environment.

The last application in use is the search engine. Web Server site search engines typically index the site either automatically or by manual intervention. The search engine creates a relatively small index of what is available on the site. The relative small size and frequency of the files associated with search engines normally allows for a high probability that the index will be cached in memory. Thus, the index server will not provide a tangible load on the disk subsystem. The index server is placed on the same disk drive as the NT Server operating system.

The server selected to support this Web Server environment is the NCR 4300. This server supports 12 internal disk drives and these drives can be split across two SCSI buses. A single 2 GB disk drive provides ample room for NT

Server files, IIS files, the index server, and a fair amount of room for growth. Another single 2 GB disk drive is allocated as use for a dedicated NT paging file disk.

DISK AVAILABILITY CONSIDERATIONS AND REQUIREMENTS

Availability is very important to Acme Rockets. Because of this concern, all areas of the disk subsystem will have some sort of fault tolerance. NT Server, IIS, and search engine files and binaries are placed across RAID 1 array consisting of two 2 GB disk drives. The HTML documents are placed onto their own RAID 1 array, also consisting of two 2 GB disk drives. Finally, the 6 GB of shareable documents are placed onto their own three 4 GB disk RAID 5 array which provides 8 GB of usable disk space. There is no real need to provide fault tolerance for the IIS logs from a data recovery perspective. However, in general, some applications may stop operating if the log files are not available or generate a high number of errors on the server that consume precious server resources. These logs are helpful when determining access and usage patterns of the Web Server. Continued operations is important, thus, the log files will be placed on their own dedicated RAID 1 mirrored array.

CPU REQUIREMENTS:

NT Minimum: Intel 80486/66
Relevant Industry Benchmark: SPECweb96
Other relevant resources: Tuning and Sizing NT Server's File Server Case Study

Processing needs can be viewed as an additive process of the different functions the server completes. The IIS process InetInfo.exe is the primary process requiring CPU processing cycles. This processing requirement is needed to provide http and, to a lesser extent, FTP services. The second largest processing requirement placed on the CPU is from the search engine. Typical search engines will index the website periodically or on demand. As user requests increased their site searches requests, the amount of CPU processing increases greatly. The third CPU processing requirement is the load placed on the server for the transfer of the shared document files via FTP.

To support the 250 Web Server operations per second, one-fourth of the referenced 2 CPU NCR 4300 SPECweb96 benchmark results are required. This indicates that half of a Pentium Pro CPU will suffice in supporting 277 web operations/sec. Unfortunately, attempting to size the amount of CPU power that the search engine requires is more of a challenge since SPECweb96 is not helpful. The SPECweb96 benchmark only tests static HTML pages, not search engine types of activities. This is where stress testing, or at a minimum, following the tuning methodology is key. Monitoring the search engine CPU usage activities is helpful for determining how much CPU horsepower is required. In lieu of not having any of this historical information available at this time, we will estimate that the other half of the CPU will be sufficient to support search engine activities.

For the FTP or file server portion of the CPU processing needs, reference the Perfmon results from File Server Configuration 3. Reviewing these logs indicates that the File Server activity at the 30 user level consumes 45 percent of the single 200 MHz/512 K Pentium Pro CPU's capacity. If you haven't been keeping count, we now need 1.45 200 MHz/512 K Pentium Pro CPUs to support the projected workloads. Slicing a single CPU in half is a bit difficult, so two 200 MHz/512 K Pentium Pro CPUs are configured into the Acme Rockets' Web Server solution. The extra available CPU processing power could be used for possible surges in Web Server activity.

In the long run, adding dynamic web content will drive additional processing overhead. Note that additional operations per second are not projected. With additional processing overhead incurred by the dynamic web page generation, the server can easily become CPU bound. The CPU capacity is sized to support the currently projected Web Server workload. Tracking if the server is developing a bottleneck becomes important for long term capacity planning. Utilize the techniques reviewed for tracking CPU bottlenecks in Chapter 2, "NT Server and CPU Performance."

Selection of the initial server is critical. Moving an entire Web Server to a new hardware platform takes time and will result in the Web Server being off-line for a considerable amount of time, which is unacceptable for Acme Rockets. If additional CPU capacity is the bottleneck, selection of a server that will allow additional CPUs to be added becomes important. The Web Server running NT Server 4.0 will still require a short shutdown and reboot period, but the amount of time for a CPU upgrade is much lower than getting a completely new Web Server on-line.

Bottlenecks contributed by NT Server itself, Web Servers (IIS), or Web applications are more elusive to sleuth out. Closely monitor the Perfmon object Process: Processor Time for all process instances to track which processes are placing the greatest demands on the CPU and Memory Subsystems. Once you find which process is demanding more resources, several techniques can be employed to meet these processing needs and remove the CPU bottlenecks. Web applications can be tuned or rewritten from one programming language to another, more efficient language. Additional server resources could be added or the process could be distributed to multiple servers if needed. With this in mind, Acme Rockets' selection of a server that is capable of scaling to greater than two CPUs to support not just the Web operations, but all of the background processing requirements, makes a lot of sense.

When the NT Server operating system or the actual Web Server itself (such as IIS) is the bottleneck, there are less options available. Staying abreast of the latest patches for both NT Server and the Web Server software in use becomes more important. As NT Server and IIS mature, patches and updates can improve the overall software performance. As always, try to test any software patches before deploying them into production.

When you cannot complete your own baseline tests to determine if the software patches will be helpful, refer to Industry Standard Benchmarks. The TPC-C benchmarks are good examples of how software updates can improve performance. If you review the TPC-C results closely, several vendors rerun the TPC-C benchmark with similar server hardware, but with different product release levels, Service Packs, or SCSI device driver updates. These are helpful, published examples that one can review to determine if it is a good idea to deploy a new software update. If a new software or hardware upgrade is announced but no one is publishing improved results, reconsider any plans to deploy it, unless, of course, you are stress testing it yourself to ensure you will be rewarded by your purchase.

MEMORY REQUIREMENTS:

NT Server O/S: 32 MB
NT File System Buffer Cache: 320 Mbytes
Web Server Application Buffer Space (http): 200 MB
File Server Application (ftp) Disk Buffer Space: 120 MB
Web Server Application: 16 MB
Web Server Search Engine: 16 MB

Supporting the applications minimum requirements is a no brainer—read the vendor recommendations, then sum the amount of memory required. Sizing an enterprise server is more challenging. After covering the operating system and application's minimum requirements, there are two things that you want to happen when deploying a high performing web server solution. First, ensure NT Server does not page excessively. Paging quickly slows down a web server, or any other server for that matter. Occasional paging is acceptable during heavy usage or surge periods, but should not occur on a regular basis. To achieve this state, enough memory must be provided to NT Server and its applications. NT Server must be tuned to ensure it does not hog all available memory. The applications must be tuned to ensure that they either do not have access to all of the available memory either, which will starve NT Server. Finding this balance is important and is completed by good initial sizing and proactive tuning.

Sizing the memory subsystem is an additive process even though there is some sharing of cached data, dynamic link libraries and such. It is always better to configure a little more memory than a little less. This was exemplified in the File Server case study. To determine the amount of memory to configure, we first add up the required minimum amount of memory needed for NT Server and the applications which equates to 64 MB. To determine how much memory is needed to support the IIS Web Server and concurrent FTP downloads, we look at Acme Rockets' environment and relevant Industry Benchmarks.

To provide a memory sizing starting point for the Web Server, reference the 2 CPU NCR 4300 SPECWeb96 benchmark results, since it is similar to Acme Rockets' environment. Reviewing the SPECweb96 results provides insight on the achievable number of web operations per second. Acme Rockets' plans to support 277 web operations per second. The SPECweb96 benchmarked NCR 4300 achieved just over 1100 operations/sec. Thus, to support 277 web operations per second will require one-fourth of the memory capacity of the NCR 4300 benchmark configuration. Reviewing the 4300 benchmark configuration outlined in Chapter 4 indicates that 2 GB of memory was used in the benchmark with an average response time of 20.1 milliseconds when servicing the heaviest loads. This implies that 512 MB of RAM is required to support 277 operations per second. Therefore, 512 MB of RAM is now a memory configuration starting point.

For benchmarks, the goal of vendors is to ensure that every possible data set is cached in memory. Acme Rockets has not set any actual performance metrics at this time, thus configuring for subsecond performance is potentially overkill. Reviewing Acme Rockets' environment, there is 200 MB of projected Web pages. Tuning NT Server to cache all of these pages would require 200 MB of cache space. This indicates that the 512 MBytes of RAM extrapolated from the SPECweb96 benchmark results is far more than is required for this environment. For sizing the memory subsystem, use of the SPECweb96 benchmark results is less applicable, but did provide a starting point of 512 MB. Configuring 200 MB for the Web Server is sufficient to provide a high level of Web Server performance.

To support the 30 concurrent users downloading shareable documents, reference the stress test results for File Server Configuration 3. Supporting the 32 concurrent users, 120 MBytes of RAM are used for the NT Server dynamic file system cache buffers.

Summing up the various functions on the Web Server requiring memory results in a memory configuration of 384 Mbytes. Configuring exactly 384 Mbytes on this server is possible, but it may not be the best decision. If the load on the Web Server increases, additional memory will be required. Following the memory configuration guideline for the NCR 4300 (or any Intel SHV based server for that matter) with SIMM RAM modules, the entire memory board will be populated. This will not allow for future memory growth without removing the lower density SIMMs and replacing them with higher density memory modules. What do you then do with those old memory SIMMs? You might be able to redeploy them into another server or workstation, but if you can't, they are wasted.

If higher density DIMMs are used, the memory must be incremented in 256 Mbyte chunks. Time for a decision. If you match the planned memory exactly, you lose out on your investment if you ever need to increase memory capacity. If you configure the server with higher density SIMMs, you either configure lower or higher than projected. If economics (in this case a few thousand dollars) is a driving force, configure and tune the server for use with only 256 Mbytes of RAM. Then, if needed, additional increments of RAM can be configured. For this project, this cost factor level is not greatly important to Acme Rockets. The Web Server solution will be configured with 512 Mbytes of RAM.

Even though a scientific approach was provided to determine the amount of memory required by the Web Server, providing a perfectly sized memory configuration is not realistic. Sizing the memory system provides an excellent initial memory configuration, but economics and the server architecture in use also play an important role. This exemplifies why it is important to spend an appropriate amount of time configuring a server so that you are not completely out in left field, perhaps configuring this server with only 64 Mbytes or 1 GB of RAM. Spending even more time configuring the Web Server's memory subsystem with advanced algorithms may produce a 402 Mbyte memory recommendation, but we still would have ended up with the same results. Time is valuable and details are important—avoid getting lost in too many details, it can waste your days.

NETWORK I/O REQUIREMENTS

Sizing the network requirements is an additive process similar to that of sizing the memory subsystem. Determine the bandwidth requirement for each function the server is providing, then size accordingly. If the functions provided are concurrent in nature, sum the requirements needed to obtain the bandwidth required. For Acme Rockets' environment, there are two concurrent functions to plan for: 277 web operations per second and supporting 30 concurrent users downloading shareable documents via FTP.

Sizing the amount of network bandwidth required for any web server revolves around the amount of web operations per second (hits) and the size of the data delivered per operation. Using these two factors in conjunction with some basic mathematics (or a friendly spreadsheet) you can determine how much theoretical bandwidth is required to support your website. Transferring smaller amounts of data per web operation allows the network to support a higher web operations/sec, but is less efficient due to the HTTP and TCP/IP overhead. Acme Rockets estimates their Web pages will range from 5Kbytes to 25Kbytes.

To estimate how much bandwidth is required for 277 operations/sec, all values are normalized to bits/sec, then compared against available network mediums theoretical throughput and characteristics. In a worst case scenario, all web requests will be for 25kbyte sized pages. The bandwidth required to support this scenario is: 277 operations/sec * 25Kbytes/operation * 8bits/byte = 55 Mbits/sec. If this was the only function on this server, a single 100BaseTX network interface card would suffice.

To estimate the bandwidth required to support the 30 concurrent users downloading shareable documents, reference the File Server Configuration 3 case study results. These results indicate that to support 30 users with resonable initial response times requires 35 Mbits/sec of bandwidth. From this information, the total bandwidth required in a worst case environment is 90 Mbits/sec (55 Mbits/sec + 35 Mbits/sec). A single 100BaseTX network interface card can theoretically support this bandwidth requirement. 90 Mbits per second is a worst case scenario. At this time, Acme Rockets does not feel that this level of workload, even worst case, will be very common. Thus, a single 100BaseTX network interface card is configured. However, as % utilization on Ethernet networks consistently increases past a 50–70 percent utilization level, the response time to the end users increases significantly. If this scenario is encountered, additional 100BaseTX network interface cards can be added or the network connection can be changed to FDDI (fiber distributed data interface). FDDI provides the same level of bandwidth, but supports a higher level of % Utilization than Ethernet before exhibiting serious response time degradation. Changing to another network technology such as FDDI would require changes to the existing network architecture. These changes may include changing or adding an FDDI interface to the router or switch that provides connectivity to clients using a different network technology such as Ethernet.

Initial Hardware Configuration and Tuning

Table 8.13

NCR 4300
SCSI CD-ROM
Installed on the internal motherboard Ultra Fast and Wide SCSI-2 adapter channel 1
Floppy Disk Drive
2 Pentium Pro 200 MHz/512 K cache CPUs
512 MB of 60ns SIMM RAM
1 Intel Ethernet Pro 100B 100BaseTX NIC
Installed in PCI Bus 1
2 4 GB F/W SCSI Disk Drives in a RAID 1 Mirror for NT Server, Microsoft IIS, Index Server
1 2 GB F/W SCSI Disk Drive for Paging File
2 2 GB F/W SCSI Disk Drive for IIS logs
2 2 GB F/W SCSI Disk Drives in a RAID 1 array housing the Web content files
3 4 GB F/W SCSI Disk Drives in a RAID 5 Array housing the Acme Rockets published documents to share
1 Mylex 960PG 2 Channel Ultra Fast and Wide SCSI-2 PCI RAID adapter with 16 MB of onboard battery
backed cache
Installed in PCI Bus 2

Initial Software Configuration and Tuning

SOFTWARE VERSIONS

NT Server 4.0
Service Pack 3
NT Server tcpip.sys hot fix patch
Note: Service packs and hot fixes are found at *http://www.microsoft.com*
Microsoft IIS Web Server 3.0
Microsoft Index Server 1.0

Initial Tuning

The initial tuning is the basis of the Web Server baseline experienced by the end users. Without the benefit of stress testing the Web Server before deployment, the initial software installation is completed and backed up. After this, the server is tuned to provide optimal performance. Proactively following the tuning methodology will help to ensure that the initial tuning is functioning well. Without well established workload characteristics, it is important to continually monitor and tune the server as needed to support the varied workload encountered. Many of these tuning techniques are referenced in various places throughout this book. Some of these ideas I have learned on my own or while developing solutions for various customers or troubleshooting problems. Other tunables were found from the SPECWeb96 publicly published results from *http://www.spec.com*. Once the tuning suggestions were located, I researched and tested the ones I found applicable. New technology is fun to work with, but there is an amazing amount of it. To get a jump on the tuning process, review some of the publicly available industry benchmark results. These results help to provide insight into problems you may already have, or may have in the future.

Memory Tuning

WEB SERVER MEMORY TUNING STRATEGY

The strategy behind tuning Acme Rockets' Web Server is to balance the memory usage between the NT Server operating system and the applications in use. Keeping a proper memory balance will ensure that NT Server does not incur high paging rates and allow the applications to manage their own memory spaces.

As shown in the File Server Case study above, when the NT Server's Memory Strategy is set to Maximize Throughput for File Sharing, all available memory was used for caching. If an application was also running on the File Server that required a fair amount of memory, chances are better than average it would have ran slow due to NT paging activities associated with trying to provide the requested memory resources for the application. To provide memory for an application, the working set of the File System Cache would be trimmed or, in other words, less File System cache would be made available, thus slowing the disk I/O performance.

SELECTION OF THE NT SERVER STRATEGY

For this Web Server environment, NT Server Memory Strategy is set to Maximize Throughput for Network Applications. Set the NT Server memory strategy under Start|Settings|Control Panel|Network|Services. Select Server, then click Properties, then select memory strategy: Maximize Throughput for Network Applications. This will limit NT Server's use of memory for disk buffering activities and allow the application's working set more room in memory for their own memory management. By default, NT reserves 50 percent of the server's memory for the file system buffering, but it will trim the working set of this cache if it is running out of memory [NT Server Resource Kit Version 4, Supplement 1—Electronic Version, no page number].

DETERMINING IF THE FILE SYSTEM CACHE IS EFFECTIVE

Enough memory must be configured on the Web Server to ensure that the file system cache is large enough to effectively cache the http and FTP documents. To determine if the file system cache is being effective, understand what is happening on the Web Server. Based on the currently configured 512 Mbytes, 256 Mbytes is set aside initially for file system buffering. If all web pages and usable documents (FTP) are cached, this results in the use of 320 Mbytes of memory, leaving 192 Mbytes available for NT Server and applications.

The effectiveness of the File System Cache is monitored by the Perfmon Counters: Cache faults/sec and MDL Read Hits %. The Cache fault/sec indicates that the Web page or FTP document was not found in the file system cache or elsewhere in memory, as well as faults that requires disk operations. This counter alone is not helpful unless it is reviewed in conjunction with MDL Hits % over a period of time. The MDL Read Hits % is the percentage of Cache Memory Descriptor Read requests that hit the cache, thus not requiring disk access to complete the request. The MDL Read Hits % should be relatively high, greater than 90 percent on servers with sufficient memory. When this value is high in conjunction with a lower rate of Cache Faults/sec, the cache is effective. If this is not happening, and the server is paging, consider reducing the IIS Object Cache size or adding additional memory.

TUNING THE WEB SERVER MEMORY FOR FTP SERVICE

From a memory perspective, there are few special tuning adjustments needed to be accomplished specifically for the 30 concurrent users downloading files from the Web Server. The primary tuning effort to support the FTP user load is ensuring that NT Server has a sufficient amount of memory available for the file system cache. Secondary to this, ensure that any application or services using memory space that are not needed do not run on the server.

TUNING MICROSOFT IIS REGISTRY VALUES FOR IMPROVED MEMORY PERFORMANCE

Microsoft IIS allows for numerous tuning options in the NT registry. Ensure that you properly backup the registry and understand how to recover hives if needed before tuning any registry entries. Appendix A includes a registry backup/restore refresher.

The IIS Object Cache caches objects that HTTP and FTP services use frequently, such as file object handles and directory listings. Properly setting the IIS Object Cache to take advantage of the available memory will improve the server's performance, particularly in a static web page environment. For dynamic cache environments, increasing the IIS Object Cache may be less effective. The default value of the IIS Object Cache is 10 percent of memory. For Acme Rockets' web server environment, the IIS Object is set to 64 Mbytes. To set the IIS Object Cache to this value, add the registry entry HKEY_LOCAL_MACHINE\System\CurrentControlSet\Services\InetInfo\Parameters\MemoryCacheSize=0x 3D09000. Add this value as a REG_DWORD using hexadecimal notation.

To make sure you edited the registry correctly, check the Perfmon Counter Internet Information Services Global: Cache Size once the server is rebooted and running under load. This IIS object and its associated counters are installed when IIS is installed. To determine if the IIS cache is effectively large enough, check Perfmon Counter Internet Information Services Global: Cache Hits %. How effective the cache is depends on the workload being placed on the server. Typically, if the cache hit rate percentage is less than 90 percent, then the IIS Object Cache size should be increased. Remember, before increasing the IIS Object Cache size, ensure that there is sufficient available memory.

The Web Server for Acme Rockets is sized to cache most of the HTML documents. With this in mind, there is an NT Server registry tunable that is adjusted. Since sufficient memory is configured from the start, let's insure that we use it as wisely as possible. Any cache is more effective if, when the request is placed, the relevant data is already in the cache. To increase the possibility this occurs in the IIS Object Cache, edit the following registry entry: HKEY_LOCAL_MACHINE\System\CurrentControlSet\Services\InetInfo\Parameters\ObjectCacheTTL=0x8CA0. This keeps the IIS open descriptors active for at least 10 hours. The tactic here is that during a normal person's work day (10 hours), they will refer back to the same location several times. After the 10 hour period is over, another shift—perhaps international—will access different pages.

Thus, after 10 hours, the data in the cache will be flushed making room for new data access patterns. You can monitor the effectiveness of this strategy by looking at the Perfmon counter Internet Information Services Global: Cache Flushes. If the rate of cache flushes is a high value and is associated with a high value of cache misses and page faults, the cache may be flushing too quickly. When the cache is flushed too quickly, repeated requests for the same data do not result in a cache hit when it should. If this occurs, increase the ObjectCacheTTL. Increasing the ObjectCacheTTL keeps data in the cache for a longer period of time, which increases the chances that the data required is in the cache. The converse of this can also happen, in which case you will want to increase the rate in which the IIS Object Cache is flushed.

MONITORING MICROSOFT IIS OVERALL MEMORY USAGE

Monitoring how well IIS is using memory directly influences how you might tune IIS over time. IIS runs as a process called Inetinfo.exe. If the working set of this process is not kept in memory, the web server's performance will suffer. (More discussions on how NT Server uses memory are referred to in Chapter 5.)The working set for Inetinfo.exe encompasses IIS Object Cache, data buffers for logging, and the HTTP data structures used to track active connections. It is important to monitor the following Perfmon counters:

- Memory: Available bytes,
- Process Inetinfo.exe: Working Set
- Process Inetinfo.exe: Page Faults Per second

If the available memory bytes lowers and the Inetinfo.exe processes working set stays the same, there is sufficient memory available. If the available memory bytes lowers and the Intetinfo.exe processes working set lowers, and the Inetinfo.exe page faults increase, memory is being taken away from the InetInfo.exe process. When this occurs, NT Server is paging parts of the primary Web Server process to disk, which results in slower overall Web Server performance. If this begins to occur, additional memory will be needed, either by turning off more unneeded processes, trimming the IIS Object Cache size or, as a last resort, adding additional memory.

PAGEFILE PLACEMENT (VIRTUAL MEMORY)

Note again we place the paging file on its own dedicated physical disk drive. This will improve the performance when using the paging file and when determining if there is a memory shortage. The size of the page file is set initially to 1 GB. A large page file can slow a server down slightly when searching for information in the Pagefile, but this is trivial when compared to increasing the size of the page file on the fly. When NT Server increases the size of the page file on the fly, it is resource expensive. First, the process requiring the additional virtual memory space must wait for the paging file to be increased. Secondly, creations of additional page file areas are not always appended to the end of the first paging file. If this happens, page files can become fragmented across the disk, resulting in a slower response time when it is in use.

Web Server Disk Tuning

PROPERLY GROUPING SIMILAR DISK I/O ACTIVITIES

The first step in the disk subsystem tuning process is completed during the sizing portion of the sizing methodology under: Disk Performance Considerations and Requirements. The disk characteristics of the Web Server indicate that several different disk I/O activities will occur on the server at the same time. To improve disk I/O performance, similar types of disk activities are grouped together on specific RAID arrays. This lowers the disk contention experienced by the disk device and improves potential caching by NT Server file system as it utilizes a read ahead algorithm. This Web Server case study is a good example of using various raid levels for different disk subsystem workloads. Now, it will be much easier to determine where disk bottlenecks are occurring. Also, if a logical disk drive is becoming a bottleneck, it is now much easier to pinpoint the problem and tune around it since the activity associated with each disk drive is a known factor. The separation of workloads eases the longer term tuning and sizing process as well. The disk I/O layout is implemented in Table 8.13.

Table 8.14 Disk I/O layout.

ALU Size	SCSI Bus	Physical Disk Arrangement	Web Server File Locations
2 Kbytes	1	2 Disk RAID 1 Mirror	NT Operating System, IIS, and Search Engine Binaries and Files
4 Kbytes	1	2 Disk RAID 1 Mirror	Web Server Logs
2 Kbytes	1	2 Disk RAID 1 Mirror	Web (HTML) documents
4 Kbytes	2	1 Disk JBOD	NT Paging file
64 Kbytes	2	3 Disk RAID 5 Array	Shared (FTP) Documents

PROPERLY SETTING NTFS ALU SIZE

At an even lower level, the ALU sizes for each RAID array are set appropriately. For the RAID 1 NT Server Array and the RAID 1 web document array, the ALU size is set to 2Kbytes when creating the NTFS file system. The workloads on these two arrays are characterized by generally smaller random reads. The Pagefile and log file disk drive ALU sizes are set to 4 Kbytes when creating their NTFS file system. Both of these file systems are characterized as sequential and write intensive.

The RAID 5 array which houses the larger shared document files is set to a larger 64 Kbyte ALU size when creating the NTFS file system. The RAID 5 array is strictly a read only environment. Although having multiple concurrent users favors slightly more random characteristics, which the RAID 5 design supports well, the shared documents themselves are larger. The larger files are placed onto the disk array in more of a sequential fashion. This is similar to the File Server Case Study Configuration 2, a good example of using various ALU sizes used for different disk subsystem workloads.

Web Server CPU Tuning

LOWERING LOG FILE GENERATION OVERHEAD

Busy Web Servers generate large log files if they are turned on. Acme Rockets plans to use the log files to analyze the Web Server's usage pattern over time and to determine where the web clients are originating from. IIS by default, places log data into a 64 KB buffer, then writes this data to disk every 30 seconds. This consumes CPU processing overhead and some memory. To lower this overhead and take advantage of the extra memory sized during configuration sizing phase, the buffers where the log data is placed can be enlarged and the frequency that the buffers are emptied can be decreased. To accomplish this, add the following two registry entries:

HKEY_LOCAL_MACHINE\System\CurrentControlSet\Services\
InetInfo\Parameters\LogFileFlushInterval=41 and
HKEY_LOCAL_MACHINE\System\CurrentControlSet\Services\
InetInfo\Parameters\LogFileBatchSize=0x1000000.

These changes lower how often the buffers are written to disk to every 65 seconds. Why 65 seconds? A 65 second interval causes buffers to write one half of the time, lowering the context switch overhead associated with calling the CPU to write the log data. Traditionally, various operating systems, applications, and the AT scheduler (if used) functions kick off activities on 30 or 60 second intervals. Choosing 65 seconds slightly offsets this workload. Writing more to buffers data per write also improves the efficiency of the disk subsystem.

CONTROLLING NT SERVER PERFORMANCE BOOST

The performance boost for foreground applications found under Control Panel|System|Performance boost is set to none. All of the Web Server activities are occurring in the background, thus no performance preference should be provided to the foreground applications. This change is actually questionable. According to Mark Russinovich from *http://www.ntinternals.com* who also writes for NT Magazine, the NT Performance Boost bar which is supposed to adjust the quantum (amount of CPU time provided to an active thread/process) under NT Server does not actually adjust the quantum value. Mark's investigations indicate that NT Server does not actually change the quantum when the slide bar is moved all the way to the none position. This may actually be true (which I think it is), but I change the slide bar to the no performance boost setting anyway. Worst case, it only makes you feel like you helped tuned the server, even if it does not change the quantum value. Best case, it might actually help.

TUNING MICROSOFT IIS QUEUE SIZE

Under the heavy Web loads that Acme Rockets expects, keeping the Web Server properly fed with data is important. To ensure that requests are properly presented to the server, add the following registry value:

HKEY_LOCAL_MACHINE\System\CurrentControlSet\Services\InetInfo\Parameters\ListenBacklog=0x200.

Setting this value to 512 from the default of 15 increases the maximum active connections which are held in the Web Server's queue. Whenever this queue length limit is reached, the Web Server will reject any new connections until the queue length shortens. Tune this queue length lower if a system bottleneck begins to occur; subsequently, increase this value if web requests are being rejected.

FUTURE CPU TUNING SUGGESTIONS

When Acme Rockets moves a larger portion of their Web Server activities into dynamic web page generation, they will need to decide on a development environment. Typically, a combination of CGI (common gateway interface) and ISAPI (internet server application programming interface) applications are used for dynamic page generation. Depending on what they are trying to accomplish and programming preferences, the use of ISAPI for dynamic page generation incurs a lower processing overhead onto NT Server then CGI based scripts. ISAPI is a threads based application environment where most CGI programs require generation of a new process. NT Server is much more efficient when threads are used versus handling the creation of numerous new processes. With this fact in mind, Acme Rockets is consulted to consider the user of ISAPI or other thread based development environments for their dynamic web page's generation.

Web Server Network Tuning

TUNING NT SERVER PROTOCOLS

Acme Rockets has standardized on TCP/IP. Although TCP/IP is the default protocol for NT Server, occasionally other protocols are installed. To improve the network performance, all other protocols under Settings|Control Panel|Protocols besides TCP/IP are removed. This frees up available memory space and ensures that no other protocol is accessed first in the NT Server network stack.

TUNING INTERRUPT AND DEFERRED PROCEDURE CALLS (DPCS)

Each Web request received over the network generates an interrupt to the processor requesting service. If the processor does not find the request urgent enough (a high enough interrupt level), it will defer the request. This deferred interrupt request becomes a Deferred Procedure Call (DPC). As more and more requests come into the server, the number of interrupts and DPCs increase. When an interrupt is sent to a particular CPU and it gets deferred, additional server overhead is incurred if this DPC is shipped off to another CPU in the server. This can be costly from a performance perspective. To stop this from happening, set the following registry value: HKEY_LOCAL_MACHINE\System\CurrentControlSet\Services\NDIS\Parameters\ProcessorAffinityMask to 0. This forces the CPU that handled the interrupt to also handle any associated DPCs. This also ensures that the network interface card or cards, are not needed to be associated with a specific CPU. This improves the CPUs service of interrupts and DPCs generated by the network interface card(s). (More information on interrupts and the CPU are found in Chapter 4, "NT Server and CPU Performance.") For more control on this area, consider using the NCR server Utilization Manager tool also described in Chapter 4.

TUNING TCP RELATED REGISTRY VALUES

The transmission control blocks store data for each TCP connection. A control block is attached to the TCB hash table for each active connection. By increasing the TCB timewait table, more connections can be serviced. To adjust this value, add the following registry value: HKEY_LOCAL_MACHINE\System\CurrentControlSet\Services\Tcpip\Parameters\MaxFreeTcbs=0xEA60.

This increases the TCB timewait table to 60,000 entries from a default of 2000. Now that more connections can be serviced by the web server, you must adjust the corresponding hash table which is where the TCBs are stored. Accomplish this by adding the following registry value HKEY_LOCAL_MACHINE\System\CurrentControlSet\Services\Tcpip\Parameters\MaxHashTableSize=0x8000.

This increases the TCB hash table size from 512 to 32,768, allowing more room for connection information. TCB information is stored in the nonpaged memory pool. If the Web Server is experiencing memory bottlenecks and more memory is not able to be allotted to the server, lower the above values.

SERVER ARCHITECTURE RELATIONSHIP CHECK

Now that we have created and tuned the initial server configuration, let's make a common sense review of the configuration from the perspective of the overall server architecture in place. Two Pentium Pro 200 MHz/512 K CPUs should be capable of supporting the processing requirements of the expected load and have sufficient resources to drive the 2 Ultra Fast/Wide SCSI SCSI channels servicing the disk subsystem and single 100BaseTX network interface. 512 MB of RAM is sufficient to keep the CPUs fed, provide enough memory for the IIS process and Search Engine, and cache both Web Server and FTP activities in memory.

There are two peer PCI buses in a 2–4 CPU based NCR 4300 server. A quick basic math check of the I/O subsystem indicates that the I/O subsystem is required to support 2 Fast and Wide SCSI-2 buses (80 Mbytes/sec) and a single 100 Mbit network connection. Two Peer PCI buses provide an aggregate I/O bandwidth of 266 Mbytes/sec which is more than sufficient to support the current configuration. This will provide an excellent performing Web Server solution.

Future Business and Server Architectures Check Review

From steps 5 and 6 of the sizing methodology, the server is based on current industry standards and market trends. This level of Super Server still has a significant amount of additional resources available if needed. CPUs can be expanded up to eight, memory up to 8 GB, and two additional peer PCI buses for a total of four providing a clear in-box scalability path. This is in line with Acme Rockets' strategy of supporting increased Web Server workloads in a single server.

8. Stress Test and Validate the Server Configuration

Congratulations! We now have a solid configuration that will run Microsoft IIS and should support the required rate of Web users while providing excellent performance. Unfortunately, due to time restraints at Acme Rockets, this Web Server solution will not be stress tested prior to deployment.

9. Proactively Follow the Tuning Methodology During Validations Testing

Not applicable. No stress tests are completed.

10. Deploy the Server into Production

The NT Server solution is configured, sized and tuned to meet Acme Rockets' requirements.

11. Proactively Follow the Tuning Methodology After the Server Is Deployed

Following a sound sizing methodology to develop the server configuration before production deployment increases the confidence in the solution, but end users can always change their work habits. Continuing to follow the tuning methodology after the server is deployed will help you proactively plan for and tune around future performance hurdles. This is even more important as this NT Server solution was not stress tested before initial fielding.

Summary

In this chapter, the tuning and sizing methodologies and strategies are applied from Chapters 2 and 3 to develop real world solutions with specific hands on recommendations and guidelines. By using sound and structured methodologies when developing your solution, more confidence is created that the solution will meet your requirements. The various tuning and sizing information provided in Chapters 4–7 was leveraged through these case studies to gain better understanding of the environment the solutions were developed for. It becomes much easier to intelligently tune an NT Server solution when you have an understanding of what is occurring inside of the server from both a software and hardware perspective. The tuning and sizing recommendations in this chapter can be extrapolated on for use in your particular environment.

A P P E N D I X

Registry Recovery Refresher

NT Server's registry contains NT's internal configuration information. Because of this fact, it is very important that this information be properly backed up in case the registry ever becomes corrupted. A corrupt or improperly configured registry can lead to an unstable NT Server. The registry will not normally become corrupted unless an application incorrectly sets a registry value(s), a disk drive itself becomes corrupt, or you have manually intervened to set registry values. As pointed out throughout this book, the registry or any other area by itself, is not a "magic area" that will improve the performance of your server with one click of a mouse. The registry is an integral part of the tuning process that, at times, requires intervention to maximize the performance your NT Server achieves.

Tuning and Sizing NT Servers is focused on improving the performance of your NT Server and should also be used as a guide for providing new or additional capacity for your NT Server solution. This appendix outlines some techniques for backing up and restoring the registry. There are other techniques available. Most NT administration books outline backing up and rewtoring the registry in more depth. Choose the technique that works best for you.

It is important to backup the registry before and after any changes are made to your NT Server. These changes can range from editing the registry for tuning your NT Server, adding new applications, adding new hardware, changing your disk subsystem configuration, or just installing a service pack. In the highly unlikely event your configuration change does not produce the desired results, having a before and after copy of the registry for your server allows you to fall back to a previously working configuration. I highly recommend that if you have never recovered an NT Server registry that you give it a try on a test machine that is representative of your environment. In doing so, you will help build confidence in the registry recovery process that you may need to rely on in the future.

Every environment is different. Because of this, no guarantee is provided with the following registry recovery techniques, but these techniques have worked well for me in a variety of circumstances.

Backing Up the Registry

1. From the NT Server command prompt, execute the command "rdisk /s" and select "Update repair information."
   This will save the registry information into the %SystemRoot%\repair directory. It is the information in this directory that is copied to the emergency repair diskette when "Create repair disk" is selected in the next step. The "/s" option informs rdisk to backup the user and security registry information also. When using this option for a PDC, large user databases can generate large backup registry directories.
2. From the NT Server command prompt, execute the command "rdisk /s" and select "Create repair disk."
   This command will create an emergency repair disk that contains your registry information including security information that is associated with the user database. Keep this disk in a secure location because of the sensitive nature of the user security data. If you want to act conservatively, always create two of these emergency repair diskettes, and test them to ensure they work.

Restoring the Registry

1. Boot your NT Server with the NT Setup Disk 1
2. Continue the install process by removing Disk 1 and inserting Disk 2
3. At the first interactive screen, select "repair"
4. Various facets of NT can be inspected or reviewed in the repair process; for now de-select all options except for "Inspect registry files"
5. Insert Setup disk 3
6. When prompted, provide the most recently updated emergency repair diskette from step 2 above
7. From here, the NT recovery process walks through the required additional steps

Backing Up the Complete Registry

Utilizing the emergency recovery diskette is an effective technique to backup and restore the registry. Unfortunately, some portions of the registry that are active are not properly backed up using this technique. To backup the complete registry, use the "regback" utility included with the NT Server Resource

Kit. This utility can be used to backup the complete and active registry. "Regrest" is the resource kit tool that is used to restore registry information generated by the "regback" backup utility. The NT Server Resource Kit provides specific information on how to use these commands.

NT Server also provides a tool for backing up the registry: "ntbackup." For this tool, I suggest that you review NT Server's help files.

Registry Resources

This short appendix only scratches the surface of information surrounding the registry. For more in-depth information on NT Server's Registry, consider the following resources:

- *Windows NT Registry Troubleshooting*, Rob Tidrow, New Riders
- *Essential Windows NT System Administration*, Aeleen Frisch, O'Reilly
- *Windows NT Server 4 Professional Reference*, Karanjit S. Siyan, New Riders

INDEX

N

O

P

Q

R

U

V

W

Z

LICENSE AGREEMENT AND LIMITED WARRANTY

READ THE FOLLOWING TERMS AND CONDITIONS CAREFULLY BEFORE OPENING THIS CD PACKAGE, *CORE WEB PROGRAMMING*. THIS LEGAL DOCUMENT IS AN AGREEMENT BETWEEN YOU AND PRENTICE-HALL, INC. (THE "COMPANY"). BY OPENING THIS SEALED CD PACKAGE, YOU ARE AGREEING TO BE BOUND BY THESE TERMS AND CONDITIONS. IF YOU DO NOT AGREE WITH THESE TERMS AND CONDITIONS, DO NOT OPEN THE CD PACKAGE. PROMPTLY RETURN THE UNOPENED CD PACKAGE AND ALL ACCOMPANYING ITEMS TO THE PLACE YOU OBTAINED THEM FOR A FULL REFUND OF ANY SUMS YOU HAVE PAID.

1. **GRANT OF LICENSE:** In consideration of your purchase of this book, and your agreement to abide by the terms and conditions of this Agreement, the Company grants to you a nonexclusive right to use and display the copy of the enclosed software program (hereinafter the "SOFTWARE") on a single computer (i.e., with a single CPU) at a single location so long as you comply with the terms of this Agreement. The Company reserves all rights not expressly granted to you under this Agreement.

2. **OWNERSHIP OF SOFTWARE:** You own only the magnetic or physical media (the enclosed CD) on which the SOFTWARE is recorded or fixed, but the Company and the software developers retain all the rights, title, and ownership to the SOFTWARE recorded on the original CD copy(ies) and all subsequent copies of the SOFTWARE, regardless of the form or media on which the original or other copies may exist. This license is not a sale of the original SOFTWARE or any copy to you.

3. **COPY RESTRICTIONS:** This SOFTWARE and the accompanying printed materials and user manual (the "Documentation") are the subject of copyright. The individual programs on the CD are copyrighted by the authors of each program. Some of the programs on the CD include separate licensing agreements. If you intend to use one of these programs, you must read and follow its accompanying license agreement. You may not copy the Documentation or the SOFTWARE, except that you may make a single copy of the SOFTWARE for backup or archival purposes only. You may be held legally responsible for any copying or copyright infringement which is caused or encouraged by your failure to abide by the terms of this restriction.

4. **USE RESTRICTIONS:** You may not network the SOFTWARE or otherwise use it on more than one computer or computer terminal at the same time. You may physically transfer the SOFTWARE from one computer to another provided that the SOFTWARE is used on only one computer at a time. You may not distribute copies of the SOFTWARE or Documentation to others. You may not reverse engineer, disassemble, decompile, modify, adapt, translate, or create derivative works based on the SOFTWARE or the Documentation without the prior written consent of the Company.

5. **TRANSFER RESTRICTIONS:** The enclosed SOFTWARE is licensed only to you and may not be transferred to any one else without the prior written consent of the Company. Any unauthorized transfer of the SOFTWARE shall result in the immediate termination of this Agreement.

6. **TERMINATION:** This license is effective until terminated. This license will terminate automatically without notice from the Company and become null and void if you fail to comply with any provisions or limitations of this license. Upon termination, you shall destroy the Documentation and all copies of the SOFTWARE. All provisions of this Agreement as to warranties, limitation of liability, remedies or damages, and our ownership rights shall survive termination.

7. **MISCELLANEOUS:** This Agreement shall be construed in accordance with the laws of the United States of America and the State of New York and shall benefit the Company, its affiliates, and assignees.

8. **LIMITED WARRANTY AND DISCLAIMER OF WARRANTY:** The Company warrants that the SOFTWARE, when properly used in accordance with the Documentation, will operate in substantial conformity with the description of the SOFTWARE set forth in the Documentation. The

Company does not warrant that the SOFTWARE will meet your requirements or that the operation of the SOFTWARE will be uninterrupted or error-free. The Company warrants that the media on which the SOFTWARE is delivered shall be free from defects in materials and workmanship under normal use for a period of thirty (30) days from the date of your purchase. Your only remedy and the Company's only obligation under these limited warranties is, at the Company's option, return of the warranted item for a refund of any amounts paid by you or replacement of the item. Any replacement of SOFTWARE or media under the warranties shall not extend the original warranty period. The limited warranty set forth above shall not apply to any SOFTWARE which the Company determines in good faith has been subject to misuse, neglect, improper installation, repair, alteration, or damage by you. EXCEPT FOR THE EXPRESSED WARRANTIES SET FORTH ABOVE, THE COMPANY DISCLAIMS ALL WARRANTIES, EXPRESS OR IMPLIED, INCLUDING WITHOUT LIMITATION, THE IMPLIED WARRANTIES OF MERCHANTABILITY AND FITNESS FOR A PARTICULAR PURPOSE. EXCEPT FOR THE EXPRESS WARRANTY SET FORTH ABOVE, THE COMPANY DOES NOT WARRANT, GUARANTEE, OR MAKE ANY REPRESENTATION REGARDING THE USE OR THE RESULTS OF THE USE OF THE SOFTWARE IN TERMS OF ITS CORRECTNESS, ACCURACY, RELIABILITY, CURRENTNESS, OR OTHERWISE.

IN NO EVENT, SHALL THE COMPANY OR ITS EMPLOYEES, AGENTS, SUPPLIERS, OR CONTRACTORS BE LIABLE FOR ANY INCIDENTAL, INDIRECT, SPECIAL, OR CONSEQUENTIAL DAMAGES ARISING OUT OF OR IN CONNECTION WITH THE LICENSE GRANTED UNDER THIS AGREEMENT, OR FOR LOSS OF USE, LOSS OF DATA, LOSS OF INCOME OR PROFIT, OR OTHER LOSSES, SUSTAINED AS A RESULT OF INJURY TO ANY PERSON, OR LOSS OF OR DAMAGE TO PROPERTY, OR CLAIMS OF THIRD PARTIES, EVEN IF THE COMPANY OR AN AUTHORIZED REPRESENTATIVE OF THE COMPANY HAS BEEN ADVISED OF THE POSSIBILITY OF SUCH DAMAGES. IN NO EVENT SHALL LIABILITY OF THE COMPANY FOR DAMAGES WITH RESPECT TO THE SOFTWARE EXCEED THE AMOUNTS ACTUALLY PAID BY YOU, IF ANY, FOR THE SOFTWARE.

SOME JURISDICTIONS DO NOT ALLOW THE LIMITATION OF IMPLIED WARRANTIES OR LIABILITY FOR INCIDENTAL, INDIRECT, SPECIAL, OR CONSEQUENTIAL DAMAGES, SO THE ABOVE LIMITATIONS MAY NOT ALWAYS APPLY. THE WARRANTIES IN THIS AGREEMENT GIVE YOU SPECIFIC LEGAL RIGHTS AND YOU MAY ALSO HAVE OTHER RIGHTS WHICH VARY IN ACCORDANCE WITH LOCAL LAW.

ACKNOWLEDGMENT

YOU ACKNOWLEDGE THAT YOU HAVE READ THIS AGREEMENT, UNDERSTAND IT, AND AGREE TO BE BOUND BY ITS TERMS AND CONDITIONS. YOU ALSO AGREE THAT THIS AGREEMENT IS THE COMPLETE AND EXCLUSIVE STATEMENT OF THE AGREEMENT BETWEEN YOU AND THE COMPANY AND SUPERSEDES ALL PROPOSALS OR PRIOR AGREEMENTS, ORAL, OR WRITTEN, AND ANY OTHER COMMUNICATIONS BETWEEN YOU AND THE COMPANY OR ANY REPRESENTATIVE OF THE COMPANY RELATING TO THE SUBJECT MATTER OF THIS AGREEMENT.

Should you have any questions concerning this Agreement or if you wish to contact the Company for any reason, please contact in writing at the address below.

Robin Short

Prentice Hall PTR

One Lake Street

Upper Saddle River, New Jersey 07458

BLUECURVE, INC. LICENSE AGREEMENT

License Grant. This Bluecurve product may contain up to three different types of software. The Manager Software allows you to build, run and analyze test data. The Test Dataset allows you to build test data sets in various sizes on a computer system. The Test Client Motor allows you to run a test on an actual or simulated client. The Manager Software, Test Dataset and Test Client Motor are collectively referred to in this License Agreement as the "Software."

Bluecurve hereby grants to you, and you accept, a nonexclusive license to use the Software in object code form only, and the accompanying user documentation, only as authorized in this License Agreement.

Restrictions on Use of the Software. You may install the Software only on one computer at any given time. You may transfer the Software to another computer provided it is removed from the computer from which it is transferred.

Restrictions on Use of Test Results. You acknowledge that Bluecurve has the right to preserve the integrity of the performance test results resulting from the use of the Software ("Test Results"). You may copy and distribute the Test Results only for use within your organization. You agree that you will not publish in printed or electronic form any Test Results in any commercial publication or in any product promotional material or advertisements without the express written consent of Bluecurve. In addition, you agree that your use of the Software shall be limited to your own internal use, and that you will not charge a fee or receive any consideration for the sale or disclosure of Test Results to any person or organization.

Other Restrictions. You may not use the Software for timesharing, rental or service bureau purposes. You agree that you will not assign, sublicense, transfer, pledge, lease, rent, or share your rights under this License Agreement. You agree that you shall not reverse engineer, decompile or disassemble, or otherwise translate the Software.

Ownership. You acknowledge and agree that the Software and the user documentation are proprietary products of Bluecurve. The Software is protected by copyright laws and international copyright treaties, as well as other intellectual property laws and treaties. You further acknowledge and agree that all right, title, and interest in and to the Software and the user documentation, including associated intellectual property rights, are and shall remain with Bluecurve. This License Agreement does not convey to you an interest in or to the Software or user documentation, but only a limited right of use revocable in accordance with the terms of this License Agreement. You must treat the Software and user documentation like any other copyrighted material. You may not copy the user documentation accompanying the Software.

Term. This License Agreement is effective upon your installing, copying, or using the Software and shall continue until terminated. You may terminate this License Agreement at any time by destroying the Software. Bluecurve may terminate this License Agreement upon the breach by you of any term hereof. Upon such termination by Bluecurve, you agree to destroy all copies of the Software.

No warranty. Any use of the software product is at your own risk. To the maximum extent permitted by applicable law, Bluecurve and its suppliers disclaim all warranties and conditions, either express or implied, including, but not limited to, implied warranties of merchantability, fitness for a particular purpose, and noninfringement.

NO OTHER WARRANTIES EXCEPT FOR THE WARRANTIES SET FORTH ABOVE, THE SOFTWARE IS LICENSED "AS IS," AND BLUECURVE DISCLAIMS ANY AND ALL OTHER WARRANTIES, WHETHER EXPRESS OR IMPLIED, INCLUDING, WITHOUT LIMITATION, ANY IMPLIED WARRANTIES OF MERCHANTABILITY OR FITNESS FOR A PARTICULAR PURPOSE.

Limitation of Liability. Bluecurve's cumulative liability to you or any other party for any loss or damages resulting from any claims, demands, or actions arising out of or relating to this License Agreement shall not exceed five dollars (US$5.00). In no event shall Bluecurve be liable for any indirect, incidental, consequential, special, or exemplary damages, loss of business profits, business interruption, loss of data or information, or any other pecuniary loss, even if Bluecurve has been advised of the possibility of such losses or damages. SOME STATES DO NOT ALLOW THE LIMITATION OR EXCLUSION OF LIABILITY FOR INCIDENTAL OR CONSEQUENTIAL DAMAGES, SO THE ABOVE LIMITATION OR EXCLUSION MAY NOT APPLY TO YOU.

Trademark. Bluecurve, Dynameasure and Active Measurement are trademarks of Bluecurve. No right, license, or interest to such trademark is granted hereunder, and you agree that no such right, license, or interest shall be asserted by you with respect to such trademarks.

General. This License Agreement shall be construed and governed in accordance with the laws of the State of California, except for that body of law dealing with conflicts of law. If any action is brought by either party to this License Agreement against the other party regarding the subject matter hereof, the prevailing party shall be entitled to recover, in addition to any other relief granted, reasonable attorney fees and expenses of litigation. Should any term of this License Agreement be declared void or unenforceable by any court of competent jurisdiction, such declaration shall have no effect on the remaining terms hereof. The failure of either party to enforce any rights granted hereunder or to take action against the other party in the event of any breach hereunder shall not be deemed a waiver by that party as to subsequent enforcement of rights or subsequent actions in the event of future breaches.

About the CD-ROM

The following software is included on the accompanying CD-ROM:
Bluecurve, Inc.: DynameasureFile.exe
LC Technologies: Ram Charger - rcnts-ev-us-40.exe
EEC Systems: SuperDisk - sdnti401.exe
Executive Software: Diskeeper for NT Server - us_dksrtr_i.zip

Example Perl Script used in Book
BaseLineCheck.pl

Example NT Server batch files used in book
DiskAndNetworkTest.bat
LocalDiskTest.bat
PulseTest.bat

Example Performance Monitor Work Space Files
CPU-Resources.pmw
Disk-Resources.pmw
Memory-Resources.pmw
Network-Resources.pmw
Computer Based Training Course WinNT4.0: Advanced Troubleshooting and Optimization

System Requirements

The primary requirement needed to run the software on the accompanying server CD-ROM is that you must be running Windows NT Server version 4.0 or greater. There is no minimum server hardware requirement. If NT Server is installed and operating, you are ready to go! Ok, it is recommended that at least 50MB of disk space is available if you wish to load the entire CD-ROM's contents outlined below and Perl must be loaded to run the Perl script from Chapter 2.

Technical Support

Prentice Hall does not offer technical support for this software. However, if there is a problem with the media, you may obtain a replacement copy by emailing us with your problem at: *discexchange@phptr.com*

If you have a problem with the CBT software, please contact CBT Technical Support. In the US call: 1 (800) 938-3247. If you are outside the US call 3531-283-0380.